LA PIÑATA

Junior League of McAllen, Texas

favorite recipes
collected and tested by
The Junior League of McAllen, Inc.

The Junior League of McAllen, Inc. is an organization of women committed to promoting voluntarism and to improving the community through the effective action and leadership of trained volunteers. Its purpose is exclusively educational and charitable.

Additional copies may be obtained from:

LA PIÑATA

P.O. Box 2465
McAllen, Texas 78502-2465

956-682-0743

Make checks payable to Junior League of McAllen, Inc.

First Printing	February 1976	2,000 copies
Second Printing	December 1977	2,500 copies
Third Printing	September 1980	20,000 copies
Fourth Printing	January 1981	40,000 copies
Fifth Printing	May 1986	10,000 copies
Sixth Printing	September 1988	5,000 copies
Seventh Printing	April 1994	10,000 copies
Eighth Printing	October 2002	5,000 copies

International Standard Book Number 0-9604548-0-2
Library of Congress Catalog Number 80-82158

Printed in the United States of America
TOOF COOKBOOK DIVISION

STARR ★ TOOF

P. O. Box 14607
Memphis, TN 38114

TABLE OF CONTENTS

¡SALUDOS!

Greetings!

McAllen, Texas is located at the southern tip of Texas in an area known as the Rio Grande Valley. The history of the Valley dates back further than that of Jamestown and Plymouth Rock. In the early 1500's, the Spanish exploration of Mexico and Texas eventually led to grants of large tracts of land to prominent Spanish families. The land grants gave birth to the sprawling ranches of South Texas. Even as late as the early 1900's, the Rio Grande Valley was still one of the last frontiers in the continental United States.

The geographical location of McAllen affords the area a climate that annually attracts a large number of "Winter Texans." These people from the northern part of the United States and Canada come each winter to enjoy the blue skies and sunny winter days. The warm climate helps to produce a variety of agricultural products that have enhanced the economic development of McAllen.

Agriculture is one of the major industries of the area, producing an abundance of fresh citrus fruits, vegetables, cotton, and grain. The rich soil produces, among other products; onions, cabbages, carrots, oranges, and Texas's famous Ruby Red grapefruit.

Palm trees dot the landscape throughout the Valley, giving McAllen its well-deserved name—the "City of Palms." Visitors to McAllen often comment on our tropical climate and welcome the tropical flavors that enhance our recipes.

The sand and surf of the Gulf of Mexico, located about seventy miles from McAllen, offer residents abundant fishing opportunities. Seafood recipes are a specialty and source of pride to those who enjoy the bounties of the Gulf.

Also of special interest are the tastes that only wild game can produce. This area is a famous place to hunt whitewing dove, quail, and deer. Recipes are traded among hunters and shared in this book to aid those who seek recipes for preparing wild game.

Because Mexico is only seven miles south of McAllen, Mexican recipes are local favorites. These delicious recipes collected in *LA PIÑATA* have their own unique flavors and spices.

Enjoy the freshness of our tropical climate mingled with a distinctive Mexican flair unique in the United States. Sample a bit of McAllen and try what the "City of Palms" has to offer in this delightful collection of recipes.

LA PIÑATA

Originating in 17th century France at the Court of King Louis XIV as an adult plaything, the piñata was a clay container filled with surprises for the guests. It later found its way to Spain and then to Mexico where it was adapted to gaily decorated paper forms in a variety of sizes and shapes.

Along the Texas-Mexico border of the Rio Grande Valley, the piñata plays an important role in the celebrations where people come together to share in the festivities.

The McAllen Junior League presents this cookbook in the spirit of the piñata. It is a gaily decorated paper container filled with all sorts of surprises and good things. You have but to "break it open" and share its contents with others. Viva la Fiesta—Viva la Piñata.

ENJOY

Our book is dedicated to the six women who first dreamed of writing a cookbook as a representative "piñata" of our area, full of delicacies. Their love for families and pleasure in entertaining friends has been reflected in the pages of *LA PIÑATA*. With heartfelt gratitude for all of their enthusiasm, time, and hard work, we thank:

Mrs. Jerry Fair (Zetta)
Mrs. Gary Gurwitz (Bailey)
Mrs. Leroy Lewin (Hilda)
Mrs. Jerry McGilvray (Jane)
Mrs. Richard Moore (Lynda)
Mrs. Morgan Talbot (Jane)

LA PIÑATA cover art and insignia by Pam Corcoran

Appetizers

Appetizer Ham Ball

Yield: 1 ball

2 (4½-oz.) cans deviled ham
3 Tbs. pimiento-stuffed green
  olives, chopped
1 Tbs. prepared mustard
bottled hot pepper sauce to
  taste
1 (3-oz.) pkg. cream cheese,
  softened
2 tsp. milk
crackers

Combine ham, olives, mustard and pepper sauce to taste. Form into ball on serving dish. Chill. Combine cream cheese and milk; frost ham ball. Chill. Remove from refrigerator 15 minutes before serving. Trim with parsley. Serve with assorted crackers.

Mrs. Leonel Garza, Jr. (Linda)

Bacon-Cheese Ball

Yield: 1 cheese ball

3 oz. Bleu cheese
5 oz. bacon cheese
6 oz. cream cheese
1 Tbs. pecans, finely ground
1½ Tbs. parsley, chopped
1 Tbs. dried minced onion
2 tsp. Worcestershire sauce

Mix all ingredients well. Place ball in lined bowl with foil and refrigerate. Dust with paprika before serving.

Mrs. Jack Whetsel (Martha)

Black Olive Cheese Ball

Yield: 1 cheese ball

½ lb. natural Cheddar
  cheese, grated
1 (3-oz.) pkg. cream cheese,
  softened
¼ cup pitted ripe olives,
  chopped
3 Tbs. sherry
½ tsp. Worcestershire sauce
dash each of onion, garlic,
  celery salt
½ cup parsley, coarsely
  snipped

Mixture should be made several days ahead. Mix all ingredients except parsley until well blended. Wrap in foil and refrigerate. Thirty minutes before serving, unwrap and roll with hands in parsley or in chopped pecans or walnuts if desired.

Mrs. Homero Rivas (Sonia)

3

APPETIZERS

Chili-Cheese Log

Yield: 5 logs
Freezes and refreezes

1 (8-oz.) pkg. cream cheese
2 lbs. Velveeta cheese
6-8 pods fresh garlic, minced
10 dashes of Tabasco hot
  sauce (or more)
1 cup pecans, chopped
1 tsp. ground comino
¼-½ cup Pick-a-Peppa sauce
  (optional)
Morton Nature's Seasoned
  salt, to taste
chili powder
crackers

Let both cheeses reach room temperature. With hands, mix all of the ingredients except chili powder, until well blended. Divide cheese mixture into the size logs or cheese balls that you prefer, and then roll in the chili powder to coat thoroughly. Wrap in plastic wrap and freeze for future use or refrigerate for use the following day. Serve with Triscuits, Wheat Thins or mildly seasoned crackers.

Mrs. Jerry Box (Deanna)

Easy Cheese Ball

Yield: 1 cheese ball

¾ lb. Velveeta cheese (room
  temperature)
8 oz. cream cheese, softened
8 oz. cottage cheese
½ cup pecans, chopped
  (more or less to taste)
garlic salt, to taste
1 Tbs. parsley flakes (to
  taste)

Mix all ingredients until well blended. Chill. Form into a ball. If desired, coat outside of cheese ball with chopped pecans and garnish with fresh parsley.

Mrs. Jan Klinck (Sally)

A good rule of thumb: serve strong wine when serving strong cheese.

Always serve cheese at room temperature and when serving soft cheese remember to remove from refrigerator one hour before company arrives.

Old English Cheese Ball

Yield: 1 cheese ball

2 (8-oz.) pkgs. cream cheese
10 oz. Old English cheese
4 oz. Bleu cheese
¾ cup pecans, broken, set ¼
aside for rolling finished
ball
½ cup parsley, chopped, set
¼ aside for rolling finished
ball
1 Tbs. onion, finely chopped
1 Tbs. Worcestershire sauce

Let cheeses stand at room temperature, then cream together. Add pecans, parsley, onion, and Worcestershire sauce. Mix well and form into ball. Roll in ¼ cup chopped nuts and/or ¼ cup chopped parsley, if desired. Chill.

Mrs. Gilbert Heartfield (Francesca)

Pineapple Cheese Ball

Yield: 1 large or 2 medium balls
Freezes

2 (8-oz.) pkgs. cream cheese
2 cups pecans, chopped
1 (8½-oz.) can crushed
pineapple, drained
¼ cup green pepper,
chopped
2 Tbs. onion, chopped
dash seasoning salt

Soften cream cheese and add 1 cup of pecans and all other ingredients. Chill at least 1 hour. Roll in rest of pecans. Refrigerate until ready to serve. Makes 1 large or 2 medium-sized balls.

Sesame Cheese Ball

Yield: 1 large ball

soy sauce
3 large pkgs. Philadelphia
cream cheese, softened
sesame seeds

Add soy sauce to softened cream cheese, to taste or until cheese turns brownish. Roll into ball; place in refrigerator until slightly hardened. Meanwhile toast sesame seeds. Roll ball in cooled seeds and refrigerate. Serve with crackers. Makes a large ball.

Mrs. Bruce Leahy (Susan)

APPETIZERS

Taco Cheese Ball

Yield: 1 large or 2 small balls

1 (8-oz.) pkg. cream cheese,
  at room temperature
1 pkg. taco seasoning mix
1 pkg. Leo's sliced beef
  lunch meat
1 lb. American cheese, grated
parsley, paprika, chives or
  chopped nuts (your
  preference)

Cream cheese and add taco seasoning mix. Chop lunch meat very fine and add to cream cheese mixture. Add grated cheese and mix well. Form into ball and roll in paprika, parsley flakes, chives or chopped nuts.

If you like jalapeño peppers, chop one very fine and add to cream cheese.

Mrs. Allen Beakey (Jane)

Zesty Cheese Ball

Yield: 2 cheese balls
Freezes

1 roll smoked cheese or 3 oz.
  jar
1 roll garlic cheese or 3 oz.
  jar
1 roll bacon cheese or 3 oz.
  jar
2 (3-oz.) pkgs. cream cheese
1 (4-oz.) pkg. Bleu cheese
1 Tbs. dried parsley flakes
1 Tbs. chili powder
1 Tbs. Worcestershire sauce
¾ large onion, grated
3 garlic cloves, mashed
1 green pepper, chopped
6 oz. pecans, chopped

Top:
6 oz. pecans, chopped
3 Tbs. parsley flakes
3 Tbs. chili powder

Soften cheeses. Combine all ingredients, except pecans, in electric mixer. Beat until smooth. Refrigerate for at least 2 hours, or until firm enough to mold. Form into 2 balls and roll in mixture of: pecans, parsley and chili powder. Keep in freezer until serving.

Mrs. Cameron Henry (Kathryn)

Eggplant Caviar

350 degrees
Baking sheet
Yield: about 2 cups

2 large eggplant
salt
freshly ground pepper
½-1 cup salad oil
½ onion, grated

Pierce eggplant with skewer to prevent bursting during baking. Place eggplant on baking sheet and bake at 350 degrees for about 45 minutes or until soft; cool and peel. Chop pulp coarsely; season to taste with salt and pepper. Blend enough salad oil with eggplant until oil is absorbed. Mix in onion. Serve in a bowl with black bread or wheat crackers.

Mrs. Bill Blackburn (Jeanne)

Frosted Caviar Cheese Mold

2 cup mold, greased

1 cup sour cream
1 cup cottage cheese
½ clove garlic, crushed
dash Tabasco
juice of ½ lemon
1 Tbs. soy sauce
1 Tbs. Lawry seasoned salt
1½ Tbs. gelatin
2 Tbs. sherry
4 jars imported black caviar

In blender, mix all seasonings, sour cream and cottage cheese. Mix gelatin and sherry and put over hot water to dissolve. Add to cream and cheese mixture and blend again. Put in lightly greased mold and chill in refrigerator for 24 hours. Unmold on platter and frost with imported black caviar.

Mrs. Jim Jones (Jackie)

Paté Mold

1 (8-oz.) pkg. cream cheese
1 (8-oz.) pkg. Braunschweiger cheese
1 Tbs. garlic powder
1 small jar caviar, red or black

Soften cream cheese in mixing bowl, reserving ¼. Add Braunschweiger and garlic powder. Mix well. Mold into biscuit shape. Frost with reserved cream cheese. Top with the caviar. Chill. Serve with crackers.

Mrs. W. L. Moore (Ann)

APPETIZERS

Hot Artichoke Spread

350 degrees
Small casserole dish,
lightly greased
Yield: about 3 cups
Freezes

1 (14-oz.) can artichoke
   hearts, drained and
   chopped
1 cup real mayonnaise
1 cup Parmesan cheese,
   grated
⅓-½ tsp. garlic powder
   (according to taste)

Combine all ingredients and put into a lightly greased, small casserole. Bake for 20 minutes at 350 degrees. Serve with assorted crackers.

12 ounces or 17 ounces of artichokes may be used if finding a 14-ounce can is a problem.

Mrs. Thomas B. Sammons, Jr. (Gretchen)
Mrs. Jim Thompson (Sandy)

Delicious Spread

1 (8-oz.) pkg. cream cheese
Pick-a-Peppa sauce to spread
parsley

Cover cream cheese with sauce and garnish with parsley. Spread on party crackers.

Substitute for Pick-a-Peppa: Pace's Picante, A-1 sauce, Guava Jelly, Jalapeño Jelly, chutney, or 1 can smoked oysters.

Mrs. Ruben Cardenas (Dardanella)

Crab and Spinach Dip

Yield: 15 servings

1 medium onion, chopped
1 stick margarine
1 small can crab meat
1 pkg. chopped spinach,
   cooked and drained
Parmesan cheese to taste

Sauté onion in margarine. Add crab meat and spinach and Parmesan cheese to taste.

Broccoli may be substituted for spinach. Triple this recipe for 50 people.

Mrs. Jerry McGilvray (Jane)

Artichoke Dip

Yield: about 3 cups

1 lb. canned artichoke hearts,
    drained
⅓ cup mayonnaise
6 oz. cream cheese, softened
1 Tbs. onion, chopped
salt, pepper, cayenne pepper
    to taste
3-4 slices bacon, fried crisp,
    chopped
juice of ½ lemon
corn chips

Chop artichoke hearts to pulp in blender. Add softened cream cheese to mayonnaise and mix until smooth. Add to rest of ingredients; chill. Serve with corn chips.

Mrs. Jerry McGilvray (Jane)

Avocado Bleu Cheese Dip

Yield: about 1 quart

½ pint sour cream
2 ripe avocados, mashed
1 pkg. Bleu cheese
1 pint mayonnaise
1 clove garlic, crushed
2 Tbs. dry onion soup mix
salt and lemon or lime juice
    to taste
Fritos

Mix all ingredients until well-blended. Serve with king-size Fritos.

Mrs. Thomas B. Sammons, Jr. (Gretchen)

Bleu Cheese Dip

Yield: 4-5 cups

½ tsp. garlic salt
½ tsp. celery salt
red pepper to taste
paprika to taste
2 Tbs. vinegar
1 pt. sour cream
½ cup mayonnaise
½ tsp. salt
½ lb. Bleu cheese, crumbled

Mix all ingredients except cheese together; then fold in cheese crumbled in large pieces. If it is too thin add more cheese or add a little Philadelphia cream cheese.

Mrs. Mike Frost (Sandra)

APPETIZERS

Chipped Beef Dip

350 degrees
1 quart baking dish

8 oz. cream cheese
½ cup sour cream
½ cup mayonnaise
½ cup onion, chopped
1 jar dried beef
Lawry's seasoned salt, to
  taste
pecans, chopped
Triscuits

Mix all ingredients and season to taste with Lawry's salt. Pour into baking dish and top with pecans. Bake at 350 degrees until bubbly.

Mrs. Mac Pike (Tish)

Curry Dip

Yield: about 1½ cups

1 cup mayonnaise
1 tsp. curry powder
1 tsp. onion powder
1 tsp. garlic salt
1 tsp. prepared horseradish
1 tsp. tarragon vinegar
1 tsp. sugar
¼ cup sour cream

Beat all ingredients together. Mix well. Serve with your choice of crackers or chips.

This is best made at least the day before. It will keep 2 weeks in the refrigerator.

Mrs. Robert H. Kern, Jr. (Carolyn)

Delicious Hot Cheese Dip

Yield: 6-8 servings

1 green pepper, chopped
1 onion, chopped
oil—just enough to sauté
  pepper and onion till tender
chili powder to taste
1 (1-lb.) box Old English
  cheese
1 can Ro-Tel tomatoes and
  chilies
chips

Sauté the pepper and onion in oil, just until tender. Melt cheese in double boiler and add vegetables. Add Ro-Tel tomatoes. Serve with corn chips or tortilla chips.

Mrs. Hollis Fritts (Gerrie)

10

Easy Chili Beef Dip

Yield: 4-5 cups

1 onion, chopped
1 lb. lean ground beef
bacon grease
1-2 Tbs. chili powder
salt and pepper
1 (11-oz.) can Chili Beef Soup
1 (11-oz.) can Cheddar
  Cheese Soup

Sauté onion and beef in small amount of grease. Season with salt, pepper and chili powder. Add soups and simmer 30 minutes on low heat. Stir often. Serve in chafing dish with chips.

Mrs. Jack Humphreys (Kay)

Easy Dip

Yield: approximately 1 cup

½ pint French onion dip
1 small can deviled ham
4-5 drops Worcestershire
  sauce
chips

Stir together and serve with chips.

Mrs. Ruben Cardenas (Dardanella)

Hot Broccoli Dip

Yield: 1 quart dip
Freezes

½ cup onion, chopped
½ cup celery, chopped
½ cup mushrooms, chopped
3 Tbs. butter
1 pkg. broccoli, chopped,
  cooked and drained
1 (10¾-oz.) can cream of
  mushroom soup
1 (6-oz.) pkg. garlic cheese,
  diced
juice of 1 lemon

Sauté onions, celery, mushrooms in butter until tender; add broccoli. Mix mushroom soup and cheese into broccoli mixture. Cook over low heat until cheese is melted. Serve in chafing dish.

May be prepared ahead of time, but do not heat until ready to serve.

Mrs. Mac Pike (Tish)

11

APPETIZERS

Hot Crab Dip

350 degrees
1 quart baking dish
Yield: 6-8 servings

1 (8-oz.) pkg. cream cheese
1 Tbs. milk
½ tsp. horseradish
1-2 tsp. onion, minced
1 (6-oz.) can crab meat
⅓ cup almonds, slivered
salt and pepper to taste
Ritz crackers or Melba toast

Soften cheese with milk. Add other ingredients except the almonds. Sprinkle almonds on top. Bake at 350 degrees for 15 minutes. Serve with Ritz crackers or Melba toast.

Variation:
2 Tbs. sherry

Add to dip mixture.

Mrs. Cameron Henry (Kathryn)

Picante Dip

Yield: 1 quart

2 small onions, chopped
  finely
3 Tbs. salad oil
1 clove garlic, pressed
1 (l lb. 13 oz.) can whole
  tomatoes
1 (6-oz.) can tomato paste
⅓ cup green chile peppers or
  jalapeños, minced
1 tsp. sugar
salt and pepper to taste
½ cup sharp Cheddar
  cheese, grated

Sauté onions in oil until soft; add remaining ingredients except cheese; mix well. Simmer for 2 hours. Sprinkle with grated cheese. Serve warm as a dip.

Very Spicy!

Mrs. Norman Buescher, Jr. (Patty)

Shrimp Dip

Yield: 15 servings

1 (8-oz.) pkg. cream cheese,
   softened
1 cup Brockles Dressing
   (1000 Island type)
½ cup mayonnaise
2 pimientos, minced
1 small onion, grated
¼ cup green onions, minced
3-6 tsp. Tabasco
1 Tbs. Lawry's seasoned salt
1 Tbs. horseradish
2 lbs. shelled shrimp,
   chopped and cooked
chips or crackers

Combine all ingredients and chill. Serve
with corn chips or crackers.

Mrs. Mac Pike (Tish)

Smoked Oyster Dip

Yield: 2 cups

1 can smoked oysters in oil
1 (2-oz.) can mushrooms,
   drained
1 carton sour cream
1 tsp. Worcestershire sauce
salt
pepper

Drain oysters; squeeze out oil. Drain
mushrooms. Mix all ingredients
together. It takes quite a bit of salt to
bring out the flavor.

*Double it for 10 or more people. Serve
with chips, crackers, etc.*

Soak canned shrimp in a little sherry and 2 tablespoons of vinegar for 15 to 20
minutes for a fresher taste.

APPETIZERS

Tuna Dip

Yield: 3 cups

2 cans tuna
1 (8-oz.) pkg. cream cheese,
    softened
1 tsp. onion, grated
salt and pepper to taste
½ cup mayonnaise
3 Tbs. Pace's hot sauce
2 Tbs. parsley
1 tsp. Worcestershire sauce

Blend all ingredients well and put in refrigerator overnight so flavors can mix
well. Good with a little lime juice too.

Mrs. Morgan Talbot (Jane)

Water Chestnut Dip

Yield: 2-3 cups

1 cup mayonnaise
1 cup sour cream
¼ cup parsley, chopped
2 Tbs. onion, grated
1 tsp. garlic salt
1 Tbs. soy sauce
1 small can water chestnuts,
    chopped
fresh vegetables

Mix all ingredients and keep in refrigerator at least 4 hours. Use fresh vegetables such as carrot and celery sticks,
cauliflower, yellow squash as dippers.

Mrs. Cameron Henry (Kathryn)

Anchovy Bolillos
(Mexican Hard Rolls)

Yield: 24 pieces

12 Bolilla rolls
butter
garlic salt
anchovies, chopped into
    small pieces

Cut roll in half; spread with butter.
Sprinkle with garlic salt and small pieces
of anchovy. Broil until golden brown.
Anchovy paste may be substituted for
chopped anchovies. Parmesan cheese,
grated, may be sprinkled on top when
served.

Mrs. Jerry Fair (Zetta)

14

Aceituna Española
(Spanish Olives)

2 (9-10 oz.) jars green olives
   with pits or
   pimiento-stuffed
½ cup salad oil
½ cup vinegar
3 cloves of garlic, minced
2 tsp. oregano leaves,
   crushed
2 large jalapeños, minced

Place all ingredients in glass mixing bowl and mix well. Allow to marinate at least 72 hours before serving (in refrigerator), spooning marinade over olives. Serve with toothpicks.

Divide mixture into original jars in which the olives were bought, thus making it easy to shake the mixture over the olives in each jar. Keeps 2 months in refrigerator.

Mrs. Jerry Box (Deanna)

Allan Shivers' Canapés
(Former Texas Governor)

bread slices
cucumber or small onion
   slices
Parmesan cheese
mayonnaise
grated onion
paprika or parsley flakes

Cut bread into small rounds with cookie cutter. Place on cookie sheet. Slice a cucumber or onion very thinly and place on rounds. Mix grated Parmesan cheese with mayonnaise so that it is of spreading consistency; add small amount of grated onion. Top each cucumber or onion slice with this cheese mixture. Sprinkle small amount of paprika or parsley flakes on this. Place under broiler; remove when bread browns. Serve immediately.

Mrs. Allan Shivers (Marialice)

APPETIZERS

Angel Biscuits

400 degrees
Cookie sheet
Yield: 2-3 dozen
Freezes

5 cups flour
¼ cup sugar
3 tsp. baking powder
1 tsp. soda
1 tsp. salt
1 cup shortening
1 pkg. dry yeast
¼ cup warm water
2 cups buttermilk
1 lb. browned sausage or
   cocktail sausages

Sift dry ingredients together. Cut in shortening with knife. Dissolve yeast in warm water and add with buttermilk to dry ingredients. Mix well. Roll out ¼-inch thick; cut with round biscuit cutter. Dip in melted butter and fold in half. Use cocktail sausage (or anything you prefer) put in between fold of biscuits. Bake on cookie sheet at 400 degrees for 15 minutes or until done.

These biscuits can be refrigerated or frozen and can go right from freezer to oven. Bake slightly longer if they have been frozen.

Angels in Blankets

Yield: 36 servings

18 slices bacon, cut in half
36 shrimp, cooked and
   shelled
chili sauce (optional)
garlic (optional)

Cook the bacon on one side. Wash shrimp well. Dry and wrap in half slice of bacon. Secure with toothpicks. Refrigerate, covered, until just before serving time. Broil 6 inches from heat for 3 to 4 minutes. Turn and broil for 1 to 2 minutes longer.

If desired, it can be put in a mixture of chili sauce and garlic before broiling.

16

Bacon and Rye Balls

Yield: 2 dozen

1 lb. bacon
1 (8-oz.) pkg. cream cheese, softened
¼ cup evaporated milk
1 cup fine rye bread crumbs
2 tsp. onions, finely chopped
1 tsp. Worcestershire sauce
¾-1 cup parsley, chopped

Cook bacon until crisp; drain and crumble. Combine bacon, cream cheese, milk, bread crumbs, onion, and Worcestershire; mix well. Chill 2 hours, and shape into 1-inch balls; roll each in parsley.

Mrs. Cayetano Barrera (Yolanda)

Bacon Roll-ups

375 degrees
Cookie sheet
Yield: 40 roll-ups
Freezes

¼ cup butter or margarine
½ cup water
1½ cups Stove Top cornbread stuffing mix (and half of vegetable seasoning packet)
1 egg, slightly beaten
½ lb. bulk pork sausage
½ lb. sliced bacon (more if desired)

Melt butter in water. Remove from heat; stir in stuffing, egg and sausage. Blend thoroughly. Chill about an hour, then shape into small oblongs about the size of pecans. Cut bacon strips into thirds. Wrap one piece around dressing mixture and fasten with toothpick. Place on cookie sheet and bake at 375 degrees for 35 minutes or until brown, turning once. Drain on paper towels. Serve hot. May freeze before cooking. To freeze, you must freeze them individually on cookie sheets before storing them in large containers.

Mrs. Lonnie Gegenheimer (Betty)

APPETIZERS

Barbecued Ham on Egg Rolls

Deep kettle
Yield: 100 servings

¾ cup onion, chopped
⅓ cup celery, chopped
1 clove garlic, minced
½ cup butter
3 Tbs. parsley flakes
1 bay leaf
3 Tbs. Worcestershire sauce
⅛ tsp. thyme
1 Tbs. vinegar
¼ tsp. allspice
1 (14-oz.) bottle ketchup
1 cup water
5 lbs. ham, sliced wafer thin
100 cocktail egg roll buns

Sauté the onion, celery, and garlic in butter until tender. Add parsley, bay leaf, Worcestershire, thyme, vinegar, allspice, ketchup, and water. Cook all together in deep kettle for at least ½ hour. May simmer 2 to 3 hours or it can be made the day before and then reheated. Add meat and simmer for 2 more hours. Serve in cocktail egg roll buns.

Ceviche I

Fish: red fish, red snapper,
   piggy perch (any firm fish)
   chopped—the amount
   varies with cook's choice
   and availability of fish
12 limes
2 onions, chopped
3 firm tomatoes
1 jalapeño, chopped
salt, pepper, capers, to taste
2 Tbs. cooking oil, add more
   if desired
dash vinegar
garlic, chopped (optional)
cilantro (optional)

Squeeze limes and marinate chopped fish in lime juice, covered in refrigerator for 3 days. Rinse lime juice off completely in colander. Combine other ingredients and taste for correct seasoning. Add to rinsed fish. Chopped garlic and cilantro may be added, if desired.

This dish improves as it sits in refrigerator. It will keep up to 10 days. Serve as dip, salad, or main course. It's good with saltine crackers or tortillas, fried or soft.

Mrs. Jerry Fair (Zetta)

APPETIZERS

Ceviche II

1½-2 lbs. filet of trout, red
  fish, sole, red snapper, cut
  in cubes
1 cup fresh lime juice
1 cup fresh lemon juice
¾ cup fresh orange juice
2 onions, sliced thinly
3-4 jalapeño peppers (to
  taste), thinly slivered
½ cup pimiento-stuffed green
  olives
3 Tbs. red wine vinegar
2 Tbs. salad oil or very good
  olive oil
1 tsp. chili powder
2 Tbs. ketchup
½ tsp. oregano
½ tsp. comino
½ tsp. granulated sugar
coarsely ground pepper
Krazy Jane salt or regular
  salt to taste
3 green onions (all parts),
  chopped
1 bell pepper, slivered
1 red onion, chopped
1-2 avocados, chopped

Add all ingredients except bell pepper, onions and avocados together and pour over cubed fish. Marinate at least 12 hours or overnight. Approximately 4 hours before serving, add onions, bell pepper, and marinate a few hours before serving. Avocados may be added at the last minute before serving. Drain juices off of mixture and arrange on bed of lettuce leaves. Serve with assorted crackers if desired. Triscuits are especially good.

Mrs. Jerry Box (Deanna)

Chicken Salad Balls

Yield: 2 dozen

1 cup chicken, cooked and
  chopped
1 Tbs. onion, chopped
2 Tbs. pimiento, chopped
dash of hot sauce
½ cup salad dressing or
  mayonnaise
1 cup pecans, chopped

Combine all ingredients, mixing well; chill several hours. Shape into 1-inch balls.

Mrs. Cayetano Barrera (Yolanda)

APPETIZERS

Cheese Straws

2 cups flour
2 cups sharp cheese, grated
1 cup Crisco
1 tsp. baking powder
1 tsp. red pepper
1 tsp. paprika
2 egg yolks
4 Tbs. water
pinch of curry powder

Mix all ingredients together. Using a pastry tube, form straws about 3 inches long, onto ungreased baking sheet. Bake at 375 degrees for 20 minutes.

Dough may be formed into circle shapes rather than straws to prevent breaking. They do have a tendency to burn, so it is wise to watch them carefully.

Mrs. Allen Beakey (Jane)

Cocktail Pizzas

1 lb. hot sausage
1 (6-oz.) can tomato paste
1 (8-oz.) can tomato sauce
½ tsp. salt
¼ tsp. pepper
1 tsp. Worcestershire sauce
pinch of oregano
½ tsp. sugar
dash of garlic powder
1 pkg. Pepperidge Farm Brown and Serve French Bread (2 to a pkg.)
½ cup Cheddar cheese, grated
½ cup Parmesan cheese, grated

Heat oven to 425 degrees. Crumble sausage and cook slowly pouring off grease. Add remaining ingredients, except cheeses, and simmer for 20 minutes. Slice bread thinly; spread mixture on bread rounds and top with mixed cheeses. Put on a cookie sheet and freeze; then stack in plastic bags. Bake, unthawed, for about 10 minutes and serve hot.

Keep these in the freezer for quickies.

APPETIZERS

Cocktail Reubens

400 degrees
Baking sheet
Yield: 36 appetizers

36 slices party rye bread
Thousand Island salad
  dressing
1 (4-oz.) pkg. cooked corned
  beef, thinly sliced
1 cup sauerkraut, drained
  and snipped
6 (1-oz.) slices process Swiss
  cheese

Spread each slice of rye with a little of the salad dressing. Top with a thin slice of corned beef; cover with a teaspoon of sauerkraut. Cut each slice of cheese into 6 pieces; top appetizers. Place on baking sheet; bake in 400 degree oven for 6 to 8 minutes or until cheese melts and appetizers are heated through.

Corned Beef Roll-Ups

400 degrees
Baking sheet, ungreased
Yield: 3 dozen

1 (12-oz.) can corned beef
5 Tbs. mayonnaise
5 Tbs. mustard
½ tsp. salt
¼ tsp. pepper
½ tsp. garlic salt
3 dashes Tabasco
1 loaf thin-sliced fresh bread
  (crust removed)
3 Tbs. butter, melted
Parmesan cheese, grated

Heat oven to 400 degrees. Flake corned beef, add mayonnaise, mustard and seasonings. Mix well. Roll out bread slices thinly with rolling pin. Place bread slices on board. Divide mixture and spread to ends of each slice. Roll firmly having fold on bottom. Line up on cutting board, brush with butter and sprinkle generously with cheese. Cut in thirds and place on ungreased baking sheet. Bake for 10-12 minutes until lightly browned.

Cheese will not dry out if wrapped in a cloth dampened with vinegar.

21

APPETIZERS

Creamed Shrimp

Yield: 4 servings

4 Tbs. melted butter or
  margarine
4 Tbs. flour
1½ cup cream or whole milk
8 Tbs. ketchup
4 tsp. Worcestershire sauce
2-3 lbs. shrimp, cooked and
  deveined
crackers or cooked rice

Melt butter and add flour; mix until smooth and add milk. Cook in double boiler until thick and smooth. Slowly add ketchup and Worcestershire sauce. Finally add cooked and cleaned shrimp and serve hot with crackers or over cooked rice.

Mrs. Mike Frost (Sandra)

Crisp Parmesan Strips

400 degrees
Cookie sheet
Yield: 48 strips

12 slices white bread
1 cup butter or margarine,
  melted
1½ cups Parmesan cheese,
  grated
paprika

Heat oven to 400 degrees. Trim crust from bread; cut each slice in 4 strips. Dip bread strips in butter or margarine, then into Parmesan cheese. Place strips ½-inch apart on cookie sheet. Bake 8-10 minutes or until golden brown. Remove from oven. Transfer strips to wire rack, cool. Sprinkle lightly with paprika.

Mrs. Robert H. Kern, Jr. (Carolyn)

Hot Corn Flake Cheese Cookies

350 degrees
Cookie sheet, ungreased
Yield: 500 small balls

3 sticks butter
1½ lb. sharp cheese, grated
2⅔ cups flour
2 tsp. salt
1 or 2 tsp. red pepper
1 (8-oz.) pkg. corn flakes

Combine all ingredients. Roll into balls about the size of a marble. Flatten with a fork. Bake at 350 degrees for 15 to 20 minutes on ungreased cookie sheet.

Mrs. Robert Whitis (Linda)

APPETIZERS

Curry Chicken Balls

Yield: 36 balls
Freezes

1 (8-oz.) pkg. cream cheese
2 Tbs. mayonnaise
1 Tbs. chutney sauce or
  chutney, chopped
½ tsp. salt
1 Tbs. curry powder
2 cups chicken, chopped and
  cooked
1 cup slivered, blanched
  almonds or pecans
2 (3½-oz.) cans flake coconut

Place softened cream cheese and mayonnaise in small bowl of mixer. Beat at medium speed until well blended. Add chutney sauce, salt and curry powder. Mix well. Add chicken and chopped almonds. Continue mixing on low speed for one minute. Shape in walnut-sized balls and roll in coconut. Refrigerate for about 3 hours or until firm.

Mrs. E. F. Wallace (Janet)

Electric Skillet Cheese Fondue

Yield: 4 to 6 servings

1 lb. Swiss cheese, grated
2 Tbs. flour
1 clove garlic
2 cups dry white wine
⅛ tsp. ground nutmeg
¼ tsp. salt
dash of pepper
1-2 loaves French bread,
  broken into bite-size
  pieces, preferably with a
  crust on each piece

Toss cheese with flour. Rub skillet with garlic. Pour in wine at 300 degrees and heat until wine starts to boil. Gradually add cheese, stirring constantly with wooden spoon. Reduce heat to 230 degrees and continue cooking and stirring constantly until well blended and thickened. Add nutmeg, salt and pepper. When bubbly hot, transfer to fondue pot for serving. Spear bread with long fork or skewer and dip into cheese.

Mrs. Gary Gurwitz (Bailey)

Olive Surprises

large stuffed green olives
1 (8-oz.) pkg. cream cheese,
  softened
chopped pecans

Roll olives in cream cheese, then in pecans until completely covered. Serve well chilled. Can be made a day or two ahead.

APPETIZERS

Escargot in Garlic Butter

450 degrees

1 stick butter
2-3 cloves garlic, mashed
2 Tbs. fresh parsley, very
  finely minced
1-1½ Tbs. fresh lime juice
  to taste
1-2 Tbs. fresh bacon, very
  finely minced
¼ tsp. Beau Monde
  seasoning (optional)
salt and pepper to taste
2 dozen snail shells or fresh
  large mushroom caps
2 dozen canned snails,
  drained

Mix together the butter, garlic, parsley, lime juice, bacon, Beau Monde, and salt and pepper until very fluffy, using electric mixer or wooden spoon. Put approximately ¼ tsp. of this butter mixture into snail shell or mushroom cap. Place small end or tail of snail down into shell or mushroom cap as far as possible, and then cover the opening with approximately ¼ tsp. of butter mixture. Place snails in baking dish and refrigerate for several hours or overnight, if possible.

Preheat oven to 450 degrees and place baking dish of snails in middle oven for about 10 minutes, or until butter is bubbling out of snail shells. Serve immediately. If you do not have the special escargot forks, holders or clamps, you may hold the shell steady with a fork in one hand and use a small pick to remove the snail. With the mushroom cap there is no problem.

Serve the escargot from individual plates or from a chafing dish. If using a chafing dish be sure to pour excess butter from baking dish over the snails. Let guests choose their own shells. Pieces of crusty French bread or Italian bread may be served to "sop" the garlic butter after shells have been served.

Mrs. Jerry Box (Deanna)

Hot Cheese Biscuits

300 degrees
Yield: dozens
Freezes

2 sticks margarine
4 cups sharp Cheddar
cheese, grated
½ tsp. salt
4 cups flour
cayenne pepper
coarse salt (Kosher)

Cream the margarine and cheese. Add salt and flour gradually. A half recipe at a time may be made in a food processor. Roll into size rolls desired and chill or freeze until needed. Slice very thin while cold and bake 15 minutes at 300 degrees. Place on foil covered cookie sheets instead of greasing them. Sprinkle with cayenne pepper and coarse salt (Kosher) before baking. Store in air-tight tins or freezer.

Mrs. William H. Wilson (Marion)

Hot Cheese Squares

350 degrees
Yield: 80 squares
Freezes

3 loaves Pepperidge Farm
very thin sliced bread
1 lb. real butter, not
margarine
1 Tbs. Tabasco sauce
1 Tbs. onion powder
2 tsp. dill seed
2 tsp. Worcestershire sauce
2 tsp. Beau Monde
dash cayenne pepper
4 small jars Old English
cheese

Soften butter and mix with all other ingredients, except bread. Trim crust from bread. Spread mixture on bread and put 3 slices layered together. Ice sides with mixture. Cut into 4 squares. Freeze on cookie sheet, then store in plastic bag. Bake frozen for 15 to 20 minutes at 350 degrees. Should be slightly browned on top.

These can easily be sliced in 6 squares, making lots more.

Mrs. Paul Moxley (Karen)

APPETIZERS

Marinated Mushrooms I

Yield: about 25 servings

½ lb. fresh or canned
   mushrooms
6 Tbs. olive oil
3 Tbs. wine vinegar
1 tsp. dried tarragon
dash celery salt
1 tsp. onion, grated
⅛ tsp. freshly ground black
   pepper
1 clove garlic, crushed

Wash fresh mushrooms or drain canned mushrooms. Combine remaining ingredients and pour over mushrooms. Stir to coat well. Cover and chill for 6 to 8 hours, stirring gently several times. The mushrooms will darken. Serve on toothpicks.

Mrs. Ernie Williams (Ann)

Marinated Mushrooms II

Yield: about 40

1 large can whole
   mushrooms, drained
1 bottle Italian dressing
1 clove garlic, thinly sliced

Combine all ingredients. Shake well and marinate overnight.

Mrs. Gary Gurwitz (Bailey)

Jalapeño Quiche

275 degrees
9 x 9 pyrex dish
Yield: 20 bitesize pieces or
6 generous servings

1 med. can mild jalapeños,
   seeded and cut in strips
18-20 oz. Cheddar cheese,
   grated
6 eggs, beaten
salt and pepper to taste
dash of Worcestershire sauce

Line bottom of pie plate with strips of seeded jalapeños. Fill the dish with cheese. Pat down. Add salt and pepper and Worcestershire sauce to well beaten eggs and pour over cheese. Bake at 275 degrees for 40 minutes or until bubbly. Cool 15 minutes to set. Cut into small squares for appetizers or larger for zesty luncheon dish.

Grated cheese may be half Cheddar and half Mexican white cheese.

Mrs. Mac Pike (Tish)

APPETIZERS

Hot Mushroom Canapés

Yield: about 24 servings

½ lb. fresh mushrooms
2 Tbs. butter
2 Tbs. flour
¾ tsp. salt
dash cayenne pepper
small toast rounds

Chop mushrooms. Cook in butter over low heat for 5 minutes. Sprinkle flour, salt and cayenne pepper over mushrooms and stir until it thickens. Cool. Spread mixture between 2 small rounds of toast and sauté in butter or put mixture on a single round of toast, brush melted butter on top and broil until mixture bubbles. Serve hot.

Mrs. Frank Birkhead (Janet)

Josefinas

Yield: 5 dozen

½ lb. soft butter
1 cup canned green chiles, chopped
1 clove garlic, crushed
1 loaf cocktail rye bread
½ lb. Cheddar cheese, shredded
1 cup mayonnaise

Mix butter and chilies and garlic. Spread on bread. Top with mixture of cheese and mayonnaise. Broil until brown and fluffy. Each mixture will keep in refrigerator for 2 weeks.

Mrs. Shelley Collier, Jr. (Caryl)

Marinated Shrimp

Yield: 20 to 25 servings

5 lbs. medium shrimp
4 Tbs. hot mustard
½ cup tarragon vinegar
1 cup salad oil
1 bunch green onion tops, chopped
½ cup celery, minced
1 Tbs. (heaping) paprika
2 Tbs. ketchup
½ tsp. salt
½ tsp. pepper
1 clove garlic, pressed

Boil shrimp, rinse and drain. Combine all other ingredients and mix well. Pour over shrimp, cover and refrigerate overnight.

Mrs. Gary Gurwitz (Bailey)

APPETIZERS

Mushrooms Stuffed with Crab Meat

400 degrees
Large shallow pan
Yield: 8 servings

24 large fresh mushrooms
12 green onions, chopped
4 sprigs parsley, chopped
5 Tbs. margarine
¾ tsp. Worcestershire sauce
salt and pepper to taste
1 Tbs. flour
½ cup sherry or white wine
2 cans crab meat
1 lb. sharp cheese, grated

Wash mushrooms gently under running water and drain in colander. Trim stems; then cut off stems and chop along with onions and parsley. Sauté mushroom stems, onions, and parsley in margarine in small skillet, adding Worcestershire, salt and pepper, for about 10 minutes. Stir in flour and then wine. Add crab meat last. Put mushroom tops in large shallow pan and salt lightly. Use a teaspoon to divide mixture among mushrooms. Top with grated cheese and put into 400 degree oven for about 10 minutes, or until cheese is melted.

Excellent as appetizer, entree for luncheon or garnish for filet of beef!

Mrs. Shelley Collier, Jr. (Caryl)

Oysters Ernie

Yield: 24 tidbits

24 oysters
salt and pepper
flour
butter

Dredge oysters in flour, salt and pepper mixture and grill on lightly buttered griddle on top of the stove until crisp and browned on both sides. Sprinkle oysters with melted butter while grilling on both sides. Dress with following sauce after oysters are browned and are on hot serving plate.

Sauce:
3 Tbs. butter, melted
⅓ cup fresh lemon juice
2 jiggers sherry
1 cup A-1 steak sauce
⅓ cup Worcestershire sauce

Mix all ingredients and heat before pouring over freshly grilled oysters. Serve on toothpicks. This sauce can be saved, strained, re-heated and used again.

Mrs. Frank Birkhead (Janet)

Parmesan Cheese Sticks

325 degrees
Baking sheet, ungreased

white bread
butter (about 1 stick)
½ tsp. Lawry's seasoned salt
Parmesan cheese to taste

Cut crust from bread. Cut each slice into 3 sticks. If thinner sticks desired, cut each again. Brush both sides of each stick with salted butter. Roll in Parmesan cheese. Place on ungreased baking sheet. Bake at 325 degrees for 10 minutes, turn sticks over and bake 10 minutes more. If bread is very fresh, turn off oven and leave sticks in for a few minutes to dry out—not more than 5 minutes.

Mrs. Sam Henderson (Eleanor)

Parmesan Crowns

Yield: 15-20 servings

¾ cup mayonnaise
1 cup Parmesan cheese
1 Tbs. chives, chopped
Melba toast

Combine all ingredients. Spread on Melba toast. Broil for a few minutes.

Mrs. Carl Judin (Joy)

Pineapple Roll-Ups

Yield: 40 servings

1 lb. bacon
1 medium size can pineapple
  chunks

Cook bacon on one side. Cut the bacon in half and wrap it around a pineapple chunk. Hold the bacon in place with a toothpick. Broil until brown on both sides. These are best when served immediately. Prepare ahead and then broil at the last minute.

APPETIZERS

Peanut Butter Squares

250 degrees
Cookie sheet
Yield: 162 squares

1 loaf sandwich bread
1 small jar of smooth peanut
butter
½ cup oil
cayenne pepper

Cut crust off sandwich bread and save. Cut each slice into 9 one-inch squares. Put squares and crusts in slow oven, 250 degrees, until completely dry. Combine peanut butter, oil, and cayenne to make a syrup. Put crusts in plastic bag and roll, making crumbs. Take a handful of the squares and dunk in peanut butter mixture. Remove with a spoon and put them in the plastic bag with the crumbs and shake. Remove and place on wax paper.

Pepperidge Farm Puffs

375 degrees
Cookie sheet, greased
Yield: 24 tidbits
Freezes

1 pkg. Pepperidge Farm patty
shells, thawed
1 (3-oz.) pkg. Philadelphia
cream cheese
1 egg
1 tsp. lemon juice
1 tsp. chives
½ cup Cheddar cheese,
grated
½ small can shrimp, chopped
(optional)

Roll out thawed patty shells into rectangles. Slice each shell into four pieces. Roll each piece into a square. Place a small portion of the mixture of cream cheese, egg, lemon juice, chives, grated cheese and shrimp on ½ of the square. Fold over and seal edges as for a tart. Bake on a greased cookie sheet for 30 minutes at 375 degrees.

Vienna sausage can be used instead of the shrimp.
If you wish to freeze the puffs, do so before baking them. They can be frozen on a cookie sheet and then placed into plastic bags for storing in freezer.

Mrs. Jim Corcoran (Pam)

APPETIZERS

Pickled Shrimp

5 lbs. shrimp, cooked and
    cleaned
1 large onion, sliced in rings
7-8 bay leaves

¾ cup white vinegar
1½ cups salad oil
1½ tsp. salt
2½ tsp. celery salt
2½ Tbs. capers

Alternate layers of cooked and cleaned shrimp in ceramic or glass bowl with a layer of onion rings. Place the bay leaves on top.

Mix the vinegar, oil, salt, celery salt and capers together; shake well and pour over the shrimp-onion mixture. Chill for 12 to 24 hours; mixing several times so all the shrimp are coated. Drain and serve on toothpicks.

Potato Puffs

375 degrees
Baking sheet, ungreased
Yield: about 150
Freezes well

Potatoes:
2⅓ cups instant potato buds
2 cups water
2⅓ Tbs. milk
3 Tbs. butter
¾ Tbs. salt
1 onion, finely chopped
½ stick butter or margarine
salt and pepper to taste

Dough:
3 cans refrigerated crescent
    rolls

Mix instant potato buds, water, milk, butter and salt as directed on box. Sauté onions in butter or margarine and season with salt and pepper. Add to potatoes. Roll out 2 triangles of dough into one thin rectangle. Spread with a thin layer of potato mixture. Roll up jelly-roll fashion and seal edges. With side of hand, divide into about 12 slices or balls. Using your hand provides for an automatic sealer. Form into balls by sealing any open edges. Bake for about 15 minutes or until lightly browned.

Mrs. Gary Gurwitz (Bailey)

31

APPETIZERS

Rice Krispies Cheese Wafers

350 degrees
Cookie sheet, ungreased
Yield: 80-100 wafers

2 sticks butter, softened
2 cups sharp cheese, grated
  (½ lb.)
2 cups flour
2 cups Rice Krispies
¼ tsp. salt
¼ tsp. garlic powder
⅛ tsp. cayenne pepper

Soften butter and cheese. In mixer, add the butter, cheese and all other ingredients. Roll into little balls and place on ungreased cookie sheet. Press with a fork. Bake at 350 degrees for 12 to 15 minutes.

Mrs. Jerry McGilvray (Jane)

Sausage Balls

350 degrees
Baking sheet (with sides),
ungreased
Freezes

1 lb. sharp Cheddar cheese,
  grated
1 lb. hot sausage (use
  uncooked—spicy)
3 cups biscuit mix

Combine cheese with sausage and gradually add biscuit mix. Form into 1-inch balls. Place in pan with sides, as grease will build up. Bake at 350 degrees until golden. Let cool thoroughly and may be frozen at this stage. To serve, heat in oven till warm.

For variety, this could be wrapped around a stuffed olive.

Mrs. Jerry Fair (Zetta)

Stuffed Mushrooms

325 degrees
Cookie sheet

fresh mushroom caps
1 tsp. Rondelé cheese per
  mushroom cap

Wash and prepare mushrooms. Fill each mushroom cap with 1 tsp. of cheese. Place on cookie sheet and cook for 25 minutes.

Miss Jill Jones

Shrimp Imperial

thin sliced bread
butter, melted
5½ oz. can shrimp
⅓ cup (small jar) pimiento, finely chopped
⅓ cup green pepper, finely chopped
few dashes hot sauce
1 Tbs. Worcestershire sauce
½ cup mayonnaise
Parmesan cheese
paprika

Cut thin sliced bread with 2-inch biscuit cutter. Dip in melted butter and press buttered side of two pieces together. Separate and put in small muffin tin, buttered side up. Bake in 250 degree oven until Melba toast brown (about 1 hour). Mix the pimiento, green pepper, hot sauce, Worcestershire, mayonnaise, and shrimp. Mix together and spread in cups. Make a small dent in shrimp to which may be added Parmesan cheese and paprika. Bake at 350 degrees for 10 minutes.

Mrs. John Freeland (Jayne)

Variation:
(omit shrimp)
½ cup butter
1 egg
1 jar Old English cheese

Combine ingredients and beat until smooth. Fill the cups with the cheese mixture and heat in oven as for Shrimp Imperial.

Mrs. Kenneth Landrum (June)

Water Chestnuts

¼ cup soy sauce
2 Tbs. sugar
2 (5-oz.) cans water chestnuts, drained
bacon slices

Combine soy sauce and sugar. Marinate water chestnuts in sauce, from ½ hour to overnight, the longer, the better. Wrap ½ slice bacon around each water chestnut and secure with toothpick. Bake at 350 degrees for 30-35 minutes.

Mrs. Jim Corcoran (Pam)

APPETIZERS

Shrimp Toast

350 degrees skillet
Yield: 40 pieces

1 lb. raw shrimp, minced
½ cup green onion, finely
  chopped
¼ tsp. ground ginger
1 tsp. salt
⅛ tsp. black pepper
2 egg whites, slightly beaten
10 slices bread, cut into
  triangles
bread crumbs made from
  stale bread or bread that
  has been baked in an oven
  until crisp
peanut oil

Variation:
6 minced chestnuts
2 Tbs. soy sauce
1 tsp. ginger

Mince and combine the raw shrimp, green onion, ginger, salt, and pepper with the slightly beaten egg whites. Trim crusts from 10 slices of white bread. Cut each slice into 4 triangles. Spread shrimp mixture on bread triangles and sprinkle with bread crumbs. Drop into hot peanut oil. Turn once and remove when brown. Drain on paper towels.

Add to shrimp paste.

The toast is delicious by itself or fantastic served with a Chinese plum sauce (or sweet and sour sauce) and a Chinese hot mustard for dipping. These are very similar to Chiness egg rolls without all the work in making them.

Mrs. Neal Runnels (Gayle)

Sugared Pecans

350 degrees
Yield: 3 cups

1 egg white
1 Tbs. water
3 cups pecans
½ cup sugar
⅛ tsp. nutmeg
1 tsp. cinnamon

Mix the egg white and water together, but do not beat. Add pecans and stir until pecans are well coated. Mix the sugar, nutmeg and cinnamon together and cover the pecans with the mixture. Bake on buttered foil for about 30 minutes, stirring several times.

Mrs. Steven Zenthoefer (Ann)

APPETIZERS

Texas Trash

200 degrees
Yield: 4 (2-lb.) coffee cans

1 large box Alphabets cereal
1 large box Cheerios cereal
1 large box Wheat, Rice or
  Corn Chex cereal
1 large box Captain Crunch
  cereal
1 box stick pretzels
2 lbs. pecan halves
1 large bottle Worcestershire
  sauce
4 Tbs. savory salt
4 Tbs. celery salt
4 Tbs. chili powder
2 tsp. Tabasco
4 Tbs. garlic powder
1 lb. margarine
2 cups bacon fat
2 Tbs. liquid smoke

Mix cereals, pretzels and pecans in a large roasting pan. Combine remaining ingredients and bring to boil in saucepan. Pour over dry mixture, spreading evenly and mixing well. Put in preheated 200 degree oven and stir every 10 minutes. This is very time consuming, but worth it. After 1½ hours, test to see if dry mixture has taken up all of the juice or is almost dry. Let cool well and keep in coffee cans. This will fill at least 4 two-lb. coffee cans and will keep indefinitely.

Mrs. Jerry Fair (Zetta)

Variations: Substitute peanuts, almonds, etc. for pecans.

This is a good way to clean out the cereal cabinet!

Spinach Balls

350 degrees
Yield: 75-100
Freezes (before baking)

2 pkgs. frozen chopped
  spinach (cook by
  directions—drain well)
1 (8-oz.) pkg. Pepperidge
  Farm herb stuffing
4 eggs, beaten
1 large onion, minced
½ lb. butter, melted
½ cup Parmesan cheese
½ tsp. garlic salt
½ tsp. Accent or MSG
¼ tsp. thyme
½ tsp. black pepper

Mix all ingredients. Chill. Shape into balls. Bake 20 minutes at 350 degrees. These may be frozen uncooked. Thaw 20 minutes before baking.

This recipe can be used as a stuffing for cornish hens. Add chopped celery and/or apples.

Mrs. Bob Batte (Gerry)
Mrs. Bruce Gray (Suzanne)
Mrs. Tom Moore (Pam)
Mrs. Jim Thompson (Sandy)

APPETIZERS

Spicy Stuffed Mushrooms

Yield: 36
Freezes

36 mushrooms (about 1½
  lbs.—silver dollar size)
1 stick butter or margarine
1 bunch green onions
8 oz. cream cheese, softened
½ tsp. garlic powder
1 Tbs. Worcestershire sauce
¼ cup nuts (pecans or
  walnuts), finely chopped
½ tsp. cayenne pepper (more
  or less to taste)
1 Tbs. anchovy paste (or
  mash 3-4 filets)
parsley sprigs
paprika

Clean mushrooms with damp cloth. Carefully snip off stems (save for another use). Melt ½ stick butter in large heavy skillet and sauté half of onions about 3 minutes. Add (just one layer at a time) mushrooms and very lightly sauté about 2-3 minutes on each side. Carefully remove and place "cup side up" on large cookie sheet. Repeat process for remainder of mushrooms. Mix softened cream cheese until fluffy. Add remainder of ingredients as well as the sautéed onions from skillet.

Mound filling in cups of mushrooms using teaspoon. Garnish with sprig of parsley and paprika. Broil amount desired until bubbly, about 5 minutes.

All of the directions, prior to broiling, may be done in advance of serving time. The mushrooms should then be covered and refrigerated or frozen. Allow them to reach room temperature before broiling. Serve hot, with a napkin!

Mrs. Forrest Fitch (Marion)

Sugared Peanuts

Yield: 2 cups

2 cups raw peanuts
1 cup sugar
½ cup water

Stir all ingredients together in a large skillet. Cook at medium temperature heat, stirring constantly, until water is evaporated. Spread evenly on foil to cool.

Mrs. Hulon Webb (Carole)

Beverages

BEVERAGES

Amaretto Coffee

Amaretto
coffee
semi-sweet chocolate, grated
whipped cream
orange peel, grated

Put one jigger of Amaretto (almond liqueur) into a coffee cup or ½ jigger into a demitasse cup. Add hot coffee, a heaping tablespoon of whipped cream, sprinkle with grated chocolate and grated orange peel.

Mrs. Dan Seitz (Amy)

Bellini

fresh peaches (amount will
    vary according to number
    of drinks)
sugar
champagne

Peel and seed fresh peaches. Blend in blender. Add sugar to taste. Pour in sherbert glasses ⅓ full. Add champagne to fill glass.

Hint: Strawberries can be substituted for peaches.

Mrs. W. L. Moore (Ann)

Bloody Mary Mix

Yields: 1 pint

2 Tbs. salt
2 Tbs. coarse ground pepper
2 Tbs. celery salt
1 Tbs. Tabasco
2 Tbs. cocktail onion juice
6 Tbs. Worcestershire sauce
10 Tbs. beef bouillon
Mott's Clamato juice or
    tomato juice
(Vodka or Gin)

Mix first seven ingredients and store in refrigerator. To prepare a Bloody Mary drink, use 1 tsp. of mix and 1 jigger Vodka or Gin in glass of tomato or preferably Clamato juice. Add slice of lime and give a slight squeeze.

Mrs. Mark Seitz (Diana)

39

BEVERAGES

Christmas Float

Yield: 15 servings

1 dozen eggs, separated
2½ cups sugar
1 gallon milk
vanilla or any other flavoring
  desired
nutmeg

Separate eggs, beat yolks well; add sugar and beat again. Add milk and cook over medium heat until it coats a spoon (just under boiling point). Stir while this is cooking for it scorches easily. Beat egg whites. When custard is cool, add whites and vanilla. Blend. Serve very cold. Sprinkle nutmeg on top before serving.

Mrs. Joe Stroud (Ruthie)

Claret Lemonade

Tall glass
1 serving

2 Tbs. sugar
1 Tbs. lemon juice
crushed ice
½ cup dry red wine
sparkling water
lemon twist

Put sugar and lemon juice in a tall chilled glass and stir until sugar is dissolved. Add crushed ice and ½ cup dry red wine. Fill glass with sparkling water. Garnish with lemon twist.

Mrs. Larry Dooley (Jacqui)

Coffee Punch

Yield: 12-15 cups

1 qt. coffee, already brewed
1 gal. chocolate ice cream
¼ tsp. almond or vanilla
  extract
½ pint whipping cream
nutmeg

Chill coffee and pour in punch bowl. Add ½ of 1 gallon of chocolate ice cream and stir. Add almond or vanilla extract to whipping cream and whip. Place whipped cream and rest of ice cream alternately on top of coffee. Sprinkle with nutmeg.

Mrs. Robert Whitis (Linda)

BEVERAGES

Cranberry Punch

Yield: 30 servings

½ cup water
½ cup sugar
1 bottle cranberry juice
1 cup orange juice
½ cup lemon juice
2 qts. ginger ale
add vodka to taste (optional)

Boil water and sugar to make a simple syrup. Mix all ingredients together except ginger ale. Add the ginger ale immediately before serving.

Mrs. Allen Beakey (Jane)

Dry Chocolate Mix

1 lb. instant Hershey
  chocolate mix
1 lb. powdered sugar
1 lb. Coffee Mate
1 box powdered milk (kind
  that makes 8 qts.)

Mix the ingredients together and sift. Store in air tight containers and then take out portions as needed. When using, fill cup ½ full of mix and finish filling with hot water.

Mrs. Shelley Collier, Jr. (Caryl)

Fluffy Punch

Yield: 30 servings

4 cups sugar
6 cups water
1 (6-oz.) can frozen orange
  juice, (or juice of 5
  oranges)
2 lemons, juiced
1 (46-oz.) can unsweetened
  pineapple juice
5 bananas, mashed
2-3 large bottles ginger ale

Bring sugar and water to a boil and boil for 3 minutes. Cool. When cool, add the juices and mashed bananas. Freeze mixture in plastic freezer cartons. Thaw slightly before serving. Place in punch bowl and add bottles of ginger ale. Stir to slightly slushy but almost frozen consistency.

Mixture may be tinted with food coloring before serving.

Mrs. Frank Birkhead (Janet)

BEVERAGES

French Chocolate

Yield: 16 servings

½ cup semi sweet chocolate
  pieces
½ cup white corn syrup
¼ cup water
1 tsp. vanilla
1 pint heavy cream
2 qts. milk

Prepare early in day or at least one hour before serving. Over low heat, blend chocolate pieces with syrup and water until chocolate is melted. Pour into a cup and refrigerate until cool. Add vanilla. In a large bowl, beat cream while gradually adding chocolate syrup. Beat until mixture just mounds, then spoon into crystal serving bowl—refrigerate.

Just before serving: Scald milk, pour into heated coffee pot. Arrange on tray with bowl of chocolate whipped cream mixture. Spoon some cream mixture into each cup, then fill with hot milk. Guests stir the two together before sipping.

Mrs. Shelley Collier, Jr. (Caryl)

Ginger Ale Punch

4 (½ gallon) containers
Yield: 3 gallons
Freezes

3 (3-oz.) pkgs. lime Jello
9 cups boiling water
4 cups sugar
4 cups hot water
1 (16-oz.) bottle lemon juice
2 (46-oz.) cans of pineapple
  juice
4-6 bananas, mashed
1 (18-oz.) can of crushed
  pineapple
4 qts. ginger ale

Dissolve gelatin in boiling water. Mix sugar in hot water and boil, then add it to the gelatin mix. Cool. Add juices to mix, then add bananas and pineapple. Pour into 4 (½ gallon) containers. Freeze overnight. Partially thaw and add ginger ale (2 qts. of ginger ale to each ½ of the recipe).

For a pink color, use 2 packages of strawberry Jello and one package of cherry Jello. Will keep frozen for months.

Mrs. Joe Weir (Lupe)

BEVERAGES

Frosted Pineapple Punch

Punch bowl
Yield: 40 servings

2 qts. vanilla ice cream
1 qt. pineapple or lime
  sherbert
1 qt. pineapple juice
2 qts. ginger ale

Mix ingredients together and serve.

Mrs. Joe Stroud (Ruthie)

French Mint Tea

Yield: 2 quarts

13 small tea bags
¼ cup fresh mint leaves
juice from 2 fresh lemons
1 (6-oz.) can frozen orange
  juice concentrate
1 cup sugar
water

Combine tea, mint leaves and one quart of water in saucepan. Cover and bring to boil. Then remove from heat. Let steep 30 minutes. Remove tea bags and mint. Add remaining ingredients and additional water to make 2 quarts liquid. Chill, serve over ice. Garnish with mint.

Mrs. Allen Beakey (Jane)

Grapefruit Freeze

Yield: 10 servings
Freezes

1¼ cups sugar
1 cup water
handful of fresh mint
1 (48-oz.) can of pink
  grapefruit juice

Make a simple syrup of sugar and water, by boiling the sugar and water until the sugar dissolves. Crush into the simple syrup a handful of fresh mint. Strain the mixture to remove the mint leaves. Add the grapefruit juice. Freeze in plastic container. Thaw for 2 hours before serving. Garnish with fresh mint.

Mrs. Kenneth Landrum (June)

BEVERAGES

Green Punch

Yield: 18-20 cups

1 (6-oz.) can frozen lemon
    juice
2 (6-oz.) cans frozen limeade
1 (6-oz.) can frozen orange
    juice
6 cans water
1 qt. rum
1 qt. ginger ale
green food coloring

Mix ingredients and add green food coloring to color desired. Freeze and serve. (Will freeze to a slush consistency.)

Mrs. Robert Whitis (Linda)

Holiday Hot Perk

Yield: 8-10 cups

2½ cups cranberry juice
2½ cups pineapple juice
1¾ cups water

Pour these ingredients in the bottom of an electric coffee maker.

1 tsp. whole cloves
3 sticks cinnamon
1 tsp. whole allspice
½ cup brown sugar

Place these ingredients in the basket of the coffee maker, plug in coffee maker and enjoy a warming spicy drink when perking stops.

Mrs. Glenn Jarvis (Pat)

Holiday Red Punch

Punch bowl
Yield: 30 servings

1 (32-oz.) bottle apple juice
1 (46-oz.) can Hawaiian
    punch
1 (6-oz.) can frozen pink
    lemonade
1 (6-oz.) can frozen lemon
    juice
1 (28-oz.) bottle carbonated
    Collins mixer

Mix the first four ingredients in a punch bowl. Add ice ring made from carbonated Collins mix in a 9-inch ring mold.

Mrs. Larry Dooley (Jacqui)

BEVERAGES

Orange Blossom

Yield: 4 servings

1 (6-oz.) can frozen orange
    juice
1 can gin or rum
juice from one lemon
4 tsp. sugar
crushed ice
maraschino cherries, reserving
    juice

Place all ingredients except cherries in a blender and mix with crushed ice. In each glass put a maraschino cherry on top of drink along with a tsp. or two of cherry juice.

Mrs. Jim Miller (Terry)

Piña Coladas

Yield: 16 servings

1 (14½-oz.) can sweetened
    cream of coconut (Coco
    Lopez brand is good)
2 (14½-oz.) cans pineapple
    juice
1½ (14½-oz.) cans light rum
ice
slice of pineapple
½ banana (optional)

Blend the coconut juice, pineapple juice and rum together. Can be refrigerated indefinitely at this point. When ready to use put ice in blender up to ¾ full. Add mixture ½ full in blender. Add slice of pineapple and ½ of a banana at this time if desired. Blend and serve in champagne glasses.

Mrs. Jim Corcoran (Pam)

Pineapple Punch

Yield: 6 quarts

2 qts. pineapple juice
juice of 4 lemons
juice of 2 limes
juice of 4 oranges
1 cup sugar
1 pt. sparkling water
1 qt. ginger ale
fresh fruit in season for
    decorating top of bowl
few sprigs of mint

Combine all fruit juices and sugar in a large bowl and place in the refrigerator either overnight or for a number of hours to ripen. Add sparkling water and ginger ale and serve in a punch bowl, pouring it over a block of ice.

Mrs. Billy Simpson (Ginger)

BEVERAGES

Sangria

1 (24-oz.) bottle red burgundy
  wine
2 oranges, very thinly sliced
2 limes, very thinly sliced
2 lemons, very thinly sliced
¼ cup sugar
¼-½ cup cognac or
  brandy
2 cups chilled soda

Combine all but soda and chill for several hours, allowing flavors to "marry". Add no more than 2 cups soda at last minute. Serve in wine glass with ice cube (if desired). Garnish with freshly cut lime slice in glass. (Fruit in pitcher may have become soggy, but leave in pitcher for flavor.)

Mrs. Jerry Box (Deanna)

Screwdriver Punch

1 (10-oz.) can Mandarin
  oranges
1 cup vodka
1 (6-oz.) can frozen orange
  juice
1 (28-oz.) bottle orange
  flavored carbonated soda
1 (4/5 qt.) bottle Rhine wine
1 ice ring
orange slices
lemon slices

Mix first three ingredients, and just before serving, add orange soda and wine. Add ice ring, orange segments, and thinly sliced lemons.

Mrs. Larry Dooley (Jacqui)

Tequila Slush

1 (6-oz.) can frozen lime juice
2 (6-oz.) cans frozen limeade
1 (6-oz.) can orange juice
6 (6-oz.) cans water
1 quart bottle Wink or similar
  drink
⅓-½ bottle tequila

Mix ingredients and freeze. Remove from freezer 30 minutes before serving and stir until slushy with a spoon. Can be refrozen and kept indefinitely.

Mrs. Michael D. Owens (Cissy)

BEVERAGES

Seven-Up Midnight Punch

Punch bowl
Yield: 30 servings

1 (1-lb.) can crushed
   pineapple
1 (12-oz.) pkg. frozen
   strawberries, thawed
1 (46-oz.) can pineapple juice
1 cup grenadine
6 (7-oz.) bottles 7-Up
orange rind curls

Chill fruits, juice, grenadine and 7-Up. Combine pineapple and strawberries in punch bowl. Stir in pineapple juice and grenadine and pour in 7-Up slowly. Mix gently. Add 2 trays ice cubes. Garnish punch with orange curls.

Mrs. Larry Dooley (Jacqui)

Sorority Punch

Yield: about 1½ gallons
Freezes

1 (6-oz.) pkg. any flavor jello
2 cups boiling water
1 (12-oz.) can frozen
   lemonade, undiluted
1 cup sugar
1 (46-oz.) can unsweetened
   pineapple juice
1 gal. water
½ oz. almond extract (1 Tbs.)
1 large bottle ginger ale

Dissolve jello in boiling water, add lemonade and sugar. Stir well. Add remaining ingredients except ginger ale. Freeze day before using. Take out 6-8 hours before serving (if frozen solid). Add ginger ale just before serving.

Can be refrozen if ginger ale hasn't been added.

Mrs. Walt Mielcarek (Betty)

Red jello at Valentines and Christmas. Orange at Halloween, yellow at Easter and green for St. Patrick's Day.

Mrs. Stanley Marcus (Marsha)

BEVERAGES

Spiced Tea

Yield: 6 servings

1 qt. water
2 tea bags (individual size)
½ (6-oz.) can frozen orange
   juice
½ (6-oz.) can frozen
   lemonade
1 (6-oz.) can pineapple juice
½ tsp. cinnamon
¼ tsp. allspice
½ cup sugar

Boil water and add tea bags when boiling. Remove tea from heat and let steep for 5-10 minutes. Remove tea bags. Add orange juice, lemonade and pineapple juice. Stir until all the juices have dissolved. Add cinnamon, allspice and sugar. Serve hot.

Mrs. Joe Stroud (Ruthie)

Special After Dinner Coffee

Demitasse cups

2 Tbs. (level) coffee per ½
   cup of water
cinnamon or peppermint
   candies, crushed
orange peel, shredded
fat curls of sweet baking
   chocolate
whipped cream

Brew your coffee as usual using the ½ measuring cup of water per 2 Tbs. of coffee. This dark, fragrant brew will seem even richer poured from a handsome silver pot, with the small bowls of toppings for the coffee alongside. Offer the crushed cinnamon or peppermint candies, shredded orange peel, and fat curls of sweet baking chocolate as elegant additions. Top with the whipped cream.

Mrs. Shelley Collier, Jr. (Caryl)

48

Breads

BREADS

Beer Biscuits

3 cups Bisquick
2 Tbs. sugar
¾ can warm beer

Mix thoroughly; knead on floured board; roll out and cut in small circles. Place in pan with melted shortening, bake at 450 degrees for 15 minutes or until brown.

Mrs. Larry Fritz (Libby)

Cream Biscuits

450 degrees
9 x 9 pan
Yield: 16 biscuits

2 cups flour, sifted
1 Tbs. baking powder
½ tsp. salt
¾-1 cup heavy cream
¾-1 cup milk
4 Tbs. butter

Sift together the dry ingredients. Add the milk and cream. Turn out on floured board and knead a few times. Pat or roll ½-inch thick. Cut with biscuit cutter. Melt the butter in a 9 x 9 pan. Dip each biscuit in melted butter and place in pan. Bake at 450 degrees 12 to 15 minutes or until light and brown.

Mrs. Ken Forrester (Phoebe)

Never Fail Biscuits

450 degrees
Cookie sheet
Yield: 6 dozen minimum

1 cup warm water
2 pkgs. yeast
3 Tbs. sugar
¾ cup salad oil
2 cups buttermilk
1 tsp. soda
1 tsp. salt
5 cups self-rising flour

Mix together the warm water, yeast, and sugar. When yeast dissolves, add the oil, buttermilk, soda and salt; mix well. Add the flour. Put in a covered bowl for a few hours or overnight. Stir slightly and dip out with a spoon onto a floured board. Work with hands to form a biscuit. Bake in a 450 degree oven for 10-15 minutes. This dough may be kept covered in refrigerator for a week.

Mrs. Walt Mielcarek (Betty)

BREADS

Super Biscuits

450 degrees
Baking sheet, ungreased
Yield: 16 biscuits

2 cups flour, sifted
4 tsp. baking powder
½ tsp. salt
½ tsp. cream of tartar
2 tsp. sugar
½ cup shortening
⅔ cup milk

Sift first five ingredients; cut in shortening until the mixture resembles coarse meal; add milk all at once, stir only until dough follows fork around bowl. Turn out on lightly floured surface; knead gently ½ minute. Pat or roll out ½-inch thick; cut with biscuit cutter. Bake on ungreased baking sheet at 450 degrees for 10-12 minutes.

Variation:
Super biscuit recipe above
  plus:
½ tsp. sage
¼ tsp. dry mustard
1½ tsp. caraway seeds

Sift the sage and dry mustard with the dry ingredients. Stir in the caraway seeds with the liquid ingredients. Knead, roll and bake as for Super Biscuits.

Mrs. Jerry McGilvray (Jane)

Quick Banana Bread

350 degrees
2 loaf pans, greased
Yield: 2 loaves

4 cups of packaged biscuit
  mix
1 cup sugar
½ cup flour, sifted
½ tsp. baking soda
4 eggs, beaten
1 cup sour cream
2 cups bananas, mashed
1 cup walnuts, chopped

Combine dry ingredients. Combine eggs and sour cream; stir into dry ingredients. Add mashed bananas and nuts. Pour into 2 greased loaf pans. Bake at 350 degrees for 50 minutes. Cool 10 minutes. Remove from pans.

Mrs. Jim Jones (Jackie)

BREADS

Banana Nut Bread I

350 degrees
Loaf pan, greased
Yield: 1 loaf
Freezes

1 cup sugar
1 (8-oz.) pkg. cream cheese, softened
1 cup ripe bananas, mashed (2 bananas)
2 eggs
2 cups packaged biscuit mix
½ cup pecans, chopped

In bowl, cream together the sugar and cream cheese until light and fluffy. Beat in mashed bananas and eggs. Add biscuit mix and pecans. Pour into a greased 9 x 5 x 3-inch loaf pan. Bake in 350 degree oven for 1 hour or until done. Cover with foil the last 15 minutes if bread browns too quickly. Cool thoroughly before slicing.

Mrs. Cayetano Barrera (Yolanda)

Banana Nut Bread II

350 degrees
Loaf pan, lined with wax paper
Yield: 1 loaf
Freezes

½ cup oil
1 cup sugar
2 eggs, beaten
3 bananas, mashed
2 cups flour
1 tsp. soda
½ tsp. baking powder
½ tsp. salt
3 Tbs. milk
½ tsp. vanilla
½ cup pecans, chopped

Beat the oil and sugar together. Add the beaten eggs, bananas and mix well. Sift the dry ingredients together and add to the first mixture. Add the milk and vanilla and mix well. Stir in the pecans. Bake in loaf pan, 9 x 5 x 3, that has been lined with wax paper, for about 1 hour at 350 degrees. Cool and store in airtight containers. This will keep in refrigerator indefinitely.

Mrs. David Edrington (Carol)

What to do with over-ripe bananas? Freeze them and use later in frozen banana desserts or baked breads and cakes.

BREADS

Apricot Nut Bread

350 degrees
Loaf pan, greased
Yield: 1 loaf
Freezes

½ cup dried apricots, diced
1 egg
1 cup sugar
2 Tbs. butter, melted
2 cups flour, sifted
3 tsp. baking powder
¼ tsp. soda
¾ tsp. salt
½ cup orange juice
¼ cup water
1 cup walnuts or Brazil nuts,
  chopped

Soak apricots ½ hour. Drain and grind. Set aside. Beat egg until light, stir in sugar and mix well. Stir in butter. Sift flour with baking powder, soda and salt. Add alternately with orange juice and water. Add nuts and apricots. Mix well. Bake in loaf pan, well greased, for 1½ hours at 350 degrees.

Candied ginger spread:
1 (8-oz.) pkg. cream cheese
3 Tbs. candied ginger

Combine, and spread on bread.

Mrs. Jerry McGilvray (Jane)

Carrot Nut Bread

350 degrees
Loaf pan, greased
Yield: 1 loaf
Freezes

1 cup sugar
⅔ cup oil
2 eggs
1 tsp. cinnamon
1 tsp. nutmeg
1 cup carrots, grated or
  chopped
1½ cups flour
½ tsp. baking powder
½ tsp. soda
½ tsp. salt
½ cup nuts, chopped

Cream sugar, oil and eggs; add spices and carrots, mixing well. Combine remaining ingredients and add to mixture. Bake for 1 hour at 350 degrees.

Mrs. Robert Jones (Elizabeth)

BREADS

Cranberry Nut Bread

325 degrees
1 loaf pan, greased
Yield: 1 loaf
Freezes

1 cup sugar
½ tsp. soda
2 cups flour
½ tsp. salt
1½ tsp. baking powder
2 Tbs. hot water
2 Tbs. shortening, melted
1 egg, beaten
½ cup orange juice
1 cup cranberries, coarsely
   cut
½ cup pecans, chopped

Mix the dry ingredients together; add other ingredients in order listed. Bake in a greased 9 x 5 x 3 loaf pan for 1 hour and 10 minutes at 325 degrees.

Mrs. Boone Slusher (Shirley)

Peachy Nut Bread

350 degrees
Loaf pan, greased
Yield: 1 loaf
Freezes

2 cups flour
1 tsp. baking powder
½ tsp. soda
½ tsp. salt
⅔ cup sugar
⅓ cup shortening
2 eggs, unbeaten
¼ cup buttermilk
1 cup canned peaches,
   drained and chopped
1 Tbs. orange rind, grated
¼ cup maraschino cherries,
   chopped
½ cup pecans, chopped

Sift the first four ingredients together and set aside. Blend the sugar and shortening together creaming well. Add the unbeaten eggs. Stir in the buttermilk and peaches. Stir this mixture into the dry ingredients mixture and mix just until the dry ingredients are moist. Fold in the orange rind, cherries and nuts. Do not beat. Pour batter into a greased loaf pan, 9 x 5 x 3. Bake in 350 degree oven for 50-60 minutes.

Mrs. David Edrington (Carol)

55

BREADS

Lemon Nut Bread

325 degrees
Loaf pan, greased
Yield: 1 loaf
Freezes

⅓ cup butter or margarine,
  melted
1 cup sugar
2 eggs
¼ tsp. almond extract
¼ tsp. lemon extract
1½ cups flour, sifted
1 tsp. baking powder
1 tsp. salt
½ cup milk
1 Tbs. fresh lemon rind,
  grated
½ cup pecans, chopped

Blend well the butter and sugar; beat in eggs, one at a time. Add extracts. Sift together the dry ingredients; add to egg mixture alternately with milk. Blend just to mix. Fold in lemon rind and nuts. Turn into greased 9 x 5 loaf pan and bake in slow 325 degree oven for 70 minutes or until it tests done in the center.

Glaze:
6 Tbs. (or more) lemon juice
¼ cup sugar

Punch holes with a toothpick in the top of the hot bread. Mix lemon juice and sugar and spoon over the hot lemon bread.

Do not cut for 24 hours. This bread freezes well and doubles or quadruples well. Store in refrigerator.

Mrs. Jerry Box (Deanna)

Pear Preserves

Yield: 3 (16-oz.) pint jars

4 cups pears, sliced and
  peeled
3 cups sugar
lime sliver or two (optional)

Combine pears and sugar (with lime peel, if desired) in large saucepan and begin heating until mixture begins to "candy". Cook for about 30-45 minutes or until pears turn a reddish color (about 250 degrees on candy thermometer). Pour into sterilized and hot mason jars. Pour ¼ inch of hot paraffin on top of preserves and then seal with dome lids.

Mrs. Jerry Box (Deanna)

Lemon Bread

350 degrees
Loaf pan, greased
Yield 1 loaf
Freezes

1 cup sugar
½ cup shortening
rind of one lemon, grated
2 eggs, slightly beaten
1½ cups flour
1 tsp. baking powder
¼ cup milk
¼ cup lemon juice
1 tsp. vanilla

Glaze:
¼ cup sugar
juice of 1 lemon

Cream sugar and shortening; add lemon rind and eggs; blend well. Add sifted dry ingredients alternately with milk and lemon juice. Add vanilla and blend well. Bake at 350 degrees for one hour. While loaf is very hot, spoon mixture of sugar and lemon juice over top if desired.

Loaf freezes well and is easily sliced while partly frozen.

Mrs. Bruce Leahy (Susan)

Mango Bread

350 degrees
9 x 5 x 3 loaf pan, greased
Yield: 1 loaf

2 cups flour
2 tsp. baking soda
1½ tsp. salt
2 tsp. cinnamon
1½ cups sugar
1 cup cooking oil
3 eggs
1 tsp. vanilla
1 cup raisins (or ½ cup
  raisins and ½ cup coconut)
2 cups fresh or canned
  mangos, chopped

Mix together flour, baking soda, salt, cinnamon, and sugar. Add oil, eggs, vanilla, mangos, and raisins or raisins and coconut. Bake at 350 degrees for about 1 hour. Place foil over loaf if it browns too quickly.

If you make a double recipe, use only 1 cup cooking oil.

Mrs. Morgan Talbot (Jane)

BREADS

Monterrey Cheese Bread

400 degrees
Yield: 1 loaf

1 cup real mayonnaise (one
   pint jar)
½ cup Parmesan cheese,
   grated
1 bunch green onions, all
   parts chopped
½ tsp. Worcestershire sauce
garlic powder to taste
1 Tbs. parsley, chopped
1 loaf French or Italian bread
butter or margarine

Mix first six ingredients and refrigerate for a few hours. Slice the loaf of French bread. Spread margarine or butter on one side, place on baking sheet and heat long enough to warm and melt butter. Remove from oven and generously spread one side of bread (buttered side) with the cheese-mayonnaise mixture, covering top of bread slices completely. Sprinkle paprika on top and return to oven and heat until mixture is bubbly. Serve immediately.

Mrs. Jerry Box (Deanna)

Orange Marmalade Bread

350 degrees
3 (3 x 7) loaf pans,
well greased and floured
Yield: 3 small loaves
Freezes

2 Tbs. butter
1 cup sugar
3 eggs
4 cups flour
3½ tsp. baking powder
½ tsp. salt
⅞ cup milk
2 Tbs. orange juice
1 cup pecans, chopped
1 cup orange marmalade
1 Tbs. orange rind, grated

Variation:
¼ cup sugar
3 Tbs. orange liqueur
1 Tbs. orange juice

Cream butter and sugar together. Add eggs, one at a time, beating well after each addition. Sift flour, baking powder, and salt together. Add alternately with milk and orange juice. Add pecans, marmalade and orange rind. Stir well. Spoon mixture into 3 well greased and floured 3 x 7 loaf pans. Bake at 350 degrees for 50 minutes.

Mrs. Jerry McGilvray (Jane)

Mix in small pan. Cook until sugar is dissolved. Poke holes in bread with toothpick and pour mixture over bread. Let stand 15 minutes.

Mrs. Carl Judin (Joy)

BREADS

Party Bread

325 degrees
Yield: 4-8 servings

1 loaf French or Mexican
 crusty bread
1½ sticks butter or margarine
¼ tsp. garlic salt
¼ tsp. marjoram
¼ tsp. paprika
¼ tsp. rosemary
¼ tsp. thyme

Cut the bread into one-inch slices down to ½ inch from the bottom crust so that it is not cut all the way through. Cream the remaining ingredients into a spread. Spread the butter mixture on each side of each slice of bread. If any remains, spread it across the top of the loaf. Wrap the bread in aluminum foil, and bake in a slow oven (about 325 degrees) for at least an hour, longer if you like.

This is great for dinner parties. You prepare it in advance, stick it in the oven and forget it until time to serve dinner. Leftovers are good rewarmed the next day.

Mrs. Morgan Talbot (Jane)

Tasty and Nutritious Bread

325 degrees
5 x 9 or 4 x 8 pan
greased and floured
Yield: 1 loaf

1¼ cups all purpose or
 unbleached flour
½ cup whole wheat flour
1 cup sugar
1 tsp. soda
1 tsp. salt
1½ cups bananas (3), mashed
¼ cup butter or margarine,
 softened
2 Tbs. orange juice
¼ tsp. lemon juice (optional)
1 egg
¼-½ cup raisins
½-¾ cup wheat germ
 (optional)

Lightly spoon flour into measuring cup and level off. In large bowl, blend all ingredients. Beat 3 minutes at medium speed. Pour batter into prepared pan. Bake 60 to 70 minutes, or until toothpick comes out clean. Remove from pan to cool.

If using self-rising flour, omit salt.

Mrs. Randy Davis (Lynn)

BREADS

Tennis Ball Can Nutty Spicy Bread

350 degrees
2 Tennis ball cans
Freezes

1 cup brown sugar, packed
1 cup raisins or pitted dates
½ cup margarine
½ cup strong coffee
½ cup water
2 cups flour
1½ tsp. baking soda
½ tsp. salt
1 Tbs. Homemade Sweet
  Spice Blend*
1 cup nuts, coarsely chopped

Chop nuts in food processor using steel blade. If using dates chop them in the processor also. Combine sugar, fruit, margarine, coffee and water. Boil 1 minute. Remove from heat and cool slightly. Sift flour, salt and soda into large mixing bowl. Add Spice Blend. Blend in cooled liquid mixture. Add nuts. Prepare tennis ball cans by placing a circle of wax paper in the bottom, spraying with vegetable spray and sprinkling with flour. Be sure all is well covered. Divide batter between the two cans and place upright on lower shelf of oven. Bake about 40 minutes. Test for doneness with long broom straw. Place on wire racks to cool. Breads should fall out of cans, if not, run a knife around edges.

Freeze breads in tennis cans and seal with tennis can plastic tops.

*Homemade Sweet Spice
  Blend:
1 Tbs. orange or lemon peel,
  finely grated
2 Tbs. cinnamon
1 Tbs. nutmeg
1 Tbs. ground cloves
1 Tbs. ground ginger

Grate peel. Spread on waxed paper and let stand uncovered about 10 minutes. Put grated peel and spices in food processor and whirl for about one minute till mixed thoroughly. Store in airtight container. (Makes ⅓ cup).

May add 2 or 3 tsp. of this to cakes or quick bread batters or mix with ice cream, yogurt or fruit.

Mrs. Hartwell Kennard (Mary Lou)

BREADS

Zucchini Bread

350 degrees
9 x 5 x 3 loaf pan
Yield: 1 loaf

3 cups flour
1½ cups sugar
1 tsp. cinnamon
1 tsp. salt
1 tsp. baking powder
¾ tsp. baking soda
2 cups zucchini, shredded
   and unpeeled
1 cup nuts, chopped
1 cup raisins
3 eggs
1 cup oil

In large bowl stir together flour, sugar, cinnamon, salt, baking powder, soda, zucchini, nuts and raisins. In another bowl beat eggs and oil. Pour over flour mixture and stir until moistened. Turn into greased 9 x 5 x 3-inch loaf pan. Bake in 350 degree oven 1 hour 30 minutes or until pick inserted in center comes out clean. Cool in pan 10 minutes, invert on rack, top side up and cool completely.

Mrs. Morgan Talbot (Jane)
Mrs. Joe Friend (Pam)

Corn Bread

425 degrees
Iron skillet or
muffin tins, greased

1 cup yellow corn meal
1 cup flour
2 Tbs. sugar
½ tsp. soda
1½ tsp. salt
1 tsp. baking powder
1½ cups buttermilk
2 Tbs. shortening, melted
2 eggs, well beaten

Combine dry ingredients in large bowl. In separate bowl beat buttermilk, shortening, and well beaten eggs. Add liquid to dry mixture. Stir well. Put in iron skillet or muffin tins (greased). Bake for 25 minutes.

Can be made with 1½ cups corn meal and ½ cup flour if you prefer more corn meal flavor.

Mrs. Charles Murray (Cynthia)

Rolls or bread can be freshened by wrapping in a damp cloth for 1 or 2 minutes and place in a 350 degree oven for 10 to 20 minutes.

61

BREADS

Hot Corn Bread

350 degrees
Muffin tins or 9 x 9
cake pan, greased
Yield: 9 servings
Freezes

1½ cups yellow corn meal
3 tsp. baking powder
½ tsp. salt
2 eggs
1 cup sour cream
1 cup cheese, grated
1 (8-oz.) can cream style corn
½ cup jalapeño peppers,
  chopped
½ cup shortening

Combine all ingredients as listed and put in greased muffin pans or cake pan and bake 15-20 minutes at 350 degrees.

Mrs. David Edrington (Carol)

Jalapeño Cornbread

400 degrees
Loaf pan or 9 x 9
pan, greased
Yield: 1 loaf
Freezes

3 cups cornbread mix
2¼ cups milk
½ cup oil
3 eggs, beaten
large onion, chopped
2 Tbs. sugar
1 cup cream style corn
½ cup jalapeño, chopped
1½ cup cheese, grated
¼ lb. bacon, cooked and
  crumbled
¼ cup pimiento, chopped
1 clove garlic, chopped

Mix all ingredients together and bake in a greased 9 x 9 square pan or loaf pan. Bake at 400 degrees for 35 minutes.

Mrs. Phillip Webb (Laverne)

BREADS

Bread

375 degrees
3 (6 x 10) loaf pans, greased
Yield: 3 loaves

2 cups lukewarm water
1 pkg. Fleischmann's yeast
  powder, plus 1 tsp.
4 cups flour, sifted

2 cups warm water
1 heaping Tbs. shortening
2 heaping Tbs. salt
2 heaping Tbs. sugar
6½-7 cups flour, sifted (or as
  much as it will take)

The night before (10 or 11 o'clock) set the yeast by beating ingredients with a wooden spoon. Yeast will rise and may have fallen, but this is okay.

The next morning, add the warm water, shortening, salt, sugar and flour which has been mixed together, to the yeast mixture. Mix thoroughly with wooden spoon. Grease top of dough and place near stove (warm place) to rise. Cover with clean cloth. Let rise 2 times in this bowl or crock. Punch down between risings (approximately 1 hour per rising). Grease well, 3 loaf pans. After 2nd rising, divide dough into 3 pans and let rise 1 more time. Bake at 375 degrees for 50 to 60 minutes.

Mrs. Asa Bland (Judy)

Dark Bread

350 degrees
Loaf pan, greased
Yield: 1 loaf

1½ cups buttermilk
1 tsp. salt
1 tsp. soda
⅓ cup molasses
⅔ cup honey or sugar
3 cups whole wheat flour
½ cup raisins (optional)

Combine ingredients. Pour into well greased loaf pan and bake at 350 degrees for 1 hour.

Mrs. Don Bowman (Brenda)

BREADS

Dill Cottage Bread

350 degrees
1 regular loaf pan, greased
Yield: 1 large loaf
Freezes

1 pkg. dry yeast
¼ cup warm water
1 cup cream style cottage
   cheese (small curd)
¼ cup shortening
2 Tbs. sugar
1 Tbs. onion, minced
2 tsp. dill seed
¼ tsp. baking soda
1 egg, well beaten
2¼-2½ cups flour
1 tsp. salt

Soften yeast in warm water. In sauce-pan, heat cottage cheese until luke-warm. Stir in shortening, sugar, onion, dill seed and baking soda with cheese in large bowl; add the yeast and well beaten egg. Stir in flour a little at a time to make a soft dough. Knead on lightly floured surface until smooth and elastic (about 5 minutes). Place in greased bowl, turning once to grease surface. Cover and let rise in warm place 1 hour. Punch down. Cover with cloth and let rest 10 minutes. Shape into 1 large loaf and place in greased pan. Cover and let rise until double in bulk, 30-45 minutes. Bake in 350 degree oven for 40 minutes. Remove from pan; brush with butter; sprinkle with salt.

Mrs. C. B. Herndon (Katy)
Mrs. Martha R. Clopton

90-Minute Yeast Bread

400 degrees
Loaf pan, greased
Yield: 1 loaf

1 cup warm water
1 yeast cake
1 tsp. salt
2 Tbs. sugar
1 Tbs. shortening, melted
2-3 cups flour

Dissolve yeast in water. Mix in all other ingredients. Mix into a soft but not sticky dough. Let stand 15 minutes. Using heavy mallet, pound dough for one min-ute. Form into loaf. Put into greased pan. Let stand covered for 30 minutes. Bake at 400 degrees for 30 minutes. Glaze with butter, cool, remove from pan.

Mrs. Christina Henderson

Easy Sugar Lump Bread

375 degrees
2 (5 x 9 x 3) loaf pans,
greased
Yield: 2 loaves
Freezes

1½ cups milk
½ cup butter or margarine
½ cup sugar
1 tsp. salt
2 pkgs. active dry yeast
1 Tbs. vanilla
1 egg
5½-6 cups flour

Heat milk and butter, just to melt butter. In large mixer bowl, combine milk mixture, sugar and salt; cool to lukewarm, sprinkle yeast over mixture. Add vanilla and egg; stir. Add 2½ cups flour and beat 2 minutes at medium speed. By hand, stir in remaining flour to form stiff dough. Cover, let rise in warm place until light, about 30 minutes.

Filling:
¼ cup butter or margarine, softened
1-2 Tbs. cinnamon
50 cubes sugar

Divide dough in half; roll each to a 10 x 7-inch rectangle. Spread with cinnamon-sugar filling. Place the sugar cubes on top of the filling mixture, spacing about 4-5 across and about 5-6 rows along the dough rectangle. Start from the 7-inch side and roll up. Pinch ends under to seal. Place seam side down in greased 5 x 9 x 3 loaf pans. Cover, let rise 45 minutes. Bake at 375 degrees for 30-35 minutes. If necessary, cover with foil the last 10 minutes to keep from burning the top.

Icing:
½ cup powdered sugar
3-4 tsp. milk

Remove from pan and drizzle with powdered sugar icing.

An extra special treat during the Christmas holidays.

Mrs. Kenneth Landrum (June)

A good way to test dough to see if it has properly risen, make an indentation in it with 2 fingers. It is properly risen if it does not spring back.

BREADS

Onion Herb Bread

350 degrees
Loaf pan, greased
Yield: 1 loaf

½ cup milk
1½ Tbs. sugar
½ tsp. salt
2¼ tsp. margarine
1 pkg. yeast (active dry or
    compressed)
¼ cup warm water
2¼ cups sifted all-purpose
    flour
1 Tbs. instant minced onion
1 tsp. dried dillweed,
    rosemary or other herb
melted butter
salt

Scald milk, remove from heat, and stir in sugar, salt, and margarine until dissolved. Cool to lukewarm. In large greased bowl, dissolve yeast in warm water. Add cooled milk mixture. Stir flour into yeast mixture. Add onions and dill or other herb. Stir all together until well blended. Cover and let rise in warm place about 45 minutes. Stir down and beat vigorously about ½ minute. Turn into greased loaf pan. Bake at 350 degrees about 1 hour. Brush top with melted butter and sprinkle with salt.

Mrs. Reid Thorburn (Barbara)

Ozark Cowbutter Bread

350 degrees
8-inch cast iron skillet
Yield: 1 skillet bread

1 pkg. yeast
½ cup lukewarm water
½ cup butter
¼ cup brown sugar
¼ cup granulated sugar
2 eggs
½ tsp. salt
½ cup scalded milk, slightly
    cooled
3 cups flour

Dissolve yeast in water. Cream together the butter, brown sugar, granulated sugar, eggs, and salt. Add the milk and the yeast mixture. Stir in the flour by hand. Do not knead. Cover and let dough rest in a warm place 15 minutes. Put in a heavy 8-inch cast iron skillet. Pat smooth. Do not knead. Bake in a 350 degree oven for 30 minutes.

This recipe is over 100 years old. Lynn Flowers has her kindergarten class make this every year.

Mrs. Charles E. Thompson, Jr. (Sally)

BREADS

Butter Horns

Butter horns:
12 oz. cottage cheese
2 sticks margarine
2 cups flour, sifted
dash salt

Mix cottage cheese, margarine, flour and salt in mixer until cottage cheese is not lumpy. Chill overnight in covered bowl. When ready to prepare, divide dough into thirds. Roll each portion out on floured board into a circle and cut into 12 pie shaped wedges. Roll each piece up beginning from the wide side of each. Place on greased cookie sheet and bake in 350 degree oven 30-40 minutes. Ice with butter cream glaze.

Glaze:
2 Tbs. butter
2 cups powdered sugar
1 tsp. vanilla
2 Tbs. milk

Mix together the butter, sugar, vanilla and milk. Ice the butter horns while they are warm.

Pull-Apart Whole Wheat Bread

½ cup shortening
½ cup sugar
1 yeast cake or dry yeast
1 cup warm water
1 egg, beaten
½ tsp. salt
½ cup 100% all-bran
3¼ cups flour
butter

Cream shortening with sugar, reserving about 1 tsp. sugar. Add yeast to warm water; add reserved sugar. Add egg, salt, yeast water, and bran to creamed shortening. Add flour. Place in bowl and let rise until double. Knead lightly and form into small balls. Roll in butter, stack in greased Bundt pan. Let rise until doubled; cook 45 minutes at 350 degrees.

Mrs. William H. Wilson (Marion)

BREADS

Whole Wheat Bread

350 degrees
Loaf pan, greased
Yield: 2 loaves
Freezes

3 cups whole wheat flour
¼ cup sugar
1 Tbs. salt
2 pkgs. dry yeast
2¼ cups milk
¼ cup oil
1 egg
3-4 cups white flour

Combine 2 cups whole wheat flour, sugar, salt, and yeast in large mixing bowl. In a saucepan heat the milk and oil until warm (use candy thermometer and bring milk to 120-130 degrees F.). Add egg and warm liquid to flour mixture. Beat at low speed on mixer for 3 minutes. By hand stir in more cup whole wheat flour and the white flour to form a soft dough. Knead on floured surface until smooth and elastic (about one minute. Place dough in greased 2½ quart bowl; turn dough to grease all sides; cover and let rise until double in size (45-60 minutes). Punch down; shape into 2 loaves and place in greased loaf pans. Cover and let rise in warm place until light (30-45 minutes). Bake in 350 degree oven 40-45 minutes. Remove from pans immediately.

Mrs. David Edrington (Carol)

Golden Puffs

Yield: 3 dozen

2 cups flour, sifted
¼ cup sugar
1 Tbs. baking powder
1 tsp. salt
1 tsp. nutmeg or mace
¼ cup cooking oil
¾ cup milk
1 egg
powdered sugar

Mix all dry ingredients together. Then add the cooking oil, milk, and egg. Mix thoroughly. Drop by small teaspoonful (too large a spoonful does not cook thoroughly) into deep hot oil (375 degrees). Fry about 3 minutes or until golden brown. Drain on absorbent paper. Roll warm puffs in powdered sugar. The batter may be kept in refrigerator for several days.

Mrs. Ernie Williams (Ann)

BREADS

Golden Sesame Braid

350 degrees
2 cookie sheets, greased
Yield: 2 loaves

1½ cups milk, scalded
¼ cup shortening
¼ cup sugar
1 Tbs. salt
1 pkg. active dry yeast
½ cup lukewarm water
3 eggs
7½ cups flour, sifted
1 egg, beaten
1 Tbs. water
2 Tbs. sesame seeds

Combine milk, shortening, sugar and salt. Cool until lukewarm. Sprinkle yeast on lukewarm water; stir to dissolve. Add yeast, 3 eggs and 2 cups flour to milk mixture. Beat with electric mixer at medium speed until smooth, about 2 minutes, scraping the bowl occasionally (can beat with spoon until smooth). Gradually add enough remaining flour to make a soft dough that leaves the sides of the bowl. Turn out on floured surface and knead until smooth and satiny, about 8 to 10 minutes. Place dough in lightly greased bowl. Turn over to grease top. Cover and let rise in warm place until doubled, about 1 hour. Divide dough into 6 equal parts. Roll each into 12-inch strips. Braid 3 strips together to form a loaf and place on a greased cookie sheet. Form another loaf and place on the second cookie sheet. Cover and let rise until doubled, about 45 minutes. Brush with glaze using 1 beaten egg and 1 Tbs. water. Sprinkle with sesame seeds. Bake 30 minutes or until loaves sound hollow when tapped. Remove from baking sheets; cool on racks.

Mrs. Bob Batte (Gerry)

To achieve a glossy crust on your bread: brush the top lightly with a mixture of 1 egg and 1½ tablespoons of water immediately before baking. To achieve a soft crust on your bread, brush lightly with melted butter as soon as you remove bread from the oven.

BREADS

Refrigerator Rolls

425 degrees
Baking sheet, greased
Yield: about 48 rolls
Freezes

1 qt. milk
¾ cup shortening
1 scant cup sugar
1 cake yeast
1 tsp. salt
1 tsp. soda
1 heaping tsp. baking powder
9-12 cups flour

Put milk in a saucepan with the sugar and shortening. Barely scald the milk. (stirring is permissible). Cool to blood heat or 110 degrees on a thermometer. Dissolve the yeast in the milk mixture. Add flour until mixture is the consistency of cake batter (approximately 4 to 5 cups). Add the salt. This step can be done with an electric mixer. Let batter rise 2 hours in a warm place. Work down with a wooden spoon and add the soda, baking powder, and about 6 more cups flour until the dough is very thick. (Add additional flour as needed for proper consistency). Place dough in a large greased bowl, turning in bowl to grease top, cover tightly and place in refrigerator. (You can punch it down, but it is not necessary). Make into rolls 2 to 3 hours before baking (use for Parkerhouse, cloverleaf, braided, or any roll you like). Dough keeps 2 to 3 weeks in the refrigerator.

To make Parkerhouse rolls, roll out dough about ½-inch thick on a floured board. Cut circles with a biscuit cutter, brush with shortening, fold in half and pinch together. Let rise again and bake at 425 degrees for about 20 minutes on a greased sheet.

Mrs. Charles E. Thompson, Jr. (Sally)

A small dish of water in the oven will prevent the crust of bread that is baking from getting too hard.

Basic Yeast Rolls

400 degrees
2 glass 10-inch pie pans
Yield: 25-30 rolls

2 Tbs. sugar
1 Tbs. salt
2 Tbs. Crisco
2 cups hot tap water (not boiling)
1 pkg. dry yeast
4 cups flour

In a large bowl, cream together sugar, salt, and Crisco. Add 1¾ cups of the hot water. Stir until the creamed mixture is dissolved. Dissolve yeast in remaining ¼ cup hot water and add to other mixture. Stir in flour and beat 25-30 strokes. Cover and let stand until double in bulk. Refrigerate at this point unless using immediately. Pour on a floured board and knead. Roll and cut into shapes. Melt 1 Tbs. butter in two glass pie plates. Turn rolls in butter and let stand until double in size (about 1 hour). Bake in 400 degree oven for 15 or 20 minutes, or until golden brown. Dough will keep for approximately one week in refrigerator. I sometimes use half of it and save half for later use.

Variation:
Sweet rolls:
butter
sugar
cinnamon
raisins
nuts

Use half of Basic Yeast Roll Recipe. Roll dough thin, dot with butter, sprinkle with sugar and cinnamon—add raisins or nuts. Roll like a jelly roll and cut in ½-inch slices. Follow Basic Yeast Roll Recipe for baking instructions.

Mrs. Robert Whitis (Linda)

Fig Preserves (Mock Strawberry)

Yield: 3 or 4 (16-oz.) pint jars

3 cups figs, peeled and mashed with potato masher
3 cups sugar
2 (3-oz.) boxes strawberry jello

Mix and cook until thick—about 20 minutes. Seal in jars.

Mrs. Jerry McGilvray (Jane)

71

BREADS

Potato Rolls

375 degrees
Baking sheet, lightly oiled

¼ cup plus 2 Tbs. sugar
¾ tsp. salt
1 pkg. dry yeast
¾ cup lukewarm water or
water used in cooking
potatoes
1 egg, slightly beaten
⅓ cup shortening, melted
¾ cup potatoes, lukewarm,
mashed
3¾ cups flour

Add sugar, salt and yeast to potato water and stir until yeast dissolves. Add beaten egg, shortening and mashed potatoes. Add flour about a cup at a time until a firm dough is formed. Knead 5 to 10 minutes until smooth. Form into ball, lightly oil surface, and refrigerate in covered bowl for at least 2 hours. After this time, pull out the amount you want; roll about ¼-inch thick and cut into rolls. Place rolls on baking sheet that has been lightly brushed with oil and keep in warm place about 1-1½ hours. Bake at 375 degrees about 10 to 12 minutes or until brown.

Mrs. J. W. Caldwell (Bernice)

Bran Muffins

400 degrees
Muffin tins
Yield: 6 dozen

2 cups boiling water
2 cups 100% bran
2 tsp. salt
5 tsp. soda
5 cups flour
4 cups Kellogg's All-Bran
3 cups sugar
1 cup Crisco
4 eggs, beaten
1 qt. buttermilk
2 cups raisins (optional)

Pour boiling water over 100% bran. Cool. Mix salt, soda, flour, and All-Bran. Cream sugar and Crisco together; stir in beaten eggs, buttermilk, and cooled bran. Add dry ingredients to creamed mixture. Bake in muffin tins at 400 degrees for 15-20 minutes. Store batter in covered container in refrigerator and bake as few or as many as you wish. Batter will keep in refrigerator for 6 weeks.

Mrs. Glenn Andrews (Laurie)

Your muffin batter is perfect if it contains lumps.

Kolaches

350 degrees
Baking sheet, greased
Yield: about 3 dozen rolls
Freezes

2 pkgs. dry yeast
½ cup warm water
1 Tbs. sugar
1 cup milk, scalded and
  cooled
4 cups flour, divided
2 eggs
½ cup sugar
1 tsp. salt
⅔ cup margarine, melted

Dissolve yeast in warm water and sugar. Stir it and let it rise to the top of the cup. Scald milk and then cool; add it to the yeast mixture. Add 2 cups of flour and stir until like thin cake batter. Cover and let rise about 45 minutes. To the yeast mixture add 2 beaten eggs, sugar, salt and margarine. Sift about 2 more cups of flour gradually into the mixture. Mix and stir until dough is spongy and not sticky. Cover and let rise until about double (1½ hours).

Topping:
1 cup flour
1 cup sugar
⅔ stick of butter

Combine topping ingredients until crumbly.

Filling:
Stewed apricots, stewed
  prunes, stewed apples or
  any other filling you prefer
  cooled

Now spoon out dough mixture by table-spoon on floured board. Spread out like tortilla with rolling pin. Put a heaping teaspoonful of fruit on dough, pinch the dough together to seal and put pinched side down on greased baking sheet. Brush with melted butter and sprinkle with topping. Let rise about 45 minutes. Then bake at 350 degrees for 20-25 minutes. When done, brush with melted butter and let cool.

These freeze well. When you want to use some, let thaw, then warm in oven, uncovered, for about 10 minutes.

Mrs. Jerry McGilvray (Jane)

Always cut fresh breads with a hot knife.

BREADS

Blueberry Coffee Cake

375 degrees
11 x 15 pan, greased
Yield: 20 servings
Freezes

Cake:
2 Tbs. margarine
4 cups biscuit mix
⅔ cup sugar
2 eggs
1 cup milk
1 can blueberry pie filling

Melt margarine. Mix together biscuit mix, sugar, eggs, and milk. Add margarine to biscuit mixture. Pour into greased 11 x 15 pan, then top with blueberry pie filling.

Topping:
6 Tbs. margarine, softened
¾ cup sugar
¾ cup flour

Make a crumbly mixture, to resemble small peas, of the softened margarine, sugar and flour. Crumble topping over blueberry mixture. Bake for 30 minutes at 375 degrees. Cool.

Delicious for a brunch or as a dessert. Could be made with other prepared pie fillings also.

Mrs. Leroy Lewin (Hilda)

Blueberry Muffins

350 degrees
Muffin tins, greased
Yield: 24 muffins
Freezes

⅓ cup butter
½ cup sugar
2 eggs
2⅔ cups flour, sifted
4 tsp. baking powder
1 cup milk
1 cup blueberries
cinnamon and sugar mixture

Cream together the butter and sugar until light and fluffy. Add the eggs, one at a time, beating well after each. Add the flour and baking powder alternately with the milk. Fold in the blueberries. Sprinkle the tops of each muffin with a cinnamon and sugar mixture. Bake at 350 degrees until golden brown, about 20-25 minutes.

Mrs. Jack Whetsel (Martha)

74

Cinnamon Coated Cupcakes

350 degrees
Small or large muffin tins,
greased and floured
Yield: 18 large or 36 small

Puffs:
⅓ cup margarine
½ cup sugar
1 egg
1½ cups flour
1½ tsp. baking powder
½ tsp. salt
¼ tsp. nutmeg
½ cup milk
1 tsp. vanilla

Topping:
6 Tbs. butter, melted
½ cup sugar
2 tsp. cinnamon

Mix together margarine, sugar, and egg. Sift dry ingredients and add alternately with milk; add vanilla. Fill greased and floured muffin tins ⅔ full. Bake at 350 degrees for 15 minutes (small muffins) or 22-25 minutes (large muffins). Remove from pans immediately and roll in: melted butter; then in a mixture of sugar and cinnamon. Cool on racks or serve hot.

Mrs. Michael D. Owens (Cissy)

Honey Bun Ring

375 degrees
3 (9-inch) round pans
Yield: 40 buns

⅓ cup honey
⅓ cup butter
⅓ cup brown sugar
2 cans biscuits
½ cup canned pineapple, or
   peaches, and maraschino
   cherries, (fruit crushed)

Melt honey, butter and sugar. Halve biscuits and roll into little bails. Line bottom of a round 8 or 9-inch cake pan with fruit and cherries. Pour honey butter mixture on fruits. Put biscuits on top so they barely touch. Pour the remaining honey butter mixture over this. Bake at 375 degrees for 25 minutes. Invert pan and serve at once.

Mrs. Charles E. Thompson, Jr. (Sally)

75

BREADS

Ice Box Muffins

450 degrees
Muffin pan, buttered
Yield: 12 muffins

2 cups flour, sifted
2 level tsp. baking powder
2 Tbs. sugar
½ tsp. salt
1 egg, beaten
4 Tbs. butter, melted
1 cup milk (not too cold)

Sift dry ingredients together. Mix the wet ingredients and then combine with the dry ones, stirring only enough to moisten the flour, without removing the lumps. Pour in buttered muffin pans; bake at 450 degrees for 25 minutes. These can be left in pan 12 hours before baking if covered with a damp cloth and wax paper or Saran.

Mrs. Mitchell Darby (Martha)

Mince Coffee Circle

375 degrees
9-inch ring mold, (small tube pan),
greased and floured
Yield: 8 servings
Freezes

Cake:
2 cups flour, sifted
¾ cup sugar
2½ tsp. baking powder
½ tsp. salt
⅓ cup shortening
1 egg, slightly beaten
½ cup milk
¾ cup moist mincemeat

Sift dry ingredients together. Cut in shortening to resemble coarse meal. Combine egg, milk and mincemeat. Add to dry ingredients, mixing just until the flour is moistened. Spoon mixture into a well-greased and floured 9-inch ring mold, filling it ⅔ full. Bake in 375 degree oven for 25-30 minutes.

Frosting:
2 Tbs. butter, softened
1 cup powdered sugar
milk
salt

Combine the butter and sugar. Add just enough milk to make a mixture of spreading consistency. Add a dash of salt. Mix thoroughly and drizzle over warm cake.

If desired at Christmas time, top with candied cherries and pecans.

Mrs. Jerry McGilvray (Jane)

BREADS

Refrigerator Ginger Muffins

350 degrees
Muffin tins, greased
Yield: about 36

1 cup shortening
½ cup sugar
4 eggs
1 cup dark molasses
4 cups cake flour, sifted
3 tsp. ginger
1 tsp. cinnamon
1 tsp. allspice
2 tsp. soda
1 cup buttermilk
1 tsp. vanilla

Cream together the shortening and sugar and add the eggs and molasses. Sift together the flour, ginger, cinnamon, allspice, and soda and add to the molasses mixture alternately with the buttermilk. Mix well and add vanilla. Place in a covered bowl. Will keep in refrigerator for two weeks. When ready to bake, fill greased muffin tins ⅔ full. Bake at 350 degrees for 25-30 minutes.

Mrs. Jack Whetsel (Martha)

Sock-It-To-Me Cake

325 degrees
Tube or Bundt pan,
greased and floured
Yield: 24 servings
Freezes

Streusel:
½ cup pecans, chopped
3 Tbs. brown sugar
2 tsp. cinnamon

Mix in small bowl and set aside.

Cake:
1 box butter cake mix
½ cup sugar
¾ cup vegetable oil
1 cup sour cream
4 eggs
2 tsp. vanilla

Combine cake mix, sugar, oil, and sour cream. Beat in eggs one at a time; add vanilla. Pour half of mixture into a greased and floured bundt pan. Sprinkle the batter with the streusel mixture. Add the remaining half of the batter. Bake at 325 degrees for 1 hour.

Glaze:
3 Tbs. butter, at room
   temperature
2 Tbs. milk
1 cup powdered sugar, sifted

Combine the glaze ingredients and ice cake while it is warm. Continue to scoop glaze off of plate and spoon onto cake until it begins to congeal.

Mrs. Robert Barnes (Kay)

BREADS

Streusel Coffee Cake

350 degrees
Tube or bundt pan,
greased and floured
Yield: 16 servings
Freezes

Streusel:
½ cup sugar
1 Tbs. cocoa
½ cup pecans, chopped
1 tsp. cinnamon

Mix ingredients in bowl. Set aside.

Cake:
1 box yellow cake mix
1 carton sour cream
4 eggs
½ cup oil
½ tsp. vanilla

Grease and flour bundt or tube pan well. Mix cake ingredients together and beat for 5 to 7 minutes. Pour ½ of streusel in bottom of pan, then ½ of batter, then the rest of the streusel and finish with the rest of the batter. Cut through with a knife to swirl slightly. Bake for 1 hour at 350 degrees. Let stand 10 minutes and remove from pan.

Yogurt Coffee Cake

350 degrees
9-inch tube or bundt pan,
greased and floured
Yield: 12 large servings or 24 small

Cake:
½ cup butter
2 cups sugar
2 eggs
2½ cups flour
1 tsp. baking soda
⅛ tsp. salt
1 cup plain yogurt
½ cup mixed candied fruit,
 chopped fine

Grease and flour bundt pan. Cream butter and sugar until light and fluffy. Beat in eggs well, one at a time. Sift together flour, soda, and salt and add to batter alternately with yogurt. Stir in fruit. Spoon batter into bundt pan and bake at 350 degrees for one hour. Turn out on wire rack.

continued ...

Glaze:
1 cup water
1 cup sugar
¼ cup orange juice
¼ cup ginger flavored
brandy, or Grand Marnier

Heat water and sugar, stirring in small pan until the sugar dissolves, then boil rapidly for 5 minutes. Add juice and brandy. While cake is still hot, spoon hot syrup over cake.

Mrs. C. A. Pagenstecher (Adelyn)

Ginger Waffles with Citrus Sauce

Yield: 14 waffles and 1⅓ cup sauce

Waffles:
3 cups ginger snaps, finely
crushed
4 tsp. baking powder
½ tsp. salt
3 egg yolks, beaten
1 cup milk
4 Tbs. butter or margarine,
melted
3 egg whites

In mixing bowl, combine crumbs, baking powder and salt. Combine beaten egg yolks, milk and butter or margarine; stir into crumb mixture. Beat egg whites until stiff; fold into egg yolk mixture just till combined. Bake in preheated waffle baker. Serve warm with citrus sauce and whipped cream.

Citrus sauce:
½ cup sugar
2 Tbs. cornstarch
dash of salt
¾ cup water
½ tsp. orange peel, grated
½ tsp. lemon peel, grated
½ cup orange juice
1 Tbs. lemon juice
1 Tbs. butter or margarine

In saucepan, combine sugar, cornstarch, and salt. Stir in water; bring to a boil. Cook and stir until thickened and bubbly. Stir in orange and lemon peel, juices, and butter. Heat through. Serve warm.

The citrus sauce is super on top of ice cream, too!

Mrs. Neal Runnels (Gayle)

Topping:
1 pt. whipped cream

BREADS

Swedish Tea Ring

375 degrees
Cookie sheet,
lightly greased
Yield: large tea ring

Sweet Roll Dough:
1 pkg. active dry yeast
2 tsp. sugar
2 Tbs. 105-115 degrees water
7 Tbs. lard
1 cup milk, scalded
7 Tbs. sugar
3 eggs, beaten
1 tsp. salt
4½ cups all-purpose flour

Combine yeast, sugar, and water and let stand for 3 to 5 minutes. Dissolve lard in scalded milk. Add sugar, beaten eggs, and salt to milk mixture. Stir milk and yeast mixtures together. Add flour and beat about 5 minutes. Place in a foil covered, greased bowl in the refrigerator overnight. Take out just before baking. (Use this or your favorite sweet roll dough recipe.)

Cinnamon-Raisin Filling:
4 Tbs. butter, softened
1 cup brown sugar
3-4 tsp. cinnamon
1 cup raisins
½ cup nuts, chopped

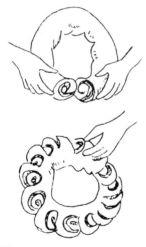

Mix together filling ingredients. On lightly floured surface, roll dough into a very large rectangle or 2 smaller 15 x 9 rectangles. Spread with filling; roll up tightly beginning at the 15 inch side—jelly roll fashion. Pinch edge of dough to seal well. Stretch roll to make even. With sealed edges down, shape into ring on lightly greased cookie sheet. Pinch ends together. With scissors make cuts ⅔ way through the ring at 1-inch intervals. Turn each section on its side. Let rise until doubled (about 1 hour). Bake until golden brown (25 to 35 minutes). If ring browns too quickly, cover loosely with aluminum foil.

Glaze:
2 cups powdered sugar
3-4 Tbs. milk
1 tsp. vanilla
cherries
nuts

Mix powdered sugar, milk, and vanilla until glaze is smooth and of desired consistency. Spread ring with glaze and decorate with cherries and nuts.

Mrs. Roger Vitko (Jolene)

BREADS

Sour Cream Coffee Cake

350 degrees
Tube or Bundt pan,
greased and floured
Yield: 16 servings
Freezes

Streusel:
¼ cup sugar
1 tsp. cinnamon

Mix sugar and cinnamon together in small bowl and set aside.

Cake:
1 cup sugar
¼ lb. butter
2 eggs
½ pint sour cream
1½ cups flour
¼ tsp. salt
1 tsp. baking soda
1 tsp. vanilla

Cream sugar and butter together. Add eggs and beat well. Add sour cream and dry ingredients alternately. Beat well; add vanilla. Pour ½ of the mixture into a greased and floured tube pan. Then sprinkle ½ of the streusel mixture on top of batter. Pour the rest of batter into pan and top with streusel. Bake at 350 degrees for 45 minutes.

Mrs. Russell Barron (Jeannie)

Orange Muffins

350 degrees
Small size muffin tins, greased
Yield: 84 bite-size muffins
Freezes

½ cup shortening
1 cup brown sugar, packed
4 eggs
2 cups flour
½ tsp. salt
1 tsp. soda
1 cup buttermilk
½ lb. dates, chopped
¾ cup pecans, chopped
1 Tbs. orange rind, grated

Cream shortening, add brown sugar; blend thoroughly. Add eggs, one at a time. Sift flour and salt together. Add soda to buttermilk. Add flour and buttermilk alternately to the creamed mixture. Then add the dates, pecans, and orange rind. Fill muffin tins ⅔ full. Bake for 15 minutes at 350 degrees. Remove from oven and while hot, dip in orange juice mixture. Drain and place on wax paper.

Orange dip:
3 cups sugar
1½ cups orange juice
orange rind, grated

Combine sugar, juice and rind. Heat, do not boil. Dip muffins.

Mrs. Kenneth Landrum (June)

BREADS

Walnut Coffee Cake

350 degrees
9 x 13 pan,
greased and floured
Yield: 20 servings
Freezes

Streusel:
⅔ cup brown sugar, packed
1 tsp. cinnamon
1 cup walnuts, chopped

Mix together in a bowl and set aside.

Cake:
2 cups flour
1 tsp. baking powder
1 tsp. soda
½ tsp. salt
1 cup butter
1 cup sugar
2 eggs
1 tsp. vanilla
½ pint sour cream

Sift dry ingredients and set aside. Cream butter, sugar, eggs, and vanilla. Beat well. Add dry ingredients alternately with sour cream. Pour half of batter in greased and floured baking dish. Sprinkle half of streusel and repeat. Bake 35 minutes at 350 degrees. If desired, ice with a powdered sugar icing.

Mrs. Blaine Holcomb (Andrea)

French Toast

Yield: 3-6 servings

6 slices of white bread
6 eggs, beaten with
  6 Tbs. milk
butter
powdered sugar

Cut each slice of bread diagonally in half. Soak each piece of bread in the egg and milk mixture. Melt a generous amount of butter on griddle or frying pan and fry the soaked bread over medium heat for about 5 minutes on each side depending upon how brown you like your toast. Total cooking time on both sides should be about 10 minutes. Remove from heat and serve with a sprinkling of powdered sugar and either jelly or maple syrup.

Mrs. Jerry McGilvray (Jane)

Cakes and Pies

continued ...

CAKES

Angel Food Cake

1 cup cake flour
¾ cup sugar
1 cup egg whites (approx. 12
  egg whites)
1 tsp. salt
1 tsp. cream of tartar
¾ cup sugar
1 tsp. vanilla
½ tsp. almond extract

Sift cake flour and ¾ cup sugar together 3 times. Set aside. Beat egg whites with wire whisk beater until stiff, not dry. Add salt and cream of tartar. Gradually fold in the additional ¾ cup sugar, vanilla and almond extract. Fold in sifted flour and sugar. Pour in angel food cake pan and bake 30 minutes. Cool cake upside down—put cone in large coke bottle.

Variation: Mango Topping
1 can mangos
1 can sweetened condensed
  milk
juice of 1 lime (or to taste)

In blender combine mangos with milk and lime juice. Chill. Serve on cake slices.

Apricot Nectar Cake

350 degrees
Bundt pan,
greased and floured
Yield: 24 servings
Freezes

Cake:
1 box yellow cake mix
6 eggs
⅔ cup apricot nectar
1 box lemon jello
1 tsp. lemon extract
⅔ cup oil

Combine cake ingredients and bake in greased and floured tube pan for 1 hour in 350 degree oven. Remove from pan and glaze with mixture below.

Glaze:
1 cup powdered sugar
2 Tbs. lemon juice

Mix powdered sugar with enough lemon juice to make a glaze and dribble over cake while hot.

So easy to make and very moist.
Mrs. Don Bowman (Brenda)

CAKES

Banana Pudding Cake

350 degrees
10-inch tube or Bundt pan,
well greased and floured
Yield: 16 slices

1-2 small, ripe bananas
1 (5½-oz.) pkg. banana cream
  or vanilla instant pudding
1 box two-layer white cake
  mix
4 eggs
1 cup water
¼ cup oil
½ cup nuts, finely chopped
powdered sugar, if desired

Slice bananas into large mixer bowl and beat until well mashed; add the pudding mix, cake mix, eggs, water, oil, and nuts. Blend, then beat at medium speed of electric mixer for 2 minutes. Pour into a well-greased and floured 10-inch tube or Bundt pan. Bake at 350 degrees for 60 to 70 minutes. Cool in pan for at least 15 minutes. Remove from pan and finish cooling on rack. Sprinkle with powdered sugar, if desired.

Cake can be baked in a 13 x 9 pan for 50-55 minutes.

Mrs. Ken Kachtik (Sue)

Brown Sugar Pound Cake

300 degrees
Tube or Bundt pan,
greased and floured
Freezes

½ cup nuts, finely chopped
3 cups flour, sifted, then
  measured
3 sticks margarine
1 lb. box light brown sugar
½ cup granulated sugar
1 cup milk
½ tsp. baking powder
5 eggs, separated

Put nuts in ½ cup of the sifted flour. Roll nuts around. Add to remaining flour. Set aside. Cream margarine and sugar. Add milk, flour mixture, baking powder and the yolks of the eggs (one at a time). Beat well. Beat egg whites separately to stiff peaks and fold by hand into cake mixture. Bake in greased and floured tube or Bundt pan at 300 degrees for 1-1½ hours, checking for doneness.

Better if flour is sifted three times.

Mrs. Charles Murray (Cynthia)

CAKES

Banana Split Cake

9 x 13 baking pan
Yield: about 12 servings

Crust:
2 cups graham cracker
  crumbs
½ cup butter or margarine

Filling:
1 cup butter or margarine
2 eggs
1 box powdered sugar
5 bananas, sliced and placed
  in pineapple juice until
  ready to use.
2 (20-oz.) cans crushed
  pineapple, well drained
9-10 oz. whipped dairy
  topping
1 cup cherries, chopped
1 cup pecans, chopped

To make crust, combine graham cracker crumbs with butter or margarine. Press into baking pan and refrigerate or freeze while preparing filling.

Cream butter or margarine; add eggs and powdered sugar. Place this mixture into crust. Add bananas, drained pineapple and dairy topping. Sprinkle with cherries and pecans. Chill 24 hours.

Mrs. John Childers (Kathleen)

Butter Cake

350 degrees
Bundt pan, greased
Yield: 16-20 servings
Freezes

¾ cup oil
½ cup sugar
4 eggs (one at a time)
1 tsp. vanilla
½ pint sour cream
1 cup pecans, chopped
1 pkg. Duncan Hines Butter
  Cake Mix
2 Tbs. brown sugar
1 Tbs. cinnamon

Add oil, sugar, eggs (one at a time), vanilla, sour cream and pecans to cake mix. Do not overmix! Pour one half of the batter into a greased and floured tube pan. Mix brown sugar and cinnamon, and sprinkle over batter. Top with remaining batter. Bake 1 hour at 350 degrees.

Mrs. Jim Jones (Jackie)

CAKES

Buttermilk Pound Cake

325 degrees
Bundt pan, greased
Yield: 16-20 slices
Freezes

4 eggs, separated
2½ cups sugar
1 cup butter or margarine
3 cups flour
¼ tsp. soda
salt
1 cup buttermilk

Beat egg whites with ½ cup sugar until stiff. Set aside. Blend butter, 2 cups sugar and egg yolks; beat until thick. Alternate flour, soda and salt with buttermilk (begin and end with flour). Fold in egg whites. Pour into greased and floured tube pan and bake in 325 degree oven for 1½ hours. Do not look at cake until 1 hour is over. For the last 30 minutes, cover with foil to keep from burning. Check to see if it is pulling away from sides of pan; then it is done.

Variation:
½ cup brown sugar
1 tsp. cinnamon
water to moisten

Mix ½ cup brown sugar, 1 tsp. cinnamon and enough water to moisten; pour about half of the cake mixture in tube pan, pour brown sugar mixture over and then remainder of cake. Bake as above.

Cassata

Yield: 12 servings

1 (9 x 5) pound cake
1 (15-oz.) carton ricotta
  cheese
1 oz. orange liqueur
1 (10-oz.) raspberry jam
1 (2¾-oz.) pkg. blanched
  almonds, finely chopped
1 (12-oz.) carton Cool Whip

Chill pound cake at least an hour. Slice the cake horizontally into 4 layers. Beat ricotta cheese until smooth. Mix together jam and liqueur. Place base layer of cake on serving platter. Spread with ⅓ ricotta cheese, jam and almonds. Repeat twice more, ending with a top layer of plain cake. Press the filled cake gently. Use a spatula to even up sides. Cover with a plastic wrap and refrigerate for 24 hours. Before serving, frost with whipped cream or Cool Whip.

Mrs. Bob McClure (Ginger)

CAKES

Carrot Cake

Cake:
2 cups sugar
1¼ cups oil
4 eggs
2 cups flour
2 tsp. cinnamon
2 tsp. baking powder
2 tsp. soda
3 cups carrots, finely grated
1½ cups pecans, chopped

Cream sugar and oil. Add eggs one at a time, beating well after each addition. Sift dry ingredients and add alternately with carrots and pecans. Pour into an ungreased Bundt pan and bake at 300 degrees for 1 hour and 10 minutes. Cool. Then remove from pan and ice with frosting listed below.

Frosting:
1 (8-oz.) pkg. cream cheese
½ stick butter, softened
1 tsp. vanilla
1 box powdered sugar, sifted

Beat together cream cheese and butter. (It helps if cheese and butter are at room temperature.) Add vanilla and continue beating while adding sifted powdered sugar.

Cake can be baked in 3 layers for 20-25 minutes at 350 degrees. Can be baked in little muffin tins at 350 degrees for 12 minutes. These are delicious for teas, coffees, etc. Ice with frosting as usual.

Mrs. Homero Rivas (Sonia)

A cup of self-rising flour contains 1½ teaspoons baking powder and ½ teaspoon salt.

The safest size egg to use in a recipe is a large egg. When using extra large eggs you may need to add a little more flour and when using a small egg you may need a little less flour.

CAKES

Chocolate Banana Cake

300 degrees
9 x 13 pan, ungreased
Yield: 20 servings

Cake:
2 cups sugar
1 cup shortening
2 eggs, well beaten
3 bananas, mashed
½ cup cocoa
2½ cups flour
2 tsp. soda
¼ tsp. salt
½ cup buttermilk
1 cup boiling water

Cream sugar and shortening; add eggs and bananas. Mix well. Sift cocoa, flour, soda, and salt and add alternately with buttermilk. Mix well. Lastly, add boiling water. Bake in 9 x 13 ungreased pan at 300 degrees about 50 minutes. Frost with 2 Minute Fudge Frosting.

Frosting:
1 cup sugar
½ cup cocoa
½ cup margarine
¼ cup milk
pinch salt
1 tsp. vanilla

Blend in saucepan the sugar and cocoa. Add margarine, milk, and salt. Cook over low heat, stirring constantly, until it boils. Then boil for 2 minutes without stirring. Remove from heat. Add vanilla and frost cake while icing is hot.

Mrs. Charles Henson (Nancy)

Chocolate Chip Fudge Marble Cake

350 degrees
Bundt pan, well greased
Yield: 16 servings

Cake:
1 box Duncan Hines Butter Cake Mix
½ cup sugar
⅔ cup oil
1 cup sour cream
4 eggs
1 generous tsp. vanilla
1 (5.5-oz.) can Hershey's chocolate syrup
½ (12-oz.) package mini milk chocolate chips

Mix cake mix, sugar, oil and sour cream. Add eggs, one at a time and vanilla. Do not mix well. Remove ½ to ¾ cup batter and to it add the can of chocolate syrup. To white batter, mix in milk chocolate chips. Pour white batter into very well-greased Bundt pan. Drop chocolate batter by tablespoons onto white batter and swirl with knife to marble. Bake at 350 degrees for 55-60 minutes. When testing, cake need not be perfectly dry. Let cool.

continued . . .

CAKES

Icing:
1 stick butter
6 Tbs. milk
4 Tbs. cocoa
1 box powdered sugar
1 tsp. vanilla
1 cup pecans, chopped

Bring to boil 1 stick butter, milk and cocoa. Remove from heat and add confectioner's sugar, vanilla and pecans. Beat to right consistency and ice cake.

Mrs. Gary Gurwitz (Bailey)

Chocolate Sheet Cake

400 degrees
16 x 11 pan,
greased and floured
Yield: 20 servings
Freezes

Cake:
4 Tbs. cocoa
1 stick margarine
¼ cup shortening
1 cup water
2 cups flour
2 cups sugar
½ cup buttermilk
1 tsp. soda
2 eggs, slightly beaten
1 tsp. vanilla

In saucepan, boil cocoa, margarine, shortening, and water. Pour this mixture over flour and sugar in a large bowl. Mix well. Add buttermilk that has been mixed with soda. Mix well. Add beaten eggs and vanilla. Pour into a greased and floured 16 x 11 pan and bake 20 minutes at 400 degrees.

Frosting:
1 stick margarine
4 Tbs. cocoa
6 Tbs. milk
1 box powdered sugar
1 cup pecans, chopped
½ tsp. vanilla

Five minutes before cake is finished, make frosting as follows: mix and boil margarine, cocoa, and milk. Add sugar, nuts and vanilla to cocoa mixture and mix well. Pour over cake while it is hot.

Mrs. Billy Simpson (Ginger)

For a chocolate cake, dust pans with cocoa rather than flour.

CAKES

Hershey Bar Cake

300 degrees
Tube or Bundt pan,
greased and floured
Yield: 18 servings
Freezes

7 (1½-oz.) Hershey bars
2 sticks margarine
2 cups sugar
4 eggs
2 tsp. vanilla
2½ cups flour
¼ tsp. soda
1 cup buttermilk
1 cup pecans or walnuts,
   chopped
powdered sugar

Melt 7 Hersheys in top of double boiler with 2 Tbs. water. Cream margarine and sugar. Add eggs and beat well. Add chocolate mixture and vanilla. Mix flour and soda, and add alternately with buttermilk. Mix well. Add chopped pecans. Pour in large tube pan that has been greased and floured and bake at 300 degrees for 2 hours. Dust with powdered sugar.

This is very moist and will keep for several days.

Mrs. Madonna Johnson

Mississippi Mud Cake

350 degrees
11 x 15 pan, well greased
Yield: 30-35 large servings
Freezes

Cake:
2 sticks margarine, melted
⅓ cup cocoa
1 (3½-oz.) can coconut
pinch salt
2 cups sugar
1½ cups flour
1 tsp. baking powder
1 cup pecans, chopped
4 eggs, beaten
1 (7-oz.) jar marshmallow
   creme

Place all cake ingredients except marshmallow creme in mixing bowl and mix well. Bake in a well-greased oblong pan for 40 minutes at 350 degrees. Take from oven and while cake is still hot, spread on marshmallow creme.

continued . . .

CAKES

Frosting:
¾ cup margarine
¼ cup milk
1 square baking chocolate
2¾ box powdered sugar
1 tsp. vanilla

Melt over low heat, the margarine, milk and chocolate. Add powdered sugar and vanilla. Spread over marshmallow creme on cake.

Mrs. Glenn Jarvis (Pat)

White Chocolate Cake

350 degrees
3 (8-9 inch) layer pans,
greased, floured, lined
Yield: 12-14 servings

Cake:
¼ lb. white chocolate
1 cup butter, softened
2 cups sugar
4 eggs, separated
1 tsp. vanilla
2½ cups cake flour, sifted
½ tsp. salt
1 tsp. baking soda
1 cup buttermilk

Heat oven to 350 degrees. Melt white chocolate in ½ cup boiling water; cool. Meanwhile cream together butter and sugar until fluffy. Add egg yolks one at a time and beat well after each addition. Add melted chocolate and vanilla; mix well. Sift dry ingredients together and add alternately with buttermilk to the creamed mixture. Beat after each addition until smooth, but do not overbeat. Beat egg whites until stiff. Fold into mixture. Pour into 3 (8-9 inch) layer pans, greased, floured and lined on the bottom with wax paper. Bake for 30-40 minutes. Cool.

Custard:
3 eggs, well beaten
½ cup sugar
1 cup milk, scalded in double boiler

Add eggs and sugar slowly to hot milk and cook until spoon is coated. Cool; spread between layers.

Icing:
1 (8-oz.) pkg. cream cheese
½ cup butter
1 box powdered sugar
1 tsp. vanilla
Angel flake coconut

Cream together all ingredients until fluffy and set in refrigerator to chill before icing cake. Press coconut into icing.

CAKES

Coca-Cola Cake

375 degrees
11 x 15 pan, ungreased
Yield: 20 servings
Freezes

Cake:
1/2 cup Coke
1/2 cup oil
4 Tbs. cocoa
1 stick butter
1 cup water
2 cups sugar
2 eggs
2 cups flour
1/2 tsp. soda
1/2 tsp. vanilla

Bring Coke, oil, cocoa, butter and water to a boil. Let cool to lukewarm. Add sugar, eggs, flour, soda, and vanilla by hand into lukewarm mixture. Pour into ungreased sheet cake pan. Bake at 375 degrees about 25 minutes.

Frosting:
1 stick butter
1/2 cup Coke
4 Tbs. cocoa
1 box powdered sugar
1/2 tsp. vanilla
1 cup pecans, chopped

Bring to a boil the butter, Coke and cocoa. Remove from heat and add powdered sugar and vanilla. Stir. Add pecans. Pour over warm cake.

Rich and delicious. Like chocolate sheet cake with coke variation!

Mrs. Neal Runnels (Gayle)

Cream Cheese Cake

350 degrees
9 x 13 pan

4 eggs
1 box yellow cake mix
1 stick margarine, softened
1 box powdered sugar
1 (8-oz.) pkg. cream cheese

Mix 2 eggs, cake mix, and softened margarine together. Spread evenly into a 9 x 13 baking pan. Mix powdered sugar, 2 eggs and cream cheese. Spread over cake mix. Bake at 350 degrees for 40 minutes.

Mrs. Paul Moxley (Karen)

Always sift cake flour before measuring.

Heavenly Hash Cake

350 degrees
9 x 13 x 3 pan, greased
Yield: 18 servings
Freezes

Cake:
1 stick butter
1 cup sugar
4 eggs
1 (1-lb.) can Hershey's syrup
1 cup flour
1 tsp. baking powder
1 tsp. vanilla

Cream butter and sugar. Add eggs, one at a time, and beat well. Add Hershey's syrup and vanilla. Add flour and baking powder which have been sifted together. Beat well. Pour into 9 x 13 x 3 greased pan. Bake at 350 for 30 minutes.

Icing:
1 bag tiny marshmallows
1 cup pecans, chopped
3 squares unsweetened
  chocolate, melted
2 sticks butter
1 tsp. vanilla
2 eggs
3 cups powdered sugar

As soon as cake comes out of oven, cover with tiny marshmallows and pecans. Melt chocolate and butter. Let cool. Add vanilla. Beat in 2 eggs and powdered sugar. Spread over cake.

This cake is delicious, but must be cut and served from the baking pan.
Mrs. Gary Gurwitz (Bailey)

Dump Cake

350 degrees
9 x 13 pan
Yield: 15 servings

1 med. can crushed
  pineapple and juice
1 (3½-oz.) can flake coconut
1 box yellow cake mix
1½ sticks butter
1 cup pecans, chopped

In the 9 x 13 pan, layer the ingredients in order given. Bake at 350 degrees for 45 minutes. Serve with ice cream while hot.
Mrs. Steven Zenthoefer (Ann)

A little sifted powdered sugar under a fresh cake will prevent it from sticking to the plate.

CAKES

Sour Cream Coconut Pound Cake

325 degrees
Bundt pan and
1 (8-inch) cake pan,
greased and floured
Yield: 24 servings
Freezes

Cake:
3 sticks butter
3 cups sugar
6 eggs
3 cups cake flour
¼ tsp. soda
¼ tsp. salt
1 (8-oz.) carton sour cream
1 (3½-oz.) can Angel Flake
  Coconut
1 tsp. vanilla

Cream together the butter and sugar. Add eggs one at a time. Sift together flour, soda, salt and add alternately with sour cream. Fold in coconut and vanilla. Bake the Bundt pan at 325 degrees for 1 hour and bake the 8 inch pan for 30 minutes.

Frosting:
1 (3-oz.) pkg. cream cheese
2 cups powdered sugar
¼ cup rum

Cream cheese; add sugar and rum alternately. Frost cooled cake.

Mrs. Carl Judin (Joy)

Short Cut Dobosch Torte

Yield: 12-14 servings
Freezes

1 Sara Lee pound cake,
  slightly frozen
2 (4-oz.) pkgs. Baker's
  German Sweet chocolate
¼ cup brewed coffee
2 Tbs. cognac
1½ cups heavy cream

With a serrated knife, cut the cake lengthwise into six layers. Do this while it is still frozen. Melt the chocolate in the coffee. Mix until very smooth, then stir in the cognac. Cool. Whip the cream and fold in the chocolate. Spread between the layers, put the cake together and cover tops and sides. Chill several hours before serving.

So easy, but elegant. Makes others think you spent hours in the kitchen.

Mrs. Larry Hofland (Marsha)

CAKES

Lemon Apricot Pound Cake

350 degrees
Tube or Bundt pan,
greased and floured
Yield: 24 servings
Freezes

Cake:
1 (3-oz.) pkg. instant lemon
   pudding mix
1 cup apricot nectar
1 box lemon supreme cake
   mix
4 eggs
¾ cup oil
1 Tbs. lemon extract

Place pudding into bowl with apricot nectar and let sit while mixing the rest of ingredients. Combine the cake mix, eggs, (beating well after each addition of egg) oil, lemon extract and then add the pudding mixture. Beat well with mixer and pour batter into well oiled tube pan. Cook at 350 degrees for 40-50 minutes. Remove from oven and take out of pan immediately. Prick top with a toothpick and spoon glaze over the cake.

Glaze:
¼ cup fresh lemon juice
¼ cup apricot nectar
1½ cups powdered sugar

Mix lemon juice, apricot nectar, and powdered sugar until smooth.

Delicious with glaze alone, but for a special treat add this icing over glaze: a box of Fluffy Lemon Frosting and 1 cup whipping cream. Mix until stiff and ice.

Mrs. Jerry Box (Deanna)

Pineapple-Cherry Cake

350 degrees
9 x 13 pan, ungreased

1 (1-lb.) can cherries for pies
1 (1-lb.) can crushed
   pineapple
1 box yellow cake mix
1 stick margarine, melted
1 cup nuts, chopped

Place cans of fruit in ungreased pan. Stir to mix. Sprinkle cake mix over top of fruit. Drizzle melted margarine over cake mix and sprinkle with chopped nuts. Bake at 350 for approximately 1 hour or until nuts are brown.

CAKES

Italian Cream Cake

325 degrees
3 (9-inch) round or
square pans, greased
Yield: 16 servings

Cake:
½ cup Crisco
1 stick margarine
2 cups sugar
1 cup buttermilk
1 tsp. soda
5 eggs, separated
2 cups flour
1 tsp. vanilla
1 (3½-oz.) can Angel Flake
  coconut
1 cup pecans, chopped

Cream Crisco, margarine and sugar, and add buttermilk in which soda has been dissolved. Separate eggs, and add yolks. Mix remaining ingredients in order. Fold in stiffly beaten egg whites last. Pour into 3 greased round or square pans. Bake at 325 degrees for 30 minutes. Let set in pans for 15 minutes after removing from oven.

Icing:
1 (8-oz.) pkg. Philadelphia
  cream cheese
1 stick margarine
1 lb. powdered sugar
1 tsp. vanilla

Soften cream cheese and margarine. Beat until creamy. Add powdered sugar and vanilla. Ice between layers and top of cake.

Mrs. Jim Jones (Jackie)

White Cake

350 degrees
2 (8-inch) cake pans,
greased and floured
Yield: 16 servings

2 cups cake flour, sifted
2 tsp. baking powder
½ cup butter
1 cup sugar
⅔ cup milk
1 tsp. vanilla
3 egg whites, beaten stiff

Sift flour, measure, add baking powder and sift three more times. Cream butter and sugar until light and fluffy. Add flour alternately with milk. Add vanilla. Fold in egg whites (that have been beaten very stiff) quickly and thoroughly. Bake at 350 degrees for 25-30 minutes in greased and floured 8-inch layer pans. Let cool.

Mrs. Jack Whetsel (Martha)

CAKES

Seven-Up Cake

325 degrees
12 cup tube pan, and
1 (8-inch) cake pan, greased
Yield: 24 servings
Freezes

3 sticks butter or margarine
3 cups sugar
5 eggs
3 cups flour
2 Tbs. lemon extract
¾ cup 7-Up

Cream butter and sugar together for 20 minutes. Add eggs, one at a time. Beat well, then add flour. Add lemon extract and fold in 7-Up. Pour into well-greased 12 cup tube pan and 1 (8-inch) cake pan. Bake in 325 degree oven for 1 hour and 15 minutes and bake 8 inch pan for 30-35 minutes.

Mrs. Jerry Fair (Zetta)

Fresh Apple Nut Cake

Cold oven
Bundt pan,
greased and floured
Yield: 20 servings
Freezes

Cake:
1 cup corn oil
3 eggs
2 cups sugar
1 Tbs. vanilla
3 cups apples, peeled and
  chopped
1 cup pecans, chopped
3 cups flour
1 tsp. salt
1 tsp. soda
1 tsp. cinnamon
1 tsp. nutmeg
1 tsp. cloves

Mix oil, eggs, sugar and vanilla together. Add apples and pecans. Mix thoroughly. Sift flour, salt, soda, cinnamon, nutmeg and cloves together and add to egg and sugar mixture; mix well. Place in a greased Bundt pan and place in a COLD oven. Bake 1 hour and 10 minutes in a 350 degree oven. Remove from pan.

Glaze:
½ stick margarine
½ tsp. vanilla
½ cup brown sugar
2 Tbs. milk

Bring margarine, vanilla, brown sugar, and milk to a boil, stirring constantly. Boil one minute. Dribble over hot cake.

Mrs. Tom Wilkins (Geen)

CAKES

German Apple Cake

350 degrees
Loaf or tube pan,
greased and floured
Yield: 16 servings

Cake:
2 large eggs
1 cup salad oil
2 cups sugar
1 tsp. vanilla
2 cups flour
2 tsp. cinnamon
1 tsp. soda
¼ tsp. salt
4 cups raw apples, peeled
  and grated

Beat eggs and oil until foamy. Add sugar, vanilla, flour, cinnamon, soda, and salt and mix well. Stir in apples. Bake at 350 degrees for 1 hour in loaf or tube pan. Remove from pan. Cool.

Frosting:
1 (3-oz.) pkg. cream cheese
3 Tbs. butter, melted
1 Tbs. vanilla
1½ cups powdered sugar

Mix all frosting ingredients together and spread over cool cake.

Very moist and improves with several days aging.

Mrs. Robert Whitis (Linda)

Gingerbread

350 degrees
9 x 12 pan, greased
Yield: 15 large pieces

½ cup butter
½ cup sugar
1 egg, beaten
1 cup molasses
2½ cups flour, sifted
1½ tsp. soda
1 tsp. cinnamon
1 tsp. ginger
¼ tsp. cloves
½ tsp. salt
1 cup hot water

Cream butter and sugar; add beaten egg and molasses; then add dry ingredients which have been sifted together. Add the hot water last and beat until smooth. The batter is soft. Bake in a greased pan for 35 minutes at 350 degrees. Serve hot with butter.

For muffins use 3 cups sifted flour. Makes about 18 muffins.

Mrs. Kenneth Landrum (June)

CAKES

Harvey Wallbanger Cake

350 degrees
Tube or Bundt pan,
greased and floured
Yield: 16-20 servings
Freezes

Cake:
1 box orange supreme cake
  mix
1 (3-oz.) pkg. vanilla instant
  pudding
½ cup oil
4 oz. frozen orange juice
  concentrate (thawed out)
½ cup water
4 eggs
3 oz. Galliano
1 oz. Vodka or white rum

Mix all cake ingredients in mixer for 5 minutes at medium speed. Pour into greased and floured tube pan. Bake at 350 degrees for 45-55 minutes. Cool in pan 15 minutes before removing.

Glaze:
1 cup powdered sugar
1 oz. orange juice
  concentrate
1½ Tbs. Galliano
1 Tbs. vodka or rum

Blend sugar, orange juice, Galliano, and vodka together; then spread over top of cake.

Mrs. Paul Haas (Maurie)

Lemon Nut Cake

300 degrees
2 small tube or Bundt pans
Yield: 20 servings
Freezes

1 lb. butter
2½ cups sugar
4 cups flour
1 Tbs. baking powder
6 eggs
4 cups pecans, chopped
2 oz. lemon extract

Mix all ingredients well. Pour into 2 small greased and floured Bundt pans. Bake at 300 degrees for 1½ hours.

Mrs. J. P. Williams (Dillie)

CAKES

Fruit Cocktail Cake

325 degrees
9 x 13 pan, greased
Yield: 12 servings
Freezes

Cake:
2 cups flour, sifted
1½ cups sugar
2 tsp. soda
2 eggs, slightly beaten
1 (No. 303) can fruit cocktail
(do not drain)

Sift together the dry ingredients. Add beaten eggs and fruit cocktail. Mix well. Bake in a slightly greased pan at 325 degrees for 25-35 minutes. Test with a toothpick.

Frosting:
1½ cups sugar
1 stick margarine
1 (5.33-oz.) can evaporated milk
1 cup coconut
1 cup pecans, chopped

Mix and boil together sugar, margarine and milk for 5 minutes. Add coconut and chopped pecans. Pour over cake while hot.

Very moist.

Mrs. Bruce Leahy (Susan)

Mincemeat Cake

275 degrees
10-inch tube pan

1 (28-oz.) jar mincemeat
2 cups raisins
2 cups pecans, chopped
1 Tbs. vanilla extract
½ cup butter or margarine, melted
2 cups sugar
3 eggs, separated
1½ tsp. soda
¼ cup water
3 cups all-purpose flour

Combine mincemeat, raisins, pecans, and vanilla. Set aside. Combine butter, sugar, and egg yolks. Beat well. Dissolve soda in water and add to batter mixture. Stir in flour and mincemeat mixture. Beat egg whites until stiff. Fold into mincemeat. Line bottom of a 10-inch tube pan with heavy brown paper. Grease paper and sides of pan. Spoon mixture into prepared pan. Bake at 275 degrees for 2 hours and 10 minutes or until cake is done. Cool cake slightly. Remove from pan and remove paper. Cool thoroughly. Wrap in foil and store in a cool place.

Mrs. Mark Seitz (Diana)

CAKES

Sugared Lemon Crown

350 degrees
Bundt pan, greased and floured
Yield: 16 servings
Freezes

2¼ cups flour, sifted
1 tsp. baking powder
½ tsp. salt
1½ sticks butter, softened
1½ cups granulated sugar
3 eggs
1 Tbs. lemon rind, grated
 (optional)
2 Tbs. lemon juice
⅔ cup milk
powdered sugar

Grease and flour Bundt pan. Sift flour, baking powder, and salt. Set aside. Cream butter, sugar, and eggs. Slowly beat in rind and lemon juice. Add flour mixture, a third at a time, alternately with milk, beating at low speed just until blended. Pour into pan. Bake at 350 degrees for 50 minutes. Cool cake in mold on wire rack 10 minutes. Loosen and invert on rack. Cool completely. Before serving, sprinkle lightly with powdered sugar.

A delicious pound cake for summertime.

Mrs. Jerry McGilvray (Jane)

Spice-Apple Cake

350 degrees
9 x 13 x 2 pan, greased
Yield: 18 servings

Cake:
3 eggs
1 box Duncan Hines Deluxe
 Spice Cake Mix
1 can apple pie filling
3 Tbs. water
½ cup pecans, chopped

Beat eggs first and add other ingredients and beat by hand just a few minutes, until all parts are moist. Pour into 9 x 13 x 2 greased baking dish.

Topping:
½ tsp. cinnamon
½ cup sugar
½ cup flour
1 stick margarine

Mix the cinnamon, sugar and flour together and cut in margarine. Put on cake in dabs before baking for 45 minutes at 350 degrees.

CAKES

Easy Pound Cake

325 degrees
Tube pan, greased and floured
Yield: 18 servings
Freezes

Cake:
1 cup butter
1⅔ cups sugar
5 eggs
2 tsp. vanilla
¼ tsp. almond extract
2 cups flour, sifted

Cream butter, add sugar and then eggs, one at a time. Add flavorings and flour. Pour in greased and floured bundt pan and bake 1 hour at 325 degrees.

Mrs. Kenneth Landrum (June)

Variation:
6 eggs
grated rind and juice of 4
  lemons
2 cups sugar
1 cup butter

Lemon Butter Sauce: In top of double boiler, beat eggs with lemon juice and sugar. Add lemon rind and butter; cook over hot water, stirring constantly, until mixture thickens. Serve on cake. Makes about 5 cups of sauce.

1, 2, 3 Cake

350 degrees
3 (9-inch) layer pans,
greased and floured

1 cup of butter or margarine
2 cups sugar
4 eggs, separated
3 cups flour
2½ tsp. baking powder
1 cup milk
½ tsp. vanilla

Cream butter and sugar. Add beaten egg yolks. Mix well. Sift flour and baking powder. Add to butter mixture. Add milk and vanilla. Fold in stiff beaten egg whites. Pour into pans and bake at 350 degrees for 30 to 40 minutes or until done.

Pineapple Frosting:
1 (20-oz.) can crushed
  pineapple
1 cup sugar
2-2½ Tbs. flour
2 Tbs. butter, melted

Drain juice from crushed pineapple. Save juice. Add sugar, flour, and butter to juice. Cook over medium heat until thick; add crushed pineapple. Spread lightly between layers and spoon remaining frosting over top of the cake.

Mrs. Morris Nelson (Carolynn)

12 Egg Pound Cake

325 degrees
Angel food cake pan, greased
Yield: 30 thin slices
Freezes

1 lb. butter, softened
3½ cups sugar
12 eggs
4 cups cake flour, sifted
¼ tsp. salt
2 tsp. almond extract
1 Tbs. vanilla

Mix the softened butter and sugar together until creamy. Add the eggs, one at a time, mixing well. Set aside. Sift the dry ingredients three times and add to the egg mixture about a cup at a time. Add the flavorings and turn into an Angel food cake pan (greased). Bake 1½ hours in a 325 degree oven. Cool before turning out of the pan.

This makes a very big cake and requires a pan larger than a bundt pan. If you wish to use a bundt pan, place a portion of the batter in an 8 inch square pan also. The cake won't be as pretty but it will taste just as good.

Mrs. E. F. Wallace (Janet)

Pumpkin Cake

350 degrees
Tube pan, greased and floured

3 cups sugar
1 cup shortening
3 eggs
1 tsp. vanilla
1 can pumpkin (2 cups)
1 tsp. soda
½ tsp. baking powder
3 cups cake flour
¼ tsp. salt
½ tsp. cloves
½ tsp. nutmeg
½ tsp. allspice
1 tsp. cinnamon
powdered sugar

Cream sugar and shortening. Add eggs, vanilla, and pumpkin. Add dry ingredients. Mix well. Bake in greased and floured tube pan at 350 degrees for 1 hour 15 minutes or until done. Cool, remove from pan, and dust with powdered sugar.

Mrs. Robert Parry, Jr. (Barbara)

CAKES

Oatmeal Cake

325 degrees
9 x 13 pan
Yield: 16 servings
Freezes

Cake:
1½ cups water, boiling
1 cup quick cooking oatmeal
½ cup butter
1 cup sugar
1 cup brown sugar
2 eggs, beaten
1½ cups flour
½ tsp. salt
1 tsp. soda
1 tsp. cinnamon

Pour boiling water over oatmeal and let stand 20 minutes. Cream together butter, sugar, brown sugar, and eggs. Blend well. Sift flour, salt, soda, and add to butter mixture. Add oatmeal and cinnamon. Blend together. Bake 325 degrees for 35-45 minutes.

Topping:
½ cup butter
¼ cup cream or milk
½ cup brown sugar, packed
1 cup pecans, chopped
1 cup coconut
½ tsp. vanilla

Heat butter, cream and sugar in pan. (Do not let it boil). Add remaining ingredients. After cake is done, pour prepared topping on cake and place back in oven under broiler until slightly browned. Let cool.

Mrs. Gilbert Heartfield (Francesca)

Vanilla Wafer Cake

275 degrees
Tube pan, greased well and floured
Freezes

2 sticks margarine
2 cups sugar
6 eggs
1 (16-oz.) box vanilla wafers, finely crumbled
1 (3½-oz.) can Angel flake coconut
1 cup pecans, chopped

Cream the two sticks of margarine and the two cups of sugar. Add six eggs, one at a time. Add the vanilla wafer crumbs, the Angel flake coconut and the cup of chopped pecans. Bake in a greased and floured tube pan at 275 degrees for 1¼ to 1½ hours. Cool about 15 minutes before removing from pan.

This is a very moist cake!

Mrs. Don Bowman (Brenda)

CAKES

Poppyseed Cake

375 degrees
2 (9 or 10-inch) cake pans,
greased and lined
Freezes

½ cup whole poppyseeds
1 cup milk
1½ cups sugar
⅔ cup butter
2¼ cups cake flour, sifted
1½ tsp. baking powder
4 egg whites, stiffly beaten

Soak poppyseeds in milk at least 3 hours. Cream sugar and butter together well. Sift together flour and baking powder. Add milk and poppyseeds to the sugar and butter mixture. Add flour mixture and mix well. Fold in egg whites. (Batter will be thick). Pour into 2 (9 or 10-inch) round cake pans, greased and lined with waxed paper. Bake for about 25 minutes or until lightly browned at 375 degrees. Remove to waxed paper lined plates to cool. Slit each layer in half horizontally to make 4 layers.

Filling:
1½ cups milk
2 Tbs. cornstarch, dissolved
  in milk
4 egg yolks
¾ cup sugar
pinch of salt
1 tsp. vanilla
½ cup nuts, chopped
  (optional)

Dissolve cornstarch in milk. Add egg yolks, sugar and salt. Cook in double boiler until thick, stirring constantly. Add vanilla and nuts, if desired. Fill between each layer of cake.

Frosting:
½ cup white Karo syrup
1 egg white
1 tsp. vanilla

Beat syrup and egg white until stiff. Add vanilla. Frost cake. REFRIGERATE CAKE.

May omit frosting and frost with whipped cream.

Mrs. Claus Eggers (Mardi)

Secure a slice of fresh bread with toothpicks to the cut sides of a cake to prevent drying or hardness.

CAKES

Red Velvet Cake

350 degrees
2 (9-inch) layer pans,
greased and floured
Yield: 24 servings
Freezes

Cake:
½ cup shortening
1½ cups sugar
2 eggs
2 (1-oz.) bottles of red cake
  color
2 tsp. cocoa
2¼ cups cake flour
1 tsp. salt
1 cup buttermilk
1 tsp. vanilla
1 tsp. soda
1 tsp. vinegar

Frosting:
5 Tbs. flour
1 cup milk
1 cup sugar
½ cup shortening
½ cup butter
1 tsp. vanilla

Cream together shortening and sugar. Add two eggs and continue to cream. Make a paste of cake coloring and cocoa and add to egg mixture. Sift together flour and salt; combine buttermilk and vanilla. Alternately add the two mixtures to the creamed mixture. Mix well. Mix soda and vinegar together and blend into batter immediately. Pour into 2 cake pans that have been greased and floured and bake 30 minutes at 350 degrees. Cool. Slice into four layers and put together with frosting.

Stirring constantly, cook until thick, the flour and milk. Cool thoroughly. Cream the sugar, shortening and butter until fluffy. Add vanilla, then combine the two mixtures and blend well. Frosting should be similar to whipped cream.

Makes a beautiful surprise red birthday cake, AND really good at Valentine's baked in heart-shaped pans.

Mrs. Paul Moffitt (Marilyn)

When creaming butter and sugar, add a few drops of boiling water for a fine-textured cake.

CAKES

Orange Cake

350 degrees
Loaf or Bundt pan, buttered
Yield: 16 servings
Freezes

Cake:
1 cup raisins
¾ cup pecans, chopped
1½ oranges
1 cup butter
1 cup brown sugar
1 cup granulated sugar
3 eggs
3 cups flour
1 tsp. soda
1 cup buttermilk

Put raisins, nuts and rind of oranges through a nut chopper. Cream butter, add sugars and eggs. Beat well. Sift together dry ingredients and add alternately with buttermilk to the creamed butter mixture. Stir in nut and fruit mixture. Turn into a buttered loaf or Bundt pan. Bake 1 hour at 350 degrees.

Glaze:
juice of 1 orange
½ cup sugar

To juice of one orange, add sugar and pour over the hot cake to glaze.

Mrs. Billy Simpson (Ginger)

Watergate Cake

350 degrees
9 x 13 pan,
greased and floured
Yield: 15 servings

Cake:
1 box white cake mix
1 box pistachio instant
   pudding
1 cup oil
1 cup club soda
3 eggs
½ cup nuts, chopped

Mix all cake ingredients together and beat for 2 minutes. Pour into greased and floured 9 x 13 pan and bake at 350 degrees for 30-35 minutes. Cool.

Frosting:
1 small box pistachio
   instant pudding
1 envelope Dream Whip
1¼ cups milk

Beat pudding, Dream Whip and milk with mixer until stiff. Ice cake.

This is pretty, green, and has an unusual flavor.

109

CAKES

Rainbow Cake

350 degrees
3 (9-inch) cake pans,
greased and lined
with waxed paper,
greased and floured, again
Yield: 20 slices

Cake:
3¼ cups plus 2 Tbs. flour
2¼ cups sugar
6 tsp. baking powder
1½ tsp. salt
¾ cup shortening
1 cup plus 2 Tbs. milk
1½ tsp. vanilla
6 egg whites, unbeaten
¼ cup plus 2 Tbs. milk

Sift flour, sugar, baking powder and salt together in a LARGE mixing bowl. Drop in shortening. Pour in 1 cup and 2 Tbs. milk and vanilla. On low speed, beat 2 minutes. Add egg whites, ¼ cup and 2 Tbs. milk and beat 2 minutes longer. Turn into greased 9-inch layer cake pans and bake 20 minutes or until done in 350 degree oven. Cool in pans on wire racks for 10 minutes. Remove from pans and peel off waxed paper. Cool completely on racks. Put cloth in between each layer and cover. Chill layers overnight. Next day split each layer in half to form 6 layers. Fill with the following fillings to form rainbow layers:

Filling:
3 cups heavy cream, whipped
½ cup pineapple preserves
¼ cup semi-sweet chocolate
  chips, melted
½ cup strawberry preserves
½ cup peeled pistachio nuts,
  finely chopped
2 Tbs. sugar
½ tsp. almond extract
½ cup apricot preserves
yellow, red, green food
  coloring

First divide the whipped cream into 5 equal portions. For the pineapple layer add one portion of the whipped cream to the pineapple preserves, tint yellow. For the chocolate layer, add one portion of the whipped cream to the melted chocolate chips. For the strawberry layer, add one portion of the whipped cream to the strawberry preserves, tint red. For the pistachio layer, mix the nuts, sugar, and almond extract with the whipped cream portion, tint light green. For the apricot layer, add one portion of the whipped cream to the apricot preserves.

continued . . .

110

CAKES

Assemble cake in the following manner:

cake. . . . . pineapple filling
cake . . . . chocolate filling
cake . . . . strawberry filling
cake . . . . pistachio filling
cake . . . . apricot filling
top with last layer of cake

Frosting:
2 egg whites, unbeaten
1½ cups sugar
5 Tbs. water
1 tsp. light corn syrup
¼ tsp. salt
1 Tbs. vanilla

Place the unbeaten egg whites, sugar, water, corn syrup, and salt in the top of a double boiler and beat with an electric mixer until thoroughly blended. Place these ingredients over rapidly boiling water. Beat them constantly until peaks are formed (like a 7-minute icing, but it takes longer than 7 minutes). Remove the icing from the heat and add the vanilla. Continue beating until the icing is the right consistency to spread. Ice the top and sides of the Rainbow cake. Once cake has been iced, refrigerate cake for at least 6 hours so that it slices nicely. Be sure to keep refrigerated until cake is all gone.

**Gold Cake
(use for egg yolks
from Rainbow Cake)**

350 degrees
3 (9-inch) cake pans, greased
Yield: 16-20 slices

3¼ cups plus 2 Tbs. flour
3 tsp. baking powder
1½ tsp. salt
1½ cups sugar
¾ cup shortening
8 egg yolks
1½ tsp. vanilla
1 cup plus 2 Tbs. milk

Sift the flour, baking powder, salt, and sugar together. Drop in shortening, yolks, vanilla and half of the milk. Beat at low speed, for 2 minutes. Add rest of milk, beat 1 minute. Pour in pans, bake at 350 degrees for 30 minutes or until done.

CAKES

Rum Cake

325 degrees
10-inch tube pan
Yield: 10-12 servings

½ cup butter, softened
½ cup shortening
2 cups sugar
4 eggs
3 cups self-rising cake flour,
   unsifted
1 cup buttermilk
3 tsp. rum extract
2 tsp. vanilla

Grease and flour tube pan. In large bowl beat with electric mixer at medium speed the softened butter, shortening and sugar until light and fluffy. Beat in the eggs one at a time. With rubber scraper or wooden spoon, stir in flour (in four parts) alternately with buttermilk (in three parts) beginning and ending with flour. Add rum extract and vanilla and stir just to combine. Turn into prepared pan. Bake 1 hour and 20 minutes or until cake tester inserted near center comes out clean. Cool in pan on wire rack 15 minutes.

Glaze:
1 cup sugar
½ cup water
2 tsp. rum extract
1 tsp. vanilla

In small saucepan combine sugar and water and bring to a boil stirring sugar until dissolved. Remove from heat and add rum extract and vanilla. Cool slightly. Remove cake from pan. Brush top with glaze. Cool thoroughly on wire rack.

Mrs. Kenneth Kachtik (Sue)

Chocolate Frosting

Yield: Frosting for
1 (9-inch) square cake

½ cup sugar
1½ Tbs. cornstarch
1 (1-oz.) square unsweetened
   chocolate, grated
dash of salt
½ cup boiling water
1½ Tbs. butter or margarine
½ tsp. vanilla

Mix sugar and cornstarch (this step is important, otherwise, frosting may lump). Add chocolate, salt and water; cook until mixture thickens. Remove from heat; add butter and vanilla. Spread on cake while hot for a glossy frosting which remains soft and smooth. Consistency will be rather thin. Will frost one 9-inch square cake and can easily be doubled for layer cake.

Mrs. Bill Blackburn (Jeanne)

CAKES

Salad Dressing Cake

350 degrees
9 x 13 pan
Yield: 20 servings
Freezes

Cake:
2 cups flour, sifted
1 cup sugar
1½ tsp. baking powder
1½ tsp. soda
¼ cup cocoa
1 cup Miracle Whip Salad
  dressing
1 cup cold water
2 tsp. vanilla
dash salt

Sift flour, sugar, baking powder, soda and cocoa together. Add salad dressing. Mix water with vanilla and stir into other ingredients. Bake in a 9 x 13 sheet cake pan in 350 degree oven for 25-35 minutes. Allow cake to cool before frosting.

Frosting:
2 cups powdered sugar
3 Tbs. cocoa
3 Tbs. butter
3 Tbs. hot coffee

Combine all ingredients. If frosting is too thick, thin with cream or evaporated milk. Spread over cake before frosting cools and thickens.

Stays moist for a week.

Mrs. J. P. Williams (Dillie)

Mocha Almond Angel Cake Icing

Yield: Icing for 1 (10-inch)
tube cake
Freezes

6 Tbs. corn oil margarine,
  softened
1 box powdered sugar,
  unsifted
¼ cup cocoa
½ tsp. instant coffee
3 Tbs. skim milk
1 tsp. vanilla extract
1 angel food cake
almonds, sliced

In a small bowl, blend together margarine, powdered sugar and cocoa. Dissolve instant coffee in skim milk. Add to margarine mixture with vanilla extract. Beat until smooth and spreadable. Use to frost a 10-inch angel food cake. Garnish top of cake with sliced almonds.

Mrs. Ann Walker

113

CAKES

Yogurt Sweet Cake

375 degrees
9 x 13 pan, well-buttered
Yield: 18 servings

Cake:
½ lb. butter
2½ cups sugar
6 eggs, separated
1 tsp. soda
1 oz. whiskey
3 cups cake flour
1 cup plain yogurt

Beat butter and sugar until creamy. Add egg yolks and yogurt and mix well. Dissolve soda in whiskey and add to above mixture, alternating with flour until all is used. Beat egg whites into stiff meringue and fold into first mixture. Pour into 9 x 13 well-buttered pan and bake 10 minutes at 375 degrees, reduce heat, and cook at 350 degrees for 30 minutes. Remove cake from oven when done and cool 10 minutes. With toothpick make several indentations in cake, and pour ½ of syrup over the cake. Let cook 10 more minutes. Pour remaining syrup over cake. Let cool. Cut into diamond-shaped pieces.

Syrup:
1½ cups sugar
1¼ cups water
½ tsp. lemon juice

Boil sugar and water for 5 minutes. Remove from heat and add lemon juice. Follow directions above for adding to cooled cake.

Mrs. Forrest Fitch (Marion)

Whipped Cream Frosting

1 cup heavy whipping cream
¼ cup powdered sugar,
  sifted
1 egg yolk
¼ tsp. nutmeg
½ tsp. vanilla

Whip cream until partially stiff. Add sifted powdered sugar and then other ingredients. Frost cake and chill for several hours. Delicious on angel food cake. Nuts can be added to top, or coconut, if desired.

Mrs. Paul Wagner (Doris)

PIES

Best Pie Crust

425 degrees
2 (9-inch) pie pans
Yield: 2 crusts
Freezes

2¼ cups flour, sifted
1 tsp. salt
¼ cup water
¾ cup shortening

Sift flour and salt into bowl. Remove ⅓ cup flour and mix with the water to form a paste. Cut shortening into remaining flour. Add paste and shape into two equal balls. Roll out on floured board. Place in pans and be sure to prick sides and bottoms with fork before baking. Can be frozen at this stage. Bake 10-12 minutes in 425 degree oven or until golden brown.

Mrs. Robert Parry, Jr. (Barbara)

Fantastic Pie Crust

400 degrees
Pie pans, ungreased
Yield: 5 crusts
Freezes

4 cups flour
1 Tbs. sugar
2 tsp. salt
1¾ cup shortening
½ cup water
1 Tbs. white vinegar
1 large egg

In large bowl stir flour, sugar and salt with fork. Cut in shortening until crumbly. In small bowl beat together water, vinegar and egg. Add this to the flour mixture. Stir until all is moistened. Divide in 5 parts. Shape in flat patties ready for rolling. Wrap in plastic and chill ½ hour. Lightly flour and roll on floured board. Fit loosely in pie pan. Prick to remove air. Makes 5 single pie shells; store in refrigerator for 2 weeks. Can be frozen but do not keep too long. Bake in 400 degree oven 18-20 minutes or until golden brown.

Mrs. Leroy Lewin (Hilda)

PIES

Meringue Recipes

2-Egg White Meringue:
2 egg whites
2 tsp. water
⅛ tsp. salt
¼ tsp. cream of tartar
4 Tbs. granulated sugar
½ tsp. vanilla

3-Egg White Meringue:
3 egg whites
1 Tbs. water
⅛ tsp. salt
¼ tsp. cream of tartar
6 Tbs. sugar
¾ tsp. vanilla

4-Egg White Meringue:
4 egg whites
1 Tbs. water
⅛ tsp. salt
¼ tsp. cream of tartar
8 Tbs. sugar
1 tsp. vanilla

Combine egg whites, water, salt, and cream of tartar in a bowl. Beat until stiff peaks form. Add sugar, 1 tablespoon at a time. Beat until stiff and add the vanilla. Starting at the edges to seal, pile the meringue on custard. Work toward the middle to make an extravagant heap of meringue. Bake in slow oven (300 degrees) for 15 to 20 minutes. When lightly browned, turn off oven and open door to allow slow cooling. (Sudden cooling shrinks the meringue). When oven is cool, remove the pie. Refrigerate.

Rules for meringue:
A meringue is beaten constantly until it is spread. Its success depends upon the proper beating of the egg whites, the slow addition of the sugar, and the slow oven in which it is baked.

Banana and Blueberry Cream Pie

9-inch pie pan
Yield: 6-8 servings

1 (9-inch) baked pastry shell
½ cup sugar
1 (3-oz.) pkg. cream cheese
1 pkg. Dream Whip
2-3 bananas, sliced
½ cup blueberry pie filling

Mix sugar with cream cheese. Whip Dream Whip according to package directions. Combine with cheese mixture. Cover bottom of shell with thinly sliced bananas. Pour cheese mixture over bananas and then add the blueberry filling. Chill several hours before serving.

Mrs. Jerry McGilvray (Jane)

PIES

Swedish Apple Pie

350 degrees
9-inch pie pan
Yield: 6-8 servings

1 (9-inch) unbaked pastry
  shell
2 cups canned apple pie
  slices
¾ cup sugar
2 Tbs. flour
¼ tsp. salt
1 egg, slightly beaten
1 cup sour cream
1 tsp. vanilla

Topping:
⅓ cup sugar
⅓ cup flour
1 tsp. cinnamon
¼ lb. butter or margarine

Mash apples slightly. Mix in sugar, flour, and salt. Add to the apples. Add the egg and fold in the sour cream and vanilla to the apples. Pour into pastry shell; bake at 350 degrees for 40 minutes. Mix the sugar, flour, cinnamon and butter to resemble crumbs. Cover the pie with topping after it has cooked 40 minutes and continue baking for 15 minutes longer.

Mrs. Forrest Fitch (Marion)

Black Russian Pie

9-inch crumb crust
Yield: 6-8 servings

1 (9-inch) crumb crust
⅓ cup Kahlua
2 envelopes unflavored
  gelatin
½ cup milk, heated to boiling
2 eggs
½ cup sugar
⅔ cup Vodka
1½ cups whipping cream

Put Kahlua, gelatin and milk into blender. Cover and blend on low speed until gelatin is dissolved. Add eggs, sugar and Vodka. Blend until thoroughly mixed. Pour mixture into large bowl and chill in refrigerator for 15 minutes or until slightly thickened; stirring occasionally. Pour cream into blender and blend on low speed until thickened. Fold gelatin mixture into whipped cream. Pour into a crumb crust. Chill until set.

Mrs. J. R. Schroeder (Molly)

117

PIES

Black Bottom Pie

9-inch pie pan
Yield: 6-8 servings

1 (9-inch) baked pastry shell
1 Tbs. unflavored gelatin
4 Tbs. cold water
2 cups milk
½ cup sugar
1 Tbs. cornstarch
¼ tsp. salt
4 egg yolks, beaten
2 oz. unsweetened chocolate, melted, (2 squares)
1 tsp. vanilla

Meringue:
4 egg whites
⅛ tsp. cream of tartar
½ cup sugar
1 tsp. sherry
1 Tbs. rum
¾ cup heavy cream
1 Tbs. unsweetened chocolate, shaved

Soften gelatin in cold water. Scald milk in double boiler. Mix sugar, cornstarch, and salt together; stir slowly into milk and cook until thick, stirring often. Add gradually to beaten egg yolks. Return to double boiler and cook 3 minutes longer. Stir in gelatin to dissolve. Divide in half; add melted chocolate and vanilla to one half of the mixture to make the chocolate layer. Pour carefully into cooled, cooked shell. Let remaining half of custard cool.

Beat egg whites until frothy; add cream of tartar; continue beating to a soft peak and gradually add sugar. Fold meringue into cooled custard, adding flavorings. Pour carefully over chocolate layer. Chill in refrigerator until set. When ready to serve, whip cream and spread on top of pie. Sprinkle with shaved chocolate.

Mrs. Jerry McGilvray (Jane)

Cherry Nut Pie

2 (8-inch or 9-inch) pie pans
Yield: 12-16 servings

2 baked pastry shells
1 can Eagle Brand milk
2 lemons, juiced
1 can cherry pie filling
1 pint whipped cream
¼ cup sugar
1 cup pecans, chopped

In one bowl combine milk, juice of lemons and cherry pie filling. In another bowl, whip cream with sugar; add chopped pecans. Fold the two mixtures together and pour into the baked pastry shells. If the shells are not filled completely, you can spread with a thin layer of whipped cream. Chill.

Very rich pie!

Mrs. Jim Thompson (Sandy)

118

PIES

Buttermilk Pie

450-325 degrees
9-inch pie pan
Yield: 6-8 servings

1 (9-inch) unbaked pastry
  shell, chilled
3 eggs
1 cup sugar
3 Tbs. flour
2 cups buttermilk
6 Tbs. butter, melted
1½ tsp. vanilla
pinch of salt

In a large bowl, beat eggs until they are light and lemon colored. Mix sugar and flour and add to beaten eggs about ¼ cup at a time, beating constantly. Stir in buttermilk, butter, vanilla and salt. Pour into the pastry shell and bake the pie on the lowest shelf of a preheated oven set at 450 degrees for 10 minutes. Reduce heat to moderately slow oven, about 325 degrees, and bake the pie for 50 minutes more or until a knife inserted in the center comes out clean. Transfer the pie to a rack and cool.

Mrs. Forrest Fitch (Marion)

Candy Bar Pie

325 degrees
8-inch pie pan, ungreased
Yield: 6 servings

Crust:
1½ cups coconut, grated
2 Tbs. margarine, melted

Combine coconut and margarine and press into an 8-inch pie pan. Bake at 325 degrees for 10 minutes or until golden brown. Cool.

Filling:
1 tsp. instant coffee powder
  or crystals
2 Tbs. water
1 (7½-oz.) bar of almond milk
  chocolate, broken into
  pieces
4 cups frozen whipped
  dessert topping, thawed

Dissolve coffee powder or crystals in water; add broken pieces of chocolate bar and stir over low heat until melted. Cool. Fold in whipped topping after chocolate mixture is cool; pile into crust. Chill in freezer for several hours or overnight. This will not freeze solidly. If you are a coconut fan, double the crust recipe and it will make a 10-inch pie yielding more servings.

Mrs. Jerry Box (Deanna)

PIES

Chocolate Cream Pie

300 degrees
10-inch pie pan
Yield: 6-8 servings

1 (10-inch) baked pastry shell
Filling:
1 cup sugar
3 Tbs. cocoa
1 pinch of salt
3 Tbs. flour
½ stick of butter
3 egg yolks
2 cups milk
1 tsp. vanilla

Mix sugar and cocoa together with salt and flour; add the butter and cream together. Beat egg yolks slightly, add to mixture; add milk and beat again. Cook in saucepan until creamy and thick. Add vanilla and pour into a large, baked pastry shell.

Meringue:
3 egg whites
¼ tsp. cream of tartar
¼ cup sugar

Beat egg whites until stiff; add cream of tartar and sugar. Beat again. Pour over pie mixture. Bake 15 minutes in a 300 degree oven.

Mrs. Beverly Levermann

Chocolate Peppermint Pie

9-inch pie pan, ungreased
Yield: 6-8 servings

14 Oreo cookies, crushed
2 Tbs. butter or margarine, melted
1 quart peppermint ice-cream, softened
2 egg whites
½ cup sugar
chocolate syrup

Mix crushed cookies with melted butter and pat into pie pan. Put in freezer 10 minutes. Fill with softened peppermint ice-cream. Beat egg whites with sugar until stiff. Spread over top of pie. Swizzle with chocolate syrup. Freeze, uncovered, for at least 4 hours.

Mrs. P. D. Terrell (Marabeth)

A meringue topping should touch the edge of the crust; otherwise, it may shrink from the side.

PIES

Chocolate Meringue Pie

350 degrees
9-inch pie pan
Yield: 6-8 servings

1 (9-inch) baked pastry shell
Filling:
2 squares unsweetened
  chocolate
2 cups milk
3 Tbs. flour
¾ cup sugar
¼ tsp. salt
2 egg yolks, beaten
1 Tbs. butter or margarine
1 tsp. vanilla

Meringue:
2 egg whites
4 Tbs. sugar
½ tsp. cream of tartar
⅛ tsp. salt
½ tsp. vanilla

Heat chocolate and milk in double boiler. Mix flour, sugar and salt thoroughly. Add some of the hot mixture to the flour mixture; mix well; add remaining hot mixture and return to double boiler. Stir until thickened (about 1 minute). Cover and cook 15 minutes. Beat well (with spoon). Pour some of this into the beaten egg yolks and mix. Combine the rest of mixture and add butter and vanilla. Pour into baked pastry shell and let stand while making the meringue.

Beat the egg whites and add sugar, cream of tartar, salt, and vanilla. Continue to beat until stiff peaks form. Spread over the chocolate filling to the edge of the crust. Bake at 325 degrees for 15 to 20 minutes or until lightly browned.

Mrs. Robert Parry, Jr. (Barbara)

French Silk Chocolate Pie

9-inch pie pan
Yield: 6-8 servings

1 (9-inch) baked pastry shell
1¼ sticks margarine
1 cup sugar
1 tsp. vanilla
2 oz. unsweetened chocolate
  (2 squares), melted
3 eggs
½ pint whipping cream

Cream margarine; add sugar, vanilla and chocolate; beat until creamy. Add eggs, one at a time, beating 3 minutes after each egg. Pour into baked pastry shell, top with whipped cream. Chill 3 hours before serving.

PIES

Fudge Pie

350 degrees
10-inch pie pan
Yield: 8-10 servings

1 (10-inch) unbaked pastry
shell
⅓ cup butter
3 squares unsweetened
chocolate
4 eggs
2 cups sugar
¼ tsp. salt
1 tsp. vanilla
⅔ cup pecans, chopped
1 half pint cream, whipped

Melt butter and chocolate. While this is melting, beat eggs and add sugar, salt and vanilla. Add the chocolate mixture to the egg mixture and beat. Add the pecans; pour into unbaked pastry shell and bake at 350 degrees for 40 minutes or until top is puffed up and crusty. (Top will fall slightly when cool.) Serve with unsweetened whipped cream on top, as pie is very sweet and very rich.

Mrs. Morgan Talbot (Jane)

Kentucky Derby Pie

325 degrees
9-inch pie pan
Yield: 6-8 servings

1 (9-inch) unbaked pastry
shell
1 cup sugar
2 eggs, unbeaten
½ cup flour
1 stick butter, melted and
cooled
1 cup chocolate chips
1 cup pecans, chopped
1 tsp. vanilla

Mix together ingredients and put into an unbaked pastry shell. Bake in 325 degree oven for 45 minutes.

Mrs. Mac Pike (Tish)

Before melting chocolate for a recipe, grease pot in which it is to be melted.

PIES

Chess Pie

425-300 degrees
9-inch pie pan
Yield: 6-8 servings

1 (9-inch) unbaked pastry
  shell
½ cup butter
2 cups sugar
3 eggs
2 Tbs. milk
2 Tbs. vinegar
2 tsp. vanilla
2 Tbs. cornmeal

Mix in order given. Bake in uncooked pastry shell for 10 minutes in 425 degree oven, then reduce heat to 300 degrees; and bake for 35-40 minutes or until center does not shake.

Mrs. Charles Murray (Cynthia)

Lemon Chess Pie

350 degrees
9-inch pie pan
Yield: 6-8 servings

1 (9-inch) unbaked pastry
  shell
3 eggs
1½ cups sugar
½ cup butter, melted
¼ cup lemon juice

Beat eggs until creamy; add about ½ of the sugar and beat well. Add remaining sugar; add melted butter; beat. Finally add lemon juice. Pour into an unbaked pastry shell and bake in 350 degree oven until firm and brown. It usually takes between 35-40 minutes to become firm.

Mrs. Jerry McGilvray (Jane)

Cranberry Pie

1 can Eagle Brand sweetened
  condensed milk
1 (4-oz.) container Cool Whip
1 (large) can frozen cranberry
  juice
1 graham cracker pie crust

Mix ingredients with a spoon. Pour into pie crust and set in freezer.

Mrs. Roger von Rosenberg (Robin)

123

PIES

Daiquiri Pie

1 (4-oz.) pkg. vanilla pie
  filling (not instant)
1 (3-oz.) pkg. lime jello
1½ cups water
⅓ cup rum
1 Tbs. lime juice
graham cracker pie crust
2 (4-oz.) containers Cool
  Whip

Combine pudding, jello and water. Cook and stir until mixture comes to a boil and is thick and clear. Remove from heat. Add lime juice and rum. Blend in well and chill until thickened. Blend in 1 small container of Cool Whip to the thickened mixture and pour into crust. Chill at least 3 hours or until firm. Top with remaining Cool Whip and graham cracker crumbs if desired.

Mrs. J. A. Morgan (Dorothy)

Fruit Pies

Yield: 12 to 14 servings

¼ cup flour
1½ cups sugar
1 (No. 2) can of pie cherries,
  drained
1 (No. 2) can crushed
  pineapple
1 (6-oz.) pkg. orange jello
½ cup pecans, chopped
6 bananas, diced small
2 baked pie shells (8 or
  9-inch)
whipped cream

In a saucepan, mix flour and sugar. Add cherries and pineapple and cook until slightly thickened. Remove from heat. Add dry jello, nuts and bananas. Pour into 2 baked shells (8 or 9-inch). Chill. Top with whipped cream.

Mrs. Robert Jones (Elizabeth)

For easy, no mess pie crust: roll between two sheets of wax paper and peel off the top paper and flip the bottom into pie pan, removing paper.

PIES

Grasshopper Pie

9-inch pie pan
Yield: 6-8 servings

16 Hydrox cookies
3 tsp. butter, melted
24 large marshmallows
¾ cup milk
1½ oz. green creme de menthe
1½ oz. white creme de cocoa
½ pint whipping cream (or large carton Cool Whip)

Crush cookies and add melted butter. Mix and press into a 9-inch pie plate. Chill. Heat 24 marshmallows and milk in double boiler. When melted remove from heat and cool. When cool add creme de menthe and creme de cocoa. Fold in ½ pint whipped cream or large carton of Cool Whip. Pour into chilled crust and chill overnight. Sprinkle more cookie crumbs over top of pie.

Mrs. Robert F. Barnes (Kay)

Hawaiian Pie

2 (9-inch) pie pans
Yield: 12-16 servings

2 (9-inch) baked pastry shells
1 (No. 2) can crushed pineapple
1 cup sugar
3 Tbs. flour or cornstarch
2 bananas
1 (3½-oz.) can flaked coconut
1 cup pecans, chopped
Cool Whip

Bake pastry shells and cool. Mix pineapple and juice, sugar, and flour and cook over low heat until thick. Let cool. Slice bananas and layer one banana in the bottom of each pastry shell. Layer ½ can of coconut in each shell. Then add ½ cup of pecans to each shell. Top with cooled pineapple mixture and then with Cool Whip.

A very pretty pie.

Sprinkle an equal mixture of sugar and flour into a pastry shell before filling to keep fruit from baking through the bottom of the shell.

PIES

Heavenly Pie

2 (9-inch) pie pans
Yield: 12-16 servings

2 (9-inch) graham cracker
shells
1 (8-oz.) pkg. cream cheese,
softened
1 (14-oz.) can sweetened
condensed milk
½ cup lemon juice
1 (9-oz.) carton whipped
topping, thawed
½ cup pecans, chopped
1 cup drained fruit
(pineapple, peaches or fruit
cocktail)

Combine cream cheese, milk and lemon
juice; beat until smooth. Fold in whipped
topping. Stir in pecans and fruit. Pour
into pie shells and refrigerate for several
hours.

Mrs. Ken Forrester (Phoebe)

Impossible Pie

350 degrees
2 (8-inch) pie pans, ungreased
Yield: 6-8 servings each

4 eggs
½ stick butter, melted
1¾ cup sugar
½ cup all-purpose flour
½ tsp. baking powder
¼ tsp. salt
2 cups milk
1 tsp. vanilla
1 (4-oz.) can shredded
coconut

Beat eggs thoroughly with mixer. Add
melted butter, sugar, flour, baking powder, salt and milk. Beat until well
blended. Stir in vanilla and coconut.
Pour into 2 ungreased 8-inch pie pans
and bake in a 350 degree oven, 35-40
minutes. Cool and cut. Mixture is rather
thin when poured into pan, but after baking it cuts evenly.

*A great favorite with those who hate to
make pie crusts.*

Mrs. Neal Runnels (Gayle)

126

PIES

Irish Coffee Pie

1 (8-inch) pie pan
Yield: 6-8 servings

1 (8-inch) baked pastry shell
1 (3½-oz.) pkg. whipped
    topping
2 tsp. instant coffee powder
½ cup cold milk
⅓ cup cold water
3 Tbs. Irish whiskey
½ cup whipping cream

In small mixing bowl, combine whipped topping mix and coffee powder. Add milk and beat at high speed of electric mixer for about 1 minute. Blend in the water and whiskey; beat at high speed 2 minutes more or until fluffy. Whip cream; carefully fold into prepared filling. Pile into baked pastry shell and chill for 3 to 4 hours. Garnish with additional whipped cream and chocolate shavings if desired.

Mrs. Gary Gurwitz (Bailey)

Lemon Meringue Pie

9-inch pan
Yield: 6-8 servings

1 (9-inch) baked pastry shell
4 Tbs. cornstarch
5 Tbs. flour
1½ cups sugar
1½ cups water
4 egg yolks
3 Tbs. butter
4 Tbs. lemon juice
1½ Tbs. lemon rind, grated

Meringue:
4-Egg White Meringue (see
    index)

Mix cornstarch, flour and sugar; stir in boiling water. Cook over direct heat, stirring constantly until mixture thickens and boils. Set over boiling water in double boiler and cook 10 minutes longer. Beat egg yolks slightly and beat in a little hot mixture, then add to the rest of the hot mixture in the double boiler. Cook 5-10 minutes stirring constantly. Remove from heat; blend in butter, lemon juice and rind. Cool. Pour into a baked pastry shell and top with a 4-Egg White Meringue.

Mrs. Bill Scurlock (Mary)

PIES

Lemon Ice Box Pie

9-inch pie pan
Yield: 6-8 servings

1 (9-inch) graham cracker
crust
1 (5.33-oz.) can evaporated
milk
2 eggs, separated
⅓ cup frozen lemon juice
½ cup sugar
1 tsp. lemon peel, grated

Chill the evaporated milk in freezer until crystals form. Beat well. Add egg yolks, lemon juice, sugar and lemon peel. Fold in beaten egg whites. Pour into graham cracker crust and place in the freezer for about 2 hours. Serve frozen.

Mrs. Tom Wilkins (Geen)

Pink Lemonade Pie

8-inch pie pan
Yield: 6-8 servings

1 (8-inch) graham cracker
crust
1 (6-oz.) can frozen pink
lemonade, thawed
2 Tbs. lemon juice
1 can Eagle Brand milk
1 (4-oz.) container Cool Whip

Mix together first three ingredients until slightly thickened. Fold in Cool Whip thoroughly. Put in graham cracker crust and refrigerate.

Mrs. Vernon Neuhaus, Jr. (Gayle)

Limelight Pie

9-inch pie pan
Yield: 6-8 servings

1 (9-inch) baked pastry shell
1 (15-oz.) can Eagle Brand
milk
¼ cup lime juice
¼ tsp. salt
⅔ cup crushed pineapple,
drained
green food coloring
½ pint cream, whipped,
sweetened
semi-sweet chocolate, grated

Mix together the milk, lime juice, salt and crushed pineapple; add few drops of green food coloring and pour into a baked pastry shell. Top with sweetened whipped cream. Sprinkle with grated semi-sweet chocolate.

A very good pie to make ahead of time and freeze.

Mrs. Bill Scurlock (Mary)

PIES

Osgood Pie

325 degrees
9-inch pie pan
Yield: 6-8 servings

1 (9-inch) unbaked pastry
  shell
½ cup butter
1 cup sugar
3 eggs
½ cup raisins
1 tsp. cinnamon
1 tsp. cloves
1 tsp. nutmeg
1 tsp. vinegar
½ cup cream

Cream butter and sugar; add eggs, one at a time; add remaining ingredients. Bake in a 9-inch unbaked pastry shell at 325 degrees for 45 minutes.

Yummy with Christmas dinner.

Mrs. Richard Moore (Lynda)

Fresh Peach Pie

450 degrees
9-inch pie pan
Yield: 8 servings

1 (9-inch) baked pastry shell
8-10 peaches, sliced (about 4
  cups)
½ cup water
1 cup sugar
3 tsp. cornstarch
1 tsp. lemon juice
dash of salt
½ pint cream, whipped

Bake 9-inch single pie crust. Place two cups of the peaches aside. In a saucepan combine the remaining two cups of peaches and other ingredients. Stir and bring to a boil (about 5 minutes); cook until thick. Set aside to cool. When cool, add the two cups of peaches and pour into baked pastry shell. Refrigerate until served. Serve topped with whipped cream.

Mrs. Tom Wilkins (Geen)

Use your basic biscuit recipe to make rich pastries; make recipe according to directions but add more shortening for a richer dough.

PIES

Pecan Pie

325 degrees
9-inch pie pan
Yield: 6-8 servings

1 (9-inch) unbaked pastry
  shell
4 eggs
1 cup sugar
1 cup light Karo syrup
2 Tbs. vinegar
2 Tbs. butter or margarine,
  melted
1 cup pecans

Beat eggs; add sugar; stir in Karo, vine-gar, and margarine. Stir in nuts last. Pour into a 9-inch unbaked pastry shell and bake at 325 degrees for 1 hour.

Mrs. Leroy Lewin (Hilda)

Mock Pecan Pie

400 degrees
9-inch pie pan
Yield: 6-8 servings

1 (9-inch) unbaked pastry
  shell
2 eggs, beaten
1 cup sugar
1 cup maple or Log Cabin
  syrup
1 cup quick Quaker oats
1 cup coconut, shredded
⅓ cup butter or margarine,
  melted

Mix all ingredients together—pour into unbaked pastry shell and bake at 400 degrees for 45-50 minutes.

Mrs. Larry Fritz (Libby)

Whipped cream will keep for a day or two in the refirgerator if while whipping you add 1 teaspoon light corn syrup for each ½ pint of cream.

Coat pastry shells with egg white before baking to prevent soggy crusts.

PIES

Texas Pecan Pie I

350 degrees
9-inch pie pan, greased
Yield: 6-8 servings

3 egg whites
1 cup sugar
¾ cup graham cracker
   crumbs
1 tsp. baking powder
1 cup pecans
1 tsp. vanilla
dash of salt
whipped cream

Beat egg whites until stiff. Slowly pour in sugar and beat until stiff again. Fold in graham cracker crumbs and baking powder; then fold in pecans, vanilla and salt. Pour into greased pan and bake 30 minutes at 350 degrees. Cool 30 minutes. Top with whipped cream.

Mrs. Jim Corcoran (Pam)

Texas Pecan Pie II

425-350 degrees
9-inch pie pan

1 (9-inch) unbaked pastry
   shell
3 eggs
⅔ cup sugar
⅓ tsp. salt
⅓ cup butter, melted
1 cup dark Karo syrup
1 cup pecans

Mix eggs, sugar; stir in salt, melted butter and dark Karo; add pecans last. Bake in pastry shell for 10 minutes in 425 degree oven. Reduce heat to 350 degrees and bake until brown, about 20 minutes.

When making pie dough, be exact on measurements because a dough that has too much flour makes the crust tough, too much shortening makes it dry and crumbly, and too much liquid makes it heavy and soggy.

PIES

Raspberry Pie

9-inch pie pan
Yield: 8-10 servings

1 (9-inch) baked pie shell
2 boxes frozen red
  raspberries (drained of
  juice—reserve)
½ cup sugar
2 Tbs. butter
1 Tbs. lemon juice
¼ tsp. salt
½ cup water
3 Tbs. plus 1 tsp. cornstarch
1 cup juice (add water if not
  enough)
Cool Whip

Cook all ingredients (except berries and Cool Whip) until thick. Remove from stove and add berries. Let cool in refrigerator until slightly chilled. Pour into baked pie shell. Store in refrigerator. Top with Cool Whip or whipped cream when ready to serve.

Mrs. Paul Moxley (Karen)

Pumpkin Chiffon Pie

9-inch pie pan
Yield: 6-8 servings

1 (9-inch) baked graham
  cracker shell
3 eggs, separated
1 cup sugar
1¼ cups canned pumpkin
½ cup milk
½ tsp. salt
½ tsp. ginger
½ tsp. nutmeg
½ tsp. cinnamon
1 envelope gelatin
¼ cup water
whipped cream or Cool Whip

Separate eggs; beat egg yolks slightly. Add ½ cup sugar, pumpkin, milk, salt and spices. Cook until thick over low heat. Soften gelatin in cold water; add to pumpkin mixture. Cool. Beat egg whites until stiff; gradually adding remaining ½ cup sugar. Fold egg whites into slightly thickened pumpkin-gelatin mixture. Pour into baked graham cracker crust. Serve topped with whipped cream or Cool Whip.

Mrs. Morgan Talbot (Jane)

132

PIES

Rum Chiffon Pie

1½ Tbs. unflavored gelatin
⅓ cup cold water
3 eggs, separated
1½ cups milk
¾ cup sugar
⅛ tsp. salt
3½ Tbs. light rum
1 baked pie shell
½ pint whipped cream
nutmeg

Dissolve gelatin in cold water, set aside. Separate eggs. Put egg whites in large mixing bowl and set aside. Beat egg yolks and add milk first, then sugar and salt. Cook over low heat until it coats spoon. DO NOT BOIL! Add gelatin and put in refrigerator or freezer until mixture thickens like jello, then fold in beaten stiff egg whites and 3½ tablespoons light rum. Put in baked pie shell, cool. For best flavor set overnight in refrigerator. Top with whipped cream and sprinkle with nutmeg.

Mrs. Bruce Gray (Suzanne)

Strawberry Pie

1 (9-inch) baked pie shell
1½-2 pts. fresh strawberries
1 cup sugar
1 cup water
6 tsp. cornstarch
½ (3-oz.) pkg. Wild Strawberry Jello
whipped cream

Fill the baked pie shell with fresh strawberries. In saucepan, cook the sugar, water and cornstarch until thick. Then add ½ package of Wild Strawberry Jello. Let cool. Pour mixture over strawberries. Top with whipped cream.

Mrs. Mark Seitz (Diana)

Mile High Strawberry Pie

9-inch pie pan
Yield: 8 servings

1 (9-inch) baked pastry shell
1 (10-oz.) pkg. frozen strawberries
2 egg whites
1 cup sugar
3 tsp. lemon juice
1 pint cream, whipped

Whip together strawberries, egg whites, sugar and lemon juice. Beat at high speed for 15 minutes; fold in whipped cream. Pour into a 9-inch baked pastry shell and freeze.

Mrs. Alan Dreyer (Kathy)

PIES

Spice Pie

350 degrees
9-inch pie pan

1 (9-inch) unbaked pastry
  shell
½ cup margarine
1 cup sugar
4 Tbs. flour
1 tsp. allspice
1 tsp. cinnamon
1 tsp. nutmeg
½ tsp. cloves, ground
4 egg yolks, unbeaten
1 cup milk
1 tsp. vanilla

Topping:
whipping cream

Cream the margarine with the sugar and flour, allspice, cinnamon, nutmeg, cloves and egg yolks. Beat together the milk and vanilla and add to the flour mixture. Pour into an unbaked pastry shell and bake at 350 degrees for 35 minutes. Serve with whipped cream or top with a meringue made from leftover egg whites and brown in the oven. Be sure and cool the pie before adding meringue.

Strawberry Glaze Pie

9-inch pie pan
Yield: 6-8 servings

1 (9-inch) baked pastry shell
6 cups fresh medium-size
  strawberries
1 cup water
¾ cup sugar
3 Tbs. cornstarch
red food coloring
whipped cream

Wash berries; remove hulls. Crush 1 cup of the smaller berries and cook with the water for about 2 minutes; put through sieve. Blend sugar and cornstarch; stir in berry juice. Cook and stir over medium heat till glaze is thickened and clear. Stir in about 5 drops of red food coloring. Spread a small amount of glaze on bottom and sides of pastry shell. Arrange half the whole berries, stem end down, in pastry shell. Spoon half the remaining glaze carefully over berries. Arrange remaining berries on first layer; spoon on remaining glaze, coating each berry. Chill 3 to 4 hours before serving. Garnish with whipped cream and a few whole strawberries, if desired.

Mrs. Gary Gurwitz (Bailey)

134

Cookies and Candy

COOKIES

Almond Crescents

325 degrees
Baking sheet, ungreased
Yield: 5-6 dozen
Freezes

1 cup butter
½ cup sugar
2 tsp. water
1 Tbs. almond extract
2 cups all-purpose flour
1¾ cups almonds, finely
   chopped
1½ cups powdered sugar,
   into which about 2 inches
   of vanilla bean have been
   scraped or pulverized in
   the blender

Cream butter and sugar until smooth and fluffy. Add water, extract, flour and almonds. Mix thoroughly with a wooden spoon or your fingers. Chill for at least one hour. Shape dough into small crescents or balls. Bake on ungreased cookie sheet at 325 to 350 degrees for 15 to 17 minutes, until just lightly colored. (Ovens vary so some may need 325 degrees and others 350 degrees). Cool slightly, then toss or roll in vanilla-scented powdered sugar. If vanilla bean is not available, omit; but it does add a definite flavor to the cookie. Cool completely and store in airtight container.

The vanilla bean may also be cut into small pieces and stored in a jar of powdered sugar. This will give the same effect as the process described above.
Mrs. Jerry Box (Deanna)

Apricot Balls

Yield: 50-60 balls

1 box apricots, dried
1 or 2 oranges
2 cups sugar
1 cup nuts
dash of salt
box of powdered sugar

Grind together the apricots (dried) and the oranges, skin and all. Add the sugar and cook for 10 minutes. Add the nuts and salt. Let cool a bit. Make mixture into small balls and roll in powdered sugar.
Mrs. Jerry McGilvray (Jane)

COOKIES

Almond Cakes

300 degrees
Cookie sheet, ungreased
Yield: 80 cookies
Freezes

4 tsp. almond extract
2 cups shortening
2 cups butter
8 cups flour, sifted
3 cups sugar
3 tsp. salt
blanched almond halves

Blend almond extract into shortening and butter, creaming until soft. Gradually work in flour, then sugar and salt. Knead to a paste. Form into a thick roll. Chill, then cut in ½-inch slices or pat into small flat cookies. Arrange on ungreased cookie sheet. Press an almond into center of each cookie and bake in a 300 degree oven about 30 minutes.

Mrs. C. A. Pagenstecher (Adelyn)

Luscious Apricot Bars

375 degrees
9 x 9 pan, greased
Yield: 30 bars
Freezes

First Layer:
½ cup butter, softened
¼ cup sugar
1⅓ cup flour, sifted

Combine butter, sugar (granulated) and 1 cup flour; mix until crumbly. Pack into greased 9-inch square pan. Bake at 375 degrees for 20 minutes.

Second Layer:
⅔ cup dried apricots
1 cup brown sugar, firmly packed
2 eggs, well beaten
½ tsp. baking powder
¼ tsp. salt
½ tsp. vanilla
½ cup almonds, chopped

Rinse apricots, cover with water; simmer 10 minutes. Drain, cool, chop, and set aside. Gradually beat brown sugar into eggs. Sift together remaining flour, baking powder and salt. Add to egg and brown sugar mixture. Mix well. Add vanilla, ¼ cup almonds and apricots. Spread on baked layer. Sprinkle with remaining nuts. Bake at 375 degrees for about 20 minutes. Cool. Cut into bars or 1½ inch squares. If you wish, dust with powdered sugar when the bars are cooled.

Mrs. Jerry McGilvray (Jane)

COOKIES

Apricot Horns

375 degrees
Baking sheet, well greased
Yield: 10-12 dozen
Freezes

Dough:
1 lb. butter or margarine
1 lb. creamed cottage cheese
4 cups flour, sifted

Blend butter, cottage cheese and flour to form dough. Add a little more flour if cheese is too watery. Shape dough into 1-inch balls and refrigerate overnight. Dough may be kept for a couple of weeks. Take out 10 to 12 balls of dough at a time. Roll into a thin circle.

Filling:
about 24 oz. apricot jam

Place a small dab of jam in the center of each circle. Roll to horn or crescent shape.

Topping:
about 3 cups confectioners sugar
about 3 cups pecans, chopped
3 egg whites

Combine 1 cup at a time, equal parts of sugar and pecans. Brush horns with slightly beaten egg whites. Roll in sugar mixture and place on baking sheet. Bake on well greased sheet for 15 to 18 minutes at 375 degrees. Remove to cooling racks, sprinkle with additional sugar.

These are time consuming, but memorable.

Mrs. Gary Gurwitz (Bailey)

It is easier to separate eggs when very cold ones are used.

139

COOKIES

Bird's Nest Cookies

350 degrees
Cookie sheet, ungreased
Yield: 84 cookies
Freezes

1 lb. butter (no substitute)
2 cups sugar
4 eggs, separated
4½ cups flour
2 tsp. vanilla
2 cups pecans, chopped fine
strawberry jam

Cream butter and sugar; add egg yolks, flour, and vanilla. Mix well. Roll into balls the size of a walnut. Dip each ball into the egg whites, then into the finely chopped nuts. Put indentation in ball with your thumb. Then put in oven for 5 minutes, remove and put a tiny bit of strawberry jam in the center of each cookie indentation and continue baking until brown (about 10 more minutes).

The reason for baking the cookies for 5 minutes and then adding the jam is that the strawberry jam stays a prettier color when it isn't baked too long.

Mrs. Wilfred Dean (Maxine)

Brandy Balls

Yield: 60 balls

2 (7½-oz.) pkgs. vanilla wafer
  crumbs
½ cup honey
⅓ cup brandy
⅓ cup white rum
1 lb. walnuts, finely ground
granulated sugar

Mix the vanilla wafers, honey, brandy, rum and walnuts together. Shape into round bite-sized balls and roll in granulated sugar. Put into airtight container and refrigerate.

This flavor improves with age! Delicious for parties.

Mrs. Hiram Tavarez (Kathe)

Marbled Brownies

350 degrees
9 x 13 pan, greased
Yield: 36 brownies
Freezes

Cream Cheese Mixture:
8 oz. pkg. cream cheese
5 Tbs. margarine
⅓ cup sugar
2 eggs
2 Tbs. flour
¾ tsp. vanilla

Soften the cream cheese and margarine and beat together. Add the sugar, eggs, flour, and vanilla; beat until smooth. Set aside.

Brownie Batter:
1 pkg. Duncan Hines Brownie Mix—family size
½ cup pecans, chopped

Prepare the cake-like brownie batter as directed on the package. Add pecans. Pour half of the brownie batter into a greased 9 x 13 pan. Pour all the cream cheese mixture over the brownie layer. Spoon the remaining brownie batter in spots over the top. Swirl the two mixtures together with a knife or spatula. Bake at 350 degrees for 35-40 minutes or until done. Cool and frost.

Frosting:
3 Tbs. butter
2 Tbs. cooca
1½ cups powdered sugar
2 Tbs. milk
1 tsp. vanilla

Melt the butter in a medium saucepan. Stir in 2 tablespoons cocoa until dissolved. Add the powdered sugar, milk and vanilla. Stir until smooth. Add more milk if necessary to make a soft spreading consistency. Frost brownies as you desire.

Mrs. Robert Crane (Baudelia)

COOKIES

Brownies

350 degrees
9 x 9 baking pan,
greased (margarine)
Yield: 16 large brownies
Freezes

1 cup sugar
2 eggs
½ cup butter
1 (6-oz.) pkg. chocolate chips
¾ cup flour
½ tsp. salt
½ tsp. baking powder
½ tsp. vanilla
1 cup nuts, chopped

In mixer, cream sugar and eggs. Melt butter and chocolate chips together and add to sugar and egg mixture. In separate bowl, mix all dry ingredients and add to mixture; blend well. Add vanilla and stir in nuts. Pour into 9-inch square pan, greased with margarine and bake in 350 degree oven for 30 to 35 minutes. Let cool before cutting.

Butterscotch Brownies

⅔ cup butter
2⅔ cups brown sugar,
  (1 box)
3 Tbs. water
2 eggs, well beaten
2 cups flour
2 tsp. baking powder
½ tsp. vanilla
1 cup nuts

Melt butter and mix in sugar and water. Add well beaten eggs. Sift flour before measuring, then measure and sift with baking powder. Beat into egg mixture. Add vanilla and nuts. Pour into a well greased 9 x 13 pan. Bake 40 minutes at 325 degrees. While warm, mark in squares. Let cool, then slice into squares as marked and remove from pan.

COOKIES

Cookie Press Butter Cookies

350 degrees
Cookie sheet, ungreased
Yield: 40 cookies
Freezes

1 lb. butter
1 cup brown sugar
5 cups flour
¼ tsp. salt

Cream the butter and brown sugar together. Add the flour and salt, one cup at a time. Mix in mixer, then knead lightly by hand. Either run them through a cookie press or cut into fancy shapes. Bake for 15 minutes at 350 degrees.

Delicious old recipe. Even better if you leave the butter out of the refrigerator to set for 3-5 days.

Mrs. Hulon Webb (Carole)

Butterscotch Cookies

400 degrees
Cookie sheet, greased
Yield: 4-5 dozen

Dough:
½ cup shortening or
   margarine, soft
1½ cups brown sugar
2 eggs
2½ cups flour
½ tsp. baking powder
1 tsp. soda
½ tsp. salt
1 cup sour cream
1 tsp. vanilla

Cream shortening and sugar together. Add eggs and dry ingredients. Add sour cream and vanilla. Chill until firm. Drop by teaspoonful, 2 inches apart, onto a greased cookie sheet. Bake 10-15 minutes at 400 degrees.

Icing:
⅓ cup butter
1½ cups powdered sugar
1 tsp. vanilla
1-2 tsp. hot water

Melt butter and blend with sugar, vanilla, and water. Ice cookies.

Mrs. Phil Hunke (Karen)

COOKIES

Butter Cookies

350 degrees
Cookie sheet, ungreased
Yield: 40-50 cookies
Freezes

1 cup butter
½ cup sugar
1 egg
½ tsp. almond flavoring
2½ cups flour
powdered sugar

Mix butter and sugar together until light and fluffy. Add egg and almond flavoring. Gradually blend in the flour. Chill dough. Roll out and cut with cookie cutters. Bake 8-12 minutes at 350 degrees. Dust with powdered sugar.

Caramel Layer Chocolate Squares

350 degrees
9 x 13 pan,
greased and floured
Yield: 36 bars
Freezes

1 (14-oz.) pkg. caramels, about 50 pieces
⅓ cup evaporated milk
1 pkg. Pillsbury German Chocolate Cake Mix
¾ cup margarine, melted
⅓ cup evaporated milk
1 cup nuts, chopped
1 cup semi-sweet chocolate chips

In saucepan, combine caramels and ⅓ cup milk. Cook over low heat, stirring constantly until caramels are melted. Set aside. Grease and flour a 9 x 13-inch pan. In large bowl, combine dry cake ingredients, melted margarine, ⅓ cup milk and nuts. Stir by hand until dough holds together. Press ½ dough into pan, reserving remaining half. Bake at 350 degrees for 8 minutes. Sprinkle chocolate pieces over this baked crust. Spread caramel mixture over chocolate pieces. Drop and lightly pat reserved dough over caramel mixture. Return to oven; bake 20 to 25 minutes. Cool slightly, then refrigerate about 30 minutes to set caramel layer. Cut into 36 bars.

Mrs. Rondel Davidson (Judy)

Carrot Cookies with Icing

350 degrees
Cookie sheet, greased
Yield: 3-4 dozen

⅔ cup shortening
¾ cup sugar
1 egg
1 cup carrots, cooked and
  mashed
2 cups flour, sifted
¼ tsp. salt
2 tsp. baking powder
1 tsp. vanilla

Cream shortening and sugar; add egg and blend; add carrots. Sift flour, salt and baking powder; add to creamed mixture; add vanilla; drop by teaspoonful onto greased cookie sheet. Bake for 8-10 minutes at 350 degrees.

Icing:
¼ cup hot orange juice
1½ Tbs. butter
rind of 1 orange, grated
2 cups powdered sugar

Mix icing ingredients together. Ice cookies while they are warm.

Mrs. Cayetano Barrera (Yolanda)

Cheesecake Bar Cookies

350 degrees
8-inch square pan, ungreased
Yield: 48 (1-inch) squares
Freezes

Crust:
1 cup flour
⅓ cup brown sugar, packed
⅓ cup butter, softened
½ cup pecans, chopped

Cream flour, brown sugar and butter until fine particles are formed. Stir in nuts. Reserve 1 cup for topping. Press remainder in 8-inch square pan (ungreased). Bake at 350 degrees for 15 minutes.

Filling:
1 (8-oz.) pkg. cream cheese,
  softened
¼ cup sugar
1 egg
2 Tbs. milk
2 Tbs. lemon juice
½ tsp. vanilla

Blend filling ingredients together well. Spread over the partially baked crust. Sprinkle with reserved crumb mixture. Bake at 350 degrees for 25 to 30 minutes. Cool. Cut into squares. Refrigerate.

Mrs. Morgan Talbot (Jane)

COOKIES

Chess Squares

350 degrees
9 x 11 pan, greased
and floured
Yield: 30 squares

1 cup margarine or butter,
  melted
1 lb. box dark brown sugar
1 cup cane sugar
4 egg yolks, beaten
2 cups flour
2 tsp. baking powder
½ tsp. salt
1 cup nuts, chopped
1 tsp. vanilla
4 egg whites
powdered sugar

Blend melted margarine, dark brown sugar, cane sugar; add beaten egg yolks and beat well. Sift flour, baking powder and salt. Add to egg mixture. Fold in nuts and vanilla. Beat egg whites until stiff and fold into other mixture. Spread batter in greased and floured pan. Bake at 350 degrees for 30-45 minutes. When done sprinkle with powdered sugar. Cut into squares.

Mrs. Jim Jones (Jackie)

Chocolate Chip Oatmeal Cookies

350-375 degrees
Cookie sheet, ungreased
Yield: 50-60 cookies
Freezes

½ cup sugar
1 cup brown sugar
1 cup shortening
2 eggs
2 tsp. vanilla
1 tsp. salt
1 tsp. baking soda
1½ cups flour
2 cups old-fashioned oatmeal
½ cup wheat germ
1 (12-oz.) pkg. chocolate
  chips
1 cup pecans, chopped

Cream sugars and shortening; add eggs, vanilla, and mix well. Combine all other ingredients, mixing well. Add to the sugar-egg mixture. Drop on ungreased cookie sheet and cook for approximately 10-12 minutes, or until cookies begin to brown. Remove from oven and take off cookie sheet immediately. Store in tightly closed cookie jar or tins.

Nuts and chocolate chips may be omitted and the recipe turns out just as good. It doubles easily, too.

Mrs. Jerry Box (Deanna)

Chocolate Mint Sticks

350 degrees
9 x 9 baking pan,
greased and floured
Yield: 36 bars
Freezes

First layer:
2 squares unsweetened
  chocolate (2-oz.)
½ cup butter
2 eggs, beaten
1 cup sugar
¾ tsp. peppermint extract
½ cup flour, sifted
dash salt

Melt chocolate and butter in saucepan. Beat eggs until frothy and stir in sugar, chocolate mixture and the peppermint extract. Add flour and salt. Mix thoroughly. Pour in pan that has been greased and floured and bake in 350 degree oven for 15-20 minutes. Cool. Spread with filling.

Filling:
4 Tbs. butter
2 cups powdered sugar
2 Tbs. cream
1½ tsp. peppermint extract

Work butter into powdered sugar. Add cream and extract. Stir. Place filling over cooked mixture and refrigerate while making glaze.

Glaze:
2 squares unsweetened
  chocolate
2 Tbs. butter

Melt chocolate and butter. Mix together, then dribble over the cooled, firm filling. Tilt the cake pan until glaze covers the cake. Refrigerate the cake 5 minutes or until set, then cut in bars.

It is like a peppermint brownie.
Mrs. Jerry McGilvray (Jane)

S'Mores

Yield: 1 S'More

1 marshmallow
2 graham crackers
4 squares of a chocolate bar
  (Hershey milk chocolate
  bar)

Toast 1 marshmallow over medium coals. Make a sandwich with 2 graham crackers, and the chocolate squares and the toasted marshmallow.
Mrs. Bill Turk (Marian)

COOKIES

Coco Kiss Cookies

375 degrees
Cookie sheet, ungreased
Yield: 4½ dozen

1 cup margarine, softened
⅔ cup sugar
1 tsp. vanilla
1⅔ cups flour
¼ cup cocoa
1 cup nuts, finely chopped
9 oz. pkg. chocolate kisses
powdered sugar

Cream margarine, sugar, and vanilla; gradually beat in the flour and the cocoa. Add nuts, beat on low speed until well distributed. Chill. Unwrap the kisses. Shape a tablespoon of chilled dough around each kiss. Roll to form a ball. Place on ungreased cookie sheet. Bake at 375 degrees 10-12 minutes. Cool slightly before removing them to wire rack. Before serving dust with powdered sugar.

Mrs. Richard Stakes (Jackie)

Congo Bars

325 degrees
9 x 13 pan,
greased and floured
Yield: 24 bars

1 lb. brown sugar
⅔ cup shortening, softened
3 eggs
1 tsp. vanilla
2¾ cups flour
2½ tsp. baking powder
½ tsp. salt
12 oz. pkg. chocolate chips
1 cup nuts, chopped
powdered sugar (optional)

Cream sugar and shortening together. Add eggs and vanilla; then add dry ingredients. Add chips and nuts. Spread in a greased and floured 9 x 13 pan. Bake at 325 degrees for 30 minutes. If desired, sprinkle powdered sugar over top when done.

Dough will be very stiff, so be prepared to use your hands and a large spoon when spreading it in the pan.

Mrs. Dan Seitz (Amy)

COOKIES

Christmas Cookies

350 degrees
Cookie sheet, ungreased
Yield: 80 cookies
Freezes

Cookie:
2 cups sugar
1 cup butter
2 eggs
3½ cups flour
1 tsp. soda
1 tsp. salt
1 tsp. baking powder
1¼ tsp. vanilla

Mix all the ingredients together and form into small marble size balls. Press down with bottom of a glass until flattened. Bake 8-10 minutes or until lightly browned.

Topping:
pecan halves, colored sugar, red hots or any other topping desired

Nuts or red hots may be added before baking cookies. Colored sugar crystals or other toppings which may melt, should be added to the cookies after removing them from the oven, while still warm.

Mrs. Richard Moore (Lynda)

Coconut Cookies

325 degrees
Cookie sheet, ungreased
Yield: 50 cookies
Freezes

1 stick butter or margarine
1 scant cup sugar—usually ¾ cup
1 egg
1 small pkg. biscuit mix
1 pkg. potato flakes
1 tsp. coconut flavoring (use vanilla if you don't like coconut)

Mix all ingredients together. Drop by spoonful onto an ungreased cookie sheet and bake at 325 degrees until brown.

Very easy for children to make.
Mrs. Kenneth Landrum (June)

149

COOKIES

Cowboy Cookies

350 degrees
Cookie sheet, greased
Yield: dozens and dozens

2 cups flour
1 tsp. soda
½ tsp. baking powder
½ tsp. salt
1 cup shortening
1 cup sugar
1 cup brown sugar
2 eggs
1 tsp. vanilla
2 cups rolled oats
1 pkg. chocolate chips
1 cup pecans, chopped

Sift together the flour, soda, baking powder and salt. Set aside. Cream together the shortening, sugars, eggs and vanilla until fluffy. Add the flour mixture and mix well. Add the oats and chips; then add pecans. Drop by teaspoonful onto greased cookie sheet and bake at 350 degrees for 15 minutes.

This recipe makes dozens and dozens and keeps well for a long time without freezing. They are great to ship to family away from home.

Mrs. Jim Corcoran (Pam)

Date Nut Tarts

375 degrees
Small muffin tins, ungreased
Yield: 50-60 tarts
Freezes

Pastry:
1 stick margarine
1 (8-oz.) pkg. cream cheese
2 cups flour
cold water

Cream margarine and cream cheese. Stir in flour. Add enough cold water to hold the mixture together. Chill one hour.

Filling:
1 stick margarine
2 egg yolks
1 cup sugar
1 tsp. vanilla
2 cups pecans, chopped
2 cups dates, chopped
2 egg whites, stiffly beaten
powdered sugar

Mix the margarine and egg yolks, add the sugar and vanilla. Mix well. Add the nuts and dates and blend well. Fold in the beaten egg whites. Line the small muffin tins with the pastry. Put 1 tsp. of filling in each cup. Bake 20-25 minutes at 375 degrees. Cool on cookie rack and dust with powdered sugar.

Mrs. Tom Wilkins (Geen)

COOKIES

Florentines

350 degrees
Cookie sheet, greased and floured
Yield: 48 cookies
Freezes

¾ cup heavy cream
¼ cup sugar
¼ cup flour, sifted
½ lb. candied orange peel,
  chopped fine
½ cup slivered almonds,
  blanched and toasted
2 (4-oz.) bars of best
  chocolate available

Stir until well blended the heavy cream and sugar. Add the flour, then add the orange peel and almonds. Mix well. Drop by teaspoon on heavily greased and floured cookie sheet. Flatten cookie with a knife. Bake at 350 degrees for 10-12 minutes until cookies are lightly browned at edges. Allow cookies to cool and remove with spatula. In a double boiler, melt the chocolate bars. Turn the cookies upside down and cover the bottom with chocolate. Allow to dry at room temperature until chocolate becomes firm.

Excellent for freezing.

Mrs. C. A. Pagenstecher (Adelyn)

Goopie Gourmets

Yield: 2 dozen

3 cups corn flakes
½ cup coconut (optional)
½ cup sugar
½ cup light corn syrup
¾ cup peanut butter

Mix cereal and coconut in large mixing bowl. Mix sugar and syrup in medium saucepan. Cook slowly until sugar dissolves and mixture comes to a full boil. Remove from heat and stir in peanut butter. Add cereal flakes and coconut. Stir well. Drop by teaspoonful onto wax paper.

Anyone who likes peanut butter will like these.

Mrs. Anne Walker

COOKIES

Fruit Cake Cookies

350 degrees
Cookie sheet, greased
Yield: 200 cookies

1 stick butter
1½ cups brown sugar, firmly
   packed
4 eggs
¾ cup whiskey
3 Tbs. milk
3 cups flour
1 tsp. cinnamon
1 tsp. nutmeg
1 tsp. cloves
1 tsp. allspice
3 tsp. soda
1½ lbs. candied cherries
1½ lbs. candied pineapple,
   (green, red and white, big
   chunks)
2 (9-oz.) boxes raisins
1 lb. dates, chopped
6 cups nuts

Cream butter and sugar. Add eggs, one at a time. Add whiskey, then milk. Sift dry ingredients and add to above mixture. (Keep 1 cup of flour to mix with fruit and nuts) Coarsely cut up fruit and nuts and mix with flour, then add to mixture. Drop by teaspoonful on greased cookie sheet. Cook at 350 degrees for 10 minutes.

Keeps for weeks

Mrs. Steven Zenthoefer (Ann)

Gumdrop Cookies

325 degrees
11 x 16 pan, greased
Yield: 36-40 squares
Freezes

2 cups flour
¼ tsp. salt
1 tsp. cinnamon
1½ cups pecans, chopped
1¼ cups orange candy
   slices, chopped
4 eggs
1 cup sugar
1 cup brown sugar
1 Tbs. cold water

Sift together flour, salt and cinnamon. Sprinkle a little over pecans and gumdrop candy. Beat eggs. Add sugars and water and beat more. Gradually add dry ingredients. Stir in floured pecans and candy. Spread in greased shallow pan. Bake 30 minutes at 325 degrees. Cool and cut in squares.

Mrs. Jim Miller (Terry)

COOKIES

Hello Dolly Cookies

350 degrees
9 x 9 pan, ungreased
Yield: 25 cookies
Freezes

½ stick butter
1 heaping cup graham
   cracker crumbs
1 heaping cup angel flake
   coconut
1 cup chocolate chips
1 cup pecans, chopped
1 cup Eagle Brand milk

Layer dry ingredients in order given, on top of melted butter in 9 x 9 pan. Pour condensed milk over ingredients. Bake at 300 degrees for 45-50 minutes. Let cool thoroughly before cutting into desired pieces.

Can be doubled in a jelly roll pan.

Mrs. Jerry McGilvray (Jane)

Kringle

325 degrees
Cookie sheet, ungreased
Yield: 48 bars
Freezes

First layer:
1 cup flour
½ cup butter
1 Tbs. water
½ tsp. salt

Mix flour, butter, water and salt like pie crust. Pat on cookie sheet in 2 long strips that are 3 inches wide.

Second layer:
1 cup water
½ cup butter
1 cup flour
3 eggs
1 tsp. almond extract

Put water in a saucepan with butter. Heat to boiling. Remove from heat and add flour. Stir until smooth, then add eggs, one at a time, beating well after each addition. Add extract and spread on top of first mixture. Bake for 60 minutes at 325 degrees. Cool.

Frosting:
2 cups powdered sugar
½ tsp. almond extract
enough cream to make a
   smooth icing
slivered almonds, toasted

Mix powdered sugar, extract, and enough cream to make a smooth icing. Frost the cooled confection, then top with toasted slivered almonds. Serve in slices the size you desire.

Mrs. Robert Kern, Jr. (Carolyn)

COOKIES

Kuchen

350 degrees
Cookie sheet, greased
Yield: about 8 dozen pieces
Freezes

4 cups flour
2 tsp. baking powder
1 cup sugar
½ lb. butter
½ pint sour cream
½ tsp. baking soda
3 eggs, separated
1 tsp. vanilla
1 (1-lb.) jar plum jam
1 cup cinnamon sugar
1½ cups pecans, chopped

Sift dry ingredients. Work in butter as in pie crust. Mix sour cream with baking soda and add to flour mixture. Add egg yolks and vanilla. Form into smooth dough. Divide dough into 8 parts, cover with plastic wrap and freeze for several hours. Defrost dough and roll out each part on well-floured board to about ¼-inch thickness. Spread with plum jam, sprinkle with cinnamon sugar and chopped nuts. Roll up jelly-roll fashion. Brush with lightly beaten egg whites and sprinkle with additional cinnamon sugar and chopped pecans. Bake at 350 Degrees for 20 minutes until golden brown. Cut in strips to serve. Do not cut in strips before freezing. Remove from freezer, heat for about 15 minutes in 350 degree oven and then cut into strips.

To keep size and shape more uniform, cut pieces of foil about 6 x 12 and fold up sides so that the bottom is about 4 inches across. Put each roll (spray foil with Pam) into the foil and bake. They won't spread all over the cookie sheet this way.

Mrs. Gary Gurwitz (Bailey)

COOKIES

Lemon Bars

300 degrees
13 x 9 baking dish, lightly greased
Yield: 36 large bars
Freezes

1st Step:
1 cup margarine
2 cups flour
½ cup powdered sugar
⅛ tsp. salt

Combine margarine, flour, powdered sugar and salt. Blend well. Pat dough into a lightly greased 13 x 9 baking dish. Bake at 300 degrees for 30 minutes or until lightly browned.

2nd Step:
4 eggs, beaten
2 cups sugar
½ cup lemon juice
¼ cup flour
⅛ tsp. salt
1 tsp. baking powder
powdered sugar

Combine eggs, sugar, and lemon juice and mix well. Add flour, salt, and baking powder. Blend well. Pour over cooked pastry. Bake at 300 degrees for 30-40 minutes. Sprinkle with powdered sugar. Let cool. Cut into bar cookies.

Mrs. Charles Murray (Cynthia)

Variation:
1½ cups powdered sugar, sifted
4 Tbs. lemon juice
2 Tbs. butter, softened

When cookies are cold, spread with glaze made by mixing these ingredients until smooth. Cut into bar cookies.

Sand Tarts

300 degrees
Cookie sheet, ungreased
Yield: 50 cookies
Freezes

1 cup butter
¾ cup powdered sugar, sifted
2 cups flour, sifted
1 cup pecans, chopped
1 tsp. vanilla
powdered sugar

Cream butter and sugar. Add flour gradually and mix well. Add nuts and vanilla and mix. Roll in balls or crescents. Bake about 30-35 minutes or until lightly browned on ungreased cookie sheet. When done and slightly cooled, roll in powdered sugar.

Mrs. Jerry McGilvray (Jane)

COOKIES

Lemon Meringue Bars

½ cup margarine
½ cup powdered sugar
2 egg yolks
1 cup flour, sifted
¼ cup almonds, finely
  ground
2 tsp. lemon peel, grated
¼ tsp. salt
2 egg whites
½ cup granulated sugar
1 Tbs. lemon juice

Work margarine in a bowl until creamy; add powdered sugar and beat until fluffy. Add egg yolks, flour, almonds, lemon peel, and salt to creamed mixture; mix well. Spread in prepared pan and bake 10 minutes. Remove from oven and cool slightly. Beat egg whites until soft peaks form. Gradually add granulated sugar and beat until stiff peaks form. Gradually add lemon juice, beating until blended. Spread over baked layer. Bake 25 minutes at 350 degrees, or until lightly browned. Cool in pan and cut into 1 x 2-inch bars.

Mrs. Morgan Talbot (Jane)

Oatmeal Cookies

350 degrees
Cookie sheet, greased
Yield: several dozen

½ cup dark brown sugar
½ cup sugar
½ tsp. salt
½ tsp. soda
½ cup oil
1 egg
1 tsp. vanilla
1 cup oatmeal
1 cup flour
1 cup pecans

If you mix exactly as follows you will have easy mixing and perfect cookies; mix sugars, salt, soda, oil, egg and vanilla together. Add oatmeal; stir well. Gradually add flour; add nuts. Mix and drop by teaspoonful onto a greased cookie sheet and bake for 10-15 minutes at 350 degrees.

Mrs. Larry Seal (Jane Ann)

COOKIES

New England Spice Cookies

375 degrees
Cookie sheet, lightly greased
Yield: 5-6 dozen

2½ cups all-purpose flour,
   sifted
2 tsp. baking soda
½ tsp. cloves
½ tsp. allspice
½ tsp. cinnamon
¼ tsp. ginger
¾ cup butter or margarine,
   softened
1 cup sugar
1 egg
¼ cup light molasses
powdered sugar

Sift flour with baking soda, cloves, allspice, cinnamon, and ginger on sheet of waxed paper. In medium bowl, with portable electric mixer, beat butter, sugar, and egg until light and fluffy. With wooden spoon, beat in flour mixture alternately with molasses; beating well after each addition. Cover dough and refrigerate for 1 hour. Shape dough into ½-inch balls, roll in powdered sugar and place on lightly greased cookie sheet, 1 inch apart. Bake at 375 degrees for 8-10 minutes, then remove to rack for cooling. Cookies may be sprinkled with powdered sugar while still warm.

Mrs. Neal King (Wileen)

Nane Sharine

300 degrees
Cookie sheet, ungreased
Yield: 30-40 cookies
Freezes

2 cups flour
1 tsp. baking powder
1 cup shortening (not butter!)
1 cup sugar
2 egg yolks
1 tsp. vanilla
1 tsp. almond extract
1 tsp. lemon extract

Sift together flour and baking powder. Set aside. Cream shortening and sugar. Blend in egg yolks, vanilla, almond extract, and lemon extract. Mix well. Gradually add the dry ingredients and mix until dough is well blended. Roll dough into round balls with hands, using about 1 tsp. dough for each ball. Place on ungreased baking sheet and flatten slightly with a fork. Bake in a slow oven, 300 degrees, for 20 minutes. These freeze well and have a very unusual flavor.

Mrs. Morgan Talbot (Jane)

COOKIES

Oatmeal Carmelitas

350 degrees
8 x 16 cake pan
or 2 (8 x 8) pans
(use no-stick spray)
Yield: 40 squares

1 (12-oz.) jar of caramel
   topping
4½ Tbs. flour
1½ cups flour
1½ cups quick-cooking oats
1⅛ cups brown sugar
¾ tsp. soda
⅓ tsp. salt
1⅛ cups margarine or butter,
   melted
1½ cups chocolate chips
1½ cups pecans, chopped

Mix caramel topping and 4½ Tbs. flour together. Set aside. Stir together 1½ cups flour, oats, brown sugar, soda, salt and butter. Press half of the crumb mixture in the bottom of pan. Bake at 350 degrees for 10 minutes. Sprinkle the chips on it, pour on caramel mixture, then cover with pecans. Sprinkle with remaining crumbs. Bake 20 minutes. Chill one hour and cut into squares.

Mrs. Leroy Lewin (Hilda)

Oatmeal-Coconut Cookies

350 degrees
Cookie sheet, ungreased
Yield: 3 to 8 dozen

1½ cups all-purpose flour,
   sifted
1 tsp. baking soda
1 tsp. salt
1 cup sugar
½ cup brown sugar
1¼ cups rolled oats,
   uncooked
¾ cup flaked coconut
1 cup butter, melted
1 egg, well-beaten

Sift together flour, baking soda, salt, and sugars. Add oats and coconut, and mix. Add butter and egg and mix thoroughly. Shape into balls, size will depend on number of dozen desired. Place on ungreased baking sheet and press down lightly. Bake at 350 degrees for 10-15 minutes or until cookies are brown. Cooking time will depend on size of balls. Cool slightly and remove with spatula.

May be easier to handle if chilled before forming into balls.

Mrs. Paul Veale, Jr. (Sandra)

COOKIES

Molasses Crinkles

375 degrees
Cookie sheet, greased
Yield: 4-5 dozen
Freezes

¾ cup shortening
1 cup brown sugar, packed
¼ cup molasses
1 egg
2¼ cups flour
2 tsp. soda
¼ tsp. salt
½ tsp. cloves
1 tsp. cinnamon
1 tsp. ginger
sugar

Mix thoroughly the shortening, brown sugar, molasses and egg. Sift the flour, soda, salt, cloves, cinnamon, and ginger together and add to the molasses mixture. Mix well. Chill dough. (You may make as many cookies as you like at one time because the dough keeps well in refrigerator.) Roll into balls the size of a walnut and dip the top in sugar. Place sugared side up, 3 inches apart, on a greased cookie sheet. Sprinkle each cookie with two or three drops of water to produce a cracked surface. Bake 10-12 minutes in quick oven (375 degrees) just until set but not hard. Makes 4 dozen (2½-inch) cookies.

Mrs. Morris Nelson (Carloyn)

Chewy Oatmeal Cookies

375 degrees
Cookie sheet, greased
Yield: 84 cookies
Freezes

1 cup shortening
2 cups brown sugar
2 eggs, well beaten
1 tsp. soda
¼ cup boiling water
½ tsp. vanilla
2 cups flour
2 cups oatmeal
¾ cup nuts
1 cup raisins (optional)

Cream shortening and sugar; add beaten eggs. Dissolve soda in boiling water; add to mixture. Add vanilla, flour, oatmeal, nuts and raisins. Drop by teaspoonful onto greased cookie sheet. Bake 10 minutes in 375 degree oven.

Mrs. Joe Friend (Pam)

COOKIES

"Igloo" Oatmeal Cookies

325 degrees
Cookie sheet, ungreased
Yield: 60 cookies
Freezes

1 cup margarine
½ cup sugar
½ cup brown sugar
1 egg
2 cups flour
½ tsp. soda
¼ tsp. salt
1½ cups oats

Beat the margarine, sugar and brown sugar until creamy and then add egg and blend. Sift together the flour, soda, and salt and mix into the sugar mixture. Fold in oats and mix well. Drop by teaspoonful on ungreased cookie sheet and bake 325 degrees for 10 minutes. Let cool, then ice.

Icing:
⅓ cup margarine
3 cups powdered sugar, sifted
⅓ cup evaporated milk
1 Tbs. light corn syrup
1 tsp. vanilla
¾ cup nuts, chopped

Brown the margarine over low heat. Cool to lukewarm and add sifted powdered sugar, evaporated milk, corn syrup and vanilla; stir in nuts. Spread on cookies.

Mrs. Hollis Fritts (Gerrie)

Salted Peanut Crisps

350 degrees
Cookie sheet, lightly greased
Yield: 72 cookies
Freezes

1 cup shortening (part butter or margarine)
1½ cups brown sugar, packed
2 eggs
2 tsp. vanilla
3 cups flour
½ tsp. soda
1 tsp. salt
2 cups salted peanuts
sugar

Mix shortening, sugar, eggs, and vanilla. Mix flour together with soda and salt. Stir into sugar mixture. Mix in peanuts. Drop rounded teaspoonfuls of dough about 2 inches apart on lightly greased cookie sheet. Flatten each cookie with the bottom of a glass dipped in sugar. Bake 8-10 minutes or until golden brown.

Mrs. Frank Birkhead (Janet)

COOKIES

Old Fashioned Raisin Bars

375 degrees
9 x 13 pan, greased
Yield: 36 large servings
Freezes

1 cup water
1 cup seedless raisins
1 cup sugar
1 egg, slightly beaten
½ cup oil
1¾ cups flour, sifted
¼ tsp. salt
1 tsp. soda
1 tsp. cinnamon
1 tsp. nutmeg
1 tsp. allspice
½ tsp. cloves
½ cup nuts, chopped
   (optional)
powdered sugar

Combine the water and raisins and bring to a boil. Remove from heat. Cool to lukewarm. Stir in sugar, egg, oil and mix well. Sift together the dry ingredients and add to the raisin mixture. Mix well. Stir in chopped nuts. Pour into a greased 9 x 13 pan. Bake in 375 degree oven for 20 minutes or til done. Cut into bars and dust with powdered sugar when cool.

Mrs. Paul Haas (Maurie)

Pineapple Bars

350 degrees
9 x 12 baking pan, greased
Yield: about 50 bars

½ cup butter or margarine,
   softened
2 cups sugar
4 eggs
1½ cups flour
½ tsp. soda
1 (No. 2) can crushed
   pineapple, well drained
1 cup walnuts, chopped
powdered sugar

Cream butter and sugar. Add eggs, one at a time, beating well. Add dry ingredients (mixed together) and then pineapple and walnuts. Put batter into greased 9 x 12 pan. Bake at 350 degrees for 35-40 minutes. Sprinkle with powdered sugar after baking. Cut into bars.

COOKIES

"Tiny Tim" Pecan Cups

325 degrees
Small fluted tart cups
Yield: 4 dozen tarts
Freezes

Crust:
1 stick butter or margarine
1 (3-oz.) pkg. cream cheese
1 cup flour

Filling:
2 eggs, lightly beaten
2 Tbs. butter or margarine
1½ cups brown sugar
2 tsp. vanilla
2 Tbs. rum or bourbon
  (optional)
1½ cups pecans, chopped
dash salt

Mix butter, cream cheese and flour together for crust and chill in plastic wrap in refrigerator for at least one hour.

Mix together the eggs, butter, sugar, vanilla, rum, pecans and salt. Press dough for crust into very small fluted tart cups and put filling (half-full) into cups. Bake at 325 degrees for 30 minutes or until filling is set. Let cool a few minutes and turn out from tart cups. May be frozen in tins or tightly closed containers.

Mrs. Jerry Box (Deanna)

Easy Praline Cookies

350 degrees
11 x 16 jelly roll pan
Yield: 24 large or
48 small cookies

12 whole graham crackers
2 sticks butter
1 cup brown sugar
1 cup pecans, chopped fine

Line bottom of jelly roll pan with the graham crackers. In saucepan, melt butter and stir in brown sugar. At medium heat, and stirring constantly, boil for 2 minutes. Add chopped pecans and pour over the graham crackers spreading as evenly as possible. Bake 10 minutes in 350 degree oven and allow to cool slightly before cutting. Each cracker should be cut in half, or fourths or eighths, according to the size you desire. If cut in half you will yield 24 cookies.

Mrs. Leroy Lewin (Hilda)

COOKIES

Lemon Almond Shortbread

350 degrees
Cookie sheet, greased
Yield: 60 cookies
Freezes

¾ cup cornstarch
5 Tbs. powdered sugar
1 cup flour
1 cup margarine

Sift cornstarch, sugar and flour together. Blend in margarine by hand. Pinch off a teaspoon of dough and roll into a ball. Place on lightly greased cookie sheet. Make indentation in center of cookie with thumb. Bake 15 minutes at 350 degrees.

Filling:
1 tsp. lemon juice
1 tsp. almond extract
3 Tbs. butter, soft
1 cup powdered sugar, sifted

Mix two flavorings in butter; then mix in powdered sugar. Fill cookies while hot with a demitasse spoon.

These break very easily!

Mrs. Sam Henderson (Eleanor)

Scotch Shortbread

400 degrees
Cookie sheet, ungreased
Yield: About 50 cookies
Freezes

4 cups flour, unsifted
1 cup butter
1 cup shortening
1 cup powdered sugar,
  heaping
pinch salt
1 tsp. vanilla

Blend flour, butter, shortening, powdered sugar, and salt together with a pastry blender or a fork. Add vanilla. Wash hands and blend mixture with fingertips until smooth and creamy. Roll out and cut in desired shapes. Place on ungreased cookie sheet and prick with a fork. Bake at 400 degrees until light brown, about 10 or 15 minutes.

Ms. Paul Moffitt (Marilyn)

163

COOKIES

Forgotten Cookies

350 degrees
Cookie sheet with foil, ungreased
Yield: 36 cookies

2 egg whites
⅔ cup sugar
pinch of salt
1 cup chocolate chips
½ cup nuts, finely chopped
1 tsp. vanilla

Beat the egg whites until stiff. Gradually add sugar, beating well. Add a pinch of salt. Fold in chocolate chips, nuts and vanilla. Drop by teaspoon onto ungreased foil lined cookie sheet and place in a preheated, 350 degree oven. Turn oven off, close the door, and leave cookies inside for about 8 hours.

Good to do overnight.

Mrs. Hulon Webb (Carole)

Variation:
¼ tsp. almond extract
¼ tsp. lemon extract
½ tsp. vanilla extract
1 cup nuts, coarsely chopped

Omit the chocolate chips and add the almond, lemon and vanilla extracts and the chopped nuts.

Mrs. Paul Wagner (Doris)

Snickerdoos

400 degrees
Cookie sheet, ungreased
Yield: 50-60 cookies
Freezes

2 sticks butter
1½ cups sugar
2 eggs
2¾ cups flour, sifted
½ tsp. salt
2 tsp. cream of tartar
1 tsp. vanilla
1 tsp. cinnamon
½ cup sugar

Cream butter and sugar; add eggs. Mix well. Add sifted flour, salt and cream of tartar; then add vanilla. Mix well. Let sit in refrigerator a few minutes. Remove and make small balls (walnut size) and roll in a mixture of cinnamon and sugar. Place about 2 inches apart on ungreased cookie sheet. Bake at 400 degrees for about 8-10 minutes.

Mrs. Bob Batte (Gerry)

COOKIES

Sugar Cookies

375 degrees
Cookie sheet, greased
Yield: 70-80 drop cookies
Freezes

'2 eggs, slightly beaten
⅔ cup butter
⅔ cup shortening
3½ cups flour
1½ cups sugar
1 tsp. salt
2 tsp. baking powder
2 tsp. vanilla
sugar (for topping)

Beat eggs, add other ingredients on slow speed of mixer. Blend well. Chill dough if you wish to use cookie cutters. Then roll out and cut; bake at 375 degrees for 7-8 minutes. If you don't wish to use a cookie cutter, drop by teaspoonful on greased cookie sheet and press flat with bottom of glass dipped in sugar. Cover the cookies with sugar crystals or candies. Cookies may be dipped in sugar after baking.

Mrs. Robert Parry, Jr. (Barbara)

Whiskey Balls

Yield: 150 small balls

1 (12-oz.) box vanilla wafers
1 cup powdered sugar, sifted
1 cup pecans, chopped fine
½ cup cocoa, sifted
3 jiggers whiskey
3 Tbs. dark corn syrup

Crush the vanilla wafers very fine. Combine powdered sugar, pecans, and cocoa with the wafers. In a separate cup, combine whiskey and corn syrup. Pour this mixture over the crumb mixture. Blend well (should be very hard). Roll into small balls and roll balls in powdered sugar.

Store in covered container in refrigerator. Will keep indefinitely.

Mrs. Steven Zenthoefer (Ann)

COOKIES

Walnut Date Bars

350 degrees
7 x 11 pan, greased and floured
Yield: 28 bars
Freezes

Date Bars:
1 cup flour, sifted
½ tsp. soda
¼ tsp. nutmeg
¼ tsp. salt
⅓ cup butter
¾ cup brown sugar
1 egg
1 Tbs. orange rind
2 Tbs. orange juice
½ cup dates, cut up
¾ cup walnuts, chopped

Orange Frosting:
¼ cup butter
1 tsp. orange rind, grated
1 egg yolk
½ tsp. vanilla
2 cups powdered sugar, sifted
2 tsp. orange juice
¼ cup walnuts, chopped

Sift flour, soda, nutmeg and salt. Cream butter and brown sugar. Add egg, orange rind and orange juice. Stir in the dry ingredients; mix well. Add walnuts and dates. Spoon mixture into a greased and floured 7 x 11 pan and bake at 350 degrees for 25-30 minutes. Cool. When thoroughly cooled, frost with orange frosting.

Cream butter and sugar. Add orange juice, egg, rind, and walnuts. Ice. Then cut into 1 x 2½ inch bars. If you double this recipe, do not double the amount of walnuts. If you like, leave the walnuts out of the icing.

Mrs. Jerry McGilvray (Jane)

Walk-to-School Cookies

325 degrees
Cookie sheet, ungreased
Yield: 50-60 cookies
Freezes

2 cups butter
1 cup granulated sugar
4 cups flour
1 tsp. vanilla
powdered sugar

Mix well all the ingredients except the powdered sugar. Pat into three rolls and chill. Slice and bake on ungreased cookie sheet at 325 degrees for 10-12 minutes. Sprinkle with powdered sugar while warm.

Mrs. Kenneth Landrum (June)

CANDY

Martha Washingtons

Candy:
2 boxes powdered sugar,
  sifted
2 sticks margarine, melted
1 can Eagle Brand milk
1 tsp. vanilla
1-2 cups pecans, finely
  chopped
1 (3½-oz.) can Angel flake
  coconut (optional)

Mix well, with hands, the candy mixture and refrigerate. Take a small portion at a time and roll into balls.

Dip:
¼ lb. paraffin
1½ boxes Baker Semi-Sweet
  Chocolate

Melt paraffin and chocolate in double boiler and dip balls into chocolate with toothpick. Set on wax paper.

Mrs. Joe Stroud (Ruthie)

Candy Bon Bons

Yield: about 100

1 can Eagle Brand milk
1 (8-oz.) can Angel flake
  coconut
1 stick margarine
4 cups pecans, chopped
1½ cups powdered sugar
1 (12-oz.) pkg. semi-sweet
  chocolate bits
¼ lb. paraffin

Mix the milk, coconut, margarine, pecans and sugar together and chill. Roll into balls and rechill. Melt chocolate and paraffin in double boiler. Dip balls in mixture and place on wax paper to set.

Mrs. Bob Whitis (Linda)

Butter the inside top rim of a pan to keep candy from boiling over.

CANDY

Chocolate Almond Candy

Cookie sheet
Yield: 1 pound
Freezes

2 sticks (or a little less)
  butter or margarine
1 cup sugar
1½ cups blanched almond
  halves
1 (6-oz.) bag semi-sweet
  chocolate pieces or a large
  milk chocolate bar

Melt butter in skillet; stir in sugar and keep stirring until all sugar is dissolved. Then add almonds slowly and cook until golden brown or almonds begin to pop, stirring constantly. Pour mixture on a cookie sheet and wait for it to harden a little (about one minute). Quickly add chocolate pieces on top of butter-almond mixture and spread evenly over the candy. Cool. Store in metal cans; will keep six months in freezer.

Mrs. Robert Crane (Baudelia)

Fudge

3 cups sugar
2 Tbs. corn syrup
3 squares unsweetened
  chocolate
⅛ tsp. salt
1 cup evaporated milk
  (undiluted)
3 Tbs. butter
1 cup pecans

Mix all ingredients except the nuts and butter and boil until soft ball stage or until 234-238 degrees on candy thermometer. Add butter. Cook until lukewarm. Beat until creamy, add nuts and pour into buttered pan.

Mrs. Ruben Cardenas (Dardanella)

Fudge Candy

2 cups sugar
2 Tbs. cocoa (heaping)
⅔ cup milk
2 Tbs. butter
2 Tbs. light Karo corn syrup
1 tsp. vanilla

Combine all ingredients except vanilla, and cook until it reaches the soft ball stage. Add vanilla and beat until creamy. Pour into buttered pan.

Mrs. Morris Nelson (Carolynn)

CANDY

Chocolate Fudge

4 cups sugar
1 can Pet milk
1 stick margarine
1 (12-oz.) pkg. chocolate
  chips
1 (7-oz.) jar marshmallow
  cream
1 cup pecans, chopped

Mix sugar, Pet milk and margarine in saucepan. Let boil 9 minutes (or until candy thermometer reaches 234 degrees). Remove from stove and add chocolate chips and marshmallow cream. Mix well, then add chopped pecans and pour in greased pan.

Mrs. George Lillard (Diane)

Chocolate Fudge Cups

350 degrees
Small teflon muffin tins,
lightly greased
Yield: 48 fudge cups
Freezes

First layer:
½ cup butter
1 cup sugar (½ cup brown
  sugar and ½ cup white)
1 egg
2 squares Baker's chocolate,
  melted
½ tsp. vanilla
¼ tsp. salt
2¼ cups flour, sifted

Cream butter and sugars together. Blend an egg into the butter and sugar mixture. Mix until smooth. Add the melted chocolate, vanilla and salt to butter mixture. Blend in 2-2¼ cups flour. Mix well and shape into balls. Press into the bottom and up the sides of the tiny muffin tins, keeping the bottom thin. Bake in 350 degree oven for 8-10 minutes.

Fudge filling:
1½ cups sugar
⅓ cup milk
¼ cup butter
1½ squares Baker's
  chocolate
3 Tbs. light corn syrup
¼ tsp. salt
1 tsp. vanilla

In a saucepan, combine the sugar, milk, butter, chocolate, corn syrup, and salt. Cook over a low heat until chocolate and butter melt. Bring to a boil and boil for 1 minute. Remove from heat and add vanilla. Beat until lukewarm and fill the muffin cups with mixture.

Mrs. Kenneth Landrum (June)

CANDY

Five Minute Fudge

Yield: platterful

butter
1 cup pecans, chopped
1 (6-oz.) pkg. chocolate chips
2 cups sugar
12 large marshmallows
1 (5.33 oz.) can Pet milk
½ stick margarine
1 tsp. vanilla
salt

Butter a large platter or flat pan. Have ready pecans and chips. In a saucepan, put sugar, marshmallows, milk, and margarine. Cook, stirring all the time over medium heat. When it starts to boil, start counting time and cook for five minutes. Remove from fire, add chocolate chips, vanilla, dash of salt and pecans. Stir until creamy, pour into dish. Cut into pieces when cool and firm.

Mrs. Joe Stroud (Ruthie)

Peanut Brittle

Jelly roll pan, buttered
Yield: about 2 pounds

2 cups sugar
1 cup light Karo syrup
½ cup water
2 cups peanuts, raw
1 tsp. vanilla
1 tsp. soda

Cook sugar, Karo and water in large heavy skillet until it spins a thread. Add raw peanuts and cook until golden brown. (Be sure it is golden brown, not golden yellow). Remove from heat and add vanilla and soda. Stir until soda is mixed in well. Pour into buttered shallow pan, such as a jelly roll pan. Cool and break into pieces.

Mrs. Bob Whitis (Linda)

Pralines I

Yield: 2-3 dozen

1 stick butter, not margarine
1 lb. *light* brown sugar
1 cup heavy cream
2 cups pecans, whole

Cook all ingredients, except pecans, to soft ball stage (about 20 minutes) stirring constantly. Remove from heat and let stand 5 minutes. Add pecans and stir until glassy. Drop on waxed paper. Cool.

Temperamental in humid weather.
Mrs. Charles Murray (Cynthia)

CANDY

Pralines II

2 cups sugar
1 cup buttermilk
1 tsp. soda
1 Tbs. vanilla
1 cup pecan halves

Combine sugar, buttermilk, and soda in a large saucepan. Cook at a medium-high temperature, stirring constantly in the same direction until it begins to darken in color. Test by dropping small amount of the hot liquid into a cup of cold water. When it forms a soft ball in the water, remove pan from heat. Add vanilla and pecans; let cool for about 5 minutes. Beat vigorously until mixture gets a creamy texture and then pour immediately by tablespoons onto a double layer of waxed paper. Remove after cooled.

Mrs. Bob Batte (Gerry)

Pralines III

**Baking sheet, buttered
Yield: 2 dozen**

2 cups brown sugar, firmly
  packed
½ cup milk
3 Tbs. butter
1 cup pecans
1 tsp. vanilla

In a saucepan combine sugar, milk and butter. Cook, stirring constantly to 236 degrees or to soft ball stage. Add pecans and vanilla. Let cool to lukewarm. Beat till creamy, but still soft. Drop in mounds on a heavily buttered baking sheet. When pralines are cold, wrap each in waxed paper.

Mrs. Wilfred Dean (Maxine)

Add 1 tablespoon corn syrup to candy that will not harden and cook a little longer.

CANDY

Chocolate Cherry Creams

Yield: 30 pieces

1 (6-oz.) pkg. semi-sweet
  chocolate chips
½ cup Pet milk
2½ cups powdered sugar,
  sifted
⅓ cup pecans, chopped
⅓ cup maraschino cherries,
  drained and cut up
1½ cups (1 can) coconut

Place chocolate chips and milk into 2 quart saucepan. Stir over low heat until chocolate melts. Remove from heat. Stir in, until well mixed, the powdered sugar, nuts, and cherries. Chill until mixture is firm (about 1 hour). Roll teaspoonfuls of mixture in 1½ cups coconut. Chill until firm, about 4 hours. Keep chilled. Makes about 30.

Mrs. Joe Stroud (Ruthie)

English Toffee

Yield: ¾ pound

½ cup peanuts, finely
  chopped
½ cup butter
1 cup sugar

Shape a pan from a 12 x 10-inch sheet of foil by turning up edges to form a rectangle about 10 x 8 inches. Sprinkle nuts in pan. Set aside in 1½ quart saucepan, melt butter over medium high heat. Immediately begin to stir in sugar gradually with long handled wooden spoon (should take about 45 to 60 seconds). Continue to cook over medium high heat about 6 to 7 minutes until mixture turns golden brown, stirring only enough to prevent burning. Pour over nuts in prepared pan. Cool; break into pieces. Makes ¾ pound candy.

Making toffee calls for vigilance. Once the syrup mixture starts to brown, the color changes very rapidly.

Mrs. Bob Batte (Gerry)

Desserts

DESSERTS

Cheese Cake

300 degrees
9-inch pie pan, buttered
Yield: 6-8 servings

Crust:
2½ cups graham crackers, crushed
¼ cup sugar
6 Tbs. butter, melted

Combine crumbs, sugar and butter. Press in buttered pie pan.

Filling:
6 Tbs. flour
⅜ tsp. salt
1¼ cups sugar
3 (8-oz.) pkgs. cream cheese
1½ cups milk
6 egg yolks, beaten
1½ tsp. vanilla
6 egg whites, stiffly beaten

Sift flour, salt and sugar. Cut cheese into sifted ingredients and add milk, egg yolks and vanilla. Beat until creamy. Fold in stiffly beaten egg whites and pour into unbaked crust. Bake at 300 degrees for about 1 hour. Test with toothpick for doneness. Chill.

Mrs. Alan Dreyer (Kathy)

Party Cheesecakes

350 degrees
Muffin tins
Yield: 18 servings

18 vanilla wafers
2 (8-oz.) pkgs. cream cheese, softened
¾ cup sugar
2 eggs
1 Tbs. lemon juice
1 tsp. vanilla extract
½ can fruit pie filling (cherry, blueberry, etc.)
whipped cream (optional)

Place paper liners in 18 muffin cups; put 1 vanilla wafer in bottom of each. Combine cream cheese, sugar, eggs, lemon juice and vanilla; beat until smooth and creamy. Fill each muffin cup ⅔ full. Bake at 350 degrees for 15 to 20 minutes. Cool thoroughly. Put a teaspoon of pie filling on top of each cheesecake. If desired, top with whipped cream.

Mrs. Bob McClure (Ginger)

DESSERTS

Chocolate Cheese Cake

350 degrees
13 x 17 x 1 baking pan
Yield: 100 squares
Freezes

Crust:
1 box chocolate wafers,
  crushed
⅔ cup butter
¼-½ cup sugar

Combine chocolate crumbs, butter and sugar. Pack evenly in baking pan.

Filling:
2 (8-oz.) pkgs. cream cheese
4 oz. bitter chocolate, melted
1⅓ cups sugar
4 eggs
6 Tbs. flour
½ tsp. salt
⅔ cup milk
⅔ cup sour cream
2 tsp. vanilla

Cream cheese and add melted chocolate, sugar and eggs. Blend in flour, salt and milk. Add sour cream and vanilla. Pour filling over crumb mixture and bake for 25 to 30 minutes at 350 degrees.

Topping:
1 pint sour cream
¼ cup sugar
1 tsp. vanilla

Combine sour cream, sugar and vanilla and spread on cake. Bake for 7 more minutes. Chill.

For variety, topping may be colored with desired food coloring and/or sprinkled with chopped nuts. For freezing: When cake is cold, cut size pieces desired and leave in pan until frozen. Then remove frozen squares and pack in boxes or tins.

Mrs. Gary Gurwitz (Bailey)

Cover pudding with wax paper while still hot to prevent a film from forming.

176

DESSERTS

Baked Custard

350 degrees
2 custard cups

1 egg
1 Tbs. sugar
1 cup milk
1 tsp. vanilla
nutmeg

Beat egg, sugar and milk with rotary beater until sugar dissolves. Add vanilla and stir. Pour into custard cups that are ovenproof. Sprinkle each custard cup with nutmeg and bake in preheated oven for 20 to 30 minutes. (When baking the custard, the cups should be set in a pan of hot water to bake, with about ½ inch of water in the pan.) Test the cups after 20 minutes of baking time with a knife. If knife comes out clean, remove from oven.

Mrs. Waite Law (Gladys)

Caramel Custard Cups

350 degrees
4 custard cups
Yield: 4 servings

4 Tbs. brown sugar
2 eggs, slightly beaten
1 cup evaporated skimmed
  milk
⅔ cup water
⅓ cup sugar
1½ tsp. vanilla
dash of salt

Press 1 Tbs. of brown sugar lightly into each of 4 custard cups that can be baked. Mix in a bowl the eggs, milk, water, sugar, vanilla and salt. Pour carefully over the brown sugar. Set cups in a shallow pan holding 1 inch of hot water. Bake for 50 minutes or until knife inserted near edge of custard comes out clean. Cool. Loosen edges with knife. Unmold.

Easy!

Mrs. Neal Runnels (Gayle)

177

DESSERTS

Brandied Caramel Flan

325 degrees
8-inch round shallow baking dish
Yield: 8 servings

Caramel:
¾ cup sugar

Place sugar in a large heavy skillet. Cook over medium heat until sugar melts and forms a light brown syrup, stir to blend. Immediately pour syrup into a heated 8-inch round shallow baking dish. Holding dish with pot holders, quickly rotate to cover bottom and sides completely. Set aside.

Custard:
2 cups milk
2 cups light cream
6 eggs
½ cup sugar
½ tsp. salt
2 tsp. vanilla
⅓ cup brandy
1 Tbs. brandy

In medium saucepan, heat milk and cream just until bubbles form around edge of pan. In a large bowl, with rotary beater, beat eggs slightly. Add sugar, salt and vanilla. Gradually stir in hot milk mixture and ⅓ cup brandy. Pour into prepared dish. Be sure to set dish in shallow pan before baking and pour boiling water to ½-inch level around dish. Bake 35 to 40 minutes or until silver knife inserted in center comes out clean. Let custard cool; refrigerate 4 hours or overnight.

To serve, run a small spatula around edge of dish to loosen. Invert on shallow serving dish; shake gently to release. The caramel acts as a sauce. Warm 1 Tbs. brandy slightly; ignite quickly and pour over flan for a flaming dish that will impress your friends.

Mrs. Neal Runnels (Gayle)

DESSERTS

Cherry Pudding Dessert

350 degrees
9 x 9 pan, ungreased
Yield: 6-9 servings

Pudding:
2 cups sugar
2 cups flour
½ tsp. salt
2 eggs
juice from can of cherries
2 Tbs. margarine
2 tsp. soda in small amount
of cold water
1 can cherries, drained
1 cup pecans, chopped

Blend the sugar, flour and salt. Add eggs and the juice from the drained cherries. Add margarine and soda and fold in cherries and nuts. Pour into ungreased 9 x 9-inch baking dish. Bake at 350 degrees for 45 to 60 minutes or until pudding is cake-like. DO NOT underbake. Prepare topping while pudding bakes. This is poured over the pudding as soon as it is taken from oven.

Topping:
2 cups brown sugar
2 cups hot water
2 Tbs. flour
1 tsp. vanilla
whipped cream (optional)

In a saucepan, cook the sugar, water and flour until thick. Add the vanilla and pour over the baked pudding.

Best served warm with whipped cream on top.

Mrs. Bruce Leahy (Susan)

Chocolate Mocha

Blender
Yield: 8 servings

1 (6-oz.) pkg. semi-sweet
chocolate pieces
5 Tbs. boiling coffee
4 eggs, separated
2 Tbs. dark rum

Place in blender the chocolate pieces and coffee. Cover and mix on high speed for 10 seconds or until smooth. Add the uncooked egg yolks and the rum. Cover and blend on high speed for 5 seconds or until well blended. Beat egg whites until stiff. Fold chocolate mixture into the egg whites. Spoon into a serving dish and chill for 1 hour. A quick no-cook recipe.

Mrs. Morgan Talbot (Jane)

DESSERTS

Trifle (from Ireland)

Yield: 8-10 servings

1 (10 x 12-inch) sponge cake
raspberry jam
1 cup sherry or port
bananas or peaches, sliced
½ pint soft custard*
½ pint cream, whipped
nuts and cherries

Split the sponge cake in half by slicing through the middle horizontally. Cover bottom layer with raspberry jam. Put layers together. Pour sherry over the cake, and allow to soak. Top cake with sliced bananas or peaches, sliced. Prepare soft custard, chill, and pour over the entire dessert. Refrigerate until cold, then frost with whipped cream and decorate with nuts and cherries.

*Soft Custard:
2 eggs
⅛ cup sugar
dash of salt
1 cup milk
½ tsp. vanilla extract, rum,
  or sherry

Beat eggs lightly; add sugar and salt. Scald and stir in the milk. Cook over hot water or very low heat until custard thickens (do not allow to boil). Add flavoring, and chill thoroughly.

Mrs. Morgan Talbot (Jane)

Mocha Pudding

7 x 11 pan
Yield: 6-8 servings

1 cup sugar
1 stick butter
4 eggs
¼ cup cold coffee
1 cup pecans, chopped
1 (12-oz.) box vanilla wafer
  crumbs
whipped cream

Cream sugar and butter until fluffy. Add eggs one at a time, beating hard after each egg. Add cold coffee. Stir in pecans. Line 7 x 11 pan with ½ vanilla wafer crumbs. Pour in coffee mixture and then top with the rest of the wafer crumbs. Chill. Serve with whipped cream. This is better after standing for at least 4 hours before serving.

Mrs. Robert Parry (Barbara)

DESSERTS

Sherry Pudding

8 x 8 baking dish
Yield: 8 servings

vanilla wafer crumbs
1 cup pecans, chopped
1 cup cream sherry
1 (8-oz.) pkg. small
  marshmallows
1 pt. whipping cream

Cover bottom of 8-inch square baking dish with part of wafer crumbs and pecans (mixed together). Combine sherry and marshmallows and melt over heat, stirring constantly. Set aside to cool. Whip cream until firm and fold into cooled sherry-marshmallow mixture, blending well. Pour mixture into prepared baking dish and top with remaining crumbs and pecans. Place in refrigerator until well set (about 1 hour) and cut into squares to serve.

Mrs. Beverly Levermann

Steamed Cherry Pudding

1½ quart pan, buttered
Yield: 10-12 servings

Pudding:
2 cups canned cherries,
  drained (or 2 cups pitted
  fresh cherries)
1½ cups flour
¼ cup sugar
dash salt
¼ cup molasses
2 tsp. soda
½ cup hot water

Combine pudding ingredients and place in a well-buttered casserole that can be placed in a steamer. Cover steamer, and steam for one hour. Be sure water is boiling in steamer. Do not disturb for one hour. Serve with hot sauce poured over each portion.

Sauce:
1 cup sugar
½ cup butter
½ cup cream
rum to taste

In the top of a double boiler, cream sugar and butter. Add cream. Cook over boiling water until sauce thickens. Add rum and serve hot.

Mrs. Morgan Talbot (Jane)

DESSERTS

Baklava

325 degrees
9 x 13 pan, buttered
Yield: 20 large diamond pieces
or 80 med. squares

4 cups (1 lb.) walnuts
½ cup sugar
2 tsp. cinnamon
1 tsp. orange peel, grated
1 tsp. lemon peel, grated
28 sheets filo—8½ x 12½
  inches (about ¾ lb.)
1¼ cups butter or margarine,
  melted
Honey orange syrup

Grind, grate, or finely chop walnuts. Mix walnuts with sugar, cinnamon, orange and lemon peels. Set aside. Cut filo to fit 9 x 13-inch pan. Cover filo with plastic film while working to prevent drying. Brush bottom of pan with melted butter. Place one sheet of filo on pan and brush with butter. Cover with second sheet and brush with butter. Repeat making a layer of five sheets for bottom of pastry. Sprinkle with ¾ cup walnut mixture patting it to an even layer. Cover with 3 sheets of filo, brushing each with butter. Repeat layers until filling is used—should be about 7 layers of filling. Top with 5 layers of filo buttering each as before. With sharp knife, carefully cut lengthwise through top of filo layers making 5 strips. Make a second row of cuts, on the diagonal, forming diamonds. Bake at 350 degrees on rack above center of oven for 1 hour or until golden. Meanwhile, prepare and cool Honey orange syrup. Let Baklava stand 10 minutes, then spoon the cold syrup over the hot Baklava. Let stand overnight to absorb syrup before serving.

Yield: 2 cups

Honey Orange Syrup:

1 cup honey
¾ cup granulated sugar
⅔ cup orange juice
1 stick cinnamon
1 Tbs. lemon juice

Combine honey, sugar, orange juice, and cinnamon. Heat to a full rolling boil, stirring until sugar dissolves. Remove from heat and stir in lemon juice. Cool thoroughly before spooning over the pastry. Remove cinnamon stick when cold.

Mrs. Bruce Gray (Suzanne)

182

DESSERTS

Apple Crisp

350 degrees
8 x 13 x 1½ casserole dish
Yield: 8 servings

6-8 apples, peeled, cored and sliced (tart and crisp apples)
I Tbs. brown sugar
3 Tbs. natural strength lemon juice
1½ tsp. vanilla
1 Tbs. rum
1 cup all-purpose flour, sifted
½ cup butter
½ cup granulated sugar
½ cup brown sugar
1 Tbs. cinnamon

Toss apples with 1 Tbs. brown sugar, lemon juice, vanilla and rum. Arrange apples in a 8 x 13 x 1½ casserole dish. To make crumb mixture, blend flour, butter, sugars, and cinnamon with a pastry blender or fork. Sprinkle crumb mixture evenly over apples. Bake at 350 degrees about one hour or until apples are tender and crust is golden brown.

A scoop of vanilla ice cream on top is delicious.

Mrs. Bob Batte (Gerry)

Cherries Jubilee

Chafing dish
Yield: 2 cups sauce; 4-6 servings

1 (1-lb.) can (2 cups) pitted black sweet cherries, reserving syrup
¼ cup sugar
2 Tbs. cornstarch
¼ cup brandy
vanilla ice cream

Drain cherries, reserving syrup. In saucepan, blend sugar and cornstarch and gradually stir in cherry syrup. Mix well. Cook and stir over medium heat until mixture thickens and bubbles. Remove from heat, stir in cherries. Turn into heatproof bowl or chafing dish. (Be sure bottom pan has hot water). Heat brandy in small metal pan with long handle. Carefully ignite brandy and pour over cherry mixture. Stir to blend brandy into sauce and serve immediately over ice cream.

Mrs. Gary Gurwitz (Bailey)

DESSERTS

Cinnamon Meringue Shell with filling

Shell:
2 egg whites
¼ tsp. salt
½ tsp. vinegar
½ cup sugar
¼ tsp. cinnamon

Cover cookie sheet with a piece of heavy brown paper. Draw an 8-inch circle in center. Beat egg whites, salt and vinegar until soft peaks form. Blend sugar and cinnamon and gradually add to egg whites. Beat until very stiff. Spread within circle making bottom ½-inch thick and mounding around edge. Bake in oven 1 hour at 275 degrees. Turn off heat and let dry in oven (door closed about 2 hours). Remove from oven and take off paper.

Filling:
1 (6-oz.) pkg. chocolate chips
2 egg yolks, beaten
¼ cup water
1 cup heavy cream
¼ cup sugar
¼ tsp. cinnamon
whipped cream
pecans

Melt chocolate in double boiler. Cool. Spread 2 Tbs. of melted chocolate over bottom of meringue shell. To the remaining chocolate add egg yolks and water. Blend. Chill until mixture is thick. Combine cream, sugar, and cinnamon. Whip until stinf. Spread half over chocolate in shell. Fold remaining cream mixture into the chilled chocolate mixture. Pour into shell. Chill several hours. Top with whipped cream and pecans.

Mrs. Hulon Webb (Carole)

Fresh Pineapple Jubilee

½ cup orange marmalade
2 Tbs. light corn syrup
2 Tbs. brown sugar
2 cups pineapple, diced
¼ cup orange liqueur
1 quart vanilla ice cream

Combine marmalade, corn syrup and brown sugar in chafing dish; stir in pineapple till warm. Heat orange liqueur in ladle or small pan. Flame and pour over the pineapple mixture. Serve over ice cream.

Mrs. Leonel Garza, Jr. (Linda)

DESSERTS

Bananas Foster

Flat chafing dish
Yield: 6 servings

1 stick butter
1 cup brown sugar, generous
dash cinnamon
1 jigger banana liqueur
4-6 bananas, diagonally
    sliced
¼ cup rum

In flat chafing dish, melt butter and add sugar, cinnamon, and banana liqueur. Cook and stir until smooth. Add peeled, diagonally-sliced bananas. Heat rum and ignite. Pour over banana mixture to flame. Spoon over bananas until flame is gone. Serve over vanilla ice cream.

Mrs. Gary Gurwitz (Bailey)

Grapefruit Alaska

350 degrees
Yield: 4 servings

6 grapefruit
½ cup Kirsch

Clean and cut top ⅓ off large grapefruit, using four of the six grapefruit. Remove sections free of membrane. Remove the sections from the other two grapefruit. This will make a more generous serving. Reserve shells in refrigerator. Marinate sections in Kirsch.

vanilla ice cream

Put grapefruit sections in shells, about ½ full. Put generous spoons of ice cream on top.

3 egg whites
2 Tbs. sugar

At serving time, beat egg whites until stiff and add the sugar. Spread meringue over grapefruit sections, sealing edges and pile high. Put on low shelf of oven and bake at 350 degrees only until tops are light brown.

Mrs. Woods Christian (Virginia Boeye)

DESSERTS

Mangos Flambé

Heat proof serving dish
Yield: 4 servings

1 (1 lb. 3-oz.) can mango
slices in syrup
¼ cup cognac
¼ cup orange marmalade or
apricot preserves
vanilla ice cream

Drain mangos, reserving ¼ cup syrup. Place fruit in a heatproof serving bowl. Warm and ignite the cognac. Pour over fruit. Combine ¼ cup of reserved juice (make up with orange juice if necessary) with marmalade or preserves and mix into fruit. Spoon over vanilla ice cream.

Note: It is fun to have each step ready and then at the dinner table, put the flambé together.

Mrs. Bobby Etchison (Willie)

Peach Cobbler

350 degrees
8 x 8 baking pan
Yield: 6 servings
Freezes

½ cup flour
½ cup sugar
½ cup milk
1 tsp. baking powder
1 stick butter
1 (2½ lb.) can freestone or
same amount of fresh
peaches

Mix together the flour, sugar, milk, and baking powder to make a paste. Pour into an 8-inch square pan. Cube one stick butter over the paste. Pour the peaches over the butter. Bake 45 minutes or until brown in a 350 degrees oven.

Mrs. Richard Moore (Lynda)

DESSERTS

Apricot Ice Cream Torte

9 x 13 pyrex dish
Yield: 18 servings

1 box vanilla wafers, crushed
1 stick butter or margarine
½-¾ lb. almonds
½ gallon vanilla ice cream
2 cups apricot preserves

Layer the ingredients into the dish in the following order, then freeze:
½-¾ of total wafer crumbs, mixed with melted margarine
⅓ of almonds
1 quart ice cream
all of the apricot preserves
⅓ of almonds
1 quart ice cream
⅓ of almonds
¼-½ of wafer crumbs

Mrs. Reid Thorburn (Barbara)

Orange Bavarian Cream

1 quart mold, oiled
Yield: 6 servings

1 Tbs. unflavored gelatin
½ cup cold water
¾ cup frozen orange juice
2 Tbs. lemon juice (or lime)
½ tsp. grated orange rind
  (sour orange is best)
⅓ cup sugar
½ tsp. salt
1 cup whipping cream
orange sections for garnish

Soften gelatin in water. Combine fruit juices, orange rind, sugar and salt. Heat to simmering. Dissolve gelatin in hot mixture. Chill, stirring occasionally, until mixture is the consistency of unbeaten egg whites. Whip cream only until stiff. Fold cream and orange sections into gelatin mixture. Pour into mold, slightly oiled, and chill until firm. Serve on polished grapefruit or orange leaf with several spoons of frozen orange juice for color.

Mrs. Woods Christian (Virginia Boeye)

DESSERTS

Strawberry No Bake Cake

Bundt pan
Yield: 12 servings

2 (10-oz.) pkg. frozen
  strawberries, thawed
1 large box strawberry Jello
1 cup hot water
2 pts. Cool Whip
1 store bought angel food
  cake

Mix strawberries into Jello that has been dissolved in the hot water. Allow the mixture to start to gel. Fold in Cool Whip. Tear angel food cake into small pieces. Using a tube pan, alternate layers of cake and strawberry mixture. Chill overnight.

Mrs. Larry Fritz (Libby)

Dulce de Leche
(Caramel Sauce)

1 can sweetened condensed
  milk

Remove label from can, place in water to cover—boil for 2½ hours. Cool, open and serve cold.

To be used as a topping for ice cream.
Rudy Pharis

Caramel Delight

350 degrees
Cookie sheet and 9 x 13 pan
Yield: 16-20 servings
Freezes

1½ cups flour
½ cup brown sugar
1½ cups nuts, chopped
1 cup butter, melted
1 (12-oz.) jar caramel topping
½ gal. vanilla ice cream,
  softened

Combine flour, sugar, nuts, and butter. Stir. Spread, in a thin layer, on a cookie sheet and bake at 350 degrees for 20 minutes or until brown. Cool and crumble. Put ½ of the crumbs in a 9 x 13 pan. Spoon ½ caramel topping over crumbs. Slice ice cream over topping. Spoon remaining caramel over ice cream. Top with remaining crumbs. Freeze until firm. Cut in squares. To serve, allow 10 minutes to soften.

Mrs. Wilfred Dean (Maxine)

188

DESSERTS

Charlotte Russe

Bundt or Angel food pan,
well-oiled
Yield: 16 servings

4 egg yolks
1 cup sugar
2 cups scalded milk
2 envelopes plain gelatin
½ cup cold water
1 tsp. vanilla
4 egg whites, stiffly beaten
2 pts. whipped cream
1 angel food cake

Cream together the egg yolks and sugar. Add the scalded milk. Cook over boiling water until mixture coats spoon. Dissolve unflavored gelatin in cold water. Add to cooked mixture. Let mixture cool and add vanilla. Fold in stiffly beaten egg whites and 1 pint whipped cream. Cut up angel food cake in approximately 1-inch squares. Oil tube cake pan, and put a layer of cake and a layer of mixture until pan is full. Chill in refrigerator for several hours. Turn out and ice with remaining pint of whipped cream.

Mrs. Paul Bergh (Betty)

Cherry-Cheese Dessert Pizza

350 degrees
12-inch pizza pan
Yield: 10-12 servings

pastry for 2 (9-inch) pie
  crusts
1 (8-oz.) pkg. cream cheese,
  softened
½ cup sugar
2 eggs
⅓ cup walnuts, chopped
1 tsp. vanilla
2 (1 lb. 5-oz.) cans cherry pie
  filling
whipped cream

On lightly floured surface roll pastry to 14-inch circle; place in 12-inch pizza pan. Flute edges; prick crust. Bake in moderate oven, 350 degrees, for 15 minutes. Blend cream, cheese and sugar; add eggs and beat well; add nuts and vanilla. Pour into partially baked crust and bake in moderate oven for 10 minutes more; cool. Spread cherry pie filling over cheese layer. Chill. Top chilled pie with dollops of whipped cream cheese or whipped cream. To serve, cut in wedges.

Mrs. Cayetano Barrera (Yolanda)

DESSERTS

Chocolate Éclairs

450 degrees
Cookie sheet, greased
Yield: 16 éclairs

Éclair:
½ cup butter
1 cup boiling water
1 cup flour, sifted
¼ tsp. salt
4 eggs

Melt butter in boiling water. Add flour and salt all at one time, stirring vigorously. Cook, stirring constantly, until the mixture forms a ball that doesn't separate. Remove from heat and cool slightly. Add eggs one at a time, beating hard after each addition until mixture is smooth. Taking a small portion, form into 3 x 1-inch éclairs and place on a greased cookie sheet. Leave about an inch of space between each éclair. Bake at 450 degrees for 15 minutes, reduce heat and continue baking at 325 degrees for 25 minutes. Cool. Cut éclairs in half and fill with custard. Frost with chocolate frosting.

Custard:
¾ cup sugar
3 Tbs. flour
3 Tbs. cornstarch
¾ tsp. salt
2 cups milk
5 egg yolks, slightly beaten
2 tsp. vanilla
1 cup whipped cream

Combine sugar, flour, cornstarch and salt. Gradually stir in milk. Cook, stirring constantly, until mixture boils and thickens. Stir a little of the hot mixture into the egg yolks; return to hot mixture. Stirring constantly, bring just to boiling. Cool. Add vanilla. Chill. Beat with mixer until smooth. Fold in whipped cream.

Chocolate Frosting:
1 egg
⅓ cup butter, melted
1½ squares unsweetened chocolate, melted
1 tsp. vanilla
1½ cups powdered sugar

Beat egg, add butter, melted chocolate, vanilla and sugar. Beat well.

Mrs. Jerry McGilvray (Jane)

190

DESERTS

Chocolate Ice Box Cake

9 x 9 pan
Yield: 9 large or
12 small servings

vanilla wafers
2 cakes German Sweet
  Chocolate
4 Tbs. hot water
4 eggs, separated
3 tsp. sugar
1 tsp. vanilla
whipping cream

Line 9 x 9 pan with vanilla wafers. Melt chocolate in hot water until smooth. Remove from heat and add egg yolks one at a time, beating after each addition. Cool. Beat egg whites until stiff and add sugar and vanilla. Fold chocolate mixture and egg white mixture together. Pour mixture over vanilla wafers and top with layer of wafers. Let set 24 hours in refrigerator. Serve with whipped cream if desired.

Mrs. Michael Owens (Cissy)

Chocolate Delight

1½ quart casserole
Yield: 8-10 servings

1 stick margarine, melted
⅝ cup sugar
3 eggs, separated
½ tsp. vanilla
4 squares semi-sweet
  chocolate, melted
1 cup nuts, chopped
6 oz. vanilla wafers, crushed
1 (6-oz.) carton Cool Whip

Cream melted margarine and sugar. Add beaten egg yolks and vanilla. Add melted chocolate to mixture. Fold beaten egg whites and nuts into mixture. Grease a 1½-quart casserole and line the sides and bottom with crushed wafers. Layer chocolate mixture, Cool Whip, wafers, etc. Let stand 24 hours in the refrigerator.

Mrs. Robert Barnes (Kay)

191

DESSERTS

Chocolate Parfait

350 degrees
Cookie sheet and
Parfait glasses
Yield: 4-6 servings

Crunch:
⅓ cup flour
¼ cup flaked coconut
2 Tbs. brown sugar
2 Tbs. butter, melted

Spread the crunch mixture on a cookie sheet and bake at 350 degrees for 15 minutes or until brown, stirring while cooking. Set aside to cool.

Pudding mix:
1 (4-oz.) pkg. instant
   chocolate pudding mix
1¾ cups milk
¼ cup crème de cacao

Stir pudding mix, milk, and crème de cacao together.

Topping:
Cool Whip
chocolate shavings

Layer the pudding mixture and the crunch in tall parfait glasses and top with Cool Whip and chocolate shavings.

Mrs. Rondel Davidson (Judy)

Basic Crepes

Yield: 20-24

1½ cups milk
2 Tbs. vegetable oil
3 eggs
1½ cups all-purpose flour
⅛ tsp. salt

There are two methods of making crepes: a blender method and a electric mixer method. Choose the method you like best as follows:
BLENDER METHOD: Place all ingredients in blender in order listed. Cover and blend on high speed until smooth.
ELECTRIC MIXER METHOD: Place eggs in a large mixer bowl and beat well on a medium speed. Add dry ingredients slowly alternating with milk and oil. Beat until mixture is smooth.

Mrs. Neal Runnels (Gayle)

DESSERTS

Chocolate Layer Dessert

350 degrees
9 x 12 pyrex dish
Yield: 12 large servings

Crust:
1 cup flour
1 stick margarine or butter, melted
½ cup nuts, chopped

Mix flour, margarine, and nuts to form crumb mixture. Pat into a 9 x 12 pyrex pan. Bake at 350 degrees for 25 minutes. Cool.

Cheese layer:
1 (3-oz.) pkg. cream cheese
1 cup powdered sugar
1 tsp. vanilla
1 cup Cool Whip

Beat cream cheese, sugar and vanilla together. Fold in 1 cup Cool Whip and spread on cooled crust.

Pudding layer:
1 large pkg. chocolate instant pudding
2 cups milk
1 tsp. vanilla

Mix instant pudding, milk and vanilla until pudding consistency. Spread over the cheese layer.

Topping:
1 cup Cool Whip
1 cup nuts, chopped (optional)

Spread Cool Whip very thinly over pudding layer. Garnish with chopped nuts, if desired. Chill.

Chocolate Mousse

Yield: 12-14 servings

¾ cup butter, softened
1½ cups sugar
3 eggs, separated
1 Tbs. brandy
½ tsp. almond extract
½ lb. semi-sweet chocolate chips, melted
¼ cup slivered almonds, toasted
2 cups whipping cream, whipped and divided
shaved chocolate

Cream butter until fluffy. Add sugar gradually, then egg yolks, brandy, and almond extract. Add chocolate and almonds. Beat egg whites until stiff and fold into chocolate mixture. Fold in whipped cream. Freeze. Remove from freezer 30 minutes before serving. Garnish with extra whipped cream and shaved chocolate.

Mrs. John Wright (Melinda)

193

DESSERTS

Ice Cream Cake

9 x 13 pan
Yield: 8-10 servings
Freezes

4 cups chocolate wafer
  crumbs
⅔ cup butter, softened
6 pts. vanilla ice cream
½ lb. peppermint sticks,
  crushed

Combine wafers and butter to make crust. Pour into large 9 x 13 pan and refrigerate until cold and set (about 1 hour). Put ice cream in large bowl and swirl in crushed candy for marbled effect. Mash ice cream into pan and put into freezer until ready to serve.

Mrs. Richard Moore (Lynda)

Lemon Ice Box Cake

9 x 9 pan
Yield: 9 servings

¾ cup sugar
¼ tsp. salt
1 Tbs. flour
3 eggs, separated
¼ cup lemon juice
1 lemon rind, grated
1 cup milk
1 Tbs. butter, melted
½ pt. whipping cream
1½ doz. lady fingers

Mix sugar, salt, and flour. Add egg yolks and beat well. Add lemon juice and rind, then milk and melted butter. Cook over a slow fire in a double boiler until thickened. Add beaten egg whites, blending gently. Cool and fold in whipped cream. Alternate with layers of lady fingers (or stale cake) in a 9-inch square pan. Chill in refrigerator.

Mrs. Paul Moffitt (Marilyn)

Strawberry Mousse

Yield: 6-8 servings

1 (3-oz.) pkg. strawberry jello
2 (½-pint) containers
  whipping cream
½ cup powdered sugar
1 tsp. vanilla
10 oz. strawberries, frozen

Make strawberry jello. Set aside. Whip cream and add ½ cup sugar and vanilla. Combine strawberries and strawberry jello mix and whipping cream. Refrigerate until set.

Mrs. Joe Hettler (Paula)

DESSERTS

Mango Mousse

Blender
9 x 9 pan
Yield: 9 servings

1 (3-oz.) pkg. lemon gelatin
1 cup hot water
3 fresh mangos
1 can sweetened condensed
  milk

Dissolve gelatin in hot water. Put fruit, milk, and gelatin in blender in that order. Blend. Pour into mold, and refrigerate until set.

Mrs. Morgan Talbot (Jane)

Mock Spumoni

8 x 8 pan
Yield: 12-16 servings
Freezes

2½ cups vanilla wafers,
  crushed
½ cup butter, melted
1 tsp. almond extract
½ cup almonds, slivered
3 pints vanilla ice cream
1 (12-oz.) jar apricot
  preserves

Mix vanilla wafers, butter, almond extract, and slivered almonds together. Line a 8 x 8 pan with part of the crumb mixture. Cover with a layer of ice cream, then spread with preserves, repeating until all the ingredients are used. The top layer should be the crumb mixture. Cover with foil and place in freezer. Serve in 1½ x 2-inch squares.

Mrs. Tom Sammons (Gretchen)

Orange Fluff

Yield: 8 servings

2 (3-oz.) pkgs. orange Jello
1 cup boiling water
1 pt. orange or tangerine
  sherbet
½ pt. whipping cream
1 (11-oz.) can mandarin
  oranges or one peeled and
  sectioned orange

Dissolve jello in boiling water. Stir in sherbet until dissolved thoroughly. Chill. Whip cream until stiff. Cut jello in cubes and fold in oranges and whipped cream. Chill until serving time.

This dessert can be served from a bowl or chilled in individual parfait glasses.

Mrs. Dan Seitz (Amy)

DESSERTS

Oreo Smush

9 x 13 pan
Yield: 18 servings

1 stick margarine
1 (19-oz.) pkg. Oreos,
  crushed
½ gallon vanilla ice cream,
  softened
2 jars Kraft or Smucker fudge
  sauce
1 large carton Cool Whip

Melt margarine in 9 x 13 pan. Crush Oreos, reserving a few crumbs. Mix crumbs with margarine and form crust in pan. Spread the softened ice cream over crust, then add layer of fudge sauce. Top with large carton of Cool Whip. Sprinkle with remaining crumbs. Keep frozen until ready to serve.

Mrs. John Wright (Melinda)

Strawberry Delight

350 degrees
9 x 9 pan
Yield: 16 servings
Freezes

1 cup flour
¼ cup brown sugar, packed
½ cup pecans, chopped
½ cup butter or margarine,
  melted
1½ cups fresh strawberries,
  sliced
1 cup sugar
2 tsp. fresh lemon juice
2 egg whites
½ pt. whipping cream,
  whipped

Combine flour, brown sugar, pecans and butter. Bake at 350 degrees for 20 minutes in a square pan, stirring often. Let cool. Combine strawberries, sugar, lemon juice and egg whites. Beat at high speed in electric mixer about 20 minutes or until light and fluffy. Gently fold whipped cream into strawberry mixture. Remove ⅓ of crumb mixture from pan. Pat remaining crumbs into smooth layer. Pour strawberry mixture over crumbs in pan and sprinkle reserved crumbs over top. Freeze. When ready to use, remove from freezer, cut into squares and serve immediately. Can be kept in freezer several days.

Mrs. P. D. Terrell (Marabeth)

Champagne Sorbet

Yield: 1 quart

¾ cup sugar
1 cup water
grated zest of ½ orange or
   lemon
⅓ cup lemon juice
½ cup orange juice
pinch of salt
2 cups champagne, chilled

Heat and stir with metal spoon the sugar and water until the sugar has dissolved; bring to boil and continue to boil until the syrup forms a thread (about 230°) between finger and thumb when a little is lifted on a spoon; cool slightly. Add the zest, fruit juices, salt; chill. Stir in the champagne; cover and freeze. After it has frozen, put in food processor and whip to break up ice crystals.

1½ Tbs. cognac, chilled
½ cup champagne, chilled

Before serving, mix cognac and champagne and stir into ice; fill chilled dishes or glasses and serve.

Mrs. Hartwell Kennard (Mary Lou)

Fruit Ice Cream

Yield: 1 gallon

juice of 3 lemons
juice of 3 oranges
3 cups sugar
1 large can apricots that have
   been run through a sieve
2 pts. of half and half
3 cups milk

Mix all ingredients except milk together and chill thoroughly. Put in ice cream freezer and blend in half-n-half. Fill can to 1 inch from top with milk (approx. 3 cups).

Mrs. Hollis Fritts (Gerrie)

Chocolate Malt Ice Cream

2 cans Eagle Brand
   condensed milk
1 cup and 2 Tbs. malted milk
   powder (Kraft or Carnation)
1 pt. whipping cream, not
   whipped
½ gallon whole milk

Mix all together and put in ice cream freezer and freeze.

The recipe may be halved and frozen in ice trays.

Mrs. John Wright (Melinda)

DESSERTS

Homemade Ice Cream

Yield: 2 gallons

8 eggs
3 cups sugar
2 cups milk
1 tsp. salt
1 can Eagle Brand milk
1 Tbs. vanilla
1 pt. half and half or cream
milk

Mix eggs, sugar, milk and salt in mixer. Cook over medium heat until just hot. Do not let boil. Stir often. Mix together Eagle Brand milk, vanilla and half-n-half in mixer. Set aside. Pour hot mixture through strainer into second mixture. Mix well. Pour into ice cream freezer can, add milk up to 2 inches from top. Cool in refrigerator for at least 2 hours. Freeze in ice cream freezer as usual.

Mrs. Ken Forrester (Phoebe)

No Cook Ice Cream

Yield: 1 gallon

2 cups dry milk powder
2 cups sugar
2 (13-oz.) cans Pet milk
1 Tbs. vanilla
dash of salt

Combine all ingredients and pour in freezer can. Finish filling can with whole or low fat milk, and freeze according to directions on freezer. If you want to add fruit, add a little less milk and puréed fruit before ice cream gets firm. Peaches or mangos are delicious used in this recipe.

Mrs. Charles E. Fox (Nancy)

Strawberry Ice Cream

Yield: 1 gallon

¾ cups sugar
4 eggs
1 can sweetened condensed
  milk
1 can Pet milk
2 cans strawberry soda
1 tsp. vanilla
strawberries, mashed
milk

Combine all ingredients in electric mixer. Pour into ice cream freezer and fill remainder of freezer with homogenized milk.

For peach ice cream, use cream soda water and peaches. For vanilla, use cream soda.

Mrs. Walt Mielcarek (Betty)

DESSERTS

Peachy Yogurt Pops

5 (7-oz.) paper cups
Yield: 5 pops

1 (16-oz.) can peaches,
  drained
1 (8-oz.) carton plain yogurt
¼ cup sugar
1 tsp. lemon juice
few drops almond extract

Place peaches, yogurt, sugar, lemon juice and almond extract in blender or food processor. Cover and process till smooth. Pour mixture into five 7 oz. paper cups. Insert wooden sticks. Freeze until firm. Peel off paper to serve.

Great for Kids. Try any fruit you have on hand.

Mrs. Glenn Jarvis (Pat)

Vanilla Ice Cream

Yield: 1 gallon

4 eggs
2½ cups sugar
6 cups milk
1 pint whipping cream
1 pint half-and-half
2 Tbs. vanilla
½ tsp. salt

Beat eggs until light. Add sugar gradually, beating until mixture thickens. Add remaining ingredients; mix thoroughly. Freeze in ice cream freezer.

Variation:
1-2 Tbs. almond flavoring
2-3 cups peaches, chopped

Substitute almond flavoring for the vanilla and add chopped peaches. You might need to reduce the amount of milk to allow about 1½ inches at the top of freezer can.

Mrs. Jerry McGilvray (Jane)

DESSERTS

Peppermint Ice Cream

Yield: 1½ gallons

1¾ cups sugar
5 eggs, well beaten
2 cans Eagle Brand milk
1 tsp. vanilla
2 or 3 half-pints of whipping
    cream
1½ (10-oz. size) bags
    peppermint, crushed
milk to fill freezer

Add sugar to well beaten eggs. Beat until smooth. Add the other ingredients. Beat well. Pour into freezer can. Fill with milk to 1½-inches from top of can. Freeze.

Variation:

Yield: 1 gallon

3 eggs
1¼ cups sugar
1 can Eagle Brand milk
1 tsp. vanilla
2 half-pints whipping cream
1 (10-oz.) pkg. peppermint,
    crushed
milk to fill freezer

Mix as for 1½ gallon freezer above.

Mrs. Bill Schurlock (Mary)

Creole Cream Cheese Ice Cream

Yield: 1 gallon

3 (24-oz.) cartons of cottage
    cheese
3 cups sugar
1 qt. whipping cream
fresh fruit (your choice)

Purée the cottage cheese until there are absolutely no lumps. Combine with the sugar and the whipping cream. Freeze as usual in ice cream freezer. Serve with fresh fruit in season.

Not real sweet. Tastes like cheese cake.

200

Entrees

continued . . .

Cheese Soufflé

300 degrees
Small soufflé dish, greased
Yield: 2 servings

¾ cup milk
3 Tbs. butter, melted
3 Tbs. flour
1 cup Cheddar cheese,
   grated
3 egg yolks, slightly beaten
3 egg whites, stiffly beaten

Scald milk and add to butter and flour, which have been combined to smooth paste. Add cheese and remove from heat. When cheese is melted, add egg yolks and fold mixture into beaten egg whites. Pour into greased soufflé dish and bake at 300 degrees for 45 minutes. This may be divided into 2 petite casseroles—reduce cooking time a little. Serve with plum jelly.

Mrs. Mitchell Darby (Martha)

Egg and Bacon Casserole

325 degrees
7 x 11 pyrex dish
Yield: 6 servings

1 lb. bacon
½ cup butter or margarine
4 cups unseasoned croutons
2 cups sharp Cheddar
   cheese, grated
8 eggs
½ tsp. dry mustard
1 tsp. salt
2 cups milk

Brown bacon until crisp, drain and crumble. Preheat oven to 325 degrees. Melt butter in pyrex dish. Pour croutons on top of melted butter, then sprinkle with grated cheese. Beat eggs, milk, salt, and mustard with fork. Pour over crouton mixture in casserole. Sprinkle with bacon. Bake at 325 degrees for 1 hour. Let stand 5 to 10 minutes before serving.

Mrs. Robert H. Kern, Jr. (Carolyn)

Small or medium eggs contain the same amount of protein as the large or jumbo eggs. The smaller eggs are laid by younger hens and have less fluid and stronger shells; therefore, they stay fresh longer.

ENTREES
Cheese and Eggs

Overnight Chile Eggs

300 degrees
9 x 12 pan, greased
Yield: 6-8 servings

8 eggs, slightly beaten
6 slices bread (no crust) cut
  in ½-inch squares
½ stick butter, cut in ¼-inch
  squares
2 cups milk
2 cups green chiles, chopped
1½ cups Monterrey Jack
  cheese, or mixture of your
  choice, grated
salt and pepper as desired

Add ingredients in order given. Mix together and pour into greased pan. Cool in refrigerator overnight or 8 hours. Cook 1 hour at 300 degrees.

Mrs. Morgan Talbot (Jane)

Eggs Parmesan

Skillet
Yield: 1 serving

2 Tbs. butter
1 oz. sherry
2 eggs
2 Tbs. Parmesan cheese
salt
freshly ground pepper

Lightly brown butter in skillet. As butter takes on color, add sherry. When liquid begins to bubble, break eggs into it. As white begins to set, remove from heat and sprinkle cheese over eggs, having seasoned them lightly. Put skillet under broiler. When eggs set and cheese begins to brown remove and serve at once. Watch eggs closely. They should not be allowed to become hard, nor cheese to burn. Great for lunch.

Mrs. William H. Wilson (Marion)

Always cook eggs at a low to moderate temperature so as not to toughen them.

Jalapeño Pie

350 degrees
9-inch pie plate
Yield: 6-8 servings

1 (10-oz.) pkg. sharp Cheddar
   cheese, grated
3-4 slivered jalapeños,
   seeded
parsley flakes
dash of Worcestershire sauce
4 eggs, slightly beaten

Line a pie plate with slivered jalapeños; add grated cheese; add slightly beaten eggs to which has been added some parsley flakes and Worcestershire sauce. Bake in 350 oven for 35 minutes. Let set for about 10 minutes before slicing in pie shaped wedges and serving at once.

Liberace Breakfast

350 degrees
9 x 12 casserole, greased
Yield: 6 servings

12 slices bread
8 oz. Cheddar cheese, grated
4 eggs
2 cups milk
salt to taste
½ tsp. English mustard
1 tsp. minced onion
6 slices tomato
6 pieces bacon

Place 6 pieces of bread (crust trimmed off) in a greased casserole. Place Cheddar cheese on bread, topping it with another layer of trimmed bread. Beat eggs. Add milk, salt, mustard and onion. Pour mixture over sandwiches and soak for 10 minutes. Bake at 350 degrees for about 30 minutes. Place a peeled tomato slice on each sandwich and top with a limp piece of cooked bacon. Brown under broiler and serve.

Mrs. Robert Parry, Jr. (Barbara)

To prepare perfect hard-boiled eggs every time, prepare as follows: Place eggs in a pan and cover with cold water to which you have added one teaspoon of salt or vinegar. Bring to a boil and remove from heat, cover and let set for 15 minutes. Drain off hot water, shake the pan back and forth causing the eggs to crack against the sides, cool with cold water and peel.

ENTREES
Cheese and Eggs

Florentine Rice Quiche

350 degrees
9-inch pie pan
Yield: 6-8 servings

4 eggs
2 cups cooked rice
⅔ cup Swiss cheese, finely
   grated
1 (10-oz.) pkg. spinach,
   chopped
2 Tbs. butter
½ tsp. salt
1 cup cottage cheese
1 cup Parmesan cheese,
   grated
6 Tbs. heavy cream
dash of hot sauce
¼ tsp. nutmeg

Beat one egg. Add to mixture of rice and Swiss cheese. Mix well and spread in pie pan. Crust may be refrigerated. Cook spinach and press out all liquid. Add butter and set aside. Beat remaining eggs. Stir in salt, cottage cheese, Parmesan cheese, cream, hot sauce and nutmeg. Add spinach and pour into rice crust. Bake 30-35 minutes at 350 degrees.

Mrs. John Maxwell (Betty)

Quiche Lorraine with Ham

350 degrees
10-inch pie pan
Yield: 4-6 servings

1 (10-inch) baked pastry shell
4 slices bacon
1 large onion, sliced
1 Tbs. bacon drippings
1 cup boiled or baked ham,
   cubed
4 paper-thin slices (4 x 8)
   Swiss cheese
3 eggs
¼ tsp. dry mustard
1 cup cream, heated
nutmeg

Broil bacon until crisp. Crumble and sprinkle over the bottom of pie shell. Sauté onion rings in bacon drippings until soft. Arrange over bacon. Place half the cubed ham and 2 slices of cheese over onions. Repeat layers of ham and cheese. Beat eggs and mustard together; add to warm cream and beat again. Pour into pie shell and let stand 10 minutes. Sprinkle on enough nutmeg to lightly cover top. Bake in a preheated 350 degree oven for 35 minutes.

This quiche will keep for about 3 days in the refrigerator. It can be warmed successfully if covered with foil. May also be served cold.

Quick Shrimp Quiche

425 degrees
10-inch quiche pan
Yield: 6-8 servings

5 cups frozen hash brown
   potatoes
1/3 cup vegetable oil
2 cups Swiss cheese, grated
1 cup shrimp
1 (13-oz.) can evaporated
   milk
4 eggs
1 tsp. salt
1/4 tsp. pepper
1/8 tsp. nutmeg
1 Tbs. dry sherry
1 Tbs. parsley flakes
1/2 cup onion, chopped

Combine potatoes and oil in large skillet. Heat, stirring until potatoes defrost. Turn into quiche pan, press potatoes down evenly making a crust. Sprinkle crust with Swiss cheese. Arrange shrimp over cheese. Beat together the milk, eggs, salt, pepper, nutmeg and sherry. Stir in parsley flakes and onion. Pour over cheese and shrimp. Bake about 35 minutes. Allow 5 minutes to set before serving.

Mrs. Robert F. Barnes (Kay)

Scalloped Cheese and Eggs

300 degrees
9 x 15 baking pan, greased
Yield: 24 servings

20 slices bread, remove crust
   and cut into quarters
1 1/2 lb. sharp cheese, grated
1 1/2-2 dozen eggs
3/4 tsp. dry mustard
2 tsp. salt
1/2 gallon milk

In large greased baking pan, arrange bread quarters. Top with grated cheese. Beat eggs slightly and add mustard, salt and milk. Pour over bread and cheese. Bake at 300 degrees for 1 hour.

Mrs. Blaine Holcomb (Andrea)

Stretch your scrambled egg servings by adding bread crumbs. This also can add a new taste depending on the seasoning used on the crumbs.

ENTREES
Cheese and Eggs/Sandwiches

Shrimp Eggs

10-inch skillet
Yield: 4-6 servings

1 (10¾-oz.) can cream of
celery soup
8 eggs, slightly beaten
1 cup cooked shrimp,
chopped
½ tsp. dried dill leaves,
crushed
⅓ cup green onion, chopped
2 Tbs. butter or margarine

In bowl, stir soup until smooth. Gradually add eggs. Stir in shrimp and dill. In skillet, cook onion in butter until tender. Pour eggs into skillet. Cook over low heat. Do not stir. As mixture begins to set around eggs, gently lift cooked portion with spatula, so the uncooked portion can flow to bottom. Continue this until eggs are completely set, but still moist, about 8 minutes.

Mrs. P. D. Moore (Hortense)

Welsh Rarebit

Double boiler
Yield: 8 servings

3 Tbs. butter
3 Tbs. flour
¼ tsp. dry mustard
½ tsp. salt
1 tsp. Worcestershire sauce
2 cups milk
3 cups American cheese,
grated
2 eggs, beaten
paprika

Melt butter in double boiler; add flour, mustard, salt, and Worcestershire sauce. Add milk and cook until thickened; add cheese and cook until cheese is melted; add eggs and cook 3 minutes. Serve on toast. Sprinkle with paprika.

Mrs. Glynn Andrews (Laurie)

Hot Ham and Swiss Cheese Sandwiches

350 degrees

¼ cup mayonnaise
1 Tbs. poppy seeds
2 Tbs. horseradish
2 Tbs. onion, grated
thinly sliced ham
Swiss cheese
rye bread or rye buns

Mix the mayonnaise, poppy seeds, horseradish and onion together. Spread the mixture on ham and Swiss cheese sandwiches. Wrap in foil. Heat 30 minutes at 350 degrees.

Mrs. Jack Whetsel (Martha)

Baked Chicken Sandwiches

425 degrees
Baking sheet
Yield: 4 servings

4 slices bread, buttered
2 cups chicken or turkey,
　chopped
½ cup celery, chopped
¼ cup bell pepper, chopped
1 Tbs. onion, chopped
2 tsp. lemon juice
⅓ cup mayonnaise
½ tsp. salt
dash pepper
¾ cup American cheese,
　grated

Butter and toast bread on one side. Combine all ingredients, except cheese. Spread on untoasted side and sprinkle with cheese. Bake in 425 degree oven for 20 minutes.

Mrs. Hollis Fritts (Gerrie)

French Bake
(A Luncheon Dish)

375 degrees
Yield: 10 servings

2 cans solid water pack tuna,
　drained and flaked
½ cup sweet pickle relish
½ cup black olives, sliced
4 hard boiled eggs, cubed
2 cups Old English Cheese
　(¾ pounds) grated
1 cup mayonnaise
1 loaf French bread
butter, as needed

Slice bread in half lengthwise, scoop out, leaving ¾ inch. Reserve the crumbs for topping. Butter well, fill with mixture made of all other ingredients. Sprinkle top with buttered crumbs. Bake at 375 degrees for 45 minutes or until bubbly and browned slightly.

Note: If using food processor in preparation, first make bread crumbs, using steel knife then grate cheese using shredding disk. Slice olives last using slicing disk with very light pressure.

Mrs. George Rabinowitz (Johanna)

ENTREES
Beef

Beef Curry with Curry Rice

Quart pot
Yield: 4 servings

Beef:
2-3 lbs. chuck roast, cut into cubes
1 Tbs. curry powder
¼ cup fresh ginger root, chopped (if not available, 1 tsp. of powdered ginger will do)
2 Tbs. oil
1 (6-oz.) can tomato paste
salt and pepper to taste
2 cups water

Brown meat in oil, salt and pepper. Add ginger root, tomato paste, curry powder and water. Stir. Cover and cook on low heat for 35 minutes or until meat is tender. Serve over rice.

Can add hot fresh peppers.

Rice:
1 cup rice
1 Tbs. butter
1 tsp. curry powder
1½ cups water

Melt butter and stir in rice and curry powder. Add water when rice is coated. Cook until done.

Hint: Can bring rice to boil and turn off burner. Let set for 15 minutes.

Mrs. Jitendra Gohil (Dianne)

Beef Tenderloin in Claret Wine

300 degrees
Flaming dish
Yield: 6-8 servings

1 (3-lb.) piece of beef tenderloin, trimmed
salt and pepper
4 green onions, chopped
4 Tbs. butter
½ cup claret wine
½ cup beef consommé
1 Tbs. cornstarch
½ tsp. lemon juice
2 Tbs. brandy

Roast the tenderloin, rubbed with salt and pepper in 300 degree oven. Sauté onions in butter, add claret and cook until reduced by half. Add the consommé mixed with cornstarch and simmer until thickened. Add lemon juice and pour over filet. Run under broiler until bubbling. Add 2 Tbs. brandy at the table and light.

Mrs. Neal Runnels (Gayle)

Boeuf Bourguignonne

325 degrees
Large, flat baking dish
Yield: 4 servings

1½ lbs. round steak
6 slices bacon
2 Tbs. bacon drippings
1 Tbs. flour
1 beef stock cube
¼ cup water
5 oz. red wine
1 bay leaf
½ tsp. dried mixed herbs
  (Italian seasoning)
salt and pepper to taste
sprig of parsley
3 medium onions, quartered

Trim off fat and cut steak into 1½-inch cubes; chop bacon. In large skillet, brown bacon in drippings. Place bacon in casserole. Sauté steak in drippings until golden and place in casserole. In 2 Tbs. drippings, blend in flour and cook until browned. Stir in beef cube dissolved in ¼ cup water. Add wine and simmer until thickened. Stir in herbs, parsley, salt and pepper. Pour over meat and bake in 325 degree oven for 1½ hours. Add onions to casserole and cook for one hour or until meat is tender.

Mrs. Bob Batte (Gerry)

Beef-Steak Fromage

Large skillet
Yield: 4 servings

1 large round steak
¼ cup flour
½ tsp. salt
⅛ tsp. pepper
¼ tsp. garlic salt
3 Tbs. drippings
¼ cup onion, chopped
¾ cup water
⅓ cup Cheddar cheese,
  grated
2 Tbs. parsley

Cut round steak into serving size pieces, tenderized. Combine next four ingredients. Dredge meat in flour mix and brown in hot oil. Add onions and water, sprinkle remaining flour mixture over the top. Cover and simmer for an hour to 1½ hours. Remove cover, sprinkle on grated cheese and parsley.

Mrs. Jerry Leadbetter (Tonii)

ENTREES
Beef

Smokey Brisket

225-250 degrees
9 x 15 baking pan
Yield: 8-10 servings

brisket
3 Tbs. Liquid Smoke (or
   substitute soy sauce)
3 tsp. garlic salt
2 tsp. onion salt
2 tsp. celery salt
pepper
3 Tbs. Worcestershire
   sauce

Make a paste with the Liquid Smoke, garlic salt, onion salt and celery salt. Paint the brisket with paste. Wrap tightly in foil and seal. Marinate in refrigerator overnight. Before cooking, pepper and baste with 3 Tbs. Worcestershire sauce. Rewrap in foil. Place in shallow pan and bake at 225 to 250 degrees for 6 hours. Remove brisket from juice, (save) and chill. Before serving, slice with electric knife in thin slices. Return brisket to pan with drippings that have fat skimmed off top. Heat thoroughly.

This dish may be prepared several days in advance.

Mrs. Jim Henderson (Karen)

Variation:
1 tsp. onion salt
1 tsp. celery salt
1 tsp. garlic salt
salt
1½ cups barbecue sauce

Follow directions above noting difference in amounts of salts to be used. In last 1½ hour, open foil, add plain salt and barbecue sauce. Partially close foil and continue to cook.

Mrs. Paul Moxley (Karen)

Copenhagan Cabbage Casserole

350 degrees
Casserole, greased
Yield: 4-6 servings

1 lb. ground beef
¼ cup onion, chopped
1 (8-oz.) can tomato sauce
1 tsp. salt
⅛ tsp. cinnamon
⅛ tsp. ground cloves
1 tsp. black pepper
4 cups cabbage, shredded

Brown meat and onions. Blend remaining ingredients except cabbage and add to meat. Put 2 cups of cabbage in casserole and top with half of the meat mixture. Cover with remaining meat and cabbage mixture. Cover and bake for 45 minutes at 350 degrees.

Mrs. Madonna Johnson

212

Chop Suey

3 Tbs. oil (or bacon
   drippings)
1 lb. meat (½ pork, ½ veal)
   diced
1 cup onion, diced
1½ cups celery, diced
1 cup water
salt and pepper to taste
1 (16-oz.) can chop suey
   vegetables
1 (small) can whole
   mushrooms
3 Tbs. flour (or cornstarch)
1½ tsp. brown sauce (Bead
   molasses)
3 Tbs. soy sauce

Sear meat and onions quickly in 3-4 Tbs. oil. Add celery and water; cook covered about 20-30 minutes. Salt and pepper to taste. Add chop suey vegetables and mushrooms. Stir in thickening made of flour and sauces. Simmer slowly for 15 minutes, stirring constantly. Serve over rice, noodles, or both.

Variation:
1 can water chestnuts,
   drained

Add to meat mixture when adding chop suey vegetables.

Mrs. Neal Runnels (Gayle)

Mock Chop Suey on Rice

1 onion, chopped
1 small green pepper,
   chopped
1 cup celery, diced
1 cup water
1 lb. ground meat
2 Tbs. flour
1 (small) can tomatoes or
   tomato sauce
1 Tbs. chili powder
1 Tbs. sugar
salt and pepper to taste

Stew onion, green pepper and celery in water. Meanwhile brown meat. Add flour and mix well. Add vegetables and liquid in which they were cooked. Add tomatoes and seasonings. Cook all this together about 30 minutes to 1 hour very slowly. Stir occasionally. Serve over steamed rice.

Mrs. Joe Stroud (Ruthie)

ENTREES
Beef

Chow Mein-Cashew Nut Casserole

350 degrees
Shallow 4 cup casserole
Yield: 4 servings

3 oz. can chow mein noodles
1 Tbs. soy sauce
1 tsp. garlic powder
1 Tbs. butter, melted
Tabasco hot sauce, few
  drops

Toss contents of can of noodles with soy sauce, garlic powder, melted butter, and the Tabasco. Set aside.

1 (10¾-oz.) can cream of
  mushroom soup
1 (7-oz.) can of tuna, drained
¼ lb. lightly salted cashews
1 cup celery, finely chopped
¼ cup onions, chopped
butter
¼ cup water

Mix soup, tuna, cashews, and celery. Sauté onion in a little butter until golden, then add to soup mixture along with water. Turn into casserole. Top with noodle mixture. Bake for 45 minutes at 350 degrees.

Mrs. J. R. Schroeder (Molly)

College Casserole

350 degrees
Large casserole
Yield: 6 servings

1 lb. ground beef
1 onion, diced
salt, pepper and garlic
  powder
1 cup carrots, sliced
1 cup potatoes, sliced
1 (10¾-oz.) can cream of
  mushroom soup
1 cup Cheddar cheese,
  grated

Brown beef in skillet with onion. Add salt, pepper and a little garlic powder to taste. Layer in casserole, the beef, carrots, and potatoes, ending up with the beef. Heat the soup and pour on top. Sprinkle the grated cheese on top. Bake at 350 degrees for 1¼-1½ hours.

Mrs. Glenn Jarvis (Pat)

Easy Day Casserole

350 degrees
Large casserole
Yield: 6-8 servings

1 cup rice, uncooked
1 regular sized can whole
  kernel corn, drained
salt and pepper
1 (8-oz.) can tomato sauce
½ can water
½ cup onion, diced
½ cup green pepper, diced
1 lb. ground meat, uncooked
1 (8-oz.) can tomato sauce
¼ cup water
4 strips bacon

In a casserole layer the ingredients in the order given. Top with the bacon strips. Cover with foil and bake for one hour at 350 degrees. Uncover casserole and bake an additional 30 minutes.

Mrs. Tom Wilkins (Geen)

Flank Steak

Large skillet
Yield: 6 generous servings

3 (1 lb.) flank steaks
2 sticks butter or margarine
3 tsp. minced onion
3 tsp. Worcestershire sauce
salt and pepper
1½ cups water

Score meat and brown in butter, one steak at a time. When all are browned, lower heat and add onions, seasonings, and 1½ cups water to meat. Cover and let simmer for 30 minutes. Slice on the diagonal and serve with remaining sauce poured over top.

Sliced fresh mushrooms are a nice addition to the sauce.

Mrs. Jerry Fair (Zetta)

ENTREES
Beef

Frankfurt Bar-B-Q

Skillet
Yield: 6 servings

¼ cup onion, chopped
1 Tbs. oil
1 cup ketchup
½ cup water
2 Tbs. brown sugar
½ tsp. salt
dash of pepper
2 Tbs. vinegar
¼ cup lemon juice
3 Tbs. Worcestershire sauce
1 Tbs. prepared mustard
12 frankfurters

Sauté onions in oil until tender. Combine remaining ingredients (except frankfurters) and add to onion. Simmer covered for 20 minutes. Prick frankfurters and add to sauce. Cover and simmer about 15 minutes.

Mrs. Kenneth Kachtik (Sue)

Ground Beef Casserole

350 degrees
Large casserole
Yield: 6-8 servings

1 lb. ground beef
¾ cup uncooked rice
2 cups uncooked celery,
  finely chopped
½ cup uncooked onions,
  finely chopped
1 (10¾-oz.) can cream of
  mushroom soup
2 soup cans water
2 Tbs. soy sauce

Brown beef, drain, then add other ingredients. Bake at 350 degrees for 1½ to 2 hours.

Mrs. Ken Forrester (Phoebe)

Dot Hamburgers
(for campfires)

Yield: 1 serving

1 hamburger patty
1 onion slice
1 green pepper ring
1 potato, sliced
1 carrot, sliced

Arrange ingredients in foil with patty on bottom. Seal tightly. Place on medium coals for approximately 15 minutes. Check often to see if it is being cooked evenly. Turn entire packet over until potato is tender.

Really great for first night out, as packets may be prepared in advance and frozen until time to leave home.

Mrs. Bill Turk (Marian)

Burger Stuffed Onions

350 degrees
9 x 9 baking pan
Yield: 6 servings

6 large onions, peeled
1 lb. ground beef
2 Tbs. green peppers,
  chopped
2 Tbs. dry bread crumbs
½ tsp. chili powder
½ tsp. salt
⅓ tsp. pepper
American cheese slices
1 (8-oz.) can tomato sauce

Peel onions and cook in boiling salted water about 30 minutes or until tender yet firm. Drain and cool. Slice off top third of onions. Cut out centers to make cups. Combine ½ cup chopped onions with beef and green pepper. Sauté for about 5 minutes. Add bread crumbs, chili powder, salt and pepper. Fill onion cups with meat mixture and place in baking dish. Top each onion with a slice of cheese. Pour tomato sauce over all. Bake at 350 degrees for 20 minutes or until done.

Mrs. Kenneth Kachtik (Sue)

ENTREES
Beef

Lasagne

375 degrees
Large Lasagne pan
Yield: 12 servings
Freezes

Meat Sauce:
1½ lbs. lean ground beef
2 pkgs. spaghetti sauce mix
   (instant type)
1 tsp. oregano
½ tsp. garlic powder
3 (8-oz.) cans Hunt's Special
   tomato sauce
5 (8-oz.) cans of water
1 (8-oz.) box Lasagna
   noodles

Brown meat. Add remaining ingredients and simmer for 30 minutes. Cook noodles according to directions.

Cheese Sauce:
6 eggs
24 oz. large curd cottage
   cheese
8 oz. Monterrey Jack Cheese,
   grated
5 Tbs. parsley flakes
8 oz. Mozzarella cheese,
   grated

Beat six eggs. Add cottage cheese, Monterrey Jack cheese and parsley. In large pan, layer ingredients: meat sauce, noodles, cheese mix, meat sauce, noodles, meat sauce. Bake 45 minutes at 375 degrees. Add grated Mozzarella cheese and bake additional 15 to 20 minutes.

Variation:
mushrooms and/or black
   olives

Mushrooms and/or black olives may be added between layers.

If freezing do so before baking.

Mrs. Jon Gillespie (Jeanine)

To remove excess fat from your food, place a few lettuce leaves in the pot and the fat will cling to them. Remove when saturated.

Easy Lasagne

1½ lbs. lean ground beef
1 (28-oz.) can whole tomatoes
1 (12-oz.) can tomato paste
2 tsp. garlic salt
1½ tsp. oregano leaves
1 tsp. basil leaves
2 cups creamed cottage
  cheese
1 cup Parmesan cheese
12 oz. Mozzarella cheese,
  grated
12 oz. cooked lasagne
  noodles

Brown meat. Add tomatoes and mash. Stir in tomato paste, garlic salt, oregano and basil leaves. Heat to boiling and simmer, uncovered 20 minutes. In small bowl combine cottage cheese and ½ cup Parmesan cheese. Set aside 1 cup meat sauce and ½ cup Mozzarella cheese. In casserole layer noodles, meat sauce, and cheese mixture. Top with reserved meat sauce, Parmesan and Mozzarella cheese. Bake at 350 degrees for 45 minutes.

Mrs. Allen Beakey (Jane)

German Meat Balls

350 degrees
Baking dish, covered
Yield: 6 servings
Freezes: without
milk and soup

1 lb. ground beef
½ cup cornflake crumbs
½ small onion, chopped
2 eggs
⅓ cup cream
1 tsp. salt
1 tsp. pepper
¼ tsp. dry mustard
¼ tsp. oregano
¼ tsp. allspice
1 (10¾-oz.) can cream of
  mushroom soup
1 soup can of milk

Mix together all ingredients except milk and soup. Form beef mixture into round balls and brown slightly on all sides. In a baking dish, dilute soup with milk. Add browned meat balls and bake covered for 30 minutes at 350 degrees.

Note: For party, make small balls. For main dish, make larger balls.

Mrs. Hiram Tavarez (Kathe)

ENTREES
Beef

Green Chile Lasagne

350 degrees
2 (9 x 13 x 2) pyrex dishes
Yield: 24 servings
Freezes

16 oz. medium noodles
1 tsp. butter
3 lbs. lean ground beef
oil
5 (8-oz.) cans tomato sauce
1 Tbs. sugar
1 tsp. garlic salt
½ tsp. pepper

Cook noodles according to package directions. Drain and add the butter. In a skillet, brown beef in small amount of oil in pan. Set aside. In a large saucepan, combine the tomato sauce, sugar, salts, and pepper. Add browned meat and simmer until meat is tender (about 30 minutes). Skim off any grease.

2 cups cottage cheese, large curd
1 (8-oz.) pkg. cream cheese
1 cup sour cream
2 (4-oz.) cans green chiles, chopped
1 cup green onions and tops, thin sliced
Parmesan cheese

Mix ingredients until soft and creamy. Fill the two pyrex dishes in this order: ¼ of the cooked noodles in bottom, cover with ¼ of meat sauce, ½ of cheese mixture, ¼ noodles, ¼ meat sauce, and finish with a heavy topping of grated Parmesan cheese. Cover with foil and refrigerate. Cook in 350 degree oven for 45 minutes. This is better if prepared the day before and then cooked when ready to use.

Saturday Night Casserole

350 degrees
9 x 13 glass baking dish
Yield: 6 servings

1 lb. ground beef
½ cup onions, chopped
½ cup green peppers, chopped
1 pkg. noodles
1 (10¾-oz.) can cream of mushroom soup
1 (10¾-oz.) can cream of celery soup
1 can Chinese noodles

Brown meat, onion and peppers. Cook noodles as directed on the package. Using ½ of each ingredient, spread in layers as follows: noodles, meat, mushroom soup and celery soup; repeat. Garnish with the Chinese noodles on top and bake 30 minutes at 350 degrees.

Mrs. Bill Turk (Marian)

Lasagne Napoli

350 degrees
Medium-size skillet
9 x 13 baking dish
Yield: 6-8 servings

1 medium onion, finely
  chopped
1 clove garlic, minced
2 Tbs. olive oil
1 lb. ground chuck
1 (4-oz.) can sliced
  mushrooms with juice
1 (8-oz.) can tomato sauce
1 (8-oz.) can tomato paste
2 tsp. salt
1 tsp. dried oregano
¾ cup water
2 eggs
1 (10-oz.) pkg. frozen
  chopped spinach, thawed
1 cup cream-style cottage
  cheese
⅓ cup Parmesan cheese,
  grated
1 (12-oz.) pkg. lasagne,
  cooked and drained
  according to package
  directions
1 (8-oz.) pkg. American
  cheese slices, cut into
  strips

In a frying pan, slightly brown onion and garlic in 1 Tbs. of the oil; add ground chuck and break apart, cooking until meat is browned. Blend in mushrooms, including the juice, tomato sauce, tomato paste, 1 tsp. of the salt, oregano, and water; simmer for 15 minutes. Meanwhile mix 1 of the eggs with the spinach, cottage cheese, Parmesan cheese, remaining 1 Tbs. oil, and 1 tsp. salt. Beat the second egg slightly and toss with the cooked lasagne. Pour half of the meat sauce into the baking dish and cover with a layer of half of the lasagne. Spread all of the spinach mixture over the lasagne. Complete layers with remaining lasagne and meat sauce. Cover and bake for 45 minutes at 350 degrees. Remove cover from dish and arrange strips of the American cheese on top; bake uncovered for 15 minutes longer. Serve hot.

Mrs. Forrest Fitch (Marion)

ENTREES
Beef

Liver Fantastique

Yield: 4-6 servings

6 pieces bacon
1½ lbs. calves liver, sliced
⅓-½ cup seasoned flour
1⅓ cups brown sugar
1½ cups vinegar
1 tsp. onion salt
1 tsp. marjoram
1 tsp. rosemary leaves,
  crushed
pepper
1 bell pepper, sliced
1 onion, sliced

Fry bacon until crisp—drain and keep warm. Add enough bacon drippings or salad oil to drippings in pan to make ⅓ cup. Dredge sliced liver in seasoned flour and brown in drippings. Drain on paper towels and set aside. Make a roux of ⅓ cups seasoned flour and bacon drippings. Add all the remaining ingredients, except bell pepper and onion. Stir till thick as gravy consistency and add up to 1⅓ cups hot water if desired. Add liver to gravy mixture and cook over low heat for 30-40 minutes. Add pepper and onion during the last 15 minutes. Serve with bacon crumbled on top.

Chili Liver Fingers

Large skillet
Yield: 6 generous servings

1 cup flour
1 tsp. garlic powder
salt and pepper to taste
1½-2 lbs. calves liver, thinly
  sliced into "fingers"
½ cup bacon grease, adding
  more if needed
2 Tbs. chili powder
1 Tbs. Worcestershire sauce
5 pods garlic, chopped
4 cups hot water

In plastic bag place flour, 1 Tbs. of the chili powder, garlic powder, salt and pepper to taste. Dredge liver in bag of flour to coat thoroughly. Heat about ½ cup bacon grease and brown liver on both sides, slightly. Place liver on paper towel to drain. Stir into the bacon grease ½ cup seasoned flour from bag, 1 Tbs. chili powder, Worcestershire sauce, garlic and hot water. Make a roux with flour and seasonings before adding water. After the gravy has thickened, return liver to pan with gravy and cook slowly over very low heat for 30 minutes or until ready to eat. May be served with chopped crisp bacon and onions. Serve over rice or noodles.

Mrs. Jerry Box (Deanna)

Stuffed Manicotti

350 degrees
Large baking dish
Yield: 6-8 servings

Tomato-Meat Sauce:
1 lb. ground meat
¼ cup olive oil
½ cup onion, chopped
1 clove garlic, minced
2 (6-oz.) cans tomato paste
2 cups water
1½ tsp. salt
dash of pepper
2 Tbs. parsley, chopped

Brown meat in olive oil. Add remaining ingredients and simmer uncovered for 45 minutes. Stir occasionally.

Stuffing:
¾ lb. fresh ricotta or 1½
  cups cream-style cottage
  cheese
⅓ cup Romano or Parmesan
  cheese, grated
1 egg, beaten
2 Tbs. parsley, chopped
¼ tsp. salt
dash of pepper
1 (8-oz.) pkg. manicotti

Combine ingredients to make cheese mixture. Cook manicotti in boiling, salted water till tender. Drain and rinse in cold water. Cut pasta lengthwise and fill with cheese mixture. Pour half the tomato-meat sauce into baking dish. Arrange stuffed manicotti and top with remaining sauce. Sprinkle with Romano cheese. Bake at 350 degrees for 25-35 minutes. May be made ahead and popped in the oven for the final step at the last minute.

Mrs. Kenneth Kachtik (Sue)

Corsica Ribs

375 degrees
Glass or enamel baking dish
Yield: 4 servings

1 plank or slab spare ribs,
  split lengthwise and cut
  into rib pieces
1 cup molasses
1 Tbs. ketchup
1 Tbs. brown sugar
1 Tbs. soy sauce

Place ribs in glass or enamel baking dish. Cover with all ingredients. Bake, basting as necessary, until done (about 45 minutes).

ENTREES
Beef

Meat Loaf

400 degrees
9 x 9 pan, greased
Yield: 6 servings

⅔ cup cracker crumbs (about 16 crackers)
1 cup milk
1½ lbs. ground beef
½ lb. pork sausage
2 eggs, beaten
¼ cup onion, grated
1 tsp. salt
pepper to taste
½ (No. 303) can tomatoes

Soak cracker crumbs in milk while preparing meat. Mix beef and sausage, add beaten eggs, onion, salt and pepper. Mix well. Add cracker-milk mixture and blend thoroughly. Spread in greased 9-inch square pan. Pour tomatoes on top. Bake for 1½ hours in a 400 degree oven.

Mrs. P. D. Terrell (Marabeth)

Meat Loaf Topping

1 small onion, diced
1 small green pepper, diced
1 small can mushrooms stems and pieces, drained
1 (8 oz.) can tomato sauce
½ cup ketchup

Combine all ingredients and cook over med.-low heat about 5 minutes. Stir often. Pour into bottom of meat loaf pan—put your favorite meat loaf mixture on top and bake. After removing meat loaf from pan, pour sauce on top.

Mrs. Ken Kachtik (Sue)

Silta

Long shallow pyrex dish

5 lbs. baby beef (or veal)
2 lbs. pork hocks
3 lbs. pork roast with bone
12 peppercorns (whole)
12 whole allspice
1 tsp. salt

Take fat off pork. Cut all meat in pieces and cook in water with peppercorns, allspice and salt. Cook about 2 hours. Strain juice and put juice in refrigerator. Cut up meat in very small pieces. Take grease off top of juice. Boil meat and juice about 5 minutes. Put mixture in dish. Chill and serve when set up.

Mrs. Sam Rodio (Janice)

224

Surprise Meatballs

Large skillet
Yield: 18 meatballs

1½ lbs. lean ground beef
1 cup fine dry bread crumbs
2 Tbs. onion, finely chopped
2 eggs, beaten
¼ cup milk
1 tsp. salt
½ tsp. pepper
6 oz. Bleu cheese, cut into
    small chunks
2 Tbs. shortening, melted
1 (10-oz.) can mushroom
    steak sauce
add a little beef broth to
    sauce (optional)

Lightly but thoroughly combine meat with bread crumbs, onion, eggs, milk, and seasoning. Shape into 1½-inch balls around chunks of Bleu cheese (be certain that all cheese is sealed in). Brown in small amount of melted shortening in large, heavy frying pan. Stir in mushroom steak sauce, cover and simmer about 20 minutes.

A different kind of cheese can be used instead of Bleu cheese.

Mrs. Cayetano Barrera (Yolanda)

Meatza

375 degrees
9-inch pie pan
Yield: 5-6 servings

1 lb. ground beef
⅔ cup evaporated milk
½ cup dried bread crumbs
1 tsp. garlic salt
⅓ cup tomato paste or
    ketchup
1 (2-oz.) can sliced
    mushrooms
¼ tsp. oregano
1 cup sharp Cheddar cheese,
    grated
2 tsp. Parmesan cheese

Mix meat, milk, bread crumbs and garlic salt. Pat evenly on bottom and sides of pie pan and pinch a slight edge around rim. Spread tomato paste over meat and sprinkle with mushrooms. Top with oregano and cheese. Bake at 375 degrees for 25 minutes.

Mrs. Steven Zenthoefer (Ann)

ENTREES
Beef

Pepper Steak

Large skillet
Yield: 4 servings

1 lb. round steak, cut in
  serving pieces
2 Tbs. fat
¼ cup onion, chopped
1 clove garlic, halved
1 tsp. salt
dash pepper
1 beef bouillon cube
1 cup hot water
1 (1-lb.) can (2 cups) stewed
  tomatoes
1 large green pepper, thinly
  sliced in rings
2 Tbs. cornstarch
¼ cup cold water
2 Tbs. soy sauce

Brown meat slowly in hot fat; add onion and garlic last few minutes. Season with salt and pepper. Dissolve bouillon cube in hot water; add to meat. Cover; simmer till meat is almost tender, 60 to 70 minutes. Add tomatoes and green pepper; cook 10 minutes longer. Combine remaining ingredients; stir into meat mixture. Bring to boiling; cook, stirring constantly, 5 minutes longer. Remove garlic. Serve with hot noodles.

Mrs. Bill Blackburn (Jeanne)

Chinese Pepper Steak

Skillet
Yield: 4 servings

1 lb. round steak
2 Tbs. shortening
2 Tbs. onion, minced
1 clove garlic, minced
½ cup celery, diced
1 (small) jar of pimientos,
  drained and sliced
1 (14-oz.) can beef
  consommé
salt and pepper to taste
2 large green peppers, cut
  into strips
2 Tbs. cornstarch
½ cup water
1 tsp. soy sauce

Cut steak into narrow and long strips. Brown in shortening. Add onions, garlic, and celery and sauté until soft. Add pimientos, consommé, salt and pepper. Simmer in covered skillet (electric or other) one hour, adding water as needed. Add green pepper strips and cook about 30 minutes more. Thicken with mixture of cornstarch, water and soy sauce. Serve over rice or noodles.

Mrs. P. D. Terrell (Marabeth)

Meat Balls and Spaghetti

Heavy Dutch oven
Yield: 12 servings
Freezes

¼ cup olive oil
1 lb. ground beef
1 sm. onion, chopped fine
1 clove garlic, chopped fine
2 eggs, beaten
1 cup (plus) bread crumbs
salt and pepper
½ cup milk

Heat olive oil in heavy iron skillet. Mix all ingredients in order given. Form into small balls and brown on all sides in olive oil. Brown slowly and set aside. Save oil.

Sauce:
4 small onions
3 cloves garlic
6 (10¾-oz.) cans tomato soup
6 small cans tomato purée
1 (4-oz.) can mushroom
   slices and juice
2 Tbs. Worcestershire sauce
¼ tsp. Tabasco
¼ tsp. cayenne pepper
12 peppercorns (whole)

Herbs:
¼ tsp. marjoram
¼ tsp. thyme
½ tsp. basil
4 bay leaves

3 pkgs. spaghetti, prepared
   according to directions

Finely chop onions and garlic and brown in same oil. Add remaining ingredients and stir well to insure thorough mixing. Cover and cook over slow fire for 5 hours, stirring occasionally to prevent sticking. At the end of 3 hours remove lid from skillet and add browned meat balls and herbs. Cook slowly 2 more hours adding water as needed. NOTE: total time is 5 hours.

This sauce may be used as a pizza base. Will double easily.

Mrs. Frank Schultz (Marilyn)

Spear garlic pods or cloves with a toothpick before placing in pot of stew or soup. When recipe is finished simply stir and locate garlic for easy removal.

ENTREES
Beef

Spaghetti Casserole

325 degrees
Large casserole dish
Yield: 10-12 servings

3 lbs. ground beef
½ cup olive oil
3 cloves garlic, minced
1 cup onion, chopped
1½ cup green pepper,
  chopped
¾ cup celery, diced
2 large cans whole tomatoes
2 bay leaves
2 pinches oregano
2 Tbs. Worcestershire sauce
1 can mushroom buttons,
  drained
1½ cups stuffed green olives,
  sliced
1 (10-12 oz.) pkg. spaghetti

Heat oil and brown hamburger meat until just done. Add onions, garlic, green peppers, celery, tomatoes, bay leaves, oregano and sauce. Cover and simmer for 3 hours. During the last half hour, add the olives and mushrooms. Cook spaghetti according to directions. Rinse and drain. Place in large shallow baking dish or large casserole. Cover with sauce and bake 325 degrees for about one hour.

Mrs. P. D. Terrell (Marabeth)

Spaghetti for 40

Electric Roaster
Yield: 40 servings

5 lbs. ground beef
2 tsp. garlic powder
1¼ cups olive oil
¼ lb. butter
2 cups onions, chopped
5 (1-lb.) cans of tomatoes
13 (6-oz.) cans of tomato
  paste
12½ cups water
¼ cup sugar
12½ tsp. salt
7½ tsp. pepper
4 lbs. spaghetti

Brown meat, seasoned with garlic powder, in olive oil in electric roaster. Sauté onions in butter; add to meat and garlic. Then add the tomatoes, paste, water, sugar, salt and pepper. Mix well. Cover and simmer 6-7 hours. About one hour before serving, boil spaghetti until tender in salt water. Take out 2 quarts meat sauce and save to add later. Add spaghetti to meat sauce and cover. Turn to warm on your roaster setting. (Allow at least one hour to cook 4 lbs. of spaghetti.) Top with remaining sauce.

Spaghetti a la Niña

350 degrees
Casserole
Yield: 6-8 servings
Freezes

1 cup onion, chopped
1 clove garlic, finely chopped
   (optional)
1 cup celery, chopped
1 lb. ground beef
½ cup (approx.) butter or
   margarine
1 (small) can sliced
   mushrooms
1 Tbs. chili powder
1 (10¾-oz.) can tomato soup
1 soup can water
1 (8-oz.) can Italian tomato
   paste
1 (8-oz.) can water
¾ cup green pepper,
   chopped
2 tsp. salt
1 tsp. cumin
1 (small) box spaghetti
salt
½ lb. American cheese,
   grated

Cook onions, garlic, and celery in butter a few minutes before adding meat. Add meat and cook until slightly brown, and then add all other ingredients except spaghetti and cheese. Blend all together well and simmer a few minutes. Cook spaghetti according to instructions on box, season with salt. Drain well when done and add to the meat mixture. Pour into large casserole, cover with grated cheese and bake at 350 degrees for 45 minutes.

This is a hearty dish.

Mrs. Randy Davis (Lynn)

Steak-A-Bobs

15 skewers
Yield: 4 servings

1 round steak, tenderized and
   cut in 1 inch squares
bacon slices, quartered
onions, quartered or wedged
seasoned flour (seasoned
   salt, pepper and other
   favorites)

On wooden skewers, alternate pieces of steak, bacon, steak, onion, etc. Dredge in seasoned flour and fry in hot oil.

Tastes like chicken fried steak and french fried onion rings.

Mrs. Dudley Roberts (Carol Ann)

ENTREES
Beef

Beef Stroganoff

375 degrees
12 quart enamel roasting pan
Yield: 20 servings

8 lbs. sirloin tip
Adolph's meat tenderizer
4 lbs. fresh mushrooms
5 large onions, chopped
½ lb. butter
4 (10½-oz.) cans beef
  bouillon
¾ cup flour
1½ pints sour cream
2 cups tomato juice
1 cup Rhine wine

Slice meat into thin strips about 1½ inches wide and 2-3 inches long. Sprinkle lightly with tenderizer, toss and refrigerate. Cut off mushroom stems even with the caps and slice mushrooms. Sauté ¼ of the onions in 3 Tbs. butter until almost clear, but not brown. Add ¼ of the mushrooms and sauté until just tender. Remove to a 12 quart enamel roasting pan. Sauté remaining onions and mushrooms in same manner, i.e., in four batches. You may need to add a little butter each time. In same skillet in which vegetables have been cooked, brown meat a little at a time with a minimum of butter, removing it to the roasting pan as it browns. Put in 2 cans of bouillon and the flour in a blender and blend until smooth. Set aside. Pour remaining cans of bouillon into skillet and stir and scrape to deglaze the pan. Add bouillon and flour mixture, stirring as you add to keep smooth. Add tomato juice and Rhine wine. Pour over the meat and vegetables in roasting pan. Season to taste. About 1½ hours before serving, place in a 375 degree oven and bring to a simmer, stirring occasionally. Just before serving, add sour cream and a splash of Rhine wine. Serve with buttered noodles or long grain and wild rice.

Can easily be halved. Great recipe for a crowd.

Mrs. Mac Pike (Tish)

Beef and Beer Stew

¼ cup flour, unsifted
3½ tsp. salt
½ tsp. pepper
2 lbs. chuck, cut in one inch cubes
½ cup salad oil
2 lbs. onions, peeled and sliced
1 clove garlic, crushed
1 (12-oz.) can light beer
1 Tbs. soy sauce
1 Tbs. Worcestershire sauce
1 Tbs. steak sauce
2 bay leaves
1 tsp. dried thyme leaves
2 lbs. potatoes
2 Tbs. parsley, chopped

In large bowl combine flour, 2½ tsp. salt, and pepper. Add chuck, tossing to coat. Set aside. Heat ¼ cup oil in 4 quart Dutch oven or kettle. In oil, sauté onion and garlic until tender, 8 to 10 minutes. Remove from Dutch oven. Heat remaining oil. Add chuck, brown well on all sides. Return onion and garlic to Dutch oven, along with beer, soy sauce, Worcestershire sauce, steak sauce, bay leaves, and thyme. Mix well. Bring mixture to boiling. Reduce heat; simmer, covered 2 hours or until meat is tender. Meanwhile, pare potatoes, cut into quarters. Add potatoes and 1 tsp. salt to 1 inch boiling water; simmer, covered 20 minutes or until potatoes are tender. Drain potatoes well. Toss with parsley. To serve, turn stew mixture into serving dish. Surround the stew with potatoes.

Mrs. Morgan Talbot (Jane)

Stay-A-Bed Stew

2 lbs. beef stew meat, cubed
1 (17-oz.) can tiny peas
1 cup carrots, sliced
2 onions, chopped
1 tsp. salt
dash pepper
1 (10¾-oz.) can cream of tomato soup
½ soup can water
1 big raw potato, sliced

Mix all ingredients together in a large casserole dish and cover tightly. Put casserole in 275 degree oven. Let cook for 5 hours, without checking.

This can be cooked in a crock pot.

ENTREES
Beef

No-Peek Stew

300 degrees
1½ quart casserole
Yield: 4 servings

1 pkg. Lipton onion soup mix
1 (small) can mushrooms
1 (10¾-oz.) can cream of
  mushroom soup
1-2 lbs. stew meat
½ cup sherry
cooked rice

Mix onion soup mix, mushrooms, mushroom soup, meat and sherry in casserole. Cover and bake in 300 degree oven for 3 hours. NO PEEKING!! Serve over cooked rice.

Teriyaki Shish Kabobs

Marinade:
2 cloves garlic, mashed
2 Tbs. brown sugar
1 tsp. ground ginger
1 tsp. coarsely ground black
  pepper
4 Tbs. water
½ cup soy sauce
2 Tbs. cooking oil

Mash garlic and combine with sugar. Add ginger, black pepper, water, soy sauce and cooking oil, mixing well. Marinate beef kabobs in this mixture at least one hour. Use as a basting sauce during cooking for meat and vegetables.

Kabobs:
chuck roast—carefully cut
  kabobs, about 1 inch
  square eliminating all
  gristle, fat and bone
cherry tomatoes, whole
fresh mushrooms, soaked in
  salt water
green peppers, cut in 1½
  inch squares
onions, fresh or canned
zucchini slices, if desired

The amount of beef and vegetables depends on how many you are feeding. To make the shish kabobs, thread marinated meat alternately with vegetables on skewers. Barbeque over coals until meat reaches desired doneness.

This is a fabulous party dish served with green rice, a green salad and herb bread. Also, all gristle, fat and bone can be used later for soup stock.

Can parboil green peppers and onions if desired.

Mrs. Morgan Talbot (Jane)

Beef Stroganoff
(Inflation style)

Yield: 4 servings

1½-2 lbs. round steak
salt and pepper
6 Tbs. butter or margarine
1 cup fresh mushrooms,
   sliced, or 4 oz. can drained
1 large onion, sliced
2 Tbs. flour
2 cups beef bouillon
3 Tbs. sherry
2 Tbs. tomato paste
1 tsp. dry mustard
⅔ cup sour cream
rice or noodles

Trim all fat and gristle from meat, and cut in narrow strips about 2 inches long, ½ inch wide. Dust strips with salt and pepper. Melt about 3 Tbs. butter in heavy skillet and sauté mushrooms and onion until tender. Remove and set aside. Add rest of butter to skillet, and when bubbly, sear strips of beef on both sides. Remove and set aside. Add flour to butter left in skillet and blend. Slowly add beef bouillon, stirring well. Add sherry, tomato paste and mustard. When well blended add meat, onions and mushrooms. Simmer 45 minutes to one hour. About 5 minutes before serving, add sour cream. Serve over rice or noodles.

Hamburger Stroganoff

Large skillet
Yield: 5-6 servings

1 lb. ground beef
3 slices bacon, diced
½ cup onion, chopped
¾ tsp. salt
¼ tsp. paprika
dash pepper
1 (10¾-oz.) can cream of
   mushroom soup
1 cup dairy sour cream
poppy seed noodles, buttered

In skillet, brown beef with bacon. Add onion and cook until tender, but not brown. Drain off excess fat. Add seasonings to meat mixture. Stir in soup. Cook slowly, uncovered 20 minutes, stirring frequently. Stir in sour cream and heat thoroughly. Do not boil. Serve over hot poppy seed noodles.

Mrs. Glynn Andrews (Laurie)

ENTREES
Beef

Talvina

325 degrees
3 quart baking dish
Yield: 6 servings

1 lb. ground beef
½ cup onion, chopped
½ tsp. salt
1 green pepper, chopped
2 Tbs. Worcestershire sauce
½ lb. cheese, cut in small
   pieces (American or
   Cheddar)
1 small can ripe olives,
   chopped
1 (16-oz.) can cream-style
   corn
1 (8-oz.) can tomato sauce
1 (8-oz.) pkg. large noodles,
   cooked

Cook meat, onion, salt, green pepper and Worcestershire for 15 minutes. Mix remaining ingredients with meat mixture and layer in baking dish with one package cooked large noodles and bake for 1 hour.

Mrs. T. B. Waite, Jr. (Thelma)

Tegarini

Large skillet
Yield: 6-8 servings

2 lbs. ground beef
2 medium onions, chopped
1 garlic pod, chopped
2 tsp. oregano
1 tsp. chili powder
1 (1-lb.) can tomatoes, do not
   drain
1 (8-oz.) can tomato sauce
1 (8-oz.) pkg. noodles
1 (regular sized) can Niblets
   corn, do not drain
3 (small) cans mushrooms,
   drained
1 (4-oz.) can black olives,
   chopped and drained
8-12 oz. cheese, grated
salt to taste

Brown meat with onion and garlic. Add oregano and chili powder. Add tomatoes and tomato sauce, plus a little water. Pour in uncooked noodles and let boil in juices. When noodles are nearly done, add corn and juice, mushrooms and olives. You may need to add water from time to time to prevent sticking, but make sure that the noodles are cooked. Blend in cheese. Eat immediately or set in 350 degree oven for a short while.

Good as leftovers.

Mrs. Charles Murray (Cynthia)

Chicken Amandine

8 chicken breasts, boned
flour for dredging
salt and pepper
8 Tbs. margarine
1 (3-oz.) pkg. almonds
1 small can mushrooms
¼ cup sherry
¼ cup half and half

Dredge seasoned chicken in flour. Sauté in margarine until golden. Remove chicken to casserole. Add almonds to pan drippings and sauté for 4-5 minutes, stirring to brown evenly. Add mushrooms, with liquid, and sherry. Over low heat, slowly add half and half. Remove from heat as soon as cream is well mixed and pour over chicken. Bake uncovered at 300 degrees for 45 minutes or until tender. May be frozen before baking.

Mrs. Joe Weir (Lupe)

Chicken and Asparagus

2 chicken breasts, boned,
 skinned and halved
1 tsp. salt
¼ tsp. pepper
1½ tsp. MSG
½ cup corn oil
2 (10-oz.) pkgs. frozen
 asparagus
1 (10¾-oz.) can cream of
 chicken soup
½ cup mayonnaise
1 tsp. lemon juice
4 tsp. curry powder
Parmesan cheese

Sprinkle chicken with salt, pepper and MSG. In skillet, heat oil and add chicken. Sauté slowly, about 6 minutes or until white and opaque. Drain. Cook asparagus according to package directions. Line bottom of pan with asparagus and place chicken on top. Mix remaining ingredients and pour over chicken. Sprinkle cheese on top. Cover with foil and bake in 375 degree oven for 30 minutes.

Mrs. Jim Jones (Jackie)

ENTREES
Chicken

Avocado and Chicken Bombay
Yield: 6 servings

1 small onion, chopped
1 small apple, peeled and
 chopped (optional)
2 Tbs. butter
1 (10¾-oz.) can cream of
 chicken soup
2 tsp. curry powder
2 cups chicken, cooked
6 avocado halves, peeled
cooked rice

Sauté onion and apple in butter. Stir in cream of chicken soup and curry powder. Heat over low flame until smooth. Add chicken. Place avocado half on bed of rice. Fill with chicken curry mixture.

Mrs. Joe Friend (Pam)

Chicken Breasts Vienna Style
Skillet
Yield: 6 servings

3 whole chicken breasts,
 skinned, deboned, and
 halved
salt and freshly ground black
 pepper
flour for dredging
2 eggs, beaten
1 cup fresh bread crumbs,
 finely crumbled
½ cup butter
6 lemon slices
parsley, chopped

Place the chicken breasts between pieces of waxed paper and pound until thin. Sprinkle both sides with salt and pepper; dredge with flour and dip into the beaten eggs. Coat with the bread crumbs and tap lightly with the flat edge of a knife to make the crumbs stick to the chicken. Refrigerate for one hour or more. In a skillet, heat the butter, add the chicken, and cook until brown on both sides. Garnish with lemon slices and parsley.

All steps in this recipe may be prepared early in the day, waiting to cook the chicken when ready to serve. The chicken is a good substitute for veal, which is sometimes hard to find in some meat markets.

Mrs. Bill Blackburn (Jeanne)

Chicken Breasts in Wine Sauce

325 degrees
9 x 15 casserole
Yield: 6 servings

3 whole chicken breasts,
  halved
1 cup sour cream
3 Tbs. flour
1 cup mushroom soup
1 (small) can whole or
  chopped mushrooms,
  drained
½ cup cream sherry
salt to taste
paprika

Place chicken breasts in casserole. Mix remaining ingredients and pour over chicken. Bake uncovered for 1½ hours at 325 degrees. Sprinkle with paprika before serving. May be kept at low temperature before serving.

Mrs. Mike Frost (Sandra)

Creamy-Rich Chicken Breasts

325 degrees
Shallow baking dish
Yield: 12 servings

6 chicken breasts, halved
pepper
12 slices bacon
1 pkg. dried beef, not corned
  beef
2 (10¾-oz.) cans cream of
  chicken soup
1½ cups sour cream
3 oz. cream cheese
4 cups hot rice

Pepper, but do not salt, chicken breasts. Wrap slice of bacon around each half of chicken breast. Place layer of dried beef in bottom of baking dish. Arrange bacon-wrapped chicken on beef slices. Cover with mixture of chicken soup, sour cream and cream cheese. Cover pan tightly with foil. Place in oven for 2 hours. When tender, remove foil and let brown slightly. Serve on bed of hot rice.

Mrs. Jerry McGilvray (Jane)

ENTREES
Chicken

Poulet de Broccoli

350 degrees
Casserole dish
Yield: 6-8 servings

6-8 chicken breasts, boiled,
  skinned and deboned (may
  use thighs) cut into chunks
2 pkgs. frozen broccoli
  spears (fresh if you prefer)
2 (10¾-oz.) cans cream of
  chicken soup
1 cup mayonnaise
1 tsp. lemon juice
½ tsp. curry powder
1¼ cups sharp Cheddar
  cheese
1¼ cups soft bread cubes
2 Tbs. butter, melted

Cook chicken and broccoli until tender. Layer in a buttered casserole and cover with sauce made from soup, mayonnaise, lemon juice and curry powder. Cover sauce with cheese and bread cubes that have been mixed in butter. Bake 30 minutes at 350 degrees.

Mrs. Roger von Rosenberg (Robin)

Variation: Generously sprinkle tarragon leaves across the top before baking.

Mrs. Rondel Davidson (Judy)

Chicken-Broccoli Casserole

375 degrees
1½ quart casserole
Yield: 6 servings

1 (10¾-oz.) can cream of
  chicken soup
½ cup mayonnaise
½ tsp. lemon juice
¼ cup butter, melted
1 pkg. frozen broccoli,
  partially cooked and
  drained
2 cups cooked chicken,
  sliced
1 cup bread crumbs

Combine soup, mayonnaise, lemon juice and melted butter until smooth. Place broccoli in casserole. Add chicken and pour sauce on top. Sprinkle with bread crumbs. Bake in 375 degree oven for 15-20 minutes.

Mrs. Margaret Colley

Chinese Chicken

Wok
Yield: 4-6 servings

1 Tbs. peanut oil
8 oz. chicken, diced, raw
4 oz. water chestnuts, diced
4 oz. cabbage, diced
1½ Tbs. soy sauce
1 tsp. sugar
2 Tbs. dry white wine
rice or Chinese noodles

Marinade:
1½ Tbs. soy sauce
1 tsp. sugar
1 Tbs. dry white wine
1 Tbs. cornstarch

Variations:
bean sprouts,
   celery,
   red pepper, or
   green pepper may be
   substitutes for the
   vegetables

Marinate the chicken for at least 30 minutes before cooking. Preheat the wok to a very high temperature, put oil in the wok, then add the chicken immediately. Be sure to heat the wok before adding the oil, or your food will stick to the wok. Stir-fry the chicken until half done. Add the water chestnuts, cabbage, and other seasonings and continue cooking until the chicken is done. Serve with rice or crispy Chinese noodles.

Important note:
Your wok must be very dry and clean. A very short period of time, from 2-3 minutes, is all that is needed for good Chinese stir-frying in a wok. Since you won't have time to measure all the seasonings when you want to add them, they must all be ready beforehand. Using small containers, measure out the oil, soy sauce, sugar, and wine you will use while cooking. Then place them in easy reach in order of use. Add the seasonings separately with an interval of at least five seconds between them, stirring constantly. Bring the food from all directions to the center of the wok so that it will be evenly blended and cooked.

Mrs. Dan Seitz, Jr. (Amy)

ENTREES
Chicken

Cheesy Chicken

350 degrees
Small casserole, greased
Yield: 4 servings

4 chicken breasts, boned and
  skinned
Monterrey Jack cheese,
  sliced
cracker crumbs
1 Tbs. flour
salt and pepper to taste
3 Tbs. Parmesan cheese
1 egg, beaten
3 Tbs. water
parsley flakes
2 Tbs. butter

Put slice of cheese in each breast; fold over. Roll breast in mixture of crackers, flour, salt and pepper. Dip in egg, Parmesan, parsley and water mixture. Sauté in butter until brown, place in greased baking dish and bake 40 minutes at 350 degrees.

Mrs. Jerry Leadbetter (Tonii)

Chicken Cheesy Strata

325 degrees
8 x 8 pan
Yield: 3-4 servings

6 slices day old bread
4 oz. sharp Cheddar cheese,
  grated
1½ cups cooked chicken,
  diced
1 (10¾-oz.) can cream of
  chicken soup
2 eggs, beaten
1 cup milk
2 Tbs. onion, chopped
¼ cup bread crumbs
2 Tbs. butter, melted
¼ tsp. paprika

Trim crust from bread slices; cut in half diagonally. Put half of the bread in 8 x 8 pan. Sprinkle with cheese. Top with chicken. Add rest of bread. Combine soup and eggs, stir in milk and onion. Spoon the soup mixture over the bread. Cover and chill 6-24 hours. Before serving, combine crumbs, butter and paprika. Sprinkle over casserole. Bake at 325 degrees for 1-1¼ hours. Let set 10 minutes before serving.

Mrs. Walt Mielcarek (Betty)

240

Chicken Crepes

325 degrees
9 x 13 casserole
Yield: 6 servings
Freezes

Crepes:
1 cup cold water
1 cup cold milk
4 eggs
½ tsp. salt
2 cups flour, sifted
4 Tbs. butter, melted

Put water, milk, eggs, and salt into a blender jar. Add the flour, then the butter. Cover and blend at top speed for 1 minute. If bits of flour adhere to sides of jar, dislodge with a rubber scraper and blend for 2 to 3 seconds more. Cover and refrigerate for at least 2 hours. (The batter should be a very light cream, just thick enough to coat a wooden spoon. If, after the first crepe is made, the batter seems to be heavy, beat in a bit of water, a spoonful at a time. Your cooked crepe should be about 1/16 inch thick.) Brush the crepe pan or small iron skillet lightly with oil. Set over moderately high heat until pan is beginning to smoke. Quickly tilt the pan in all directions to run the batter over the bottom of the pan in a thin layer. Pour off any excess batter. Return the pan to the heat for 1 minute. Then flip the crepe to the other side and brown lightly for about ½ minute. Slide crepe onto a plate and begin the operation again.

Chicken Filling:
1 stewing chicken (3-4 lbs.)
1¼ lbs. Swiss cheese, grated
1 jalepeño pepper, seeded
 and chopped
1 tsp. salt
1 tsp. pepper
1 pint whipping cream

Cook chicken, bone and dice. Combine chicken, all but 1 cup of the grated cheese, jalepeños, salt, and pepper. Mix well. Place a large spoonful of the mixture on each crepe, then roll up. Arrange filled, rolled crepes in shallow baking dish (9 x 13) and top with remaining cheese. Pour cream over all. Cook in 325 degree oven about 20-30 minutes, or until thoroughly heated. If frozen, thaw out before cooking.

Mrs. Jerry McGilvray (Jane)

Cumin Baked Chicken

350 degrees
3 quart casserole
Yield: 6 servings ·

2½-3 lbs. chicken, cut-up
¼ cup flour
¼ tsp. salt
⅛ tsp. pepper
2 tsp. salad oil
1 (10¾-oz.) can cream of
chicken soup
1 (10¾-oz.) can cream of
celery soup
1 (16-oz.) pint sour cream
1 Tbs. parsley flakes
2 tsp. cumin seed (or ground)

Dredge chicken in mixture of flour, salt and pepper. Sauté in hot oil until golden on all sides. Transfer to 3 quart casserole. Combine soups, sour cream, parsley and cumin. Pour over chicken. Cover and bake in 350 degree oven for 45-60 minutes or until tender.

The sauce is great over rice.

Mrs. Dan Seitz (Amy)

Easy Chicken Dish

400 degrees
Large baking dish
Yield: 6-8 servings

1½ cups rice, uncooked
1 (10¾-oz.) can cream of
celery soup
1 (10¾-oz.) can cream of
mushroom soup
1 (10¾-oz.) can cream of
chicken soup
1½ soup cans of milk
1 fryer, cut up
salt

Stir rice and soups together with milk. Pour into large baking dish. Place salted pieces of chicken on top. Bake in 400 degree oven for at least 1¼ hours. Test chicken before serving to be sure it is tender. This dish may be held at warm in the oven before serving.

Mrs. Robert Crane (Baudelia)

Allow roasted meat or fowl to stand at room temperature for about 15 minutes before carving.

Easy Quick Chicken Curry

Yield: 8 servings

2 cups onion, chopped
2 tsp. curry powder
4 Tbs. butter
2 (10¾-oz.) cans cream of
   chicken soup
1½-2 soup cans milk,
   depending on thickness
   desired
4 cups cooked chicken,
   chopped
4 cups sour cream
noodles or rice

Simmer onion, curry and butter until onion is clear. Add soup and milk. Stir over low heat until smooth. Add chicken and sour cream. Heat, but do not boil. Serve over noodles or rice.

Mrs. Charles E. Thompson, Jr. (Sally)

Chicken Jambalaya

Large skillet
Yield: 8 servings
Freezes

1 lb. seasoned *hot* Jimmy
   Dean sausage
4 cups cooked chicken, diced
2 cups ham, diced
1 cup green onions, chopped
1½ cups green pepper,
   chopped
2 cloves garlic, minced
4 scant cups chicken stock
1½ tsp. salt
½ tsp. pepper
½ tsp. Tabasco
½ tsp. thyme
1½ cups raw rice

Brown sausage in large skillet. Add chicken and ham and brown additional 5 minutes. Remove meat from skillet, draining off excess fat. Cook onions, peppers and garlic in same skillet until tender. Add remaining ingredients. Pour rice evenly over mixture. Then spread meat over rice and cover. Cook at lowest heat for approximately 30-40 minutes or until rice is done.

Mrs. Paul Moxley (Karen)

Chicken and Dumplings

Yield: 6-8 servings

1 large fryer or hen, boiled

Boil hen until tender; remove and debone, return to broth.

Dumplings:
3 cups flour
½ tsp. baking powder
1 tsp. salt
1¼ cups hot water
2 tsp. corn oil

Sift the dry ingredients together and add the hot water and oil to them. Mix together, but DO NOT OVERMIX. Roll out on a floured board about ⅛ inch thick (the thinner the better). Cut into strips and cut strips into several pieces. Drop into hot boiling chicken and broth and cook for 20 minutes.

Mrs. Jim Corcoran (Pam)

Chicken 'n Dumplings

Large Dutch oven
Yield: 6-8 servings

1 large hen or 3 lb. fryer
salt and pepper to taste

Cook chicken in enough water to cover until tender. Remove and debone. Reserve chicken broth.

Dumplings:
2 cups flour
1¼ tsp. salt
½ tsp. pepper
2 Tbs. butter
chicken broth
½ cup milk

Sift together flour, salt and pepper. Add enough chicken broth to form soft dough. Roll out on well-floured board to pie dough thickness. Cut in strips. Add 2 Tbs. butter to remaining broth. Bring to boiling and add ½ of the dumplings. Cover and cook 5 minutes. Don't peek! Repeat. Remove lid and continue cooking dumplings for 10-15 minutes. Check for doneness. Add chicken and milk and heat thoroughly.

Mrs. Bill Scurlock (Mary)

Chicken Kiev

Yield: 12 servings

1 cup butter, softened
2 Tbs. parsley, chopped
1 tsp. rosemary
¾ tsp. salt
⅛ tsp. pepper

Combine butter and seasonings in a small bowl; blend thoroughly. Shape butter mixture into 2 sticks; cover and put in freezer for 45 minutes or until firm.

6 whole chicken breasts,
  split, boned, and skinned
¾ cup all-purpose flour
3 eggs, well-beaten
1½-2 cups bread crumbs

Place each half of breast on a sheet of wax paper; flatten to ¼-inch thickness using meat mallet or rolling pin. Cut each stick of butter mixture into 6 parts; place a pat in center of each half of breast. Fold long side of chicken over butter; fold ends over and secure with toothpick. Dredge each piece of chicken in flour, dip in egg and coat with bread crumbs. Cover and refrigerate about 1 hour.

salad oil
rice

Fry chicken in heated salad oil. Cook 5 minutes on each side or until browned, turning with tongs. Place in warm oven until all chicken is browned. Serve over warm rice.

Mrs. Ken Forrester (Phoebe)

Lusicous Lemon Chicken

Large skillet
Yield: 5-6 servings

2 lbs. chicken pieces
2 Tbs. shortening
1 cup cream of chicken soup
½ tsp. salt
2 Tbs. lemon juice
½ tsp. tarragon leaves,
  crushed
dash of pepper
lemon slices

In skillet, brown chicken, remove from pan, pour off fat and combine remaining ingredients, except lemon slices. Return chicken to skillet, cover, cook over low heat 45 minutes or until tender. Garnish with lemon slices.

Mrs. Larry Dooley (Jacqui)

ENTREES
Chicken

Chicken Mornay

Yield: 1½ quarts sauce

Sauce:
¼ lb. butter
1 cup flour
4 cups milk
2 lbs. Velveeta cheese, cut in
  small pieces
1 can beer

Melt butter, add flour and cook until bubbly. Add milk and cook until smooth. Boil 1 minute. Beat the cut up cheese into hot cream sauce with an electric beater. Beat about 15 minutes, the longer the better. Add beer a little at a time to obtain desired consistency.

canned asparagus spears,
  4-5 per serving
baked chicken or turkey,
  sliced
sauce

Arrange 4 to 5 asparagus side by side. Top with 2 to 3 slices baked chicken or turkey. Top with Mornay Sauce (completely covering meat). Put under broiler until sauce is lightly browned.

Sauce may be kept for several days. It is good on any desired fish, meat, or vegetable.

Mrs. Jim Miller (Terry)

Oriental Chicken

350 degrees
Saucepan and baking pan
Yield: 6-8 servings

⅔ cup soy sauce
½ cup sherry
6 Tbs. sugar
3 Tbs. powdered ginger
4 Tbs. prepared horseradish
1 medium onion, chopped
12-20 pieces of chicken

Cook first 6 ingredients in saucepan over low heat for 5 minutes. Brush the chicken pieces with the mixture and let stand at least 15 minutes. (It is much better if you do this early in the day and put the basted chicken into the refrigerator until ready to cook.) Bake in oven for about 45 minutes and baste once or twice. This can be prepared by broiling, but it takes careful watching.

Mrs. Robert Crane (Baudelia)

Not Hard, Not Fattening
Not Expensive, Not Bad Chicken

350 degrees
Baking dish

chicken pieces
seasonings
flour
boiling water seasoned with
 chicken stock base or
 bouillon cubes
paprika

Select your favorite pieces of chicken, (cook more than you need because it is good the next day cold). Sprinkle on both sides with favorite seasoning— lemon pepper and garlic salt or curry and tarragon or just salt and pepper. Sprinkle a little flour in the bottom of as many pans as you need and put the chicken in, skin side down. Pour in boiling water that has been seasoned with chicken stock base or bouillon cubes until the chicken pieces are almost covered. Bake at 350 degrees for 45 minutes. Turn pieces over, sprinkle with paprika, and bake another 30-45 minutes.

This is tender enough for the baby, good enough for the daddy, low calories for the dieters, and will wait in a warm oven till the last straggler comes home!

Chicken Parisienne

350 degrees
11 x 7 x 1½ baking dish
Yield: 6 servings

6 medium chicken breasts
1 cup cream of mushroom
 soup
3 oz. (⅔ cup) broiled
 mushroom crowns
1 cup sour cream
½ cup cooking sherry
paprika

Place chicken breasts, skin side up, in a 11 x 7 x 1½ baking dish. Blend remaining ingredients including mushroom liquid and pour over chicken. Sprinkle with paprika. Bake at 350 degrees for 1¼ hours, uncovered, or until tender. Serve with wild rice.

Mrs. Ed Wallace (Janet)

247

Chicken Pancakes

1 small skillet
1 large skillet
Yield: 10 servings

1 cup pancake mix
2 eggs, beaten until light
1 cup milk
1 Tbs. brandy
2 Tbs. butter, melted
2 Tbs. vegetable oil

In mixing bowl, combine pancake mix and well-beaten eggs. Add milk, brandy and butter. Beat until smooth. Melt 1 Tbs. oil in a 6-inch skillet. When it begins to bubble, pour in 2 Tbs. batter and tilt pan to spread evenly. When light brown, turn to cook other side. Repeat. The pancakes should be about 5-inches in diameter.

Chicken filling:
½ cup butter
⅓ cup flour
3 cups milk
1½ tsp. salt
¼ tsp. pepper
2 Tbs. parsley, chopped
2 cups chicken, cooked and minced
1 small can mushrooms
½ cup Swiss cheese, shredded
pinch cayenne pepper
2 Tbs. instant cream

Melt butter in pan over moderate heat. Stir in flour. Gradually add milk and cook until smooth and thick, stirring constantly. Add seasonings. Cook 5 minutes. Set aside 1 cup sauce. To remaining sauce, add parsley, chicken and mushrooms. To the reserved sauce, add Swiss cheese and cayenne pepper. Cook until cheese melts. Then add instant cream. Fill each pancake with chicken mixture and place in large shallow baking pan. Pour cheese sauce on top. Cook under broiler until sauce is brown and bubbly—about 3 minutes.

Mrs. Wilfred Dean (Maxine)

An old hen will taste like a spring chicken if soaked in vinegar for several hours before cooking.

Chicken Paprika

350 degrees
Dutch oven
Yield: 12-16 servings

1 medium onion, chopped
½ stick butter or margarine
salt and pepper
2 Tbs. paprika
2 cups chicken broth
12-16 chicken breasts or
    thighs
2 Tbs. cornstarch
1 cup sour cream
hot cooked rice

Sauté onion in butter. Add salt and pepper to taste. Add paprika and broth (or water). Bring to boil and add chicken. Bring to a rolling boil and place in a dutch oven and bake for 1½ hours at 350 degrees. Remove the chicken from the broth and stir in the cornstarch. After broth thickens add the sour cream. Bring to a rolling boil and remove from heat. Place chicken on rice and pour sauce over or serve rice separately.

Mrs. Robert Crane (Baudelia)

Plantation Chicken

325 degrees
1½ quart baking dish
Yield: 4 servings

1 cup celery, diced
1 onion, chopped
2 Tbs. green pepper, diced
2 Tbs. butter
5 Tbs. flour
2½ cups milk
1 (10¾-oz.) can mushroom
    soup
2 cups diced chicken, cooked
    and deboned
2 cups ham, diced
2 Tbs. pimientos
1 cup dry bread or cracker
    crumbs
½ cup Cheddar cheese,
    grated

Boil celery in separate pan until tender; drain. In skillet, sauté onion and green pepper in butter. Add flour and stir until smooth. Add milk, soup, chicken, ham and drained celery and pimientos. Cover with crumbs and cheese. Bake until brown at 325 degrees.

Mrs. Ben Bilbrey (Lucille)

ENTREES
Chicken

Sunday Chicken Pie

450 degrees
Large, deep baking dish
Yield: 8-10 servings

1 large chicken, cut in pieces
water
salt
1-2 (10¾-oz.) cans chicken
  soup
flour
butter
salt and pepper
rich biscuit dough

Cut chicken, as for frying. Cover well with water, add salt and simmer until tender. Remove skin and separate meat from the bones but DO NOT cut up fine. Leave it in pieces just as it comes from the framework. Cool the broth and extend it by adding chicken soup as needed for plenty of gravy. Skim all grease from the top of the cooled broth before continuing. Now cook a thickening mixture of flour and butter (6 Tbs. to 1 quart of liquid). Reheat broth and when warm, add the thickening gradually and cautiously, stirring until thick enough. Season with salt and pepper to taste. Put chicken portions back into the hot gravy and be sure to keep it hot. Make rich biscuit dough. Roll the dough out lightly into a shell about ½ inch thick. Put hot chicken and gravy into a casserole, cover with the crust, fitting carefully around the edges and slitting the top. Bake in oven, 450 degrees until crust is brown and done.

Mrs. Billy Simpson (Ginger)

A slightly frozen chicken will skin and bone more easily.

Easy Hawaiian Chicken

Large skillet
Yield: 4 servings

1 chicken, cut up
chicken seasoning (to taste)
1 bell pepper, chopped
1 (20-oz.) can pineapple
  chunks (canned in own
  juice)
1 cup fresh mushrooms,
  sliced, or 1 jar mushrooms,
  sliced
½-1 cup fruit juice (optional)
  orange, apple or pineapple
rice

Liberally season chicken pieces with chicken seasoning. In a large non-stick skillet, slowly brown chicken very well on all sides. When well browned, pour off all grease that cooks out of chicken. Add bell pepper, pineapple, and mushrooms. Simmer for 1 to 1½ hours. As it is cooking, add fruit juice as necessary to prevent drying out. Serve over rice.

Mrs. Jan Klinck (Sally)

Chicken Parmesan

350 degrees
2-3 quart pyrex dish
Yield: 6-8 servings

2 lbs. chicken breasts,
  deboned and halved
2 medium eggs, beaten
¾ cups Italian seasoned
  bread crumbs
8 oz. Mozzarella cheese,
  shredded
¼-½ cup grated Parmesan
  cheese
1 (16-oz.) jar Ragu Italian
  cooking sauce

Dip chicken in eggs and bread crumbs. Brown in oil. Layer chicken in 2-3 quart pyrex dish. Sprinkle with Mozzarella and one-half of Parmesan cheese. Pour Ragu Sauce over chicken. Sprinkle with remaining Parmesan cheese. Bake at 350 degrees uncovered for about 30 minutes or until bubbly.

Mrs. Stanley Marcus (Marsha)
Mrs. Larry Fallek (Patty)

Chicken and Rice Casserole

350 degrees
8 x 8 casserole
Yield: 4 servings

flour for dredging
2½ lb. fryer, cut up
¾ cup uncooked rice (not minute)
salt and pepper to taste
1 (3-oz.) can mushrooms, chopped
1 Tbs. onion, grated
2 chicken bouillon cubes, dissolved in 2½ cups hot water
½ stick margarine

Flour and brown chicken in small amount of oil. Place rice and seasonings in bottom of greased casserole. Add mushrooms, juice and onion. Place chicken pieces on top and pour bouillon over all. Dot with margarine. Cover with foil. Bake 1 hour at 350 degrees.

Mrs. Allen Beakey (Jane)

Sherried Chicken

350 degrees
Dutch oven
Yield: 3 servings

3 whole chicken breasts, halved
seasoned salt as needed
3-4 Tbs. butter
½ cup sherry
1 (4-oz.) can button mushrooms
1 pkg. chicken gravy mix
1 cup sour cream

Lightly sprinkle chicken with seasoned salt. Brown in butter in Dutch oven. Add sherry and liquid from can of mushrooms. Cover and bake in 350 degree oven 45 minutes to 1 hour. Remove chicken to serving platter. Measure pan juices and add water, if necessary, to make 1¼ cups liquid. Carefully blend liquid and chicken gravy mix in Dutch oven. Bring to a boil, reduce heat and simmer uncovered 5 minutes, stirring continuously. Blend in sour cream and add button mushrooms. When sauce is smooth and hot, pour over chicken breasts. Serve with fluffy rice or mashed potatoes.

Mrs. James Humphrey (Jane Ellen)

Chicken and Wild Rice

350 degrees
Large casserole
Yield: 8 servings

2 cups cooked chicken, diced
1 pkg. Uncle Ben's Long
  Grain and Wild Rice mix,
  cooked according to
  directions
1 (1-lb.) can French cut green
  beans, do not drain
1 can water chestnuts,
  drained and sliced
1 (10¾-oz.) can cream of
  celery soup
1 (small) jar pimientos
2 Tbs. onions, chopped
½ cup mayonnaise
½ cup mushrooms (optional)

Mix all ingredients together in large casserole. Heat in a 350 degree oven for
about 20-30 minutes.

*May be mixed a day ahead and refriger-
ated. Heat longer if refrigerated.*

Mrs. Jack Hart (Darlene)
Mrs. Joe Friend (Pam)

Hot Chicken Salad

350 degrees
Large casserole
Yield: 6-8 servings

3 lb. fryer, cooked and
  deboned
1 cup celery, chopped
1 Tbs. onion, chopped
3 boiled eggs, chopped or
  sliced
1 cup Miracle Whip
1 (10¾-oz.) can cream of
  chicken soup
1 (small) pkg. slivered
  almonds
1 cup raisins (optional)
1 cup potato chips, crushed

Mix ingredients together except chips.
Place in casserole and top with crushed
potato chips. Bake 45 minutes at 350
degrees.

Mrs. Cameron Henry (Kathryn)

Sweet 'n Sour Chicken

Very large skillet
Yield: 6-8 servings

2 lbs. chicken, boned and
  skinned
chicken seasoning* (to taste)
1 tsp. fresh ginger, finely
  chopped
3-4 cloves of garlic
3 carrots, sliced
1 (8-oz.) can water chestnuts,
  drained and sliced
½ medium onion, cut up
1 medium bell pepper,
  chopped
1½ cups fresh mushrooms,
  sliced
1 (20-oz.) can pineapple
  chunks in natural
  juice—DO NOT DRAIN
1 large orange, sectioned
  without membrane or 1 can
  mandarin oranges
  (optional)
½-1 cup fruit juice (apple,
  orange or pineapple)
1 Tbs. vinegar
1-1½ Tbs. soy sauce
1 Tbs. sugar (optional)
2 Tbs. cornstarch
2 Tbs. water
rice

Cut chicken into bite-sized pieces and season liberally with chicken seasoning.* In a VERY LARGE non-stick skillet, slowly brown the chicken pieces well on all sides. Remove chicken from pan and set aside. Cook ginger and garlic in juices left from browning the chicken. Add the next 7 ingredients, one at a time in the order listed. With each addition, add enough fruit juice to keep pan from drying out, and cook until crisp-tender. Carrots may take from 5 to 10 minutes, others much less. Add vinegar, soy sauce and sugar. Stir well. Dissolve cornstarch in water and add just enough to thicken mixture. Add chicken and heat through. Serve with rice.

*Use any seasoning you prefer with chicken. Example: Cavender's Greek seasoning or mixture of garlic salt, pepper, monosodium glutamate, oregano, rosemary, parsley and thyme.

Mrs. Jan Klinck (Sally)

Our Favorite Chicken Spaghetti

Large saucepan
Yield: 8-10 servings

1 qt. or more chicken broth
1 (12-oz.) pkg. spaghetti
2 cups cooked chicken,
   chopped in small pieces
1 (14-oz.) can tomatoes
1 (10-oz.) can tomatoes and
   chiles
pimiento
salt
2 cups Old English Cheese,
   grated

Cook spaghetti in broth until tender. Add all ingredients except cheese. Simmer until thick. Place in serving bowl and sprinkle with 2 cups grated cheese.

Mrs. Hollis Fritts (Gerrie)

Chicken Tetrazzini

350 degrees
2 casseroles
Yield: 4-6 servings
Freezes

1 large chicken
4 cups water
½ stick margarine
1 (5-oz.) pkg. vermicelli
1 cup celery, chopped fine
1 cup onion, chopped fine
1 cup cheese, grated (save
   some for topping)
2 (10¾-oz.) cans cream of
   chicken soup
dash of garlic salt

Boil chicken; bone and cut into small pieces. Return chicken to stock adding margarine and vermicelli and cook until tender. Cook, celery and onion in oil until tender, then add to broth. Add cheese, soup and garlic salt. Put into 2 casseroles. Sprinkle cheese on top and bake for 50 minutes.

Mrs. Phillip Webb (Laverne)

ENTREES
Chicken/Pork

Chicken Soupreme

400 degrees
2 (13 x 9 x 2) baking dishes
Yield: 10 servings

5 lbs. chicken parts
½ cup flour
1 tsp. paprika
½ tsp. salt
⅛ tsp. pepper
½ cup butter, melted
3 (10¾-oz.) cans cream of
   mushroom or cream of
   chicken soup (or a mixture
   of both)
½ cup water

Dust the chicken parts with a mixture of the flour, paprika, salt and pepper. Put in a single layer (skin side down) in baking dishes (13 x 9 x 2). Dribble melted butter over chicken. Bake in hot oven, 400 degrees for 20 minutes. Turn chicken and bake 20 minutes longer. Stir the soups together with the water until smooth. Pour over the chicken and bake 20 minutes longer or until tender.

Mrs. F. H. Mangum (Maree)

Jambalaya

Large kettle
Yield: 8 servings

1 fryer, about 2½ lbs.
2 cups water
3 tsp. salt
¼ tsp. pepper
1 bay leaf
2 large onions, chopped
1 large clove garlic, crushed
¼ cup butter or margarine
1 lb. cooked ham, cubed
1 (1-lb. 12-oz.) can whole
   tomatoes
1 large green pepper,
   chopped
½ tsp. thyme, crumbled
¼ tsp. cayenne
1 cup uncooked rice

Place chicken in large kettle, add water, salt, pepper and bay leaf. Bring to boil, reduce heat and simmer 45 minutes or until tender. Remove chicken from broth, reserve broth. When cool enough to handle, bone chicken and cut into cubes. Pour broth into 2 cup measure. Add water if necessary to make 2 cups. Remove bay leaf. Sauté onions and garlic in butter in kettle. Add ham, tomatoes, green pepper, thyme, cayenne, chicken and reserved broth. Heat to boiling and add rice. Cover and simmer 12-15 minutes, until rice is tender. Serve in large bowls. Sprinkle with chopped parsley.

Mrs. Ivan Kuhl (Ruth)

Carbonara

4 slices of bacon
¼ lb. cooked ham, or more if
  desired
1½ Tbs. butter or margarine
1½ Tbs. olive oil
1 (8-oz.) pkg. thin spaghetti,
  cooked and drained
  according to pkg.
  instructions
½ cup Parmesan cheese,
  grated
2 eggs, slightly beaten
3 Tbs. parsley, chopped

Cut bacon and ham in julienne strips. Brown bacon pieces lightly in large skillet; drain on paper towels; pour off fat in skillet. Sauté ham slowly in butter or margarine and olive oil for 4-5 minutes. Remove from heat; add hot spaghetti, reserved bacon, cheese, eggs, and parsley. Toss quickly to coat spaghetti evenly and thoroughly. Serve immediately.

Mrs. Joe Friend (Pam)

Hawaiian Ham

2 cups ham, cubed or strips
1 cup pineapple tidbits
2 Tbs. brown sugar
1½ Tbs. cornstarch
1 tsp. Accent
¾ tsp. vinegar
2 tsp. prepared mustard
¾ cup water
1 green pepper, cut in strips
salt to taste

In a skillet, brown ham in small amount of hot fat. Drain pineapple, reserving syrup. Mix next five ingredients. Stir in syrup and water, mixing well. Add this mixture to the ham in skillet. Cook and stir until mixture thickens; cover and simmer for ten minutes. Add pineapple and green pepper. Simmer 5-8 minutes, and salt to taste. Serve with rice.

Mrs. J. R. Schroeder (Molly)

To prevent fat from splattering when frying, sprinkle a small amount of salt over oil before adding meat.

ENTREES
Pork

Ham Loaf

350 degrees
Loaf pan
Yield: 6-8 servings

1 lb. ground fresh pork
1 lb. ground smoked ham
2 eggs
1 cup cracker crumbs
½ cup milk

Sauce:
¾ cup brown sugar
½ cup mustard
¼ cup vinegar
½ cup water

Mix meats, eggs, crumbs and milk thoroughly. Form into a loaf pan and bake 1½ hours at 350 degrees. Baste frequently with sauce.

Mrs. Tim Johnstone (Mel)

Corn Stuffed Pork Chops

325 degrees
9 x 15 x 2 baking dish
Yield: 8 servings

8 (1-inch) thick pork loin
   chops, with pockets
1 cup celery, chopped
½ cup onions, chopped
4 Tbs. butter
4 cups soft bread crumbs
1 (7-oz.) can whole kernel
   corn, drained
½ tsp. salt
½ tsp. sage
dash pepper
paprika (optional)

Season chops with salt and pepper. Cook celery and onion in butter until tender, but not brown. Combine vegetables and remaining ingredients. Spoon into each chop which has been split to form a pocket. Cover and bake at 325 degrees for 45 minutes. Uncover and bake 30 minutes more. Sprinkle with paprika if desired.

Mrs. Dan Seitz (Amy)

Pork Chops with Amber Rice

350 degrees
12 x 10 x 2 baking dish
Yield: 6 servings

6 pork chops
1⅓ cups rice
1 cup orange juice
1 (10¾-oz.) can chicken-rice
   soup

Brown pork chops. In baking dish, spread rice evenly. Arrange browned pork chops on top and cover with liquids. Cover. Bake at 350 degrees for 45 minutes. Uncover and continue baking for 10 minutes.

Mrs. Hulon Webb (Carole)

Egg Fu Yung with Mushroom Sauce

Skillet
Yield: 12 medium-sized
pancakes

1 pkg. Fried Rice-A-Roni,
   prepared according to
   directions
6 eggs
1 Tbs. soy sauce
1 (16-oz.) can bean sprouts
½ cup green onion, sliced
1 cup ham or shrimp, cubed

Prepare Rice-A-Roni. Allow to cool while beating eggs. Drain bean sprouts. Add all ingredients together. Drop mixture by large spoonfuls in skillet which has been generously greased. Brown on each side.

Mushroom sauce:
1 cup fresh mushrooms or 1
   small can
2 Tbs. flour
2 Tbs. soy sauce
1½ cups water

Sauté 1 cup mushrooms. Set aside. Combine flour, soy sauce, and water. Cook until thick. Add mushrooms to gravy. Serve over Egg Fu Yung.

Mrs. Leroy Lewin (Hilda)

ENTREES
Misc.

Egg Rolls

Wok or large skillet
Yield: 20-24 rolls

1 can water chestnuts,
  drained
1 cup fresh mushrooms
2 carrots
¼ lb. green beans or pea
  pods
2 cups Chinese cabbage
2 stalks celery
½ lb. bean sprouts
¼ cup onion
2 Tbs. peanut oil
1 lb. ground beef
3-4 chicken breasts
1 clove garlic, finely chopped
2 tsp. sugar
1 Tbs. cornstarch
2 Tbs. sherry
2 Tbs. soy sauce
salt
¼ tsp. ginger root, grated
1 egg, beaten
prepared egg roll skins
  (1 pkg.)
paste made with flour and
  water
peanut oil for frying

Chop vegetables into small, even-sized chunks. Put peanut oil in wok or large skillet and brown ground meat at highest heat. Add chicken and vegetables plus garlic. Cook down, about 5 minutes, maybe more. Add sugar, cornstarch, sherry, soy sauce, salt and ginger root. Toss lightly. Take off heat and add egg and mix. Fill egg roll skins and seal with paste of flour and water. Deep fry egg rolls in hot peanut oil till brown. Serve immediately.

Nothing has to be exact. Use leftovers or whatever is in the refrigerator.

Best if made the day before—but they stick easily, so roll in flour and store on floured cookie sheet in refrigerator.

continued . . .

Sweet and Sour Sauce:

½ cup packed brown sugar
1 Tbs. cornstarch
⅓ cup wine vinegar
⅓ cup chicken broth
¼ cup green pepper,
   chopped
2 Tbs. pimiento, chopped
1 Tbs. soy sauce
¼ tsp. garlic powder
¼ tsp. ground ginger

Mix all ingredients and heat until boiling and thickened.

Mustard Sauce:

¼ cup boiling water
¼ cup dry mustard
2 tsp. cooking oil
½ tsp. salt

Pour water into mixture of other ingredients. Stir.

Mrs. Jim Corcoran (Pam)

Lamb and Rice Casserole

350 degrees
Large casserole
Yield: 6 servings

2 cups canned beef broth
1 cup canned tomatoes
1 onion, chopped
2 cups leftover lamb, diced
1 tsp. salt
¼ tsp. pepper
1 Tbs. margarine
½ cup uncooked rice
2 Tbs. Worcestershire sauce

Combine broth, tomatoes, onion, lamb, salt and pepper in casserole. Place in a 350 degree oven for 10 minutes. Melt margarine in skillet and add rice. Brown lightly. Combine rice and Worcestershire sauce with meat mixture. Continue baking for 30 minutes or until rice is tender. Serve directly from casserole.

Mrs. Morgan Talbot (Jane)

ENTREES
Misc.

Veal with Wine

Large skillet
Yield: 8 servings

flour for dredging
salt and pepper
8 veal cutlets, pounded flat
1 egg, beaten
8 Tbs. unsalted butter
1 cup dry white wine
juice of 2 lemons

Salt, pepper and dredge in flour the veal cutlets. Dip the floured veal into a beaten egg and place the meat directly into the pan of butter; sauté 3 minutes on each side. Remove the cutlets to a warm platter. Add a little more butter (about 1 Tbs.) to the pan with the wine and lemon juice. Stir and simmer for about 3 minutes. Pour mixture over cutlets and serve immediately.

Mrs. Joe Weir (Lupe)

Paella

350 degrees
Dutch oven
Yield: 8 servings
Freezes

⅓ cup salad oil
2 whole split chicken breasts
4 chicken legs
1 cup onion, chopped
2 cloves garlic, crushed
2 (14-oz.) cans chicken broth
1 tsp. white pepper
3½ tsp. salt
½ tsp. paprika
½-1 tsp. saffron
2 cups raw regular rice
1 (16-oz.) can tomatoes
3 links sausage (Polish,
   Spanish or Pepperoni)
1½ lbs. shrimp, deveined
1 (10-oz.) can whole clams
1 (10-oz.) pkg. frozen peas
1 (7-oz.) can artichoke hearts

Put salad oil in Dutch oven and sauté chicken pieces until golden brown on all sides. Remove and set aside. In same oil sauté onion and garlic until golden. Add chicken broth, pepper, salt, paprika and saffron. Bring to a boil. Add rice. Cook covered until about half of the liquid is absorbed. Now add tomatoes, sliced sausage, shrimp and chicken. Simmer, covered for about 30 minutes or until rice is almost dry. Heat clams and cook peas as package directs. Add peas and artichoke hearts to rice mixture and toss. Serve heaped in a large casserole and garnish with clams.

This can be increased for larger crowds and put in enamel covered roaster at 350 degrees just before adding rice and continue recipe. Reheat carefully.

Mrs. Gary Gurwitz (Bailey)

262

Artichoke-Crabmeat Casserole

350 degrees
2 quart casserole
Yield: 6 servings

1 (14-oz.) can artichokes,
  well-drained and quartered
½ cup mayonnaise,
  store-bought
2 cups medium white sauce
4 egg whites, beaten stiff
1 lb. crabmeat, well-drained
Parmesan cheese

Line bottom of 2 quart casserole with artichokes. Mix mayonnaise into white sauce. Gently fold mixture into stiffly beaten egg whites. Next, fold crabmeat into this mixture. Place in casserole and sprinkle generously with Parmesan cheese. Bake at 350 degrees for 30 minutes or until cheese is lightly browned.

Mrs. Gilbert Heartfield (Francesca)

Crab Casserole

350 degrees
1½ quart casserole, buttered
Yield: 8 servings

2 (7-oz.) cans crabmeat
2 Tbs. chives, chopped
2 tsp. lemon juice
8 oz. Velveeta cheese, cubed
3 cups French bread, cubed
3 Tbs. butter, melted
1¾ cups milk
3 eggs, beaten
½ tsp. salt
3 drops pepper sauce
½ tsp. dry mustard
chives for garnish

Toss crabmeat with chives and lemon juice. In buttered casserole, arrange layers of cheese, crab, bread and drizzle with butter. Combine milk, eggs, salt, pepper sauce and mustard. Pour over crab mixture. Cover with foil and refrigerate overnight. Bake uncovered at 350 degrees for 50-60 minutes.

Mrs. Ernie Williams (Ann)

For a fresh-caught flavor, thaw fish in milk.

ENTREES
Seafood

Crabmeat Crepes

400 degrees
2 large rectangular pyrex dishes
Yield: 8 servings
Freezes

Prepare 16 crepes from any basic crepe recipe.

Melt butter in a large skillet. Stir in minced green onion, minced water chestnuts, then crab. Toss lightly and cook a few minutes. Add salt, pepper and garlic powder. Add Vermouth and boil rapidly until liquid is almost evaporated. Scrape into a bowl and set aside.

Filling:
1 stick butter, melted
½ cup green onions, minced
½ cup water chestnuts, minced
2 lbs. fresh lump crabmeat (1 quart)
salt and white pepper to taste
dash garlic powder
½ cup Vermouth

Add Vermouth to the same skillet and boil rapidly until reduced to 2 Tbs. Remove from heat and stir in cornstarch and milk which have been mixed together. Return to low heat and add cream slowly with salt and pepper. Cook several minutes until slightly thickened. Stir in 1½ cups grated cheese and cook until melted and well blended.

Sauce:
⅔ cup Vermouth
¼ cup cornstarch
¼ cup milk
4 cups heavy cream
salt and white pepper to taste
2½ cups (12 - oz.) Swiss cheese, grated—more if desired (divided: 1½ cups and 1 cup)
butter

Blend ½ of the sauce with the crabmeat. Put a large spoonful on each crepe and roll. Place seam side down in buttered dish. This recipe will fill 2 large rectangular pyrex dishes. Spoon remaining sauce over crepes and sprinkle with remaining 1 cup cheese. Dot with butter. Bake 20 minutes at 400 degrees until hot and bubbly.

May be made the day before and refrigerated. Take out 30 minutes before baking.

Mrs. Allen Beakey (Jane)

Crab Eddy

350 degrees
9 x 12 casserole
Yield: 12 servings
Freezes

1 lb. mushrooms, sliced
butter
2 cups mayonnaise
1 cup milk
1 cup cream
2 lbs. backfin crabmeat
(large chunks)
2 Tbs. onion, chopped
2 Tbs. parsley, chopped
4 hard-boiled eggs, chopped
1 pkg. Pepperidge Farm
stuffing

Sauté mushrooms in a bit of butter. Mix mayonnaise, milk and cream together. Mix crab and all ingredients except half of the stuffing, including the mushrooms and the mayonnaise and cream mixture. Put in a 9 x 12 casserole dish and top with remaining half of the stuffing. Dot with butter and bake at 350 degrees for 30 minutes.

Can be frozen before cooking.

Crab and Shrimp Royale

350 degrees
9 x 15 baking dish
Yield: 10-12 servings

1 onion, diced
1 stalk celery, diced
1 small green pepper, diced
½ cup margarine
1 lb. fresh mushrooms, sliced
1 (10¾-oz.) can cream of
mushroom soup
⅓ cup sherry
salt and pepper to taste
1 lb. crabmeat, fresh or
canned
1 lb. cooked shrimp
½ can water chestnuts,
sliced
1 tsp. allspice
1 tsp. tarragon
dash of hot pepper sauce
1 small jar pimientos
bread crumbs

Sauté onion, celery and green pepper in half of margarine until onion is transparent. Stir in mushrooms and cook for several minutes. Pour in soup, sherry, salt and pepper. Add crabmeat, shrimp, and sliced water chestnuts. Cook until heated through. Stir in allspice, tarragon and pepper sauce. Pour in casserole. Dot with pimientos and sprinkle generously with bread crumbs. Melt remaining margarine and pour over bread crumbs. Bake at 350 degrees for 30 minutes.

Mrs. Madonna Johnson

ENTREES
Seafood

Hawaiian Fried Fish

375 degrees
Skillet
Yield: 4 servings

3 pkgs. frozen flounder filets
½ cup soy sauce
½ cup flour
½ cup cornstarch
1 cup milk
1 egg
3 tsp. baking powder
1 tsp. salt
½ tsp. pepper

Cut flounder in small 1½-inch pieces, being careful to eliminate any skin or bones. (You can feel bones along edges.) Marinate in soy sauce for 30 minutes. Combine flour, cornstarch, milk, egg, baking powder, salt and pepper to make a thin batter. Dip fish in batter and fry in 1½ inches of hot cooking oil (375 degrees) until golden and crisp. Drain on brown paper, keeping warm. If desired, serve with pineapple sauce.

Sauce:
1 Tbs. cornstarch
¼ cup water
2 (1-lb. 4½-oz.) cans
    pineapple chunks
¾ cup sugar

To make sauce, dissolve cornstarch in water. Heat pineapple, juice, and sugar in a saucepan. Add cornstarch mixture and cook until thickened.

Mrs. Morgan Talbot (Jane)

Quick Fish-Potato Supper

350 degrees
12 x 7 x 2 baking dish
Yield: 6 servings

1 (12-oz.) pkg. frozen hash
    brown potatoes, thawed
4 eggs, beaten
2 cups milk
1 Tbs. instant minced onion
1¼ tsp. seasoned salt
1 tsp. dried dillweed
⅛ tsp. pepper
4 oz. sharp Cheddar cheese,
    shredded
1 (14-oz.) pkg. frozen fish
    sticks (16 sticks)

Break potatoes up; set aside. In bowl, combine eggs, milk, onion, seasoned salt, dillweed, and pepper. Stir in potatoes and cheese. Turn into 12 x 7 x 2-inch baking dish. Arrange fish sticks atop. Bake in 350 degree oven for 55-60 minutes or until the center is nearly set. Let stand 10 minutes before serving.

Mrs. Cayetano Barrera (Yolanda)

Baked Stuffed Flounder

375 degrees
Large flat pan
Yield: 8 large servings

¼ lb. butter
1 lb. fresh crabmeat (or frozen)
½ lb. raw shrimp, peeled and deveined
1 cup onion, finely chopped
½ cup parsley, snipped
½ cup green onion tops, chopped
1 tsp. lemon juice
¼ tsp. lemon rind, grated
1 lb. button mushrooms or 6 oz. can button mushrooms
2 cups seasoned, fine bread crumbs
2 eggs, beaten
salt, red pepper, black pepper to taste
8 fresh flounder, with good-sized pocket, cut by butcher

Basting:
¼ lb. butter, melted
1 tsp. lemon juice
½ cup dry white wine

Melt butter, add crabmeat and shrimp. Cook over low heat until shrimp are pink. Add vegetables. Cook until onions are transparent and wilted. Add lemon juice and rind. Add mushrooms. Cook about 5 minutes. Remove from heat. Add bread crumbs, beaten eggs and seasonings. Mix thoroughly, but gently. Open flounder pockets and fill cavities generously with stuffing. Arrange on large flat pan and bake uncovered in 375 degree oven. Baste well with the basting sauce of the melted butter, lemon juice and wine. Do not turn flounder. Lower temperature to 300 degrees after 20 minutes. Cook 15-20 minutes longer.

Mrs. Bill Davis (Jean)

ENTREES
Seafood

Seafood Artichoke Bake

375 degrees
2 quart casserole
Yield: 6 servings

6 Tbs. margarine
1 clove garlic, finely chopped
2 Tbs. onion, finely chopped
¼ cup flour
½ tsp. pepper
¾ cup milk
½ lb. sharp Cheddar cheese, grated
⅔ cup white wine
2 (7½-oz.) cans crabmeat
1½ lbs. shrimp, boiled and cleaned
1 (14-oz.) can artichoke hearts
½ lb. fresh mushrooms, sliced
2 Tbs. cornflakes, crushed

In 2 Tbs. margarine, sauté garlic and onion. Remove from heat. Stir in flour, pepper and milk. Bring to a boil, stirring constantly. Remove from heat and add ½ of the cheese. Stir until melted. Add wine. Drain and flake crabmeat. In casserole, combine sauce, crab, shrimp, artichokes, mushrooms and remaining cheese. Mix lightly. Sprinkle with cornflakes and dot with remaining margarine. Bake 30 minutes at 375 degrees.

Mrs. Philip Chaleff (Elsie)

Fisherman's Luck

500 degrees
28-inch length aluminum foil
Yield: 4 servings

½ cup green pepper, chopped
½ cup onion, chopped
2 Tbs. butter
½ cup ketchup
½ tsp. garlic salt
fish fillets (4 servings)
salt and pepper

Cook green pepper and onion in butter until they are tender, but not brown. Add ketchup and garlic salt. Simmer 10-15 minutes. For each person, cut foil and fold it in half. Place 1 serving fish in foil, just off center; sprinkle with salt and pepper. Pour ¼ of the sauce over each serving and seal tightly. Cook over glowing coals or place in shallow pan and bake at 500 degrees for 15-20 minutes.

Excellent and very easy. You may also use hamburger patties or chicken pieces instead of fish.

Mrs. Kenneth Kachtik (Sue)

268

Coquilles Saint Jacques

400 degrees
Baking shells or dish
Yield: 5 appetizers or
4 luncheon servings

7 Tbs. butter
6 shallots or green onions,
   minced
bouquet garni: stalk of
   parsley, bay leaf, good
   pinch thyme
1½ lbs. scallops or shrimp
1 cup dry white wine
½ lb. mushrooms, minced
⅓ cup water
½ tsp. salt
freshly ground pepper
3 Tbs. flour
1 cup heavy cream
2 egg yolks
juice of ½ lemon
good pinch cayenne pepper
Parmesan cheese, grated

Melt 2 Tbs. butter and add shallots or onions, bouquet garni, scallops or shrimp, and enough wine to cover. Simmer only and do not cook further. Drain and reserve the broth. If scallops are used, cut them in half. Melt 2 Tbs. butter in the same saucepan, add mushrooms, water, salt, and several grinds of pepper. Bring to boil and simmer until all liquid is boiled away. Combine with the scallops and set aside. Return broth to saucepan and bring to boil. Reduce liquid to 1 cup. Make a paste of the remaining butter and the flour. Add, bit by bit, to the broth, whipping constantly, and cook until you have a thick sauce. Whip the cream and yolks together. Dribble into the sauce, stirring constantly. Stir in lemon juice and cayenne to taste, bring just to a boil and remove from the heat. Spoon a little sauce into each shell or into baking dish. Add the scallop mixture, dividing it equally. Top with remaining sauce and sprinkle with cheese. Bake 5-10 minutes in 400 degree oven.

Mrs. Gary Gurwitz (Bailey)

Creamy Salmon Soufflé Pie

375 degrees
9-inch pie pan
Yield: 6-8 servings

pastry for 9-inch pie
1 (7¾-oz.) can salmon
1 (6-oz.) pkg. cream cheese
2 Tbs. lemon juice
¼ tsp. salt
½ cup heavy cream
4 eggs, separated

Line a 9-inch pie plate with pastry. Drain salmon, reserving the liquid, and sprinkle salmon chunks over the bottom of the pastry. Combine the cream cheese and lemon juice. Gradually beat in reserved salmon liquid, salt and cream. Beat egg yolks lightly and stir into the cheese mixture. Beat egg whites until stiff, but not dry, and fold gently but thoroughly into the egg-cheese mixture. Spoon over salmon and bake at 375 degrees for 45 minutes.

Mrs. J. W. Caldwell (Bernice)

Salmon Crunchies

Skillet
Yield: 6 servings

1 egg
1 (15-oz.) can salmon,
  reserve liquid
½ cup flour
1 heaping tsp. baking powder
oil

Add egg to drained salmon, mix well. Add flour and mix thoroughly. Add baking powder to ¼ cup of reserved liquid. This should foam up to ¾ cup mark. Add to salmon and mix. Fry in hot oil by teaspoonfuls. Very light and crunchy. Serve with red cocktail sauce. May be served as a main dish or as an appetizer.

Mrs. Dudley Roberts (Carol Ann)

Fresh Boiled Shrimp, Padre Island Style

Very large pot

chili sauce
onion salt
lime or lemon juice
horseradish
ketchup
1 pkg. crab boil
¾ lb. fresh shrimp per
    person

Mix chili sauce, onion salt, lime juice and horseradish with ketchup to taste. Chill. Bring water to a boil in a very large cooking pot. Add crab boil and boil for 5-10 minutes. Add fresh shrimp and cover. Remove from heat and let stand until shrimp turn soft pink and rise to the top. Do not overcook. Drain. You can either peel and devein them yourself or try letting everyone peel and clean their own. Serve with the ketchup mixture.

This, plus a green salad and a loaf of hot French bread, makes a delicious meal—on Padre Island or anywhere!

Shrimp Casserole

350 degrees
3 quart casserole
Yield: 8-10 servings
Freezes

2 (10¾-oz.) cans cream of
    shrimp soup
½ cup mayonnaise
1 onion, diced
¾ cup milk
1 (5-oz.) can water chestnuts,
    sliced
1½ cups celery, diced
1½ cups rice, cooked
paprika
1 tsp. nutmeg
red pepper and salt
3 lbs. shrimp, cooked and
    cleaned

Combine all ingredients, blend well, seasoning heavily. Pour into casserole. Bake for 30 minutes at 350 degrees.
Mrs. Gilbert Heartfield (Francesca)

ENTREES
Seafood

Shrimp Jerry

Yield: 6-8 servings

1 cup Minute Rice
1 green pepper, chopped
4 whole green onions,
   chopped
3 Tbs. olive oil
2 lbs. raw shrimp, peeled and
   deveined
½ cup dry white wine
salt
½ cup soy sauce
1 tomato, chopped

Stir-fry rice, green pepper, and onion in oil (use wok or similar utensil) until rice browns. Add shrimp, wine, salt and soy sauce. Stir and cover. Cook only until shrimp turns white. Uncover, add tomato and cook until liquid disappears.

Mrs. Jerry Leadbetter (Tonii)

Shrimp Newburg

Saucepan
Yield: 6 servings

1 lb. shrimp
1 medium onion, finely
   chopped
¼ cup butter
1 pt. half and half
½ tsp. nutmeg
½ cup Parmesan cheese
dash cayenne pepper

Boil shrimp; shuck, clean and set aside. Sauté onions in butter. Add other ingredients to make a medium white sauce. Add shrimp to mixture. Heat thoroughly. Serve over rice.

Mrs. Hulon Webb (Carole)

Easy Shrimp Newburg

Yield: 8 servings

2 (10¾-oz.) cans cream of
   shrimp soup
1 cup milk
2 cups cooked shrimp
1 (1 lb.) can Le Seur peas
½ cup sherry
2 oz. Cheddar cheese,
   shredded

Heat soup with milk. Add shrimp and peas and continue to heat, stirring, until just simmering. Cook slowly about 5 minutes. Stir in sherry and cheese and heat until cheese melts. Serve over rice or toast points.

Mrs. Joe Friend (Pam)

Shrimp Creole

Large skillet
Yield: 4 servings

1½ Tbs. butter or margarine
½ cup onion, chopped
1 clove garlic, finely minced
½ cup green pepper,
    chopped
2 cups canned tomatoes,
    drained
½ tsp. salt
2 bay leaves
½ tsp. sugar
1½ tsp. chili powder
1 cup cooked shrimp,
    deveined and chopped
3 cups cooked rice

Melt butter in skillet. Add onion, garlic and green pepper; cook uncovered about 10 minutes, or until vegetables are soft, stirring occasionally. Add tomatoes, seasonings, and shrimp. Cover and simmer for about 5 minutes. Serve over cooked rice.

Mrs. Cayetano Barrera (Yolanda)

Lemon Shrimp Oriental

Yield: 6 servings

1 lb. frozen shrimp, shelled
    and deveined
2 cups fresh mushrooms,
    sliced (5-oz.)
1 medium green pepper, cut
    in strips
1½ cups celery, bias-sliced
¼ cup green onion, sliced
2 Tbs. cooking oil
1 (6-oz.) pkg. frozen pea pods
2 Tbs. cornstarch
1 tsp. sugar
1 tsp. salt
1 tsp. chicken bouillon cube
½ tsp. pepper
1 cup water
½ tsp. lemon peel, grated
3 Tbs. lemon juice
hot cooked rice

Cook shrimp, mushrooms, green pepper, celery, and onion in hot oil for 5-6 minutes, stirring constantly. Add pea pods; cook and stir 1-2 minutes more. Combine cornstarch, sugar, salt, bouillon, and pepper; blend in water, lemon peel and juice. Stir into shrimp mixture. Cook and stir until thickened and bubbly. Serve over hot rice.

Mrs. Cayetano Barrera (Yolanda)

Shrimp and Wild Rice Casserole

300 degrees
9 x 9 baking dish, buttered
Yield: 6 servings

½ cup onion, thinly sliced
¼ cup green pepper, thinly sliced
½ cup mushrooms, thinly sliced
¼ cup butter
1 Tbs. Worcestershire sauce
few drops of Tabasco
2 cups cooked wild rice
1 lb. cooked shrimp
2 cups thin white sauce (using chicken broth instead of milk)

Sauté onions, green pepper and mushrooms in butter until soft. Add seasonings, rice, shrimp and white sauce. Place in buttered casserole and bake at 300 degrees until thoroughly heated.

Mrs. Frank Birkhead (Janet)

Shrimp Wiggle

Yield: 4 servings

1 lb. fresh or frozen shrimp
¼ cup butter or margarine
¼ cup flour
2 cups milk
1 tsp. salt
pepper to taste
⅛ tsp. Worcestershire sauce
¼ tsp. dry mustard
1 Tbs. soy sauce
1 pkg. frozen peas
Chinese noodles or rice

Clean shrimp. Melt butter and stir in flour. Add milk slowly and cook until smooth and thick. Add remaining ingredients. Cook over medium heat until shrimp and peas are tender. Serve over Chinese noodles or rice.

Shrimp Panama

375 degrees
Cookie sheet, oiled
Yield: 2-4 servings

1 lb. fresh jumbo shrimp
(10-12), peeled and
deveined
¼ lb. king crabmeat
¼ lb. real butter, softened
2 cups bread crumbs
½ cup dry sherry
dash of garlic powder
salt and pepper to taste

Butterfly shrimp and place on oiled cookie sheet. Combine other ingredients in bowl. Butter must be soft (not melted). Stuff shrimp. Bake for 10 minutes at 375 degrees. Serve with drawn butter and lemon.

Mrs. Larry Seal (Jane Ann)

Pepper Shrimp

Yield: 6 servings

2 lbs. of shrimp (shells on)
2 sticks butter or margarine,
melted
juice of one lemon
2 pressed buds of garlic
1 jigger of white wine
1 (4-oz.) bottle of olive oil
3-4 Tbs. black pepper (small
can)

Lay fresh shrimp in a shallow cake pan. Mix all ingredients, except pepper and pour over the shrimp. Sprinkle with black pepper (one small can—should be heavy). Oven broil for 7 minutes—turn shrimp and broil for another 6 or 7 minutes. Take out and serve in a large bowl with French bread.

Have a fun party with this. Serve shrimp on newspaper and furnish lots of napkins! Peeling the shrimp at the table is fun for all, but a little messy.

Mrs. Bill Davis (Jean)

ENTREES
Seafood

Shrimp Sue

Yield: 4 servings

1 stick margarine
3 Tbs. Worcestershire sauce
garlic powder
½-1 lb. shrimp, cleaned
onions, sliced

Melt margarine; add Worcestershire sauce, garlic powder (to taste) and cleaned shrimp. Top with sliced onions and cover to cook over low heat for 30 minutes.

May cook much longer if guests are late.

Mrs. Kenneth Kachtik (Sue)

Chopstick Tuna

375 degrees
8 x 8 baking dish
Yield: 4-5 servings

1 (10¾-oz.) can cream of
  mushroom soup
1 (3-oz.) can mushrooms
  (stems and pieces)
1 can chow-mein noodles
1 (9¼-oz.) can tuna
1 can chop suey vegetables
¼ cup onion, chopped
dash pepper

Mix soup and mushrooms together with a small amount of water. Add 1 cup noodles, tuna, chop-suey vegetables, onion, and pepper. Toss lightly. Place in ungreased baking dish. Sprinkle with remaining noodles. Bake at 375 degrees for 30 minutes.

Mrs. Kenneth Kachtik (Sue)

Tuna Casserole Oriental

350 degrees
8 x 8 baking pan
Yield: 4 servings

1 cup celery, chopped
1 (6-oz.) can tuna, drained
½ cup fried onion rings
1 (10¾-oz.) can cream of
  mushroom soup
1 (2-oz.) jar pimiento
cashew nuts
1½ cups chow mein noodles

Chop celery and add to tuna. Mix in onion rings. Combine mushroom soup, pimiento, and 1 cup noodles. Add nuts and place mixture in baking dish. Sprinkle with remaining noodles and cashew nuts to taste. Bake 45 minutes at 350 degrees.

276

Quick Tuna Squares

350 degrees
9 x 9 baking pan, greased
Yield: 9 servings

3 (6-oz.) cans tuna, drained
18 saltine crackers, finely
  crushed
3 eggs
1 sm. onion, grated
1 cup celery, finely chopped
1 cup milk
¾ tsp. salt
¼ tsp. pepper

Combine all ingredients until smooth and well-mixed. Pour into greased baking pan. Bake at 350 degrees for 40 minutes or until knife inserted in center comes out clean. Cut into squares. Serve hot or may be refrigerated to serve cold later.

Mrs. Morgan Talbot (Jane)

Tuna Casserole

375 degrees
1½ quart casserole
Yield: 4-6 servings

1 (4-oz.) can shoestring
  potatoes
1 (10¾-oz.) can cream of
  mushroom soup
1 (6-oz. or 9-oz.) can tuna,
  drained
⅔ cup evaporated milk
1 (3-oz.) can broiled, sliced
  mushrooms, drained
¼ cup pimientos, chopped

Reserve 1 cup potatoes for topping. Combine remaining potatoes with other ingredients. Pour into casserole. Arrange reserved potatoes on top. Bake uncovered in 375 degree oven for 20-25 minutes.

Mrs. Charles Henson (Nancy)

Oven temperatures for baking: very slow—250-275 degrees; slow—300-325 degrees; moderate—350-375 degrees; hot—400-425 degrees; and very hot—450-475 degrees.

ENTREES
Game

Rio Grande Whitewings

300 degrees
9 x 13 x 2 baking dish, ungreased
Yield: 8 servings
Freezes

16 whitewing doves
salt and pepper
garlic powder
flour
1 lb. butter or margarine
1 small bottle Worcestershire
  sauce
1 cup cream sherry
1½ cups water

Season birds with salt, pepper and garlic powder. Dredge heavily with flour. Melt butter in a large skillet, preferably iron, until nearly burning. Cook birds quickly on both sides and place in ungreased baking dish. Pour butter left in skillet over birds. Mix Worcestershire sauce, sherry, water, more salt and pepper and a dash of garlic powder; pour over birds. May be frozen at this point, after cooling. Seal carefully and tightly. When ready to prepare (if frozen), bake uncovered for approximately 4 hours at 300 degrees. If birds are not frozen, bake uncovered at 300 degrees for 2 to 3 hours, depending on desired tenderness of birds.

Mrs. Jerry Fair (Zetta)

Smothered Doves

450-400 degrees
9 x 15 x 2 pan
Yield: 4 servings

12 doves
butter
salt and pepper
3 Tbs. flour
6 Tbs. Worcestershire sauce
6 slices bacon

Clean birds well and rub breast with a little butter. Sprinkle inside and out with salt, pepper, and a little flour. Place breast side down in shallow baking dish. Sprinkle with sauce and lay ½ slice bacon on each bird. Add enough water to half cover. Bake at 450 degrees for 25 minutes. Reduce heat to 400 degrees and continue to cook for about 45 minutes or until tender. Add enough water if needed during baking to keep from becoming too dry.

Mrs. Glenn Jarvis (Pat)

Barbequed Dove

hot bacon grease
doves
barbecue sauce

Using a glass syringe with a large needle, shoot hot bacon grease on each side of the breast bone of doves and cook for 15-20 minutes on pit, breast side up and do not turn. Baste with favorite barbecue sauce. The doves will puff up like quail and will stay moist. (The bacon grease is the secret to keeping the birds moist. Do not omit this step!!)

Mrs. Bill Davis (Jean)

Doves and Quail

350 degrees

doves or quail
onion, thinly sliced
salt and pepper
bacon
water

Place doves, breast-side up, in a casserole. Place thinly sliced onions and salt and pepper over the birds. Put a strip of bacon over each row of birds. Add about ¼ inch of water to casserole. Cover tightly with foil and bake at 350 degrees for about 2 hours or longer.

Mrs. Bill Davis (Jean)

Quail in Wine Sauce

Yield: 4 servings

salt
pepper
flour
12 quail
shortening
3 (10¾-oz.) cans cream of
   mushroom soup
1½ cups sauterne

Salt, pepper and flour cleaned quail. Fry in shortening until golden brown and place in a covered casserole. Cover quail with the following sauce: mix the mushroom soups and sauterne and cover quail. Cook at 350 degrees for 1½ hours, covered. About ½ hour before the quail are done, remove the casserole lid.

Mrs. Bill Davis (Jean)

ENTREES
Game

Quail Breasts

Large skillet
Yield: 4 servings

4-6 quail breasts (may use
  dove, but increase
  amounts)
salt and pepper
flour
butter
¼ cup onion, finely chopped
½ cup mushrooms, finely
  chopped
1 Tbs. parsley, finely
  chopped
½ cup white wine
½ cup heavy cream
wild rice

Wash, dry, and rub quail with salt and pepper. Dust with flour and sauté in butter. Remove birds and add onion, mushrooms and parsley. Sauté until tender. Return birds and add white wine. Cook, covered, basting frequently for 30 minutes. Add cream and heat thoroughly. Serve with wild rice.

Mrs. Jim Corcoran (Pam)

Baked Wild Duck

450-350 degrees
Roasting pan
Yield: 1 bird/2 servings

salt
wild duck, cleaned and slit
  with pocket
onion, sliced
celery, sliced
apple, sliced
bacon
water
wild rice

Salt outside and cavity of each bird. Stuff with raw vegetable slices. Place in roasting pan, breast side up. Place a strip of bacon on each bird. Pour two cups boiling water over bird. Bake at 450 degrees for 30 minutes, covered. Lower temperature to 350 and continue baking for two hours. Remove lid during last 30 minutes. Serve with wild rice or rice pilaf.

Mrs. Mike Frost (Sandra)

Wrapped Whitewing Delight

Yield: 6 servings

12 whitewing doves
6 slices bacon, halved
salt and pepper
lemon juice
garlic
butter
wild rice

Season birds inside and out. Wrap each bird with ½ slice of bacon; secure with toothpick. Grill over charcoal slowly; for about 1 hour. Baste with a lemon, butter and garlic sauce. Serve with wild rice.

Mrs. Charles Stewart (Betty)

Cornish Game Hens I

350 degrees
10 x 14 baking pan
Yield: 6 servings

1 box Uncle Ben's wild and
  white rice
½ cup celery, chopped
¼ cup onion, chopped
¼ cup parsley, chopped
3 Cornish game hens, halved
water, seasoned with:
  garlic pods
  onions, sliced
  celery stalk
  salt and pepper
Beau Monde
  (optional)
margarine, melted

Cook rice as directed on package. Set aside, after adding celery, onion, and parsley to rice. Clean hens and put giblets into water and make stock. Cook until done in seasoned water. Chop meat from neck, livers and gizzards after giblets are completely done and add to rice mixture. Reserve stock in which giblets are cooked. Season hen halves with pepper, garlic salt, a dash of Beau Monde seasoning, if desired. Spread rice mixture over bottom of baking pan (10 x 14), pushing rice away from sides of pan and more into middle to prevent over-cooking of rice. Put in oven with hens on top of rice mixture and bake for ½ hour at 350 degrees. Brush with melted margarine and add more stock to rice, if needed. Cook for ½ hour more, take out and brush tops of hens with melted margarine—add more moisture if needed (stock). Cover and seal with foil and replace in oven for 30 minutes or more, if needed.

Mrs. Jerry Box (Deanna)

ENTREES
Game

Cornish Game Hens II

425 degrees
Baking pan
Yield: 4 servings

4 game hens
1 cup onion, minced
½ cup celery, minced
¼ cup butter
¼ cup sherry
1 tsp. salt
2 cups cooked wild rice
butter, melted

Thaw, rinse and pat dry four game hens. Sauté onion and celery in butter. Add sherry, salt and rice. Stuff in birds—tie legs. Brush with melted butter and wrap in foil (double). Place on rack in shallow pan. Roast 1 hour at 425 degrees. Uncover birds and allow to brown, about 15 minutes.

Mrs. Greg Morrow (Debbie)

Barbequed Deer

deer ham
meat tenderizer
bacon
barbecue sauce

Take one deer ham and cover with meat tenderizer for at least 30 minutes. Cut at least 3 or 4 deep crosswise cuts in the ham. Be sure the cuts are as close to the bone as possible, for venison is extremely lean. In each cut, place a slice of bacon. Cover the top side of the ham with bacon slices and wrap with string. Wrap ham in foil which has several slits in top side. Smoke ham for at least five hours or longer, depending on size of deer ham. The last hour or so, baste often with favorite barbecue sauce.

Mrs. Bill Davis (Jean)

Wild birds are very dry and have little fat, so this must be substituted in cooking. Strips of bacon will add moistness.

Mexican Food

continued . . .

MEXICAN FOOD GLOSSARY

Arroz—the Spanish word for rice; the Mexican preparation is usually fried first with liquids added later

Bolillo—Mexican hard roll; usually pointed at both ends

Buñuelos—thin fried Mexican cookies

Cabrito—the meat from a very young goat

Canela—cinnamon in stick form

Chile ancho—heart-shaped chile usually 2½-3 inches long, deep reddish brown in color and used in making red chile sauces or ground into a powder for seasoning

Chile colorado—a sweet red chile pepper

Chili con carne—meat with a chili sauce

Chile con queso—a melted cheese and chile pepper dip served with chips or refried beans

Chile jalapeño—a dark green chile about 2½ inches long; one of the hottest of the chiles; available either fresh or canned, but they are usually pickled

Chile manzano—a milder pepper than the jalapeño; about the same size but yellow-green in color

Chile molida—packaged pure ground red chile powder

Chile serrano—a little hotter than the jalapeño and not quite so big; available in cans

Chile sauce—a broad term used in reference to red or green enchilada sauce, red or green taco sauce, or a salsa picante

Chile verdes (or green chiles)—milder, more like pimientos and about the same size; packed in El Paso, Texas, the flavor is muy sabroso (very flavorful)

Chile pequin—sometimes labeled "small red chiles"; a small dried red chile that is very hot; available in small boxes in spice sections of the super market

Chilpetin—It's been said these peppers are hotter than a branding iron and will burn a hole in your hat; these little red peppers about the size of a match head are grown near the Rio Grande River and along clear springfed streams of Central Texas

Chile rellenos—fried green chiles stuffed with a meat and cheese mixture

Chorizo—a highly seasoned Mexican sausage that may be substituted with Italian sausage

Cilantro—called Chinese parsley; these are the leaves of the coriander plant

Comino—(cumin) seed; yellow-brown or yellow-gray in color; used for flavoring

continued . . .

Coriander—also called Chinese parsley in this country and cilantro in Mexico and South America; a strong flavored herb that resembles parsley only with a larger leaf; use sparingly; it is particularly good in soups and pinto beans

Frijoles—pinto beans

Frijoles refritos—refried beans; boiled pinto beans that have been mashed and then fried in hot lard or shortening

Fajitas—tender cuts of meat from the beef short plate sometimes called skirt steaks

Flan—a Mexican custard usually with a brown sugar carmel sauce on top

Guacamole—a mashed salad or dip made of avocados

Jicama—a large root vegetable with a gray-brown skin that when removed exposes a white crispy meat much like a turnip in appearance; it may be cut into slices or strips, sprinkled with salt and lemon juice and served raw as an appetizer or in salads; flavor somewhat like a radish

Molcajete or matate—Mexican version of mortar and pestle or spice grinder

Mango—a yellow-orange tropical fruit; used for salads or for desserts; can be found fresh or canned

Masa Harina—moist coarse-grained dough; several brands of dry masa meal are available in grocery stores; dry meal can easily be made into a soft dough (dough does sour quickly even in the refrigerator); this dough can be made into corn tortillas

Masa Trigo—a dry mixture for making flour tortilla dough; can be purchased in grocery stores

Oregano—wild marjoram

Pepitas—pumpkin seeds that are toasted and salted

Picante—usually referring to something very hot or highly seasoned

Quesadillas—fried tortillas with cheese

Queso—cheese

Ro-Tel Tomatoes—brand name of a tomato and green chile combination that is manufactured in Donna, Texas

Sopa—soup

Sopaipilla—light puffed-up fritters that have been deep-fried; may be served as a bread or as a dessert when sprinkled with powdered sugar or filled with honey

Tamale—spicy meat mixture surrounded by a cornmeal covering

Tortilla—a saucer-sized thin pancake made of masa; can be hand-made or machine-made and bought in packages or cans; can be made of cornmeal or flour; heat in a well covered container, butter them generously, sprinkle lightly with salt, roll up cigarette fashion pinching lower end to keep the butter from dripping; can also be used in making taco shells and enchiladas

Border Buttermilk

1 (6-oz.) can frozen pink
   lemonade
1 (6-oz.) can pineapple juice
1 juice can of tequila (or less)
crushed ice

Place all ingredients in blender. Fill with crushed ice, up to ¾ full. Blend until ice is mushy and serve immediately.

Popular regional drink served to visiting dignitaries.

Border Sunshine

1 (6-oz.) can of frozen orange
   juice concentrate (thawed)
3-4 oz. rum or to taste
2 tsp. vanilla or to taste
2 tsp. sugar
crushed ice
orange sections, mint sprigs
   or cherries (optional)

Blend first four ingredients. Add ice to make four to five cups of mixture. Blend until you have obtained slush. Serve in small glasses. If desired, garnish with orange sections, mint sprigs or cherries.

Mrs. Whitney Jones (Ruth Ann)

Campechano
(like Pico de Gallo)

5 avocados, diced
5 green onions, with tops
   chopped
7 tomatoes, diced
1 lb. boiled shrimp, cut
1 small bunch cilantro
juice of 10 or so limes
garlic salt, salt and pepper to
   taste
corn or flour tortillas
   (optional)

Combine avocados, green onions and tomatoes. Peel and devein shrimp. Add to vegetables along with finely chopped cilantro. Season with lime juice, salt, garlic salt and pepper to taste. Serve with warm corn or flour tortillas for a delicious treat.

Mrs. Robert Whitis (Linda)

MEXICAN FOODS
Appetizers

Chalupas

375 degrees
Cookie sheet, ungreased
Yield: 4-6 servings

6 corn tortillas
oil for frying
1 (15-oz.) can refried beans
1 (15-oz.) can chili (no beans)
1 cup Cheddar cheese,
  grated
chopped lettuce, tomatoes,
  avocado (optional)
hot sauce to taste

Fry tortillas flat and one at a time in a skillet of hot oil until crisp. Drain well on paper towels. Spread tortillas with refried beans, then chili. Sprinkle cheese over the chili. Place all six on ungreased cookie sheet and bake until cheese has melted. When removed from oven, add lettuce, tomatoes, avocado and hot sauce if desired.

Mrs. Philip Chaleff (Elsie)

Super Chalupa Dip

400 degrees
9 x 13 casserole, greased

1½ lbs. ground beef
1 cup onions, chopped
salt to taste
pepper to taste
chili powder to taste
garlic powder to taste
1 (17-oz.) can refried beans
1-2 (4-oz.) cans green chiles,
  chopped
3-4 cups Cheddar cheese,
  grated
1 (7-oz.) can green chile salsa
  or green taco sauce
1½ bunches scallions,
  chopped
1 (4¼-oz.) can black olives,
  chopped
2 cups guacamole dip
8 oz. sour cream

Brown meat, add onions and seasonings. Add beans and chiles. Mix well. Pat meat mixture into greased casserole. Top with cheese. Sprinkle the green chile or green taco sauce over the top. If desired, refrigerate until ready to serve. Bake at 400 degrees for 20 to 30 minutes. Make circles around the top of the casserole with the chopped scallions, then chopped black olives, then guacamole dip, then sour cream. Make circles until the top is covered. Serve with tostados, nacho chips, or corn chips.

Mrs. Gary Gurwitz (Bailey)

288

Chili Con Queso Dip

Yield: 1 quart

1 can Ro-Tel chilies and
  tomatoes
2 lbs. Velveeta cheese
1 Tbs. mayonnaise
tortilla chips

Spray double boiler with no-stick substance. Melt cheese; add drained can of Ro-Tel and mayonnaise. Place in chaffing dish and serve with tortilla chips.

Mrs. Leroy Lewin (Hilda)

Chiles

350 degrees
9 x 12 baking dish
Yield: 12 servings

9 (4-oz.) cans Ortega chiles
  (mild or hot)
1½ lbs. Cracker Barrel sharp
  Cheddar cheese (yellow
  label), grated
6 eggs
6 oz. cream
salt to taste

Wash and devein peppers and drain on paper towels. Grate cheese. Layer peppers and cheese in baking dish and end with cheese. Beat eggs, cream and add salt. Pour over chiles and cheese. Bake at 350 degrees until it bubbles and then at 250 degrees for 20 minutes.

Chili Cheese Pick-Ups

400 degrees,
reduce to 350 degrees
9 x 13 pan, greased
Yield: 117 one-inch squares

10 eggs
½ cup flour
1 tsp. baking powder
½ tsp. salt
8 oz. jalapeños, drained and
  chopped
½ cup margarine, melted
1 pint cottage cheese
1 lb. Cheddar cheese, grated

Beat eggs lightly. Mix dry ingredients and add to eggs. Add jalapeños, margarine, cottage cheese and Cheddar cheese to the egg mixture. Blend slightly. Pour into greased 9 x 13 pan. Bake at 400 degrees for 15 minutes. Reduce to 350 degrees and bake for 20-25 minutes. Cool and slice into small squares.

Mrs. Neal Runnels (Gayle)

MEXICAN FOODS
Appetizers

Guacamole Dip

Yield: 6 servings

3 avocados, mashed
juice from 1 lime or lemon
2 Tbs. bottled hot sauce
  (Picante or Tabasco)
dash Lawry's salt
garlic powder to taste
dash onion powder
corn chips

Combine all ingredients and serve with corn chips.

Mrs. Larry Seal (Jane Ann)

Nachos

375 degrees
Cookie sheet, ungreased
Yield: 6-8 servings

4 tortillas
oil for frying
4 oz. pkg. of cheese, grated
jalapeño peppers to taste

Quarter tortillas. Fry until crisp, then drain well on paper towels. Sprinkle grated cheese over crisp pieces. Place jalapeño slivers over each. Place all on ungreased cookie sheet and bake until cheese is completely melted.

Mrs. Philip Chaleff (Elsie)

Picante Sauce

4 large serranos (this can be
  increased or decreased for
  your own taste)
1 medium onion
5 large tomatoes
1½ Tbs. cilantro (alter to
  taste)

Combine serranos and onion and chop (not purée) in blender. Place in a bowl and set aside. Chop (not purée) tomatoes, several at a time. Combine these with the serranos and onion. Add cilantro and mix. Will keep in refrigerator for several days.

Mrs. Larry Seal (Jane Ann)

Flour Tortillas

4 cups flour
1½ tsp. salt
⅛ tsp. baking powder
¾ cup shortening
1 cup and 1 Tbs. warm water

In medium mixing bowl, hand mix the flour, salt, and baking powder. Cut in shortening until it is completely mixed. Slowly add warm water while mixing. Mix until the dough can be gathered into a ball. (If needed add more water or if too sticky add a little more flour.) Knead dough until it is smooth and elastic. Let dough rest 15 minutes. Divide dough into 20-24 portions, and shape into balls. On a lightly floured surface roll each ball into a thin circle. Cook on ungreased skillet over medium heat. Cook lightly on first side, turn, completely cook second side, then turn back to first side and finish cooking. (Turn a total of two times.) Serve hot, with butter, if desired.

Mrs. Leonel Garza, Jr. (Linda)

Salsa Picante (Hot Sauce)

1-2 (or 3 if really hot flavor is desired) jalapeños
1 large or 2 small pods fresh garlic
½ tsp. comino
½ tsp. salt
1 (16-oz.) can tomatoes
1-2 Tbs. oil from canned jalapeños
ground black pepper

Put into blender for 35 seconds at high speed, the jalapeños, the garlic, comino, salt, juice from tomatoes. Stop blender and add the can of tomatoes and blend on low speed for 2 to 3 seconds, to sauce consistency. Add oil from jalapeño can and pepper. Store in glass jar. Will keep for several weeks in refrigerator.

This sauce is good for preparing huevos rancheros, on sandwiches, mixed with cottage cheese, for quick stews, snacks or use your imagination.

MEXICAN FOODS
Appetizers

Picadillo Dip

Skillet
Crock pot

1 lb. ground beef
½ cup onions, chopped
2 lbs. Velveeta cheese
1 (10-oz.) can tomatoes and
　chiles
1 (8-oz.) can mushrooms,
　stems and pieces
1 (6-oz.) can pitted black
　olives, sliced
dash of cumin and garlic
　powder
salt and pepper to taste
Fritos or Doritos

Brown ground beef and onions in skillet. Melt cheese with tomatoes and chiles. Add cooked beef, mushrooms, olives and seasonings to the cheese mixture. Serve hot in crock pot with Fritos or Doritos.

This is also good on hamburgers, eggs or vegetables, such as broccoli.

Variations:
1 pkg. dry onion soup mix

Omit the onions with the beef and add one package of dry onion soup mix instead. Taste before adding salt to finished dish.

1 pkg. frozen broccoli,
　cooked and chopped

Omit ground beef and add one package of frozen, chopped, cooked broccoli instead.

Mrs. Howard Pebley (Rosann)

Pico de Gallo I

Yield: 6 servings

2 avocados, chopped
1 cup onion, chopped
½ tsp. pepper
1 Tbs. lemon juice
2 fresh green chiles, chopped
2 tomatoes, finely chopped
1½ tsp. salt
1 Tbs. cilantro, chopped
　(coriander)
2 Tbs. bottled Italian dressing
corn tortillas

Mix together and serve rolled up in corn tortillas. It's good without the chiles if you don't like hot!

Mrs. Jerry Leadbetter (Tonii)

Pico de Gallo II

Yield: 6 servings

2 medium onions
3 firm avocados
4 firm tomatoes
1 bunch cilantro (coriander)
1 Tbs. olive or salad oil
1 Tbs. (or more) lime juice
salt and pepper

Chop onions, avocados, and tomatoes. Combine. Leave avocado seeds in mixture to keep green. Mince cilantro, add to avocado mixture with oil, and lime juice. Salt and pepper to taste. This will keep in refrigerator for a week.

This can also be used with tostados or saltines as a dip. With shrimp chunks, could be a main dish.
A little red hot sauce on top adds zing.

Mrs. Jerry Fair (Zetta)

Quesadillas
(Tortilla Turnovers)

Frying pan
Yield: 12

12 Masa Harina tortillas
8 oz. Monterrey Jack cheese; plain or with jalapeños, grated
corn oil for frying
picante sauce (optional)

Make 12 tortillas according to the directions on the Masa Harina package. Do not cook on hot griddle—soft masa must be used. Place the tortillas on wax paper. Grate the cheese. Put about 1½ tsp. cheese on the center of the tortilla and fold, using wax paper to handle as they are very delicate before being cooked. Transfer to wax lined cookie sheet and seal with a fork on the edges, like an empanada. May be chilled before cooking for easier handling. Fry in hot corn oil until golden brown, turning once. When serving, pass picante sauce, if desired.

Good as a luncheon dish with salad or Pico de Gallo. May be made into cocktail size also.

Mrs. William H. Wilson (Marion)

MEXICAN FOODS
Appetizers/Soups and Vegetables

Sopa de Mesa

Yield: 4 servings

3½ cups corn (frozen or
   canned)
¾ cup chicken stock
4 Tbs. butter
2 cups milk
2 Tbs. mild green chiles,
   chopped (canned)
½ tsp. oregano
¼ tsp. garlic powder
salt
1 cup cooked chicken, diced,
   skin free
1 tomato, diced
1 cup Jack cheese or
   Muenster cheese, cubed

Put corn and chicken stock in blender. Blend well and pour through a fine sieve, extracting as much liquid as possible. Discard the remaining solids. Pour mixture into a pot, add butter and simmer for 5 minutes, stirring often to prevent corn from sticking. Add milk and bring to a boil. Add chiles, oregano, garlic powder and salt to taste. Before serving, add the chicken, tomato, and cheese. Stir well. When the cheese is melted and soup is very hot, serve topped with fried tortilla squares.

Tortilla Squares:
6-8 tortillas
oil

Stack the tortillas and cut them into ½-inch squares. Drop squares into pan of hot oil and stir with a wooden spoon until crisp and golden. Drain on paper towels.

Queso Flameado

½ small onion, chopped
1 tsp. butter
2 tomatoes, peeled and
   chopped
½ tsp. hot peppers, diced
1 lb. chorizo (Mexican
   sausage)
8 oz. Monterrey Jack cheese,
   grated
1 pkg. corn tortillas,
   quartered and fried

Sauté onion in butter. Add tomatoes and peppers. Sauté until tomatoes are very soft to make picante sauce. Cook chorizo separately. Let stand a few minutes; drain grease off using paper towels. On a platter, place half of the cheese. Place chorizo on top. Top with remainder of cheese. Put picante sauce on top. Warm in oven until cheese melts. Put fried tortilla chips around the dish and serve hot.

continued . . .

Picante Sauce:
1 small onion, chopped
2 tsp. butter
4 medium, ripe tomatoes,
  peeled and diced
½ tsp. jalapeño peppers,
  diced

Sauté onions in butter. Add diced tomatoes and hot peppers. Continue to sauté until tomatoes are very soft.

Great for football Sundays.
Mrs. Tom Wilkins (Geen)

Tortilla Soup

Yield: 8-10 servings

1 medium onion, chopped
2 cloves garlic, chopped
2 Tbs. vegetable oil or olive
  oil
2 cans beef bouillon or 3
  cups water and 3 beef
  bouillon cubes
2 cans chicken broth or
  homemade meat stock
½ cup tomato juice or tomato
  sauce
1 tsp. ground cumin
1 tsp. chili powder
1 jalapeño, chopped
1 tsp. salt
¾ tsp. Worcestershire sauce
1 cup cooked chicken, diced
1 large tomato, peeled and
  diced
tortilla strips, fried crisp
avocado slices
Monterrey Jack cheese,
  grated

Sauté onion and garlic in oil. Add beef and chicken broth, tomato sauce, cumin, chili powder, jalapeño, salt and Worcestershire. Bring to boil, cover and simmer one hour. Add chicken and tomato. Cook 5 minutes. Cut tortillas in narrow strips. Fry crisp. Place a few in bowls. Fill with the hot soup. Garnish with more tortilla strips, avocado slices, and cheese.
Mrs. Howard Pebley (Rosann)

Variation:
Parmesan cheese

Omit grated Monterrey Jack cheese and top with Parmesan cheese instead.
Mrs. Joe Friend (Pam)

MEXICAN FOODS
Soups and Vegetables

Sopa de Pollo Con Elote
(Chicken Soup With Corn)

Yield: 4-6 servings

2-3 cloves
2 pods garlic, minced
½ small onion, diced
1 tomato, chopped
1 (4-oz.) can mushrooms, if
   desired
2 Tbs. butter
1 cup chicken, cooked and
   diced
1 cup chicken stock
1 can cream-style corn
1 (10¾-oz.) can cream of
   chicken soup
1 can milk (or water)
2 Tbs. Pace's hot sauce
sprinkling of cilantro
   (optional)

Sauté the cloves, garlic, onion, tomato and mushrooms in butter until onions are tender. Then add all other ingredients, except the hot sauce, and blend over low heat, stirring gently. Salt and pepper to taste. Simmer about 10 or 15 minutes. Stir in the hot sauce, if desired, just before serving.

Mrs. Dan Seitz (Amy)

Sopa Tampiqueña

Yield: 4 servings

chicken broth or several
   chicken bouillon cubes
1 large baking potato
1 large white onion
1 large carrot
2 Tbs. butter
2 cups milk

Cook the potato, onion and carrot in enough chicken stock to cover or use water with several bouillon cubes. Cook until tender. When tender, put in blender with the butter and milk. Blend and add more, or less milk as desired. Serve either hot or cold.

Mrs. Woods Christian (Virginia Boeye)

A few squeezes of lime juice on top of soup cuts grease.

MEXICAN FOODS

Chili Beans

Yield: 4-6 servings

1½ cups pinto beans (soak
  overnight)
½ tsp. dry ginger
¼ tsp. dry mustard
2 Tbs. sugar
salt to taste
1 lb. ground meat
1-2 Tbs. chili powder
1 tsp. paprika
1 small can tomato juice
  (optional)
2-3 cloves garlic (optional)

Soak beans overnight. Add water to cover. Add ginger, mustard, sugar and salt to taste. Cook until tender. In a skillet cook ground meat until slightly brown. Add chili powder and paprika. Pour meat into beans; add more hot water if needed. The small can of tomato juice can be added at this time, also cloves of garlic. Simmer about one hour.

Mrs. Joe Stroud (Ruthie)

Spanish Rice

Frying pan
Yield: 10-12 servings

hot bacon grease
1½ cups rice
½ tsp. garlic powder
2 tsp. cumin seed
½ tsp. pepper
bell pepper to taste
1 (8-oz.) can tomato sauce
3 cups salted, boiling water

In hot bacon grease, cook 1½ cups rice until golden brown. Add the garlic powder, cumin seed, pepper, bell pepper and tomato sauce. Pour all this into 3 cups salted, boiling water. Reduce heat, cover and cook 10 to 15 minutes. Remove from heat, leave covered and let steam a few minutes before serving.

Hamburger can be browned and added on top of rice for a main dish.

Mrs. Charles Fox (Nancy)

MEXICAN FOODS
Soups and Vegetables

Jalapeño Carrots

Yield: 2 pints

1½ bags of carrots
1 tsp. dill seed
½ tsp. celery seed
1 tsp. mustard seed
1 jalapeño
1 pod garlic
1 pint water
½ pint vinegar
¼ cup salt

For each pint jar of sliced carrots, add the measurements of dill seed, celery seed, and mustard seed. One half of the jalapeño and half a pod of garlic is used per jar. Bring water, vinegar and salt to a boil; pour into jars.

Mrs. John Maxwell (Betty)

Mexican Squash Dish

350 degrees
Yield: 6-8 servings
Freezes

5-8 yellow squash
3 Tbs. instant minced onion
6 Tbs. butter
1-1½ cups Cheddar cheese, grated
½-1 can Ro-Tel tomatoes and green chilies
salt and pepper to taste
cracker crumbs

Peel the squash and slice, and cook with the minced onion until tender. Drain the squash and place in a casserole with 4 Tbs. of butter, cheese, tomatoes and green chilies and salt and pepper. Stir all ingredients. Melt remaining butter and pour over squash adding cracker crumbs last. Bake at 350 degrees for 30 minutes or until bubbly.

Mrs. Jim Thompson (Sandy)

Beans

Yield: 12 large servings

2 lbs. pinto beans
several chunks salt pork
6 cloves garlic, chopped
2 tsp. oregano
8-9 chile pequins, mashed
2 Tbs. salt

DO NOT SOAK BEANS. Fill large bean pot or Dutch oven ½ full with water. Bring beans to boil and simmer uncovered 1 hour. Add several chunks of salt pork and simmer for another hour. Add oregano and chile pequins and simmer for.another hour. Add salt and cook 1 hour more.

Mrs. Gary Gurwitz (Bailey)

Mexican Cheese Soufflé

350 degrees
9 x 13 x 2 baking dish
Yield: 6 servings

12 slices bread
butter
1 (12-oz.) can corn
1 (4-oz.) can Ortega chile
  peppers
2 cups Monterrey Jack
  cheese, grated
3 cups milk
4 eggs, slightly beaten
salt

Early in the morning, butter the bread slices and cut in half. Layer half of the bread in a 9 x 13 x 2-inch pyrex dish, then layer corn, chiles, and cheese. Add second layer of bread. Combine milk, eggs with salt, and pour over bread. Let rest several hours in refrigerator. Bake for 45 minutes.

Mrs. Morgan Talbot (Jane)

Mexican Omelet

325 degrees
10-inch oven-proof skillet/bowl
Yield: 4-6 servings

¾ cup avocado, chopped
¼ cup dairy sour cream
2 Tbs. green chiles, chopped
1 Tbs. green onion, chopped
1 tsp. lemon juice
¼ tsp. salt
dash bottled hot pepper
  sauce
2 Tbs. butter or margarine
1 corn tortilla, torn into
  pieces
6 eggs, beaten
4 oz. Monterrey Jack cheese,
  shredded

Combine avocado, sour cream, chiles, onion, lemon juice, salt and pepper sauce; set aside. In 10-inch oven-proof skillet, melt butter or margarine; add tortilla. Cook until tortilla is soft. Pour in eggs; cook 3-5 minutes, lifting eggs to allow uncooked mixture to flow under. Remove from heat. Sprinkle with cheese. Bake in 325 degree oven 3-4 minutes or until cheese melts. Spread avocado mixture atop half of omelet. Return to oven 5-7 minutes more. Fold omelet in half and serve at once.

MEXICAN FOODS
Entrees

Migas
(Eggs and Tortillas)

Yield: 4-6 servings

6 Tbs. bacon drippings
8-10 tortillas, cut into 1-inch
 squares
1 small onion or 2-3 green
 onions, chopped
1 large or 2 small tomatoes,
 chopped
1½ Tbs. chili powder
½ tsp. comino powder
salt to taste
6 eggs, beaten

Heat bacon drippings in skillet and fry tortilla pieces until they begin to brown, stirring constantly. Drain some of the fat off and push tortillas to side of pan. Add onion, tomato and seasonings and sauté until onion is transparent. Mix altogether with tortillas and add eggs. Stir gently until eggs appear done.

Arroz Con Carne
(Rice With Meat)

Frying pan
Yield: 6-8 servings

1 cup rice (long grain)
¼ cup oil
1 lb. hamburger meat
½ medium onion, diced
¼ tsp. garlic powder
1 tsp. ground comino
¼ tsp. ground black pepper
1½ tsp. salt
1 (8-oz.) can tomato sauce
2½ cups hot water

Fry rice in hot oil until golden brown. Drain off excess oil, add uncooked hamburger and fry until browned at medium temperature. Add diced onion to taste and continue frying. Stir to avoid sticking. Add garlic, comino, black pepper, salt, tomato sauce and hot water. Bring to a boil, cover, and continue cooking at low to medium heat for 25 minutes, or until rice is cooked. Keep covered until ready to serve.

Excellent meal for children. Serve with flour tortillas.

Mrs. Leonel Garza, Jr. (Linda)

MEXICAN FOODS

Entrees

Cabrito
(Baby Goat)

325 degrees
Large roasting pan
Yield: 5-6 servings

1 cabrito, quartered
2 bell peppers, sliced
3 onions, sliced
3-4 carrots, sliced
2-3 sticks margarine
2 cloves garlic
1 lemon and juice
5 Tbs. Worcestershire sauce
2 Tbs. liquid smoke

Place quartered cabrito in roasting pan. Salt and pepper to taste. Place sliced vegetables on top. Make a sauce of the last five ingredients and pour over cabrito. Roast for 2-3 hours, until tender at 325 degrees. Baste every 10 minutes during the last hour.

Mrs. Bill Scurlock (Mary)

Chicken Casserole

250 degrees
3 quart casserole, greased
Yield: 8-10 servings

1 onion, sliced
2 (4-oz.) cans Ortega diced
   green chiles
1 (15-oz.) can enchilada
   sauce, either mild or hot
2 cups chicken broth
1 chicken, cooked, deboned
   and cut into small pieces
2 cups Cheddar cheese,
   grated
salt to taste
1 pint half and half
2 dozen corn tortillas

Simmer onion, chiles, enchilada sauce and chicken broth. Add diced chicken and cheese. When heated thoroughly, add half and half. Tear tortillas in pieces and place in greased casserole dish, alternating layers with chicken mixture, ending with tortillas. Add last of sauce to moisten top layer and bake covered in 250 degree oven about 1½ hours.

Can be baked early in the morning and saved until evening, when you can re-heat it. It can also be made the day before and refrigerated until needed. Flavors blend better and it is a time saver.

Mrs. Gilbert Heartfield (Francesca)

MEXICAN FOODS
Entrees

Carne y Chilaquiles

350 degrees
11 x 15 pan
Yield: 8-10 servings
Freezes

2 onions, chopped
1 clove garlic, minced
2 Tbs. oil
1 lb. ground beef
2 (14½-oz.) cans tomatoes
salt and pepper to taste
1 (4-oz.) can green chile
  peppers
1 dozen corn tortillas
oil-one inch deep in skillet
2 lbs. Monterrey Jack cheese,
  grated
1 pint sour cream

Sauté onion and garlic in 2 Tbs. oil until clear. Brown ground meat in small amount of fat and add to onions and garlic. Add tomatoes, salt and pepper and simmer until tomatoes are cooked. Add chile peppers that have been cut into strips. Cut tortillas in fourths and dip in hot oil in skillet. Remove immediately and drain on paper towels. Put layer of tortillas in 11 x 15 dish, top with a layer of tomato and hamburger sauce, then a layer of grated cheese. Continue layering until dish is full; top with grated cheese. Heat in oven until cheese melts and mixture bubbles. Just before serving, top with sour cream.

Mrs. Carl Judin (Joy)

Green Chile Casserole

350 degrees
Large deep casserole
Yield: 4 servings

1 dozen corn tortillas
½ cup hot oil
1 (10¾-oz.) can cream of
  chicken soup
1 small can green chiles,
  chopped
1 cup milk
1 onion, chopped
2 cups cheese, shredded

Dip tortillas in hot oil one at a time on both sides. Heat mixture of soup, chiles, and milk and pour a little of this mixture in casserole dish. Stack tortillas on top of each other with onions and cheese between each layer. Pour remaining soup mixture over tortillas. Bake uncovered at 350 degrees for 30-40 minutes.

Mrs. Glynn Andrews (Laurie)

302

Chili Rellenos Casserole

350 degrees
10 x 6 x 1½ baking dish
Yield: 6-8 servings

1 lb. ground beef
½ cup onion, chopped
½ tsp. salt
¼ tsp. pepper
2 (4-oz.) cans green chiles,
  cut in half crosswise,
  seeded
1½ cups sharp Cheddar
  cheese, shredded
¼ cup all-purpose flour
½ tsp. salt
4 eggs, beaten
1½ cups milk
¼ tsp. bottled hot pepper
  sauce (optional)

Brown beef and onion in skillet; drain off fat. Sprinkle meat with salt and pepper. Place half of the chiles in 10 x 6 x 1½ baking dish; sprinkle with cheese; top with meat mixture. Arrange remaining chiles over meat. Mix flour and salt in bowl. Combine eggs, milk and hot pepper sauce; add egg mixture to flour gradually, beating until smooth. Pour over meat-chili mixture. Bake in preheated 350 degree oven 45 to 50 minutes or until knife inserted just off-center comes out clean. Let cool 5 to 10 minutes. Cut in squares to serve.

Mrs. T. B. Waite, Jr. (Thelma)

Chili

Large pot
Yield: 6 servings

2 lbs. ground beef
1 large onion, chopped
2 cloves garlic, minced
salt to taste
ground comino (cumin) to
  taste
4 Tbs. Masa Harina
4 Tbs. chili powder
2 (8-oz.) cans tomato sauce
1 quart water

Sauté meat, onion, and garlic until meat browns and onions are soft. Add salt. Grind whole comino (or powdered comino may be used) in a malquehete or matate (Mexican version of the mortar and pestle), using a bit of the water called for in the recipe to get all of the comino out of the malquehete when putting into the meat mixture. Add comino to meat and Masa Harina, cooking for 5 minutes. Add chili powder and tomato sauce and water. Simmer all day.

Mrs. Keith Tyler (Anne)

MEXICAN FOODS
Entrees

Slapdash Chili

Yield: 6 servings
Freezes

2 lbs. ground beef
1 onion, peeled and chopped
1 green pepper, seeded and
   chopped
2 (15-oz.) cans kidney beans
2 (16-oz.) cans tomatoes
1 (15-oz.) can corn
2 heaping Tbs. shortening
1 tsp. salt
1 tsp. chili powder

Brown meat in skillet along with onion that has been chopped and the green pepper. Pour the cans of beans, tomatoes, and corn, including liquid, into a large cooking pot. (Meat can be drained with a slotted spoon as you transfer it.) Add the shortening; about 1 tsp. salt and chili powder and stir to mix. Bring the chili mixture to a boil over a high or medium high heat. When it is bubbling, turn down the heat until the chili is barely boiling. Stir a few times. Cook the chili for about 2 hours stirring occasionally to keep the chili from sticking to the bottom of the pan.

Mrs. Anne Walker

Jailhouse Chili

Large saucepan
Yield: 8-10 servings

2 lbs. beef or venison, diced
oil
3 Tbs. chili powder
1 Tbs. salt
3 cloves garlic
1 Tbs. ground cumin
⅔ tsp. marjoram
1½ Tbs. paprika
2 onions, diced
1 bell pepper, diced (optional)
1 lb. can tomatoes or tomato
   juice
3 cups water

Cook meat in a small amount of oil. Add remaining ingredients and water. Cook slowly for several hours. If desired, thicken by adding a flour and water mixture and stir until flour is done and mixture is consistency you want.

Mrs. Bobby Etchison (Willie)

Chili and Beans

Large Pot
Yield: 4 servings
Freezes

1 lb. ground round
3 slices bacon, cut fine
1 onion, diced
1 green pepper, diced
2 Tbs. oil
2 (15-oz.) cans kidney beans
  or 4 cups prepared pinto
  beans
2 cans of tomato soup
1 (15-oz.) can chili (without
  beans)

Brown ground round, bacon, onion and green pepper in the oil. Add beans, tomato soup and can of chili and cook slowly, stirring frequently for 30-45 minutes.

Mrs. Joe Friend (Pam)

Empanadas

350 degrees
Yield: about 3 dozen
Freezes

Dough:
3 (3-oz.) pkgs. cream cheese,
  softened
½ cup butter
1½ cups flour

Filling:
2 Tbs. oil
½ medium onion, chopped
1 clove garlic, crushed
½ lb. ground beef
½ lb. ground pork
salt and pepper to taste
½ cup raisins (small)
¼ cup slivered almonds
1-2 small cans tomato
  purée
1 egg for sealing

Blend cream cheese, butter and flour in large mixing bowl until soft dough forms. Wrap in wax paper and refrigerate at least one hour. While dough chills, prepare filling.

Sauté onion, garlic and meat in oil. Season with salt and pepper. Add raisins, almonds; stir in tomato purée and simmer 10 minutes.

Roll out dough to ¼-inch thick and cut with biscuit cutter. Put a spoonful of meat mixture on dough round and fold over in half. Press edges with fork. Beat egg with a little ice water and brush on to seal dough. Bake at 350 degrees for 10-12 minutes or until golden brown.

Mrs. Neal Runnels (Gayle)

MEXICAN FOODS

Entrees

Enchiladas I

Yield: 12-18 enchiladas

1-1½ dozen tortillas
1 medium onion, chopped
12-16 oz. Colby or Cheddar
  cheese
1 recipe of enchiladas sauce*

If tortillas are tough, first fry in hot grease for a second or heat in microwave oven on high for 10 seconds per tortilla. Then dip in sauce. Roll chopped onion and grated cheese in tortillas. Top with sauce, more onion, and cheese. Heat until hot.

*Sauce:
2 Tbs. bacon drippings
2 Tbs. Chili Quik
2 Tbs. flour
1 cup tomato sauce
2 cups water
½ tsp. comino seed
1 bouillon cube

Melt bacon drippings and stir in Chili-Quik and flour. Add rest of ingredients and simmer about 15-20 minutes.

Mrs. Michael D. Owens (Cissy)

Enchiladas II

375 degrees
Baking pan
Yield: 4-6 servings
Freezes

1½ cup onion, chopped
½ cup oil
1½ Tbs. garlic salt
1 tsp. chili powder
1 tsp. Gebhardt's Chili Quik
3 Tbs. flour
2 cups water
4½ cups Cheddar cheese,
  grated
2 cups onions, chopped
1 dozen corn tortillas

Cook 1½ cups chopped onions in oil in skillet until glazed and soft but not brown. Add garlic salt, chili powder, and Chili Quik. Stir in flour and 2 cups water to make a smooth sauce. Add 1½ cups grated cheese and stir. Combine 3 cups cheese and 2 cups onion to make filling. Dip tortillas on both sides in sauce. Fill each one with 2 Tbs. filling and roll. Place side by side in pan and cover with remaining sauce and sprinkle on remaining filling. Bake at 375 degrees for 30 minutes.

Can be frozen for 2 months. If frozen, allow additional baking time.

Mrs. Leroy Lewin (Hilda)

MEXICAN FOODS

Entrees

Chicken Enchiladas with Sour Cream and Cheese

325 degrees
8 x 8 casserole, greased
Yield: 6-8 servings
Freezes

2½-3 lbs. chicken
1 med. onion, chopped
2 Tbs. margarine
1 (10-oz.) can Ro-Tel
  tomatoes and green chilies
  (drained)
4 cups sour cream
4 chicken bouillon cubes
1 doz. corn tortillas
½ stick margarine
½ lb. Monterrey Jack cheese,
  grated

Wash, cut up and boil the chicken; debone and cut into bite-sized pieces. Set aside. Sauté onion in 2 Tbs. margarine in a large skillet. Add chicken and tomatoes with chilies; simmer together until heated throughout. While above ingredients are simmering, heat the sour cream until the bouillon cubes are dissolved. Heat the tortillas, one at a time, in margarine. Place a small amount of chicken mixture in each tortilla, roll up, and arrange in a well-greased 8 x 8 casserole. Pour the sour cream sauce over all. Top with grated cheese. Bake for 15-20 minutes in a 325 degree oven.

Mrs. Rush Milam (Elizabeth)

Chicken Enchiladas with Sour Cream

350 degrees
9 x 13 casserole
Yield: 6 servings
Freezes

½ pint sour cream
1 (10¾-oz.) can cream of
  mushroom soup
1 (4-oz.) can jalapeños,
  seeded and chopped
1 medium onion, chopped
1 (3-lb.) chicken, boiled and
  boned
1 dozen flour tortillas
Velveeta cheese (as much as
  desired)

Mix sour cream, soup and half the jalapeños together. Mix onion, the rest of the jalapeños, and chicken together. Put chicken mixture in tortillas and roll up. Place these in casserole dish. Pour the soup mixture over the enchiladas and top with grated Velveeta cheese. Bake covered at 350 degrees for one hour.

Mrs. Ron Miller (Austin)

MEXICAN FOODS
Entrees

Swiss Enchiladas

350 degrees
Baking dish
Yield: 6 servings

1 onion, chopped
2 Tbs. oil
1 clove garlic, crushed
2 cups tomato purée
2 (4-oz.) cans green chiles,
  chopped
2 cups chicken, cooked and
  chopped
1 dozen flour tortillas
6 chicken bouillon cubes
3 cups cream
½ lb. Jack or Swiss cheese,
  grated
avocado slices, hard-cooked
  eggs, radishes, or ripe
  olives

Sauté onion in oil until soft. Add garlic, tomato purée, green chiles and chicken. Simmer 10 minutes. Fry tortillas in about 1 inch hot oil. Do not let them get crisp, as they are to be rolled. Dissolve bouillon cubes in cream. Dip each tortilla in this, cover generously with chicken filling and roll up. Arrange rolls in baking dish and pour remaining cream mixture over them. Top with grated cheese. Bake for 30 minutes. Garnish with avocado slices, hard-cooked eggs, radishes, or ripe olives.

Mrs. James Humphrey (Jane Ellen)

Cheese Enchiladas

350 degrees
9 x 13 baking dish
Yield: 4 servings

2 (15-oz.) cans chili (without
  beans)
1½ cups water
1 dozen corn tortillas
12 oz. Cheddar cheese,
  grated
2 medium onions, chopped

Begin with one can chili, diluted with ½ cup water and heat until it begins to boil. Reduce heat and place a tortilla in chili for a short time, to soften. When it becomes limp, remove to plate, and put 2 Tbs. cheese and 1 Tbs. onion across center of tortilla. Roll and place in baking dish. Prepare remaining tortillas, using the rest of the chili and water as needed. Sprinkle remaining onions on enchiladas and pour remaining chili over them. (There must be enough diluted chili to cover enchiladas.) Sprinkle approximately ½ cup cheese over tortillas. Cook approximately 30 minutes, or until chili bubbles.

Mrs. Ralph E. Crawford, Jr. (Pam)

MEXICAN FOODS
Entrees

Easy Enchilada Casserole

9 x 13 casserole

2 lbs. ground beef
1 stick margarine
1 onion, chopped
1 (10¾-oz.) can cream of
  mushroom soup
1 (10¾-oz.) can cream of
  chicken soup
1 (8-oz.) can taco sauce
1 (15-oz.) can enchilada
  sauce
2 cups Cheddar cheese,
  grated
1 pkg. corn tortillas

Brown ground beef. Sauté onion in the margarine. Add sauces and soups to the onion and meat mixture. Layer the meat mixture and tortillas in a large casserole and top with grated cheese. Bake at 350 degrees for approximately 30 minutes.

Tortillas can be torn into fourths and added to the meat mixture instead of layering. Bake as above.

For microwave, cover with plastic wrap and cook 15 minutes on roast.

Mrs. Don Bowman (Brenda)

Green Enchiladas

350 degrees
9 x 12 pyrex dish
Yield: 6 servings
Freezes

1 lb. ground meat
1 tsp. salt
¼ tsp. garlic salt
½ cup onion, chopped
1 (10¾-oz.) can cream of
  chicken soup
¾ cup evaporated milk
1 (4-oz.) can green chiles,
  chopped
1 (2-oz.) jar pimientos,
  chopped
½ lb. American cheese,
  grated
½ lb. Longhorn cheese,
  grated
1 dozen corn tortillas
Wesson oil

Brown the meat in skillet with the salt, garlic salt and onion. In a saucepan put the soup, milk, chilies, pimientos and American cheese. Heat this mixture until the cheese melts. To the meat mixture, add the Longhorn cheese and mix. Heat the oil and "fry" the tortillas in it just to soften them, not crisp. In each softened tortilla, roll an even amount of the meat mixture. Place them in a 9 x 12 casserole dish and pour the cheese sauce over the tortillas. Bake ½ hour at 350 degree oven.

Mrs. Joe Stroud (Ruthie)

MEXICAN FOODS
Entrees

Fajitas

Fajitas are rich, tender cuts of meat from the forequarter inside of the beef short plate. Fajitas literally translate "little belts" or "sashes" from Spanish, and are often called "beef skirts." Your local butcher can identify the cut as #121D in the *Meat Buyers' Guide*.

Something every visitor must try, fajitas are a real Valley treat. They are so popular in the Rio Grande Valley that local residents have "fajita cook-offs" instead of the traditional Texas "chili cook-offs." Usually a mainstay of a Mexican feast, fajitas are complemented by beans, guacamole, corn or flour tortillas, and hot sauce. To really enjoy such a feast, wrap a piece of fajita in a hot tortilla, add a little hot sauce or guacamole, and enjoy!

Due to their thin cut and relatively short cooking time, fajitas are a barbeque favorite and are delicious with nothing more than a dash of meat tenderizer and seasoned salt sprinkled on them. Or, try one of these delicious variations, allowing about one-half pound fajita per person.

Barbeque Sauce for Fajitas   Barbeque pit

2 cups ketchup
1 cup brown sugar
1 cup zesty Italian dressing
1 cup Cattleman's BBQ
  Sauce
¼ cup vinegar
¼ cup soy sauce
1½ Tbs. garlic powder
3 large onions, chopped
salt
pepper
beer (or water)

Mix the first eight ingredients together, and then add salt and pepper to taste. Marinate meat in this sauce at least two hours before barbequing. Add beer or water to make enough liquid to cover the meat.

The heated sauce may be served with the fajitas.

Mrs. Ken Kachtick (Sue)

Fajitas

Barbecue Pit

fajitas
lime juice

Fajitas are delicious barbequed with only fresh lime juice squeezed on each side.

Mrs. Kenneth Landrum (June)

Fajitas de Truett

Barbeque Pit
Yield: 6-10 servings

3-5 lbs. fajitas
lemon pepper
seasoned salt
garlic salt
meat tenderizer
Wishbone Italian dressing

Remove excess fat from the fajitas, and any skin or membrane that may have been left by the butcher. Moisten the meat and sprinkle both sides with lemon pepper, seasoned salt and garlic salt. Cover with damp cloth for 1 or 2 hours. Approximately 30 minutes before cooking, sprinkle both sides with meat tenderizer and puncture meat with dinner fork about every inch. Coat each side with Italian dressing, roll meat into rolls and store in pan, covered with damp cloth, until ready to cook.

Sauce:
1 medium onion, diced
½ stick butter or margarine
¼ cup Worcestershire sauce
1 (18-oz.) bottle Smokey
   Cattleman's BBQ Sauce
½ cup ketchup
½ can beer
1 tbs. brown sugar (or to
   taste)

Make sauce while the meat is marinating. Cook meat over hot coals approximately 10 minutes on each side, less if meat is thin. Slice meat, cross grain, into one inch strips. Put meat back into pan, pour sauce over it, and stir well. Cover pan and let simmer for 10 to 15 minutes on low heat.

Sauté onions in butter; add the two sauces, beer, and ketchup. Simmer on low heat 45 minutes, adding brown sugar the last 15 minutes. Add more beer if needed for thinner consistency.

Mrs. Dan Seitz, Jr. (Amy)

MEXICAN FOODS

Entrees

Pozole
(Mexican Pork Stew)

Large soup pot
Yield: 8 servings

10-12 regular cut pork chops
salt, pepper, flour
4 Tbs. bacon drippings
2 medium onions, chopped
1 pod garlic, diced
5 Tbs. fresh cilantro,
   chopped
2 fresh tomatoes, cubed
2 serrano peppers, sliced
   (hot)
2 tsp. soy sauce
5 cups water
1 can tomatoes, stewed
1 (14-oz.) can hominy
green onions
lime

Cube pork chops. Discard bone and fat. Salt, pepper and flour cubes of pork. Brown in hot bacon drippings. Add onion, garlic, cilantro, peppers and fresh tomato after meat is slightly browned. Add soy sauce and cook for another three minutes, stirring constantly. Add water, stir, cover and allow to simmer for one hour. Add the canned tomatoes and hominy. Cover and simmer for another 30 minutes. Serve with a few chopped green onions floating on the top. Lime juice may be squeezed on top to prevent grease from forming.

Variation: May be served on a bed of shredded lettuce.

Mrs. Phil Hunke (Karen)

Frijoles y Tortillas
(Beans and Tortillas)

375 degrees
1½ quart casserole
Yield: 4-6 servings

⅔ cup onion, chopped
1 small clove garlic, chopped
   fine
2 tsp. chili powder
½ tsp. oregano
2 Tbs. salad oil
2 (1-lb.) cans Campbell's
   Beans and Ground Beef in
   Barbeque Sauce
8 corn tortillas
⅔ cup Longhorn cheese,
   grated
onion, chopped
lettuce, shredded

In covered skillet, cook onion, garlic, chili powder and oregano in oil until onion is tender. Stir in beans. Heat. Cover bottom of casserole with 4 tortillas, torn in thirds. Add ½ bean mixture and ⅓ cheese. Repeat with remaining tortillas, beans and cheese. Bake for 15 minutes. Serve with chopped onion and shredded lettuce.

Tip: An extra ½ lb. of ground beef may be cooked with onion for a more beefy dish.

Mrs. John Childers (Kathleen)

MEXICAN FOODS

Entrees

Frito Pie

350 degrees
2 quart casserole,
lightly greased
Yield: 6-8 servings

1 small package regular size
    Fritos
2 **(15-oz.) cans chili with**
    beans
1 **large onion, chopped**
8 **oz. Monterrey Jack cheese,**
    grated

Lightly grease casserole dish. Cover bottom of dish with layer of Fritos. Empty one can of chili over Fritos. Cover with ½ of the chopped onion and ½ of the grated cheese. Add another layer of Fritos and then repeat the other layers. Top with Fritos and remaining cheese. Bake at 350 degrees for 35 to 40 minutes.

Works great in microwave.

Mrs. Tom Moore (Pam)

Gringo Pies

Large, deep skillet
Yield: 10 servings
Freezes

2½ **lbs. ground meat**
2 **(4-oz.) cans green chiles,**
    chopped
1 **Tbs. dried onion**
1½ **(10¾-oz.) cans cream of**
    chicken soup
½ **tsp. salt**
5 **cups cheese, grated**

Sauté meat until well done. Add remaining ingredients except cheese and simmer for 1 hour. Before filling masa pastry, add grated cheese.

Masa Pastry:
1 **cup Masa Harina**
1 **cup flour**
1 **tsp. baking powder**
1 **tsp. salt**
½ **cup (rounded) shortening**
10 **oz. milk**

Mix dry ingredients. Add shortening with pastry blender until mixture resembles small peas. Add milk. Roll very thin as if for fried pies. Fill with meat mixture and seal carefully. Fry in hot deep fat.

Note: May be made into smaller pies as appetizers for parties.

Mrs. Charles Stewart (Betty)

MEXICAN FOODS
Entrees

King Ranch Casserole

350 degrees
2½ quart casserole, greased
Yield: 8 servings

1 fryer
1 (10¾-oz.) can cream of
mushroom soup
1 (10¾-oz.) can cream of
chicken soup
1 (10-oz.) can Ro-Tel
tomatoes and green chilies
½ can chicken broth
1 dozen corn tortillas
1 onion, chopped
2 cups cheese, grated

<u>Variation:</u>
turkey
1½ cups mushrooms,
chopped

Cook chicken in small amount of water, lightly salted, until tender. Bone and cut into pieces. To make a sauce, blend until smooth the following: the two cans of soup, can of tomatoes and green chilies and chicken broth. Set aside. Into a 2½ quart casserole (greased), place a layer of chicken, ½ of the tortillas, cut into pieces, ½ of the onion, ½ of the cheese, and ½ of the sauce. Repeat the layers, ending with the grated cheese. Bake uncovered for 1 hour.

Mrs. Frank Birkhead (Janet)

A great way to enjoy that left over Thanksgiving or Christmas turkey. To prepare for a party, a 12-15 pound turkey works perfectly for 25-30 people, increasing the other ingredients accordingly. Repeat the layers 3 or 4 times in a large roasting pan and bake approximately 2 hours at 350 degrees. This makes a perfect entree with a minimum amount of time in the kitchen for the hostess.

Mrs. Bob Batte (Gerry)

Do not rinse canned chiles since much of the taste will go down the drain with the water. If they are packed in vinegar they may be rinsed.

Jalapeño Cornbread
With Hamburger

350 degrees
Large iron skillet or 2 quart
Corning dish, greased
Yield: 8 servings

Batter:
1½ cups corn meal
1 (No. 2) can creamed corn
2 eggs, beaten
1½ cups buttermilk
½ tsp. soda
¾ tsp. salt
½ cup bacon drippings

Mix batter ingredients together and set aside.

Filling:
1 lb. hamburger meat
1 onion, chopped fine
1 lb. American cheese, grated
3 jalapeño peppers, seeded
  and chopped
1 (2-oz.) jar chopped
  pimiento
2 Tbs. cornmeal

Sauté hamburger meat. In separate bowls, have onion, cheese, jalapeño, and pimiento. Grease large skillet or Corning dish. Sprinkle 2 tablespoons of cornmeal in skillet and brown. Pour ½ of the batter in the pan and then layer jalapeño, cheese, meat, onion, and pimiento. Pour remaining batter on top and bake at 350 degrees for 45 minutes until done in center.

Mrs. Joe Friend (Pam)

Hot Mexican Rice Casserole

Large skillet
Yield: 6 servings

½ cup raw rice
1 green pepper, diced
1 cup onion, diced
1 clove garlic, minced
1 small chile pepper,
  chopped
¼ cup vegetable oil
1 lb. ground meat
¼ tsp. seasoned salt
¼ tsp. seasoned pepper
2 tsp. salt
1 Tbs. chili powder
1 cup stewed tomatoes

Sauté first five ingredients in oil until just tender. Add meat and brown. Add remaining ingredients and cook over medium heat, covered, for about 25 minutes. Add water if necessary.

Mrs. Julian Zipper (Sue)

315

MEXICAN FOODS

Entrees

Mexican Casserole I

350 degrees
9 x 11 casserole
Yield: 6-8 servings

1½-2 lbs. ground meat
2 onions, chopped
2 (15-oz.) cans Ranch Style
  beans
1 (15-oz.) can Spanish rice
1 cup Cheddar cheese,
  grated

Brown ground meat with half of the chopped onion. In a large casserole mix 2 cans ranch style beans and 1 can Spanish rice. Add browned meat and mix. Cover the top with remaining chopped onion and grated cheese. Bake 45 minutes at 350 degrees.

Good if served with flour tortillas and tossed green salad.

Mrs. Jack Humphreys (Kay)

Mexican Casserole II

375 degrees
2 quart casserole dish
Yield: 6 servings
Freezes

1 lb. ground beef
1 (15-oz.) can kidney beans,
  drained
1 (15-oz.) can mild enchilada
  sauce
1 (8-oz.) can tomato sauce
1 Tbs. instant minced onion
1 (6-oz.) pkg. corn chips
8 oz. Cheddar cheese, (2
  cups) shredded
1½ cups sour cream

In skillet, brown beef. In mixing bowl combine beans, enchilada sauce, tomato sauce and onion. Set aside 1 cup corn chips and ½ cup cheese. Add remaining cheese, chips, and meat to beans. Stir to blend. Pour into a 2 quart casserole and bake in a preheated 375 degree oven for 20-25 minutes, uncovered. Spread top with sour cream. Sprinkle with reserved cheese. Ring the remaining corn chips around the edge of the casserole dish. Return to oven for 3-4 minutes until the cheese melts. Serve immediately.

Can be doubled successfully. This can be frozen before adding the sour cream. Thaw before cooking.

Mrs. E. F. Wallace (Janet)

316

MEXICAN FOODS

Entrees

Mexican Stew

Yield: 6 servings

1½-2 lbs. meat (leftover roast
   or fresh chili ground beef)
1 clove garlic, crushed
2 onions, chopped
2-3 stalks celery, chopped
1 large potato, cubed
2 cups tomatoes, canned or 2
   large ripe tomatoes, cut up
1½-2 Tbs. chili powder
½ tsp. comino powder
½ tsp. oregano powder or
   leaves
3 Tbs. bacon drippings
1 cup water
rice

Fry meat in bacon drippings and add other ingredients. Cook for 30 minutes or until done. Serve over rice or with Spanish rice and salad.

Mexican Toss Up

Large bowl
Yield: 6-8 servings

1 lb. ground beef
1 (15-oz.) can kidney beans,
   drained
¼ tsp. salt
1 medium onion, chopped
4 tomatoes, chopped
1 head iceberg lettuce,
   broken into bite-sized
   pieces
4 oz. Cheddar cheese, grated
6-8 oz. Thousand Island or
   French dressing
1 medium bag tortilla chips,
   broken
1 large avocado, sliced
hot sauce

Brown ground beef. Add drained beans and salt. Cover and simmer 10 minutes. While sauce is simmering, combine remaining ingredients in large bowl and toss. Season to taste with hot sauce. Add simmered sauce to cold salad and serve immediately.

Mrs. Jim Jones (Jackie)

MEXICAN FOODS

Entrees

Mexican-Frito Dish

Yield: 6 servings

Meat Layer:
1 lb. lean ground beef
1 Tbs. cumin seed
½ Tbs. chili powder
1 Tbs. margarine, melted
1 green pepper, chopped
1 onion, chopped

Brown the meat in a small amount of oil. Add cumin seed and chili powder. In separate skillet, cook pepper and onion in margarine until clear. Add to meat and cook for 20 minutes.

Salad layer:
½ head lettuce, chopped
1 tomato, chopped
1 onion, chopped or sliced
1 avocado, cut up
green olives to taste

Combine all salad ingredients.

Chili Con Queso Layer:
2 lbs. Velveeta cheese
1 (10-oz.) can Ro-Tel
   tomatoes and green chilies

Melt the queso ingredients together.

Fritos

Layer in a warm plate the following: Fritos on bottom, then the salad mix, then hot meat and finally top with hot cheese mixture. Serve immediately.

Mrs. John Maxwell (Betty)

Mexican Style Steak

325 degrees
Shallow baking dish
Yield: 6 servings

2 lbs. round steak, about
   ½-inch thick
3 Tbs. all-purpose flour
1½ tsp. salt
pepper
2 Tbs. salad oil
1 (6-oz.) can broiled
   mushroom crowns, drained

Cut steak into 6 serving pieces. Combine flour, salt and dash of pepper; dredge meat in mixture. Heat oil. Brown meat on both sides in hot oil. Remove meat and arrange in shallow baking dish. Pour half the salsa (listed below) over meat. Cover and bake in slow oven, 325 degrees, for 2 hours, or until tender. Add mushrooms the last 10 minutes. Skim off excess fat.

continued . . .

Salsa:

¼ cup salad oil
1 clove garlic, crushed
1 cup onion, chopped
1 (No. 2½) can whole
   tomatoes, mashed
1 (4-oz.) can green chiles,
   chopped (½ can if using
   seeds)
1 tsp. salt

Heat oil until very hot. Add garlic and onion. Stir while mixture cooks. When garlic and onion are browned, add the remaining ingredients. Simmer uncovered 30 minutes or to good sauce consistency. Salt to taste.

Serve with fried rice. Heat remaining salsa and pass it with the meat.

Mrs. Neal Runnels (Gayle)

Panuchos

**Skillet and saucepan
Yield: 4 servings**

8 corn tortillas
1-2 cups pinto beans,
   mashed
5 Tbs. or more cooking oil

Split tortillas into two layers by gently inserting knife in edge of tortilla. Be careful not to split all of the way around, making a "pocket" in the tortilla only. Insert mashed beans in the "pocket" in the tortillas, and fry the stuffed tortillas in the hot oil. Remove from oil and drain on absorbent paper. Top with chicken in tomato sauce.

Chicken-tomato sauce:

1½ cups fresh tomatoes,
   mashed
4 Tbs. cooking oil
2 cups cooked chicken, finely
   chopped
cumino, garlic, pepper, and
   salt to taste

Fry tomatoes in oil until cooked. Add seasonings and chicken. Let mixture come to a boil, and pour over stuffed tortillas. Top with onion rings if desired.

Onion rings:

1 large onion, sliced and
   separated into rings
olive oil
vinegar to taste
oregano leaves to taste

Slice onion and sauté in oil until tender. Season with vinegar and sprinkle oregano over onions.

Mrs. Dario V. Guerra, Jr. (Carmen)

MEXICAN FOODS

Entrees

Stuffed Peppers

Yield: 6 servings

6 large green hot peppers
  (the type used in making
  Chile Rellenos)
4 Tbs. or more cooking oil
2 cups white cheese, grated
5 eggs, separated
¾ cup flour, approximately
salt, pepper and garlic
  powder, to taste

Fry peppers, one or two at a time, in hot fat, turning often. As they heat, skin will crinkle and turn slightly brown. When they are crinkled all over, remove from oil and wrap in paper towels. Cool and peel; remove seeds, being careful not to tear pepper when you slit it. Stuff peppers with cheese and close with toothpicks. Beat egg whites until stiff; add yolks to whites and beat together. Add enough flour to make a thin batter (approximately 3 or 4 Tbs.). Season with salt, pepper and garlic powder. Dip stuffed pepper in rest of the dry flour and then in the batter. Fry in the same oil in which peppers were fried. The batter will puff and turn a delicate brown.

Sauce:
1 small carton sour cream
1 small carton half and half
  or whipping cream
1 cup Monterrey Jack cheese,
  grated

Mix sour cream, whipped cream and grated cheese; heat and salt to taste. Serve sauce mixture with stuffed peppers.

Seasoned ground meat may be used for the stuffing in place of the cheese.

Mrs. Dario V. Guerra, Jr. (Carmen)

Hot Tamale Pie

350 degrees
2 (1½ quart) casseroles
Yield: 8-10 servings

Cornmeal Mush:
6 cups water
1½ tsp. salt
1½ cups yellow corn meal
1-1½ Tbs. chili powder

Blend the water, salt, corn meal and chili powder together in a saucepan. Boil 20 minutes, stirring constantly. Spread cornmeal mush on bottom and sides of casseroles.

continued ...

MEXICAN FOODS
Entrees

Filling:
1 lb. round steak, ground
¼ lb. lean pork, ground
2 Tbs. fat
2 onions, chopped
3 Tbs. cumin seed (or ground comino)
1 Tbs. chili powder (more if you like it HOT)
1 (1 lb. 12-oz.) can tomatoes
2 tsp. salt
2 cloves garlic, minced
¼ tsp. red pepper

Fry the ground round steak, ground pork and onions in the fat in skillet. Add the seasonings and tomatoes; stir well. Pour over the mush and bake at 350 degrees for 45 minutes.

Mrs. John Wright (Melinda)

Fiesta Tamale Casserole

350 degrees
Large flat baking dish
Yield: 6 servings
Freezes

½ lb. pork sausage
1 cup onions, minced
¾ cup green pepper, chopped
½ lb. ground beef
1 cup whole kernel corn (or hominy)
⅓ cup ripe olives, sliced
1½ cups tomato sauce
2 (15-oz.) cans of tamales
¾ cup American cheese, grated

Brown sausage, drain and set aside. In 3 Tbs. drippings, sauté onion and pepper until tender. Add ground beef and sauté until done. Return sausage to mixture. Add corn, olives, 1 Tbs. liquid from corn, and tomato sauce. Simmer 15 minutes. Pour mixture in baking dish and top with tamales. Bake uncovered until well heated, about 15-20 minutes. Sprinkle grated cheese on top and return to oven until cheese is melted.

Mrs. Allen Beakey (Jane)

MEXICAN FOODS

Entrees

Sombrero Tacos

Large pot
Yield: 16 servings

5 lbs. ground beef
2 large onions, chopped
1 small carrot, finely chopped
2 large bell peppers, chopped
3 large cloves garlic, minced
3 large ribs of celery,
  chopped
2 (4-oz.) cans mushrooms,
  drained
1 (6-oz.) can ripe olives,
  chopped and drained
2 (28-oz.) cans tomatoes,
  drained
1 (16-oz.) can tomato sauce
2 (15-oz.) cans kidney beans,
  drained
2 (14-16-oz.) cans whole
  kernel corn, drained
1 cup red wine (Spañada)
1 tsp. chili powder
1 can Ro-Tel tomato and
  green chilies
2 jalapeños, chopped
salt, pepper, and ground
  cumino to taste
American cheese, grated
lettuce, shredded
chopped onion for topping
corn chips

Brown ground beef and drain well. Combine beef and all other ingredients (with the exception of cheese, lettuce and reserved onion) in large pot and simmer several hours. Serve over corn chips and top with grated cheese, chopped onion, and shredded lettuce.

Mrs. Paul Bergh (Betty)

MEXICAN FOODS
Entrees

Cream Tacos

**Saucepan and skillet
Yield: 4 servings**

4 onions, minced
1 clove garlic, minced
2 cans green chiles, chopped
1 (No. 2) can tomatoes,
  chopped
1 cup cheese, grated
3 cups half and half
salt to taste
oil for cooking
1 dozen corn tortillas
sour cream

Sauté onions and garlic. Add chiles, tomatoes, salt and simmer. Add ½ cup of the grated cheese. Add half and half to this mixture just before serving. Fry tortillas in very hot oil. Drain. Dip drained tortillas in sauce to lightly cover (half and half having been added at this point). Place tortillas on individual plate and cover with more of the sauce. Add grated cheese and a spoonful of sour cream. Stack 2 or 3 layers of tortillas per person, alternating sauce, cheese, and sour cream. Must prepare and serve immediately.

Mrs. Jim Jones (Jackie)

Taco Salad

**Large salad bowl
Yield: 6-8 servings**

Meat mixture:
1½ lbs. ground meat
1 cup green pepper, diced
1 cup onion, chopped
2 tsp. chili powder
8 shakes cumin powder

Mix and brown.

Cheese mixture:
1 lb. Velveeta cheese
1 can Ro-Tel tomatoes and
  chilies

Melt over low heat.

Salad:
1 head lettuce, chopped
2 tomatoes, chopped
1 pkg. Fritos

Toss together in large salad bowl with meat and cheese mixture.

A one dish dinner!

MEXICAN FOODS

Entrees

Cheesy Crescent Tostada Pie

375 degrees
9 inch pie pan
Yield: 8 servings

1 lb. ground meat
1 pkg. chili mix
1 (15-oz.) can refried beans
1 can crescent rolls
1 Tbs. corn meal
Cheddar cheese, grated
lettuce, chopped
tomatoes, chopped

Brown 1 lb. ground meat. Add package of chili mix. Mix well. Add can of refried beans. Mix well and simmer a few minutes. Line pie pan with crescent rolls pressing together to form a crust. Sprinkle with corn meal. Add meat mixture. Sprinkle top with grated cheese. Bake 20 min. at 375 degrees. At serving time top with chopped lettuce and tomatoes.

Mrs. Jack Humphreys (Kay)

Red Snapper Vera Cruz

9 x 9 baking dish
Yield: 6-8 servings

1 small tomato, peeled,
   seeded and chopped
½ cup onion, chopped
½ green pepper, chopped
4 Tbs. butter
1 (3-oz.) can mushrooms,
   drained
3 Tbs. chili sauce
2 Tbs. lemon juice
2 Tbs. capers
1 Tbs. parsley, chopped
1 clove garlic, chopped
½ Tbs. dried thyme
¼ tsp. salt
2 lbs. snapper fillets
1 (4½-oz.) can shrimp
¼ cup dry white wine

Combine ingredients except for fish, shrimp and wine in a baking dish. Cook in microwave 5-6 minutes or until tender. Stir in shrimp and wine. Place fillets on top. Spoon some of the sauce over the fish, cover and continue cooking for four minutes or until fish flakes with a fork.

A microwave dish!

Mrs. Jerry Leadbetter (Tonii)

Stuffed Mexican Squash

350 degrees
Baking dish
Yield: 2 servings

1 medium Mexican squash
¼ stick butter
1 medium onion, chopped
1 medium bell pepper,
  chopped
1 rib celery, chopped
1 pod garlic, chopped
½ lb. ham, cooked and
  chopped (about 2 cups)
1 cup stale French bread
  soaked in milk
1 bay leaf
¼-½ tsp. thyme (to taste)
⅛ cup fresh parsley, finely
  chopped
salt and pepper to taste
½ cup seasoned bread
  crumbs

Cut squash in half and remove seeds. Place in large pot. Cover with water. Bring to boil, lower heat and cook 15-20 minutes until tender. (Check with fork.) Remove all pulp into a bowl and reserve. Set aside. Melt butter in large skillet. Add onion, bell pepper, celery, garlic and sauté until lightly brown. Add ham, squash pulp and bread (squeeze all moisture from bread), bay leaf, thyme and parsley. Season to taste. Cook briskly until most of the liquid evaporates and mixture is thick enough to hold its shape. Spoon filling into shells heaping in center. Place in oven-proof dish. Top with seasoned bread crumbs. Bake at 350 degrees for 15 minutes until heated through and slightly brown. Serve immediately.

Variation: Shrimp may be substituted for ham.

Rudy Pharis, Director 1968-1978
McAllen International Museum
Contributed title for *LA PINATA*

Squeezing lime or lemon juice over avocados helps to keep them from turning dark. You can also place an avocado seed in the middle of a guacamole salad and cover the seed with the mixture to prevent its darkening.

MEXICAN FOODS
Entrees/Desserts

Tortilla Roll Ups

Yield: 16-20 servings

1 large onion, diced
2 raw, medium potatoes,
  peeled
oil
1½-2 lbs. chuck roast,
  cooked and cut into small
  pieces
1 pkg. dry onion soup
garlic, salt and pepper to
  taste
flour tortillas

Dice onion and raw potatoes and sauté in small amount of oil for 5 minutes. Add roast, gravy and package of onion soup. Add seasonings to taste. Add enough water to cover. Cook covered until diced potatoes are tender. Stir often and add more water if needed. Place a small amount of mixture inside the flour tortillas and roll up.

This recipe is good for leftover roast. Use gravy if you have it on hand. Can be reheated later. These are good when left in oven so tortillas become crispy.

Mrs. Greg Morrow (Debbie)

Mexican Candy

Yield: 2 dozen

1 cup white sugar
1 cup brown sugar
7 Tbs. milk
1 cup pecans, whole or
  broken

Combine sugar and milk in heavy saucepan and cook until a soft ball will form in water. Add nuts. Beat until mixed. Drop spoonfuls onto wax paper.

Mrs. Joseph Hettler (Paula)

Bolitas de Almendra
(Almond Candies)

Moderate oven
Cookie sheet, buttered
Yield: one dozen

1 cup almonds, blanched and
  ground
½ cup powdered sugar
½ tsp. vanilla
1 egg white, stiffly beaten

Mix the ground nuts with the sugar and vanilla and add the stiffly beaten egg white. Form into small balls and bake on a buttered cookie sheet in a moderate oven for 5 minutes.

A sweet from Durango.

Mrs. Tom Moore (Pam)

326

Buñuelos I
(Christmas Fritters)

Rosette wheel
Yield: 60

2 eggs
2 tsp. sugar
1 cup milk
1 cup flour, sifted
¼ tsp. salt
1 tsp. vanilla
oil
powdered sugar, cinnamon
   or syrup

Add sugar to eggs and beat. Add milk and continue beating. Add sifted flour and salt to above mixture while beating. Add vanilla. Fry in hot oil using a Rosette wheel. May be dusted with powdered sugar, cinnamon or served in bowls with syrup.

Delicious with coffee for breakfast or bridge parties. Buñuelos are a special Christmas tradition in many areas in Old Mexico. In one city, the fritters are served in bowls with syrup and after eaten the empty bowls are smashed on the ground for good luck.

Mrs. Neal Runnels (Gayle)

Buñuelos II

Yield: 2 dozen

4 cups flour
¼ cup shortening
1½ cups hot water
cooking oil
sugar
ground cinnamon

Mix flour, shortening and add water—blend like bread or tortilla dough. Let sit for about 20 minutes, covered. Shape into quarter size balls, let sit 20 minutes more. Roll out very thin pulling with hands if necessary (should be about 6 inches in diameter and paper thin). If dough is sticky sprinkle flour on the rolling area. In a frying pan place 1 inch of oil and allow it to get very hot. Place buñuelo in pan, let brown to a golden brown on each side. Remove and quickly sprinkle sugar and cinnamon mixture on both sides. Do not cover the buñuelos or they will get soggy.

Mrs. Leonel Garza, Jr. (Linda)

MEXICAN FOODS
Desserts

Caramel Flan
(Mexican Custard)

350 degrees
6 cup mold
Yield: 6-8 servings

½ cup sugar
4 eggs, beaten
1 can sweetened condensed
  milk
2 cans (milk cans) filled with
  water
1 tsp. vanilla

Melt ½ cup sugar in heavy saucepan over medium heat until caramel color liquid results. Pour into 6-cup corning, pyrex or jello mold to cover bottom of container. Beat eggs together with milk and water. Add vanilla. Do not beat more than two minutes. Pour mixture over cooled, melted sugar in container. Place mold in another container that is half-filled with water so that the flan will bake in a water bath. Bake, covered, at 350 degrees for 1½ hours. Continue to bake an additional 30 minutes uncovered or until done. Test with toothpick. Flan is done when toothpick comes out clean.

The ingredients can be doubled to fill a bundt cake pan and will serve 16-20 people. Uncovered baking time must be increased. Check with toothpick.

The most important thing to remember is to pour the melted sugar into the mold when it turns to caramel color. If the sugar cooks and liquifies too quickly it will burn, and remember that the liquified sugar is very hot, so be careful.

Amaretto, Kahlua, or brandy can replace ¼ can of water if desired for a different taste for this flan.

Mrs. Larry Fallek (Patty)

Salads and Dressing

continued . . .

SALADS and DRESSINGS
Fruit Salads

Angel Salad

3 quart mold or
pyrex dish
Yield: 12 servings

1 (6-oz.) pkg. lime jello
2 cups boiling water
2 (3-oz.) pkgs. cream cheese
1 (8-oz.) can crushed
pineapple, drained
1 cup celery, diced
1 (2-oz.) jar pimientos,
chopped
1 cup pecans, chopped
½ pint whipping cream,
whipped

Dissolve jello in boiling water and let cool. Mash cream cheese, and add pineapple, celery, pimientos, and pecans. Fold into cooled jello and place in refrigerator until it becomes thick but not firmly gelled. Whip cream and fold in. Pour into mold, rinsed in cold water, and chill until firm.

Mrs. Charles Ridlehuber (Dorothy)

Variation:
1 (3-oz.) pkg. lemon jello
1 cup boiling water
1 cup ripe olives, sliced
1 (4-oz.) jar pimientos,
chopped
½ cup sugar

Omit lime jello, 1 cup water, celery and 2-oz. pimientos as listed above. Prepare recipe, from new ingredients listed in variation, according to directions above beating in ½ cup sugar with the whipping cream stage.

Mrs. Don Bentsen (Nell)

Apricot Nectar Congealed Salad

9 x 9 pan
Yield: 9 servings

2 (3-oz.) pkgs. lime gelatin
2 cups hot water
1 (3-oz.) pkg. cream cheese
1 can apricot nectar
½ cup pecans, chopped
1 small can crushed
pineapple

Dissolve gelatin in hot water, add the cream cheese and stir well to blend. Add apricot nectar, pecans, and pineapple. Refrigerate and stir just enough to mix when salad begins to congeal.

Mrs. Billy Simpson (Ginger)

SALADS and DRESSINGS
Fruit Salads

Blueberry Congealed Salad

6 cup mold
Yield: 8-10 servings

1 (15-oz.) can wild
   blueberries, drain and
   retain juice
1 (8¼-oz.) can crushed
   pineapple, drain and retain
   juice
2 (3-oz.) pkgs. black cherry
   gelatin
1 tray of ice cubes
1 cup sugar
2 (3-oz.) pkgs. cream cheese
1 tsp. vanilla
½ pint sour cream
chopped nuts

Use fruit juices and enough water to make two cups liquid. Heat until boiling. Add gelatin, dissolve and let stand for a few minutes. Melt tray of ice cubes in gelatin. Remove unmelted cubes after a few minutes. Add drained blueberries and pineapple. Congeal. Cream together the sugar, cream cheese and vanilla. Fold in ½ pint sour cream. Spread on top of congealed salad. Sprinkle nuts on top and refrigerate.

Mrs. John Childers (Kathleen)

Bing Cherry Salad

8 x 8 dish or
small ring mold
Yield: 6-8 servings

1 can sweet Bing cherries,
   drain and reserve juice
¼ lb. pecans, halved
1 (3-oz.) pkg. raspberry
   gelatin
mayonnaise to grease muffin
   tins
lettuce leaves

Place cherries stuffed with pecans in molds or muffin tins greased with mayonnaise. Make gelatin as directed using cherry juice to substitute for the water. Pour over cherries and refrigerate until set. Unmold on a bed of lettuce. Good with turkey or chicken main dishes. Top with mayonnaise if desired.

Mrs. Cameron Henry (Kathryn)

A sure way to unmold your congealed salads is to always grease the mold first with mayonnaise.

SALADS and DRESSINGS
Fruit Salads

Cranberry Salad

7 x 11 dish
Yield: 6-8 servings

½ pkg. cranberries
1 cup sugar
1 (No. 2) can crushed
  pineapple, well drained
½ pkg. small marshmallows
1 cup pecans, chopped
1 cup whipped cream or Cool
  Whip

Chop or grind the cranberries coarsely and set overnight in the sugar. Add the pineapple and other ingredients. Put in dish and set several hours.

Mrs. Robert F. Barnes (Kay)

Cranberry Congealed Salad

8 x 8 pan
Yield: 6-8 servings

1 (3-oz.) pkg. cherry gelatin
1 cup boiling water
1 can whole cranberry sauce
½ cup celery, cut fine
1 cup sour cream
¼ cup pecans, chopped

Dissolve gelatin in boiling water. When dissolved, add remaining ingredients. Cool in refrigerator until solid.

Mrs. Billy Simpson (Ginger)

Cranberry Ribbon Loaf Salad

Yield: 8 servings

1 (1 lb.) can whole cranberry
  sauce
2 Tbs. lemon juice
¼ cup confectioner's sugar
½ cup crushed pineapple,
  drained
½ pint heavy cream, whipped
⅔ cup nuts, chopped

Combine cranberry sauce and lemon juice. Pour into refrigerator tray. Blend together remaining ingredients and place this over cranberry sauce. Freeze until firm. Serve in slices as salad or dessert.

Mrs. Jerry McGilvray (Jane)

SALADS and DRESSINGS
Fruit Salads

Thanksgiving Cranberry Salad

Yield: about 5 cups

1 sack raw cranberries
2 whole oranges
2 cups sugar
1½ cups boiling water
1 (3-oz.) pkg. cherry gelatin
½ cup nuts, chopped
  (optional)

Grind cranberries and oranges (skin and all) in a food grinder. Marinate the cranberries and oranges with sugar. Dissolve gelatin in boiling water. Cool, and add 1 cup of cranberry-orange mixture to gelatin. Add chopped nuts for extra flavor. Chill.

Remaining cranberry-orange mixture can be frozen in 1-cup portions for later use. This provides for quick salads.

Mrs. Michael D. Owens (Cissy)

Cherry Salad Supreme

9 x 9 x 2 inch baking dish
Yield: 12 servings

1 (3-oz.) pkg. raspberry-
  flavored gelatin
1 (3-oz.) pkg. lemon-flavored
  gelatin
1 (21-oz.) can cherry pie
  filling
1 (3-oz.) pkg. cream cheese
⅓ cup mayonnaise
1 (8¾-oz.) can crushed
  pineapple
2 cups water
1 cup miniature
  marshmallows
½ cup whipping cream
2 Tbs. nuts, chopped

Dissolve raspberry gelatin in 1 cup boiling water; stir in pie filling. Turn into 9 x 9 x 2-inch baking dish. Chill until partially set. Dissolve lemon gelatin in 1 cup boiling water. Beat together cream cheese and mayonnaise. Gradually add lemon gelatin. Stir in undrained pineapple. Whip ½ cup whipping cream; fold into lemon mixture with the tiny marshmallows. Spread over cherry layer; top with 2 Tbs. chopped nuts. Chill until set.

Mrs. Neal Runnels (Gayle)

SALADS and DRESSINGS
Fruit Salads

Frosted Salad

9 x 13 pyrex dish
Yield: 18-20 servings
12-16 servings

2 (3-oz.) pkgs. lemon jello
2 cups boiling water
2 cups Seven-Up
1 (20-oz.) can crushed
   pineapple
1 cup miniature
   marshmallows (optional)
2 large bananas, sliced

Dissolve jello in water. Stir in Seven-Up. Chill until partly set. Drain pineapple, saving juice for topping. Fold in pineapple, marshmallows, and bananas into jello mixture. Pour into 9x13 dish and chill until firm.

Topping:
½ cup sugar
2 Tbs. flour
1 cup pineapple juice (saved
   from jello part)
1 egg, slightly beaten
2 Tbs. butter
1 cup Cool Whip
shredded American cheese
   (optional)

Combine sugar, flour and stir in pineapple juice. Add egg and cook over low heat until thick. Remove from heat and add butter. Chill thoroughly. Fold in Cool Whip. Frost jello with topping. Sprinkle with cheese if desired.

Note: Seven-Up may bubble over so use large bowl to mix in.

Mrs. David Sulzbach (Judi)

Cool Gelatin Salad

2 quart mold
Yield: 12 servings

1 (3-oz.) pkg. lemon jello
1 (3-oz.) pkg. lime jello
1 cup boiling water
1 (14-oz.) can Eagle Brand
   Milk
1 pint large curd cottage
   cheese
1 (15-oz.) can crushed
   pineapple in heavy syrup
1 cup mayonnaise

Dissolve jello in boiling water and add all other ingredients. Refrigerate. Garnish with fresh fruit or vegetables.

Mrs. Fred Braunig (Joyce)

SALADS and DRESSINGS
Fruit Salads

Frozen Fruit Salad

Muffin paper cups
Yield: 6-8 servings

1 pint sour cream
1 large can crushed
   pineapple, drained
1 jar maraschino cherries,
   drained and chopped
2 bananas, sliced
1 cup pecans, chopped
¾ cup sugar (optional)

Mix ingredients together. Mold in muffin paper cups. When frozen, take out of paper cups and put in plastic bag and keep in freezer.

Mandarin Orange Salad

Mold or casserole dish
Yield: 8 servings

1 large container Cool Whip
1 large container small-curd
   cottage cheese
1 (6-oz.) pkg. orange gelatin
   (dry)
2 small cans mandarin
   oranges

Mix all ingredients together (including juice from oranges). Pour into a mold or casserole dish. Chill at least 2 hrs.

Mrs. Frank Birkhead (Janet)

Orange Sherbet Salad

9 x 13 inch dish
Yield: 12 servings

2 (3-oz.) pkgs. orange gelatin
2 cups hot water
1 pint orange sherbet
1 small can mandarin
   oranges, with juice
2 bananas, sliced

Dissolve gelatin in hot water. Add remaining ingredients, mixing well. Chill until set.

Mrs. Hiram Tavarez (Kathe)

SALADS and DRESSINGS
Fruit Salads

Mango Mold

11 x 15 pyrex dish
Yield: 12-15 servings

3 (3-oz.) pkgs. lemon gelatin
2½ cups boiling water
1 (29-oz.) can mangos with
  juice
1 (8-oz.) pkg. cream cheese
¼ cup lemon juice

Dissolve gelatin in boiling water. Blend mangos, juice, cream cheese and lemon juice. Combine and pour into a mold or large shallow pan. Let congeal for 24 hours. Tastes a bit like lemon pudding.

You can substitute one package of orange gelatin for one lemon.

Mrs. Jim Miller (Terry)

Pear-Orange-Cherry Mold

9 x 9 pan or ring mold
Yield: 9 servings

1 (6-oz.) pkg. jello (any kind)
2 cups boiling water
⅛ tsp. salt
1 (1 lb.) can pear slices, save
  juice
1 small jar cherries, drained
1 small can mandarin
  oranges, drained
2 (3-oz.) pkgs. cream cheese,
  softened

Dissolve jello in water and add salt. Take syrup from pears and add enough water to make a 1½ cup mixture of syrup and water. Pour this into the dissolved gelatin. From this total mixture of syrup, water and gelatin, set aside 1½ cups for later use. Pour remainder of mixture into a greased mold and add drained fruit. Chill until this layer is thick enough to hold the next layer without leaking through. Take reserved gelatin and mix with softened cream cheese. (Use blender or food processor and run through strainer.) Pour this over partly thickened jello testing to be sure that the bottom layer is ready and no leaking will occur. Chill until completely set.

Mrs. Greg Morrow (Debbie)

SALADS and DRESSINGS
Fruit Salads

Pineapple Marshmallow Congealed Salad

Large pyrex dish
Yield: 12-14 servings

4 cups water
1 (3 oz.) pkg. lemon Jello
1 (3 oz.) pkg. lime Jello
1 (No. 303) can crushed
   pineapple, drained
23 large marshmallows
1 (12 oz.) carton small-curd
   cottage cheese
1 pint whipping cream
1 cup walnuts or pecans,
   chopped

Bring 2 cups water to a boil in a large pan. Remove from heat and dissolve Jello in it. Add 2 cups of cold water and boil for 2 minutes. Add pineapple and boil 2 more minutes. Remove from heat and dissolve marshmallows in it. Chill until mixture begins to thicken and add cottage cheese, whipped cream and nuts. Chill until firm.

Mrs. Don Bowman (Brenda)

Pet Milk Salad

9 x 12 pyrex dish
Yield: 12 servings

1 (3-oz.) pkg. lime gelatin
1½ cups boiling water
17 marshmallows, cut small
1 small can Pet milk,
   thoroughly chilled, whipped
1 medium can crushed
   pineapple, drained
½ cup pecans, chopped

Mix gelatin into boiling water. While gelatin is hot, add marshmallows, and stir until melted. Chill. When gelatin mixture starts to gel, fold in Pet milk that has been whipped with electric mixer. Add pineapple and nuts. Pour in mold and chill until congealed. Use 12 individual molds or one large salad mold.

Spiced Peach Salad

9 x 9 dish
Yield: 8 servings

1 can spiced peaches
1 (6-oz.) pkg. lemon gelatin
1½ cups liquid (use peach
   juice, 1 Tbs. lemon juice,
   and water)

Cut peaches from seed and purée in blender. Dissolve gelatin in 1 cup hot water and mix in ½ cup peach syrup and peaches. Pour into mold and chill.

Mrs. Robert F. Barnes (Kay)

SALADS and DRESSINGS
Fruit Salads

Sausalito Fruit Salad

Yield: 6 servings

4 avocados
1 cup cantaloupe balls
1 cup strawberry halves
1 cup grapefruit sections
French dressing, Poppy
    Seed, or your choice of
    dressing
lettuce leaves

Make balls or cubes of one of the avocados. Combine the avocado balls, cantaloupe balls, strawberries and grapefruit sections and enough dressing to moisten. Peel remaining avocados and make halves. Fill with fruit mixture. Serve on lettuce-covered plate with additional dressing.

Mrs. Gilbert Weisberg (Suzy)

Surprise Salad

6 cup mold
Yield: 8 servings

1 (3-oz.) pkg. lemon jello
1 cup boiling water
¼ cup sugar
1 (8¼-oz.) can crushed
    pineapple, do not drain
1 cup Cheddar cheese,
    grated
1 cup cream, whipped
1 cup pecans, chopped

Add jello to boiling water, set aside. In small saucepan bring to a boil sugar and pineapple. Add to jello and let stand until ready to set, then add grated cheese, whipped cream and nuts. Mix well and refrigerate.

Mrs. Mark Seitz (Diana)

Texas Pineapple Salad

9 x 9 pan or
7 x 11 oblong
Yield: 10-12 servings

1 large can crushed
    pineapple
2 (3-oz.) pkgs. lemon gelatin
1 medium can sweet cherries
    (drained) or 1 small can
    fruit cocktail
1 small pkg. Dream Whip
½ cup nuts, chopped

Heat pineapple to boiling. Add gelatin to dissolve. Chill to congeal slightly. Add cherries or fruit cocktail. Prepare Dream Whip according to package directions, and fold into congealed mixture along with nuts. Put in pan or individual molds and chill to set.

Mrs. Steven Zenthoefer (Ann)

SALADS and DRESSINGS
Fruit Salads

Twenty-Four Hour Salad

Yield: 10-12 servings

2 cups white cherries, halved
and pitted
2 cups pineapple, diced
2 cups orange sections
2 cups marshmallows,
quartered
¼ lb. almonds, blanched and
chopped
2 eggs
2 Tbs. sugar
¼ cup light cream
1 lemon, juiced
1 cup heavy cream, whipped

Combine well-drained fruits. Add marshmallows and nuts. Beat eggs until light. Gradually add sugar, light cream and lemon juice. Mix; cook in double boiler until smooth and thick, stirring constantly. Cool; fold in whipped cream. Pour custard mixture over mixed fruit, and mix lightly. Chill 24 hours. Do not freeze.

Mrs. Morris Nelson (Carolynn)

Two-Layer Salad

9 x 13 pyrex dish
Yield: 12 servings

First layer:
1 (3-oz.) pkg. lemon gelatin
(or lime for Christmas)
1 cup boiling water
1 (3-oz.) pkg. cream cheese
1 cup marshmallows
1 pkg. Dream Whip
2 Tbs. salad dressing
1 cup crushed pineapple,
drained

Dissolve lemon gelatin in boiling water. Beat in marshmallows and cream cheese with an electric mixer. Chill until syrupy. Then mix 1 pkg. Dream Whip as directed on package and 2 Tbs. salad dressing. Mix with thickened lemon mixture, then add pineapple. Pour into dish to congeal.

Second layer:
1 (3-oz.) pkg. strawberry or
raspberry gelatin
1½ cups hot water
1 pkg. frozen strawberries or
raspberries

Dissolve strawberry gelatin in hot water. Add fruit; mix well, and pour on top of congealed lemon mixture.

Mrs. Jerry McGilvray (Jane)

SALADS and DRESSINGS
Fruit/Vegetable Salads

Strawberry Jello Mold

9 x 13 baking dish
Yield: 15-18 servings

2 (3-oz.) pkgs. strawberry
  Jello
1½ cups boiling water
1 (No. 2) can crushed
  pineapple
1 pkg. frozen strawberries
  (thawed)
1 cup nuts, chopped
1 cup sour cream

Dissolve Jello in boiling water. Drain pineapple, reserve juice. Add ½ cup pineapple juice to dissolved Jello. Add strawberries, pineapple and nuts. Put one-half of the mixture into a mold, and allow to harden. Spread sour cream over congealed portion. Chill. Then add remainder of Jello over sour cream. Chill to set.

Mrs. Larry Fallek (Patty)

Watergate Salad

7 x 11 pyrex dish
Yield: 6-8 servings

1 (9-oz.) Cool Whip
1 box instant pistachio
  pudding
1 (No. 2) can crushed
  pineapple
1¾ cups miniature
  marshmallows
½ cup pecans, chopped

Mix the Cool Whip and the instant pudding together. Add crushed pineapple, marshmallows, pecans. Mix all together and pour into a 7 x 11 pyrex dish and refrigerate.

Asparagus Salad

Yield: 6-8 servings

¾ cup sugar
1 tsp. salt
½ tsp. dry mustard
½ tsp. paprika
⅓ cup vinegar
1 cup salad oil
1½ Tbs. poppy seed
2 tall cans asparagus
1½ Tbs. onion, grated

Blend the sugar, salt, dry mustard, and paprika. Add the vinegar. Gradually blend in the oil and poppy seed. Marinate the asparagus and onion in this mixture for at least 12 hours. Refrigerate.

Mrs. Charles Fox (Nancy)

341

SALADS and DRESSINGS
Vegetable Salads

Marinated Asparagus

Yield: 4 servings

1 lb. fresh asparagus
½ cup light salad oil
⅓ cup white wine vinegar
1 tsp. sweet basil
1 tsp. Beau Monde seasoning
1 tsp. Italian seasoning
  (dried)
1 tsp. oregano
½ tsp. cracked pepper
2 cloves garlic, sliced thin

Blanch asparagus in boiling salted water for 2 to 3 mintues, until a bright green color. Drain and place in shallow dish. Combine all other ingredients and pour over asparagus. Refrigerate overnight. If marinade does not completely cover asparagus, turn the asparagus once or twice. Drain to serve and may be arranged on a bed of lettuce leaves.

Mrs. Gary Gurwitz (Bailey)

Artichoke Salad

6 cup ring mold

1 envelope plain gelatin
¼ cup boiling water
1 cup mayonnaise (not salad
  dressing or Miracle Whip)
¼ cup cold water
1 (10-oz.) can hearts of
  artichoke, well drained
1 (16-oz.) can tiny peas, well
  drained
1 Tbs. lemon juice
1 small jar pimientos,
  chopped
2 green onions, chopped fine

Soften gelatin in cold water. Add hot water, then mayonnaise and stir until smooth. Add all other ingredients and mix well. Put in ring mold and refrigerate. Unmold on tray, surround with crisp lettuce and serve with mayonnaise.

Mrs. Thomas B. Sammons, Jr. (Gretchen)

Lettuce and celery will keep longer if stored in the refrigerator in paper bags instead of cellophane ones.

SALADS and DRESSINGS
Vegetable Salads

Creamy Avocado Mold

3 cup mold,
lightly greased

1½ Tbs. (1½ envelopes)
  unflavored gelatin
1 cup cold water
¾ cup boiling water
2 Tbs. lemon juice
1¼ tsp. salt
1 tsp. onion, grated
2 or more dashes Tabasco or
  Mexican hot sauce
2½ cups ripe avocado,
  mashed
1 cup sour cream
1 cup mayonnaise

Lightly grease mold. Soften gelatin in cold water; dissolve in boiling water. Add lemon juice, salt, onion, and Tabasco. Let cool to room temperature. Stir in avocado, sour cream, and mayonnaise. Pour into mold. Chill until firm (5 to 6 hrs. or overnight).

Mrs. Dan Seitz (Amy)

Bean Salad

Yield: 16-20 servings

2 cups vinegar
2½ cups sugar
1 Tbs. salt
1 (16-oz.) can whole green
  beans, drained
1 (16-oz.) can waxed beans,
  drained
1 (16-oz.) can kidney beans,
  drained
1 (16-oz.) can lima beans,
  drained
1 small jar whole carrots,
  drained
1 head of cauliflower

Boil vinegar, sugar, and salt until slightly thickened and syrupy. Pour syrupy mixture over beans and carrots. Cook cauliflower separately in boiling water for 5 minutes. It needs to be crisp. Drain and break into small flowers. Add to the bean mixture. Mix all well and keep in covered dish in the refrigerator for 3 days before serving.

This mixture could be put into individual jars and stored in the refrigerator until ready to serve.

Mrs. Jim Jones (Jackie)

SALADS and DRESSINGS
Vegetable Salads

Four Bean Salad

1 (16-oz.) can cut green
   beans, drained
1 (16-oz.) can wax beans,
   drained
1 (16-oz.) can red kidney
   beans, drained
1 (16-oz.) can garbanzo
   beans, drained
1 small can pickled beets,
   drained
1 medium onion, sliced thin
¼ cup green pepper,
   chopped
mushrooms and sliced water
   chestnuts (optional)

Drain the green beans, wax beans, kidney beans, garbanzo beans, and pickled beets. Add chopped onion and green pepper. If desired, add mushrooms and sliced water chestnuts.

Marinade:
½ cup cider vinegar
⅓ cup oil
½ cup sugar
1 tsp. salt
1 tsp. pepper

Place vinegar, oil, sugar, salt and pepper in a jar and shake. Pour over bean mixture and marinate in refrigerator at least 8 hours.

Easy Bean Salad

1 (16-oz.) can Blue Lake
   green beans
1 (16-oz.) can kidney beans
6 green onions, sliced (use
   the tops too) or one
   medium onion, diced
1 (16-oz.) can wax beans
2 carrots, scraped and sliced
3 stalks celery, diced
bottled red wine vinegar & oil
   salad dressing

Mix vegetables. You can add other "crunchies" like diced water chestnuts, green peppers, etc. Early in the day marinate in plenty of dressing. Stir to mix every time you pass by the refrigerator. Serve cold.

Leftovers may be used in a tossed salad.

Mrs. Morgan Talbot (Jane)

Green Bean Salad

Yield: 6-8 servings

⅔ cup vinegar
⅔ cup cooking oil
⅔ cup sugar
1 (No. 2) can French style
  green beans
1 (No. 2) can bean sprouts

Mix vinegar, oil, and sugar. Bring to a boil. Add beans and sprouts. Bring to a boil. Simmer about 5 minutes. Cool. Let stand in juice overnight. Drain before serving.

Mrs. Jerry Fair (Zetta)

Cauliflower Salad

Yield: 6 servings

Dressing:
1 cup mayonnaise
1 cup sour cream
1 pkg. garlic-cheese salad
  dressing mix

Mix ingredients together for dressing.

Salad:
1 large head cauliflower
1 cup radishes
½ cup cucumbers (don't
  peel)
¼ cup green onions

Slice vegetables and combine. Add dressing, stirring to coat each one well. Chill 1 to 2 hours before serving.

Mrs. Hulon Webb (Carole)

Crinkle Cut Carrot Salad

Yield: 10 servings

2 (20-oz.) pkgs. crinkle cut
  carrots (frozen)
1 green pepper, sliced
1 large onion, sliced

Cook and cool carrots. Combine with green pepper and onion.

Dressing:
¾ cup salad oil
¾ cup vinegar
¾ cup sugar
1 tsp. mustard
1 tsp. Worcestershire sauce

Mix dressing and pour over vegetables. Allow to stand in refrigerator overnight.

Mrs. Richard Moore (Lynda)

SALADS and DRESSINGS
Vegetable Salads

Cabbage Salad with Apple Dressing

Food processor
Yield: 10-12 servings

3 apples, peeled and cored
½ cup sour cream or yogurt
1½ tsp. Dijon mustard
3 Tbs. mayonnaise
½ tsp. salt
2 Tbs. lemon juice
pinch white pepper
1 medium head cabbage
chopped parsley for garnish

Place grating disk in food processor and grate apples. Remove. Place in steel knife and add apples, sour cream or yogurt, mustard, mayonnaise, salt, lemon juice and pepper. Flick and whirl until smoothly blended. Shred cabbage with slicing disk, remove. Put in steel knife, and add cabbage in thirds and flick about 3 times to chop cabbage. Cabbage can be held in plastic bag until ready for use. Toss cabbage with dressing and garnish with chopped parsley.

Mrs. Hartwell Kennard (Mary Lou)

Molded Cheese Salad

9 x 13 mold
Yield: 20 servings

Cooked dressing:
2 eggs, beaten
½ cup vinegar
½ cup sugar
½ tsp. salt

Mix and cook over low heat until thick, stirring often. Cool before using.

2½ envelopes plain gelatin
1½ lbs. American cheese
⅔ cup cold water
1 (4-oz.) jar pimiento
4 eggs, hard-boiled
1 small onion
1½ pints whipping cream

Soak gelatin in cold water and put in double boiler until melted. Add to cooked dressing mixture. Grind cheese, eggs, pimiento and onion. Add cooked dressing and cream that has not been whipped too stiff. Pour into mold.

Mrs. Bob McClure (Ginger)

SALADS and DRESSINGS
Vegetable Salads

Elegant "No Wilt" Salad I

9 x 13 pyrex dish
Yield: 6 servings

½ large head lettuce, torn
1 can water chestnuts,
   drained and sliced
½ cup celery, chopped
½ cup green onions,
   chopped
1 pkg. frozen peas, unthawed
4 Tbs. Bacon Bits
⅓ jar mayonnaise,
   approximately
4 Tbs. Parmesan cheese

Line bottom of 13 x 9 in. glass pan with lettuce. Mix water chestnuts, celery and green onions, and place atop lettuce. Thaw peas just enough to separate. Pat ice and water off with paper towels. Place atop preceding 3 ingredients. Sprinkle bacon bits on peas. Seal with mayonnaise and sprinkle with Parmesan cheese. Place in refrigerator, uncovered, for several hours, or overnight. When ready to serve, toss.

Mrs. Ralph E. Crawford, Jr. (Pam)

Elegant "No Wilt" Salad II

Salad bowl or
9 x 12 pyrex dish
Yield: 6 servings

Salad:
1 head lettuce
1 pkg. fresh spinach
6 hard-boil eggs, chopped
6 slices bacon, fried and
   crumbled
1 pkg. cooked English peas,
   drained
salt and pepper to taste

Carefully wash lettuce and spinach and tear into bite-sized pieces. In a large salad bowl layer the ingredients in the following order: lettuce, spinach, eggs, bacon, peas; seasoning each layer slightly to taste. Spread the dressing over top layer to seal.

Dressing:
1 pkg. Hidden Valley Ranch
   dressing mix
1 bunch green onions,
   chopped
1 cup sour cream
2 cups mayonnaise

Mix all ingredients together for dressing.

Mrs. Mac Pike (Tish)

SALADS and DRESSINGS
Vegetable Salads

Elegant "No Wilt" Salad III

9 x 12 pyrex dish
Yield: 6 servings

1 small head lettuce, torn
1 cup celery, diced
½ cup onion, grated
1 can tender small peas,
   chilled and drained
1 cup mayonnaise
 5 or 6 strips crisp bacon,
   crumbled
Parmesan cheese

Layer the ingredients in the following order: lettuce torn in bite sized pieces, celery mixed with onions, peas. Spread mayonnaise over peas, crumble bacon on top, and sprinkle with Parmesan cheese.

This may be prepared a day ahead and kept in the refrigerator.

Mrs. Hollis Fritts (Gerrie)

Frito Salad

Yield: 8-10 servings

1 head crisp lettuce
1 medium onion, chopped
2 cups celery, chopped
2 tomatoes, chopped
2 avocados, chopped
1 bag Fritos, partly crushed
1 small can Pet milk
1 lb. Velveeta cheese
2 jalapeño canned peppers,
   mashed
2 Tbs. juice from jalapeño
   peppers

In a large bowl, tear lettuce leaves into bite-sized pieces. Add vegetables. In a double boiler, warm milk. Add peppers and cheese, stirring until cheese melts. Pour cheese sauce over cold, crisp vegetables and Fritos. Toss lightly.

Mrs. Joe Stroud (Ruthie)

Toss your salad greens with your hands so you don't bruise the lettuce.

SALADS and DRESSINGS

Green Wonder Salad

Yield: 12 servings

Marinade:
1 cup sugar
1 tsp. salt
pepper to taste
¾ cup cider vinegar

Mix sugar, salt and pepper in bowl; pour vinegar over mixture; set aside while preparing vegetables, stirring occasionally to dissolve sugar.

Vegetables:
1 (No. 303) can French-style
   green beans
1 (No. 303) can small English
   peas
1 (No. 303) can bean sprouts
1 can water chestnuts, sliced
1½ cups celery, thinly sliced
3 medium onions, thinly
   sliced

Drain liquid from vegetables and do NOT cook vegetables. Mix vegetables in large container; pour dissolved sugar-vinegar mixture over all. Cover and refrigerate several hours before serving, stirring occasionally to be sure vegetables are equally marinated.

May be made 2 or 3 days before serving as it keeps well in refrigerator for several days.

Mrs. Blaine Holcomb (Andrea)

German Cole Slaw

Yield: 4-6 servings

1 large head cabbage, cut
   fine
1 onion, chopped
½ cup sugar

Combine, and let stand while you make the dressing.

Dressing:
2 Tbs. sugar
1 tsp. dry mustard
1 tsp. celery seed
1 cup white vinegar
¾ cup oil

Boil dressing until well mixed, and while hot, pour over chopped cabbage. Let stand until cold. Then stir well. Store in refrigerator in covered container.

Better after 3 to 4 days.

Mrs. Hulon Webb (Carole)

SALADS and DRESSINGS
Vegetable Salads

Fresh Mushroom Salad

2 tsp. dry mustard
4 Tbs. salad oil
4 Tbs. vinegar
½ cup onions, chopped
¼ lb. fresh mushrooms,
  sliced
1 tsp. salt
¼ tsp. pepper
½ lemon
1 cup sweet cream
1 Tbs. chives, chopped

Mix dry mustard, salad oil, and vinegar in a large bowl until mustard is completely dissolved. Add chopped onions and mix. Add mushrooms, salt and pepper. Toss until well mixed. Strain juice of lemon through a napkin over mixture. Add sweet cream and toss. Serve on a glass plate with chopped chives on top of salad.

Mrs. James Humphrey (Jane Ellen)

Potato Salad

6 large potatoes
½ cup onions, chopped
½ cup pickles, chopped
salt
2-3 Tbs. bacon drippings
2-3 Tbs. vinegar
2-3 Tbs. Miracle Whip salad
  dressing
4 slices bacon, cooked crisp
  and crumbled
paprika

Boil potaotes with jackets on and let cool. Peel the potatoes and dice them. Add the chopped onions and pickles; mix, and salt to taste. Pour warm bacon drippings over mixture and stir. Add vinegar; stir, let sit until flavor goes through. Add salad dressing; stir, and refrigerate until time to serve. Before serving, stir in crumbled bacon and sprinkle paprika on top.

Mrs. Leonard Tesoro (Judy)

Never store mushrooms in a plastic bag as this causes a moisture build up. Instead store in paper bags and remember to select mushrooms that are closed (no gills open) as these are the freshest.

SALADS and DRESSINGS
Vegetable Salads

Hot German Potato Salad

Yield: Serves 6

6 medium-sized potatoes
6 strips of bacon
⅓ cup bacon fat
¾ cup onion, diced
2 Tbs. flour
1-2 Tbs. sugar
1½ tsp. celery salt
dash of pepper
¾ cup water
½ cup vinegar

Cook potatoes in skins. Peel and slice into large bowl. Fry bacon crisp, drain. In bacon fat, cook onion until it turns yellow. Add flour, sugar, celery salt, and pepper to onions. Mix water and vinegar, and stir into onion mixture gradually. Cook, stirring until mixture boils. Allow to boil 1 minute. Pour over potatoes. Add bacon bits (saving some for garnish.) Cover and let stand until ready to serve. Heat over hot water.

Mrs. Hollis Fritts (Gerrie)

Old Style German Potato Salad

4 medium to large potatoes
½ onion, diced
1 clove of garlic, minced
1 dill pickle, chopped
salt and pepper
4 slices bacon
vinegar, from pickles

Boil potatoes with the skin on. Peel and slice while hot. Add the onion, garlic, dill pickle, and seasonings. Marinate this mixture approximately 2 or 3 hours at room temperature. Just before serving, dice and fry the bacon until crisp. Crumble over potato mixture. Add a little vinegar from the dill pickles. Mix well and serve.

Mrs. Vernon Neuhaus, Jr. (Gayle)

Your fruits and vegetables will stay fresh for a longer period of time if you line your vegetable drawers with paper toweling.

SALADS and DRESSINGS
Vegetable Salads

Garden Rice Salad

Yield: 4½ cups

1 (6-oz.) pkg. long grain and
  wild rice mix
½ cup cucumbers, diced
½ cup mayonnaise
½ cup plain yogurt
1 cup celery, sliced
1 cup tomato, cubed
2 Tbs. parsley, chopped
⅛ tsp. seasoned salt
⅛ tsp. pepper
¼ cup dry roasted peanuts,
  chopped

Cook rice as directed on package. Omit butter or margarine in package directions. Cool. Toss lightly with next 8 ingredients. Cover; chill. Garnish with peanuts.

Mrs. Ralph E. Crawford, Jr. (Pam)

Lebanese Tabooley Salad

Yield: 12-15 servings

2 cups No. 2 cracked wheat
6 tomatoes, cut in small
  cubes
1 bunch green onions,
  chopped
2 small bunches parsley,
  chopped
1 cup mint leaves, chopped
12 Tbs. olive oil
juice of 2 large lemons
salt and pepper to taste

Wash wheat twice in cold water. Barely cover the wheat with water. Soak for two hours. The wheat will soak up all the water. Combine all other ingredients with the wheat. Serve on lettuce or grape leaves.

Mrs. Mike Moore (Janice)

Tomato Jello Salad

4 cup mold
Yield: 6 servings

1 (3-oz.) pkg. lemon jello
1 (15-oz.) can stewed
  tomatoes
¼ cup minced onion
½ tsp. lemon juice

Fix jello according to directions except use 1 cup of the liquid drained off the stewed tomatoes instead of the second cup of water. Mix all ingredients together and pour into mold.

Mrs. H. D. Gilliam (Virginia)

Salad Soufflé

**5 cup ring mold, or
6-8 individual molds
Yield: 8 servings**

1 (3-oz.) pkg. lime flavored
  gelatin
½ cup water
1 (10¾-oz.) can cream of
  asparagus soup
½ cup mayonnaise or salad
  dressing
1 Tbs. vinegar
1 tsp. onion, grated
dash pepper
½ cup cucumber, shredded,
  unpared
½ cup celery, diced
1 Tbs. parsley, snipped

In saucepan, mix gelatin and water. Gradually blend in soup; heat and stir till gelatin dissolves. Add next four ingredients. Beat smooth with rotary or electric beater. Chill till partially set. Turn into large chilled bowl; beat till thick and fluffy. Fold in vegetables. Spoon into 5 cup ring mold or 6-8 individual molds. Chill till firm.

Mrs. T. B. Waite, Jr. (Thelma)

Sea Slaw

Yield 6 servings

1½ lbs. shrimp, boiled
4 cups cabbage, shredded
½ cup green onion, sliced
½ cup celery, chopped
¾ cup mayonnaise
¼ cup fresh lemon juice
2 tsp. sugar
1 tsp. seasoned salt
½ tsp. dry mustard
½ tsp. Worcestershire sauce
¼ tsp. Tabasco
salt
¼ tsp. pepper sauce

Reserve a few whole shrimp for garnish and chop the remainder. Refrigerate until chilled. In a large bowl, toss cabbage, chopped shrimp, onions and celery. Set aside. In a small bowl, combine mayonnaise, lemon juice, sugar, seasoned salt, mustard, Worcestershire sauce, and hot pepper sauce. Pour over shrimp mixture and toss to coat. Add salt to taste. Chill Sea Slaw until serving time.

Mrs. Paul Bergh (Betty)

SALADS and DRESSINGS
Vegetable Salads

Spinach Salad
Yield: 8 servings

1 pkg. fresh spinach
1 white or red onion, sliced
  thin
¼ cup celery, diced
4 hard-boiled eggs, grated or
  mashed

Remove stems from well-washed spinach, drain well. Tear spinach into bite-sized pieces. Add onion, celery and boiled eggs. Just before serving pour dressing on top of salad and toss.

Dressing:
1 pkg. Hidden Valley Ranch
  dressing mix, made with
  buttermilk and mayonnaise
½ tsp. salt
1 tsp. pepper
1 Tbs. lemon juice (optional)

To prepared Hidden Valley dressing, add remaining ingredients. Cover and keep in refrigerator. Dressing may be made early in the day.

Mrs. Bryan Moore (Gloria)

Spinach Salad with Bacon Dressing
Yield: 4-6 servings

1½ lbs. fresh spinach leaves,
  tender, washed, torn
½ cup Bacon Dressing
2 eggs, hard-boiled, shredded

In a salad bowl, toss spinach with Bacon Dressing until leaves are well coated. Divide in salad plates and top each with shredded egg.

Bacon Dressing:
1 slice bacon, very crisp,
  cooled and blotted
1½ tsp. red-wine vinegar
½ tsp. hickory-smoked salt
¼ tsp. dry mustard
1 Tbs. water
5 Tbs. vegetable oil

Crumble the crisp bacon and add it to the vinegar in a jar with a tight lid. Add the hickory-smoked salt and dry mustard. Mix until the salt is dissolved. Add water and oil. Cover jar tightly and shake vigorously for 30 seconds. Store covered in refrigerator. Makes ¼ to ½ cup.

Mrs. Robert Parry, Jr. (Barbara)

SALADS and DRESSINGS

Sauerkraut Slaw

Yield: 4 servings

¼ cup vinegar
1 cup sugar
1 green pepper, chopped
1 cup celery, chopped
1 onion, chopped
1 (1-lb. 11-oz.) large can
   sauerkraut

Bring vinegar and sugar to a boil. Cool. Mix vegetables and pour the vinegar-sugar over them. Chill.

Mrs. F. H. Mangum (Maree)

Tomato Avocado Aspic

1½ quart mold, or
9 x 12 pyrex dish,
lightly greased
Yield: 10-12 servings

Avocado mixture:
½ cup water
1 Tbs. (1 envelope)
   unflavored gelatin
1 cup hot water
1 Tbs. sugar
1½ tsp. salt
2 cups sieved avocado
¼ cup lemon juice

Lightly grease dish or mold. Pour ½ cup cold water into a small bowl. Sprinkle 1 Tbs. gelatin evenly over water. Let stand about 5 minutes to soften. Add softened gelatin to hot water and stir until completely dissolved. Stir in the sugar and salt. Cool. When gelatin mixture is cooled, stir in a mixture of the sieved avocado and lemon juice. Turn into mold, and chill until partly set.
To prepare: 25 minutes

Tomato mixture:
½ cup tomato juice
1 Tbs. unflavored gelatin
1¼ cups hot tomato juice
½ cup ketchup
1 Tbs. lemon juice
½ tsp salt
1 tsp. Worcestershire sauce
2 drops Tabasco

Soften and dissolve gelatin in heated tomato juice as with avocado mixture. Blend in remaining ingredients. Gently layer the tomato mixture on top of the partially set avocado mixture, so that the salad is in red and green layers.
To chill: 4 hours

Pretty for Christmas.

Mrs. Morgan Talbot (Jane)

SALADS and DRESSINGS
Vegetable Salads

Squash Salad
Yield: 6-8 servings

8 yellow squash
8 ripe, fresh tomatoes

Marinade:
1 clove garlic
1 tsp. salt
2 tsp. sugar
½ tsp. dry mustard
several dashes Tabasco
2 Tbs. water
⅓ cup wine vinegar
¾ cup oil
1 large onion, chopped

Boil the squash in salt water for 10 minutes. Drain, cool, and slice. Cover with marinade and marinate overnight in refrigerator. Serve with fresh, cold tomato wedges.

Mrs. Charles E. Thompson, Jr. (Sally)

Tomato-Cheese Luncheon Salad
Yield: 8-10 servings

1 (10½ or 11-oz.) can
  condensed tomato soup
1½ Tbs. (1½ envelopes)
  unflavored gelatin
½ cup cold water
2 (3-oz.) pkgs. cream cheese
1 cup mayonnaise
1 cup celery, chopped
2 Tbs. green pepper,
  chopped
1 tsp. onion, minced
  (optional)
½ cup California walnuts,
  broken

Heat tomato soup. Add gelatin softened in cold water. Cool. Thoroughly combine remaining ingredients. Add to gelatin mixture. Chill until firm.

One pound cooked shrimp may be added.

Mrs. Morris Nelson (Carolynn)

Mixed Vegetable Luncheon Salad

1 pkg. frozen mixed
  vegetables
2 Tbs. onion, diced
1 cup celery, diced
1 cup sharp Cheddar cheese,
  diced
½ cup green pepper, diced
¼ cup pimiento, diced
¼ cup sweet pickle, chopped

Cook mixed vegetables according to package directions, cook only until tender (do not overcook). Drain and chill. Combine all vegetables and cheese; toss lightly. Just before serving, toss again with the dressing.

Dressing:
½ cup sour cream
½ cup mayonnaise
1 Tbs. lemon juice

Combine and mix well.
Mrs. Shelley Collier, Jr. (Caryl)

Vermicelli Salad

Yield: 8-10 servings

2 boxes vermicelli
1 Tbs. oil
4 Tbs. salad oil
1 Tbs. Accent or MSG
3 Tbs. fresh lime juice (or
  lemon)
1 cup celery, chopped
1 bell pepper, chopped
1 bunch green onions,
  chopped, all parts
1 large jar or can pimientos,
  drained and chopped
1 large can black olives,
  drained, and chopped
2 cups real mayonnaise
1 (10-oz.) pkg. frozen green
  peas, unthawed
coarsely ground black pepper
Beau Monde spice
  seasonings
garlic salt or powder
Catalina salad dressing
  (optional)

Boil vermicelli in salted water with oil added. Do not overcook. Drain and blanch in cold water. Marinate vermicelli overnight in salad oil, Accent, and lemon juice or lime juice. Early the next day add the celery, bell pepper, green onions, and pimientos; also add the black olives, mayonnaise and green peas. For seasoning, add to taste, black pepper, Beau Monde, garlic salt or powder. Add ¼ cup Catalina dressing for variety. Refrigerate.

This recipe may be doubled or tripled well.

Mrs. Jerry Box (Deanna)

SALADS and DRESSINGS
Meat Salads

Chicken Salad   Yield: 4 servings

3 cups cooked chicken,
  chopped
2 cups celery, chopped
½ cup (or more) stuffed
  olives, chopped
½ cup mayonnaise
salt

Combine all ingredients and refrigerate.

Mrs. Hollis Fritts (Gerrie)

Chicken Salad with a Twist   Yield: 4-8 servings

6 oz. corkscrew macaroni
2 cups cooked chicken,
  cubed
½ cup Italian dressing
½ cup mayonnaise
3 Tbs. lemon juice
1 Tbs. prepared mustard
1 medium onion, chopped
¾ cup ripe olives, chopped
1 cup cucumbers, diced
1 cup celery, diced
1 tsp. pepper
salt to taste
lettuce

Cook macaroni. Mix cooked chicken and dressing with hot macaroni. Cool. Blend mayonnaise, lemon juice and mustard. Stir in onions, olives, cucumbers, celery and pepper. Add to macaroni mixture. Salt to taste. Chill 2 or more hours to blend flavors. Serve in lettuce cups.

Mrs. F. H. Mangum (Maree)

For a garlic-flavored oil for salad dressing, store your garlic cloves in the oil. You can later use the cloves which have been kept from drying out in the oil.

Creamy Chicken Salad

Yield: 12 servings

6 chicken breasts, cooked
   and diced
½ cup salad oil
2½ Tbs. tarragon vinegar
¾ tsp. salt
¼ tsp. dry mustard
1 green onion
3 cups celery, thinly sliced
3 eggs, hard-boiled
1¾ cup mayonnaise
½ cup sour cream
½ Tbs. salt
slivered almonds (optional)

In blender, mix vinegar, oil, salt, dry mustard, and onion. Pour over diced chicken and marinate overnight. Mix chicken with sour cream, mayonnaise, salt, celery and eggs. Top with slivered almonds (optional).

Mrs. Robert Jones (Elizabeth)

Chicken Salad Mousse

6 cup ring mold
Yield: 6-8 servings

1 (10¾-oz.) can tomato soup
1 (8-oz.) pkg. cream cheese
1½ Tbs. unflavored gelatin,
   dissolved in ¼ cup cold
   water
1 cup mayonnaise
1 small onion, chopped fine
½ cup cucumber, chopped
   fine
¾ cup celery, chopped fine
½ cup stuffed green olives,
   chopped
1 cup chicken, diced

Heat soup in double boiler. Add cream cheese and stir until well blended. Add gelatin that has been dissolved in water. Let cool and add all other ingredients. Mold and serve very cold on any salad greens.

Shrimp, crabmeat, or lobster may be used instead of chicken.

Mrs. Paul Bergh (Betty)

SALADS and DRESSINGS
Meat Salads

Chicken-Pineapple Salad

Yield: 6-8 servings

1 small size can pineapple
  chunks, unsweetened
1 cup green grapes or
1 small can mandarin
  orange slices
½ cup almonds, sliced
2 large chicken breasts,
  boiled and diced
1 Tbs. onion, minced
2 Tbs. lemon juice
1 tsp. salt
1 cup celery, chopped
mayonnaise to taste

Combine the drained fruits and nuts.
(The grapes are nice in the summer, and
the oranges are nice when fresh grapes
are not available.) Add the chicken, onion, lemon juice, salt, and chopped celery to the fruit mixture. Refrigerate at
least 2 hours and just before serving,
fold in mayonnaise.

Mrs. Morgan Talbot (Jane)

Marinated Shrimp Platter

Yield: 8 servings

1 cup salad oil
1 cup white vinegar
¼ cup capers with liquid
1 Tbs. celery seed
2 tsp. salt
3 lbs. shrimp, cooked,
  peeled, and deveined
2 (7½-oz.) cans large ripe
  olives, drained
Romaine lettuce
tomato wedges

In large bowl, combine oil, vinegar, capers, celery seed, and salt. Add shrimp;
cover, and chill several hours, or overnight. At serving time, drain shrimp, reserving marinade. On oblong platter,
arrange a bed of Romaine with shrimp
down center. Make a row of olives on
either side. Spoon some of the reserved
marinade over all. Garnish with tomato
wedges.

*One medium onion, sliced into rings,
may also be used in the marinade.*

Mrs. Leonel Garza, Jr. (Linda)

SALADS and DRESSINGS

Meat Salads

Shrimp Louis

Yield: 4-6 servings

1 cup mayonnaise
¼ cup chili sauce
¼ cup French dressing
    (made with tarragon
    vinegar)
2 Tbs. parsley, chopped
2 Tbs. chives, chopped
1 tsp. horseradish
1 tsp. Worcestershire sauce
salt and pepper
2 lbs. fresh shrimp, cooked
    and deveined
½ lb. frozen crabmeat,
    thawed
lettuce, shredded
2-3 eggs, hard boiled
avocado, sliced

Combine the first eight ingredients. Serve over the shrimp and crab mixture on a bed of shredded lettuce. Top the shrimp with sliced egg and avocado.

Mrs. Bill Davis (Jean)

Shrimp Salad

Yield: 6 servings

1 (1-lb.) pkg. frozen shrimp
1 small carton cottage
    cheese
6 eggs, hard-boiled, chopped
1 pkg. Italian salad dressing
    mix, dry
1 small head Iceberg lettuce

Cook and devein the shrimp. Mix together the shrimp, cottage cheese, eggs, and dry salad dressing mix. Tear the lettuce in bite-sized pieces. Before serving, add lettuce; mix, and let stand a few minutes.

Mrs. Richard L. Moore (Lynda)

Perk up your lettuce and celery by placing them in a pan of cold water with a few raw sliced potatoes.

SALADS and DRESSINGS
Meat Salads

Avocados with Crab Stuffing

375 degrees
9 x 9 baking dish
Yield: 5-6 servings

2 (6½-oz.) cans (2 cups)
  crabmeat, drained
1 cup cheese, cubed
⅓ cup green pepper,
  chopped
¼ cup onion, finely chopped
1 tsp. salt
½ cup mayonnaise or salad
  dressing
2 tsp. lemon juice
avocados

Break crabmeat into chunks. Toss with cheese, green pepper, onion and salt. Blend mayonnaise and lemon juice. Add to crab mixture and toss lightly. Place in baking dish. Cover and bake about 30 minutes or until heated thoroughly. Stuff in avocados and serve on lettuce leaves.

Mrs. Kenneth Kachtik (Sue)

Molded Tuna Salad

2-3 cup mold
Yield: 4 servings

½ cup water
¾ cup carrots, diced
1 envelope unflavored gelatin
¼ cup water
½ cup mayonnaise
1 Tbs. lemon juice
1 tsp. prepared mustard
½ tsp. salt
1 (7-oz.) can water packed
  tuna, drained
2-4 green onions, sliced
⅓ cup stuffed olives, sliced
⅓ cup green pepper,
  chopped

Put water and carrots in 2 cup glass measure. Microwave on high 3-4 minutes. Soften gelatin in cold water, add to carrot mixture and cool. Mix mayonnaise, lemon juice, mustard and salt. Blend in gelatin mixture. Add tuna. Add remaining ingredients. Pour into 2-3 cup mold. Refrigerate at least 2 hours.

Mrs. Paul Moffitt (Marilyn)

Marinated Salmon

Deep serving dish
Yield: 4 servings

1 lb. can salmon, well drained
1 cup sour cream
2 Tbs. lemon juice (or more, to taste)
¼ red onion, minced (may use white)
red onion, thinly sliced
¼ cup green onion, minced
2 Tbs. parsley, chopped

Arrange salmon in chunks in deep serving dish. Mix next 3 ingredients and pour over salmon. Garnish with onion slices and a mixture of green onions and parsley. Chill at least one hour.

Mrs. Joe Friend (Pam)

Avocado Salad Dressing

Yield: 3 cups

1 ripe avocado
1 cup mayonnaise
1 cup sour cream
½ tsp. pepper
½ tsp. Worcestershire sauce
½ tsp. onion, grated
¼ tsp. garlic powder
½ tsp. salt

Blend in blender or with mixer. Enjoy on a tossed green salad or as a dip with your favorite chips.

Mrs. Russell Barron (Jeannie)

French Dressing

Yield 1 quart

1 (10¾ oz.) can tomato soup
¾ cup vinegar
1 tsp. salt
½ tsp. paprika
1 Tbs. Worcestershire sauce
1½ cups Wesson oil
1-3 Tbs. sugar, as desired
½ tsp. pepper
1 Tbs. mustard
1 tsp. onion juice

Put in jar and shake.

Mrs. Morris Nelson (Carolynn)

SALADS and DRESSINGS
Dressings

Fruit Salad Dressing
Yield: 2-3 cups

½ cup pineapple or orange
  juice
½ cup lemon juice
1 cup sugar
2 eggs
1 Tbs. corn starch
1-2 cups whipped cream

Mix well and cook in a double boiler until thick like custard. Just before serving over a fruit salad, add 1 or 2 cups whipped cream.

Keeps several days in a covered jar in refrigerator.

Mrs. Frank Birkhead (Janet)

Overnight Dressing

½ cup olive oil
½ cup oil
¼ cup wine vinegar
¼ cup regular vinegar
1 clove garlic, crushed
½ tsp. mustard
½ tsp. Worcestershire sauce
salt and pepper
1 green chile, minced
Parmesan cheese
croutons
raw egg
juice of ½ lemon or to taste

Mix ingredients and allow to blend overnight. Prepare green salad, and sprinkle with Parmesan cheese and croutons. Pour dressing on salad; toss to coat. Break a raw egg over the salad and squeeze the juice of ½ lemon over egg. Toss lightly to cover greens.

Mrs. Kenneth Kachtik (Sue)

Tangy Salad Dressing
Yield: about 2 cups

1 (10¾-oz.) can cream of
  celery soup
½ cup sour cream
¼ cup Bleu cheese, crumbled
2 Tbs. milk
1 Tbs. lemon juice

Combine ingredients; chill. Thin to desired consistency with additional milk.

Mrs. Gilbert Weisberg (Suzy)

SALADS and DRESSINGS

Tomato French Dressing

Yield: about 1½ cups

1 (10¾-oz.) can tomato soup
½ cup salad oil
¼ cup vinegar
½ tsp. dry mustard

Combine ingredients in a jar. Shake well before using (or mix in an electric mixer).

Variation:
4 slices bacon, cooked and
   crumbled or
½ cup sweet pickle relish

Add bacon or pickle relish to ingredients above and shake.

Mrs. Gilbert Weisberg (Suzy)

Poppy Seed Dressing

Yield: 1¾ cups

½ cup sugar
2 Tbs. honey
1 tsp. dry mustard
1 tsp. salt
⅓ cup vinegar
1½ Tbs. onion juice
1 cup salad oil
1½ Tbs. poppy seed

Mix sugar, honey, mustard, salt, and vinegar together with electric mixer. Add onion juice and stir it in thoroughly. Add oil slowly, beating constantly, and continue to beat until thick. Add poppy seeds and beat for a few minutes. Store in a cool place or the refrigerator, but do not freeze.

Delicious on top of fruit salad of any kind, and especially delicious on our Rio Grande Valley grapefruit!

Mrs. Bill Davis (Jean)

A clove of garlic added to store-bought French dressing yields a real surprise dressing.

SALADS and DRESSINGS
Dressings

1,000 Island Dressing

Yield: about 3½ cups

1½ cups real mayonnaise
  (homemade, if possible)
½ cup bottled chili sauce
1 tsp. Worcestershire sauce
8 green olives,
  pimiento-stuffed, chopped
1 dill pickle, chopped
¼ cup onion, chopped
2 hard-boiled eggs, chopped
2 Tbs. fresh parsley, chopped
¼ cup bell pepper, minced
½-1 tsp. dry mustard
1 tsp. capers, chopped
juice of ½ lime (optional)
garlic powder to taste
1 tsp. MSG
½ tsp. paprika

Combine all ingredients and refrigerate several hours or overnight before serving.

Mrs. Jerry Box (Deanna)

Roquefort Dressing

Yield: 1½-1⅔ cups

1 small triangle of Roquefort
  cheese
1 cup mayonnaise
dash of garlic salt
dash of salt
dash of sugar
1 tsp. vinegar
¼-⅓ cup of Pet milk
¼-⅓ cup Wesson oil

Crumble cheese in bowl. Add mayonnaise, then beat. Add garlic salt, salt, and sugar. Then add vinegar, along with Pet milk and equal amount of Wesson oil to desired consistency; then whip.

Mrs. George Lillard (Diane)

Broiled Peaches

Broiler pan

1 (1 lb. 13-oz.) can peach
  halves, drained
butter or margarine
nutmeg

Arrange peach halves, cut side up, on broiler pan; dot each with a small amount of butter. Sprinkle lightly with nutmeg. Broil 5 to 7 inches from heat about 4 to 5 minutes, or till browned.

Broiled canned fruit is a perfect accompaniment for any main dish.

Mrs. Shelley Collier, Jr. (Caryl)

Sautéed Apple Rings

Yield: 12 apple rings

2 Tbs. butter
1 Tbs. brown sugar
⅛ tsp. cinnamon
3 med. apples, cored and cut
  in rings

Combine butter, sugar and cinnamon. Heat until mixture bubbles. Add apples and sauté over medium heat until tender (3 to 4 minutes each side). Serve with ham, bacon or sausages. Makes 12 apple rings.

Bananas may be used instead of apples. Slice diagonally and shorten cooking time.

Mrs. Ruben R. Cardenas (Dardanella)

Cranberry-Orange Relish

Yield: 4 cups

1 lb. fresh cranberries
2 cups sugar
½ cup water
1 tsp. orange peel, grated
½ cup orange juice
½ cup slivered almonds

In saucepan, combine all ingredients except almonds. Cook, uncovered, for about 10 minutes or till cranberry skins pop, stirring once or twice. Remove from heat; stir in almonds. (A couple drops of red food coloring can be added.) Cool. Store in refrigerator in covered container.

Mrs. Robert Crane (Baudelia)

SALADS and DRESSINGS
Relishes

Cauliflower Relish

Yield: 8-10 servings

1 head cauliflower, broken
  into rosettes
2 carrots, cut in slices
1 green pepper, sliced
2 small cans mushrooms,
  sliced
4 oz. black olives, sliced
4 oz. green olives, sliced
1 large jar pimientos,
  chopped
2 stalks celery, sliced
¾ cup wine vinegar
½ cup oil
1 tsp. oregano
salt and pepper

Combine all ingredients in saucepan
and bring to a boil. Simmer 3 minutes.
Place in large bowl and cover tightly.
Cool and chill overnight. Drain before
serving.

Mrs. Madonna Johnson

Green Tomato Relish

Yield: about 4 pints

3¾ lbs. green tomatoes,
  chopped fine
6 small onions, chopped fine
¼ cup salt
½ pint white vinegar
1¾ cup brown sugar
¼ tsp. allspice
¼ tsp. cayenne pepper
¼ tsp. cloves
1 tsp. celery seed

Combine chopped tomatoes, onions,
and salt. Allow to set overnight, and then
drain well. Add the remaining ingredients. Boil hard for 15 minutes. Place in
sterile jars.

Mrs. Paul Wagner (Doris)

Add your tomatoes to the salad last as they tend to thin salad dressings.

SALADS and DRESSINGS

Relishes

Ripe Tomato Relish

5 (1 pint) jars
Yield: 5 pints

1 doz. large tomatoes, peeled
  and chopped
6 medium sweet peppers,
  chopped
6 medium onions, chopped
3 hot peppers, chopped
2 cups sugar
2 cups vinegar
1 Tbs. salt
1 tsp. cinnamon
1 tsp. allspice
1 tsp. pepper

Mix all together and cook down low on medium heat (about 3 hours). Seal in sterilized pint jars.

Good with meat, beans and blackeyed peas.

Mrs. Charles Fox (Nancy)

Marinated Onions

Yield: 4 servings

2-3 onions
fresh limes
salt and pepper
salad oil

Dice onions onto a large platter so they are in a thin layer. Squeeze fresh limes over the onions until they are all covered with the juice. Liberally sprinkle with salt and freshly-ground pepper. Drizzle oil sparingly over all. Refrigerate. About 1 hour later, mix and taste for seasonings. Correct seasonings. Chill again. Serve very cold as a salad.

Mrs. Morgan Talbot (Jane)

Hot Garlic Pickles

Yield: 1 gallon

1 gal. hamburger dills
5 lbs. sugar
1 (2-oz.) bottle Tabasco
½ jar garlic chips

Drain pickles all night. Mix sugar, Tabasco and garlic chips until pink. Layer sugar and drained pickles back into gallon jar until full. Each day (for 5 days) turn jar over once to mix.

Mrs. Neal Runnels (Gayle)

SALADS and DRESSINGS
Relishes

Nine-Month Cucumber Pickles

Yield: 1 gallon

1 gal. cucumbers, the
  pickling variety are
  preferable
4 cups sugar
4 cups vinegar
½ cup pickling salt
1½ tsp. tumeric
1½ tsp. celery seed
½ tsp. mustard seed
onions (optional)

Slice the cucumbers. Combine and cook the remaining ingredients. After this mixture boils, cool and pour over cucumber slices. Refrigerate. These pickles will last for nine months in refrigerator.

Very similar to Bread 'n Butter Pickles.

Mrs. Paul Wagner (Doris)

Pickled Green Pepper Strips

Yield: 4 pints

4 cloves garlic
4 red hot peppers (or 4
  chiles)
4 tsp. dill seed
green peppers, cut in strips
3 cups water
1½ cups vinegar
6 Tbs. salt (preferably
  pickling salt)
green food coloring, if
  desired

In each of 4 pint jars, place 1 clove garlic, 1 red pepper and 1 tsp. dill seed. Pack each jar with green pepper strips. Bring to a boil the remaining ingredients and pour over peppers. Seal and store in cool, dry place. They are better if not used before six weeks.

Mrs. Paul Wagner (Doris)

Sweet Hot Pickles

Gallon jar
Yield: 1 gallon

4 qts. sour pickles
4-5 lbs. sugar
2 bottles Tabasco sauce

Drain pickles and slice. In gallon jar put a layer of sliced pickles, a layer of sugar and some Tabasco. Continue this until all ingredients are used. Put lid on jar tightly. Each day turn jar over so as to mix. Do this for 15 days. Then pickles are ready.

Mrs. Robert Whitis (Linda)

370

Soups and Sauces

Avo-Mato Soup

¼ cup green onions,
　reserving tops
2 avocados
½ cup sour cream
2 cups tomatoes, finely
　chopped
1 cup beef broth
1 tsp. salt
1 Tbs. lemon juice
Dash hot sauce
Paprika

Blend the onions, avocados and sour cream in blender. Add rest of ingredients except tomatoes and chill. Add tomatoes, garnish with more sour cream, green onion tops and paprika.

Mrs. John Freeland (Jayne)

Cream of Artichoke Soup

1 (10-oz.) can artichokes,
　rinsed and drained (finely
　chop ¼ cup and reserve)
1 medium onion, finely
　chopped
2 Tbs. butter
2 Tbs. flour
2 cups chicken broth
1¼ cup half and half
salt and pepper
2 Tbs. parsley

Sauté onion in butter. Add flour and cook for 2 minutes, stirring. Remove from heat and add chicken broth, 1 cup artichokes and parsley. Cook on medium heat for 5 minutes. Purée in blender, put back in saucepan and add half and half, ¼ cup chopped artichokes and salt and pepper to taste. Cook on medium heat, stirring for 5 minutes. Serve hot or cold. Top with parsley.

Mrs. Carl Judin (Joy)

Bean Soup

1 lb. pinto beans
1 gal. water
3 slices bacon
1 ham hock
½ (14½-oz.) can tomatoes
2 cloves garlic
1 onion, chopped
1 bunch cilantro
salt and pepper to taste

Soak beans overnight in water. The next day, add water to the water the beans have been soaked in to equal a full gallon. Combine all ingredients and cook slowly until done. You will need at least a 6-qt. pan for this—a roaster is good.

Mrs. Charles E. Thompson, Jr. (Sally)

SOUPS and SAUCES
Soups

Chicken Okra Soup

Yield: 6-8 servings.

3 lb. chicken, diced
1 lb. okra
2 large tomatoes, peeled
1 onion, chopped
1 cup corn
⅓ cup rice

Boil the chicken with enough water to cover. Cool the broth and remove the fat. Dice the chicken meat. Add okra, tomatoes, onion, corn and rice to the broth. Bring to boil and add chicken. Simmer 30 minutes.

Mrs. John Kreidler (Kay)

Clam Chowder

Yield: 4 servings

½ cup carrots, chopped
2 potatoes, chopped
2 ribs celery, chopped
1 onion, chopped
2 Tbs. flour
2 Tbs. butter
1 cup milk
2 cans clams with juice
4 strips bacon, fried crisp
  and crumbled

Boil the carrots, potatoes, celery and onion until potatoes and carrots are done. Make a white sauce with the butter, flour and milk. Add cooked potato mixture, including liquid, to the white sauce. Add clams and juice to soup mixture. Simmer 20 minutes. Sprinkle with crumbled bacon and serve.

Mrs. Jerry Fair (Zetta)

Cream of Broccoli Soup I

Yield: 4 servings

1 lb. fresh broccoli
1 onion, finely chopped
2 Tbs. butter
2 Tbs. flour
4 cups chicken broth
½ cup whipping cream
salt
pepper

Rinse broccoli. Remove and discard woody parts of stem. Cut the remaining parts into 2-inch lengths. Sauté onion in hot butter for 3 minutes or until softened. Stir in flour and chicken broth. Add broccoli. Cover and simmer for 20 minutes. Put soup in blender and purée until smooth. Strain soup into a clean saucepan. Add whipping cream and heat. Add salt and pepper to taste and serve.

Mrs. Randy Davis (Lynn)

Cream of Broccoli Soup II

Yield: 10-12 servings

1 bunch fresh broccoli, diced
3 cups water
2 chicken bouillon cubes
5 Tbs. butter or margarine
5 Tbs. flour
1 tsp. salt
½ tsp. white pepper
¼ tsp. curry
¼ tsp. cumin
2 cups light cream

Add the diced broccoli and chicken bouillon cubes to 3 cups of boiling water and allow to boil 8 minutes. Meanwhile, make a thick cream sauce of the butter, flour and spices. Stir until well-blended. Add the cream. Cook over medium heat until thick, stirring continuously with a whisk. Add the thick cream sauce to the broccoli and water mixture. Stir and heat before serving.

It makes a richer soup when you blend half the broccoli in a blender.

Mrs. Dan Seitz (Amy)

Navy Bean Soup

4 quart Dutch oven
Yield: 3 quarts

1 lb. dry navy beans
6 cups water
1½ lbs. smoked pork butt or chunk of leftover smoked ham
1 cup onion, chopped
3 cloves garlic, minced
6 additional cups water
2 Tbs. paprika
2 tsp. caraway seeds
1½ tsp. salt
several twists freshly ground black pepper
1 cup sour cream
parsley, chopped

Place beans in large saucepan or Dutch oven with 6 cups water. Bring to a boil, and boil for 2 minutes; remove from heat. Allow to stand for one hour (or soak the beans overnight in the 6 cups water.). Add remaining ingredients, except sour cream and parsley, to beans and cooking liquid. Bring to a boil, cover and simmer 3 hours or until beans are cooked. Remove meat and dice into small pieces. Discard bone and fat, if any. Return meat to the soup, add sour cream and stir until blended. Cook over low heat until thoroughly heated, but do not boil. Garnish with parsley.

Mrs. Dan Seitz (Amy)

SOUPS and SAUCES
Soups

Gumbo

Dutch oven

For roux:
shortening (Wesson oil)
1-inch deep in a Dutch
oven
1-2 medium onions, chopped
1-2 green peppers, chopped
`2 Tbs. flour
1 tsp. salt

In a Dutch oven, cook the onions and peppers in the shortening very slowly for 30 minutes. Cool. Stir in the flour and salt, heating slowly until the flour is cooked, but not brown.

1 ripe fresh tomato (more if
desired)
2-4 bay leaves, broken
1-2 celery stalks, chopped
2-4 peppercorns
1 Tbs. Worcestershire sauce
1 tsp. Tabasco

Add and cook slowly for 30-45 minutes (don't let flour get thick or lumpy).

2 cups of vegetable juices
(vegetable juice is the
water saved from cooking
potatoes, rice, onions,
green beans, broccoli,
squash, etc.)
2 cups okra, chopped

Add to above ingredients.

2 lbs. uncooked shrimp or
crab bodies
rice

Add either uncooked shrimp (2 lbs.) or crab bodies, let set to season. Bring to boil and cook until shrimp or crab is done. Serve in bowl over rice.

Mrs. Asa Bland (Judy)

Shrimp Gumbo

2 lbs. shrimp
2 Tbs. oil
2 Tbs. flour
3 cups okra, chopped or 1
　Tbs. filé
1 bell pepper, chopped
2 onions, chopped
green onion tops
2 Tbs. oil
1 (16-oz.) can tomatoes
2 qts. water
1 bay leaf
1 tsp. salt
3 pods garlic
1 tsp. thyme
½ cup parsley, chopped
½ tsp. pepper
rice

Peel and devein raw shrimp. Make roux (dark) of flour and oil. Add shrimp to this for a few minutes stirring constantly. Set aside. Smother okra, bell pepper, onion and green onion tops in oil. Add tomatoes when okra is nearly cooked. Then add water, bay leaf, salt, garlic and other spices. Add shrimp and roux to this. Cover and cook slowly for 30 minutes. Serve with rice.

If okra is not used, add gumbo file after turning off heat.

Mrs. Bill Davis (Jean)

Seafood Bisque

1 lb. crab meat or shrimp (or
　both)
1 (10¾-oz.) can of cream of
　tomato soup
1 (10¾-oz.) can split pea
　soup
1 (10¾-oz.) can cream of
　mushroom soup
1 can milk or half-and-half
½ cup sherry
½ tsp. "Season All" (Season
　salt)

Combine all ingredients except sherry and "Season All." Stir at low temperature to avoid burning or use a double boiler. Add sherry and "Season All" just before serving.

Mrs. Mike Frost (Sandra)

SOUPS and SAUCES
Soups

Gazpacho

Yields: 6 servings

1 large tomato, peeled
1 large cucumber, peeled and
  halved
½ med. onion, peeled
¼ green pepper (optional)
2 (14-oz.) cans tomato juice
¼ cup salad oil
⅓ cup red wine vinegar
¼ tsp. Tabasco
1½ tsp. salt
⅛ tsp. coarse ground black
  pepper

Accompaniments:
½ cucumber, chopped
½ med. onion, chopped
1 avocado, chopped
¾ cup green pepper
  (optional)

In electric blender, combine tomato, half of the cucumber, the onion, green pepper and ½ cup tomato juice. Blend at high speed 30 seconds, to purée. In large bowl or pitcher, mix the puréed vegetables with remaining juice, oil, vinegar, Tabasco, salt and pepper. Cover and refrigerate until well chilled—2 hours. Meanwhile, chop separately the half cucumber, onion, avocado, and if desired, green pepper. Put in separate bowls and serve as accompaniments. Serve in chilled bowls.

Mrs. Gary Gurwitz (Bailey)

Potato Soup

Yield: 6-8 servings

4-5 large potatoes, peeled
  and cubed
1 medium sized onion,
  chopped
2 tsp. salt
4 Tbs. butter
8 oz. sour cream
2 Tbs. parsley, chopped
milk

Cover potatoes and onion with water. Add salt and cook until very soft. Mash to smooth consistency. Add remaining ingredients. Use enough milk to achieve desired consistency.

Note: Do not pour the water off the potatoes before mashing!

Mrs. Jim Miller (Terry)

Salad-Soup

1 small clove garlic, mashed
1 Tbs. sugar
1½ tsp. salt
1 (46-oz.) can tomato juice
¼ cup olive oil
2 Tbs. lemon juice
1 tsp. Worcestershire sauce
3 tomatoes, finely diced (2
  cups)
1 cucumber, finely diced
  (about 1½ cups)
1 green pepper, finely diced
1 cup carrots, shredded
1 cup celery and leaves,
  thinly sliced
¼ cup green onions, thinly
  sliced
4 cups crisp croutons

Put garlic through a press, or mash completely; combine sugar, salt, tomato juice, olive oil, lemon juice, and Worcestershire sauce in large bowl; beat with rotary beater to blend in olive oil; cover; chill while preparing vegetables. Stir in vegetables; chill again at least 1 hour; pour into serving bowl; serve with crisp croutons to sprinkle on top. Store leftovers, covered, in the refrigerator.

Mrs. Morgan Talbot (Jane)

Split Pea Soup

1 lb. green split peas
1 small ham hock (or chunks
  of ham scraps), skin
  removed
1 large onion, chopped
1 Tbs. parsley
3 cloves
2 bay leaves
about ½ stalk celery with
  leaves, chopped
black pepper to taste

Soak peas overnight. In a quart or two of cold water, put the remaining ingredients on to boil. Simmer, covered, for four hours. Strain, reserving stock. Save ham pieces, cut them up and add to the stock. Add the split peas and the water they have been soaked in. Simmer 2 hours.

Note: Can serve as is, or if you prefer thinner soup, whip in blender and add whole milk or cream. Can add 1 Tbs. sherry, if desired. Nice with croutons.

Mrs. Charles E. Thompson, Jr. (Sally)

SOUPS and SAUCES
Soups

Squash Soup

Yield: 4-6 servings

2 Tbs. butter
⅔ cup onion, grated
2 (10-oz.) pkgs. sliced yellow
    squash (frozen) or 1½ lbs.
    fresh squash, chopped
2 (10¾-oz.) cans chicken
    broth
2 Tbs. rice
1 tsp. salt
¼ tsp. pepper
½ cup heavy cream or
    condensed milk

Sauté onions in butter just until soft, not brown. Add squash, broth and rice. Simmer gently for 30 minutes. Purée with blender or food processor. Add salt and pepper to taste. Stir in cream.

Note: Can be served hot or cold.

Mrs. Claus Eggers (Mardi)

Tomato Bouillon Curry Soup

Yield: 4 servings

4 tsp. beef stock base (Spice
    Island)
2 cups boiling water
1 (10¾-oz.) can condensed
    tomato soup
½ tsp. curry powder (less if
    using Spice Island)
¼ cup cold water
½ tsp. Mei Yen seasoning

Dissolve stock base in boiling water. Add soup. Mix curry with cold water; add Mei Yen; add the curry mix to soup. Heat just to simmering. Serve hot.

Soup-With-A-Zip

Yield: 4 servings

1 (10¾-oz.) can tomato soup
1 (10¾-oz.) can beef broth
1 cup water
⅓ cup vodka
1 tsp. Worcestershire sauce
⅓ tsp. hot pepper sauce

Combine in saucepan—heat to boiling. Serve in mugs.

Mrs. Larry Dooley (Jacqui)

Vegetable Soup

Yield: 4-6 servings

1-2 lbs. soup meat with
  bones
1 (No. 303) can tomato juice
1 potato, cut up
1 carrot, sliced
1 onion, chopped
2 stalks celery, sliced
⅓ cup rice
¼ tsp. black pepper
salt to taste
1-2 tsp. paprika
1-2 Tbs. sugar

Wash meat and put in a good size pot, cover with water. Boil just above a simmer until tender. Remove meat from broth. Have vegetables ready and add to broth. Cook until tender. All is usually cooked when rice is tender. Chop meat and add to vegetables, add a can of tomato juice; add seasoning and simmer about 15 minutes.

Note: You may also add: English peas, corn, green pepper, barley, macaroni, etc.

Mrs. Joe Stroud (Ruthie)

Bar-B-Q Sauce for Chicken

Yield: enough sauce
for 2 chickens

½ cup Wesson oil
¾ cup onions, chopped
¾ cup tomato ketchup
¾ cup water
¼ tsp. chili powder
⅓ cup lemon juice
3 Tbs. sugar
3 Tbs. Worcestershire sauce
2 Tbs. prepared mustard
2 tsp. salt
½ tsp. pepper

Cook onions in oil until soft. Add the other ingredients and simmer 15 minutes. This makes enough sauce to baste 2 chickens.

Mrs. Bill Scurlock (Mary)

Freeze stocks in ice cube trays and after frozen, store in plastic bags to use when needed. Because freezing causes the ingredients to separate, the cubes or frozen stock in any form should be brought to a boil before using.

SOUPS and SAUCES
Sauces

Special Fruit Compote

350 degrees

2 (6-oz.) cans frozen
  lemonade
2 cans water
4 sticks cinnamon
12 whole cloves
4-8 canned peach halves
4-8 canned pear halves
10 or more cooked prunes
1 small can coconut

Combine first four ingredients. Drain fruit well and add to liquid. Heat in oven 30 minutes or on top of stove on low heat. Serve with poultry, ham or pork. Other fruit may be added such as pineapple, apricots, or bananas.

This keeps well in the refrigerator.

Mrs. Jack Humphreys (Kay)

Mayonnaise

Food processor
Yield: 2 pints

1 whole egg
2-3 Tbs. lemon juice
1 tsp. salt
1½ tsp. sugar
1 tsp. dry mustard
½ tsp. paprika
½ tsp. cayenne pepper
2 cups corn oil
1 Tbs. vinegar

With steel cutting blade in place, add egg and 1 Tbs. lemon juice, whip until frothy, about 5 seconds. Stop machine. Add salt, sugar, dry mustard, paprika, and cayenne. Turn machine on, slowly add 1 cup of oil until mixture begins to thicken, do not rush adding this oil. Add remaining lemon juice, vinegar, and rest of oil. Process until thick and creamy.

Mrs. Glenn Jarvis (Pat)

Horseradish Mayonnaise Sauce

Yield: 2 cups

1 pint whipping cream
1½ Tbs. horseradish
1 cup real mayonnaise
3 tsp. dry mustard
salt to taste
½ Tbs. fresh lime juice
1 cup sour cream (optional)

Whip the cream, add the horseradish and whip longer, until standing in peaks. Add all of the other ingredients and refrigerate. The addition of 1 cup of sour cream is optional, but it does make a creamier sauce. Serve with ham, turkey or roast beef.

Keeps for one week in the refrigerator.

Mrs. Jerry Box (Deanna)

Mustard Sauce

Yield: about 3½ cups

3 eggs, well beaten
1 cup sugar
½ cup butter
½ can tomato soup
½ cup vinegar
½ cup mustard

Mix well. Heat to a boil.

This sauce is great on ham and will keep a good while in the refrigerator.

Mrs. Tim Johnstone (Mel)

Mustard Sauce for Ham

Yield: about 1½ cups

¼ cup dry hot mustard
¼ cup brown sugar
¼ cup water
1 egg, lightly beaten

Mix together and cook over low heat until mixture thickens. Serve with cooked ham. Keep in refrigerator and re-heat. If you wish to double this recipe use 3 eggs, but double all other ingredients.

Mrs. Jerry Box (Deanna)

Shrimp or Oyster Cocktail Sauce

6 Tbs. lemon juice
  (or 3 Tbs. lemon juice &
  3 Tbs. spiced wine-vinegar)
½ cup tomato ketchup
1 Tbs. horseradish
3 drops Tabasco sauce
⅛ tsp. salt
½ tsp. celery salt
½ tsp. sugar
dash ground cloves

Blend lemon juice (or lemon juice and vinegar mixture) with ketchup. Add remaining ingredients. Chill before serving.

Mrs. Billy Simpson (Ginger)

SOUPS and SAUCES
Sauces

Tartar Sauce

Yield: 1¾ cups

1 cup mayonnaise,
   homemade if possible
2 Tbs. parsley, chopped
2 Tbs. green olives, chopped
2 Tbs. onions, chopped
2 Tbs. sweet pickle relish
1 Tbs. Kraft
   Horseradish-Mayonnaise
1 tsp. dry mustard
fresh lime juice to taste, ½
   large lime
garlic powder to taste
1 Tbs. caper, chopped
   (optional)

Mix in order given and chill.

Mrs. Jerry Box (Deanna)

Curried Vegetable Sauce

4 Tbs. butter
2-3 Tbs. green onions,
   chopped
¼ tsp. curry powder
½ tsp. salt
⅓ cup flour
1⅔ cups milk
⅓ cup dry white wine
⅓ cup Parmesan cheese
toasted almonds, sliced

Sauté onions in butter. Add other ingredients; cook over medium heat until thickened. Add cheese. Can be made ahead of time. Use with asparagus, broccoli, or anything you wish. Put toasted almonds on top.

Mrs. Larry Seal (Jane Ann)

Vegetables

Asparagus-Pea Casserole

350 degrees
Casserole, greased
Yield: 6-8 servings

8 saltine crackers
2 cans asparagus spears
(reserve juice)
1 can small green peas
(reserve juice)
4 oz. almonds, slivered
½-1 cup bread crumbs,
buttered

Crumble crackers (large pieces) into bottom of well-greased casserole. Layer 1 can of asparagus, then ½ of the peas. Cover with ½ of the cheese sauce and ½ of the almonds. Repeat layers with the remaining ingredients. Put each layer of asparagus in a different direction. Top with bread crumbs and bake 45 minutes at 350 degrees.

Cheese sauce:
4 Tbs. butter
4 Tbs. flour
2 cups of liquid (milk and
juice from vegetables)
1 (5-oz.) jar Old English
pasteurized cheese

Melt butter and add flour. Add liquid and cheese. Stir until thick.

Mrs. Tom Moore (Pam)

Egg-Asparagus Casserole

350 degrees
1 quart casserole, greased
Yield: 6-8 servings

2 cups fresh asparagus,
cooked, cut in 1-inch
lengths, reserving liquid
1¼ cups bread crumbs, dry
4 eggs, hard-boiled, sliced
¼ cup butter
1 cup cheese, grated
1 (10¾-oz.) can cream of
mushroom soup
paprika

Drain asparagus, saving liquid. If necessary add water to make ⅔ cup liquid. Arrange half of asparagus in casserole. Cover with ½ cup crumbs and half of sliced eggs. Dot with butter. Sprinkle with a portion of the cheese. Repeat to form second layer. Combine asparagus liquid with mushroom soup in small saucepan. Cook over low heat and stir until well blended. Do not boil. Pour over mixture in casserole. Top with remaining crumbs and cheese. Sprinkle with paprika. Bake for 20 to 25 minutes.

Mrs. Ben Bilbrey (Lucille)

VEGETABLES

Stuffed Artichokes

350 degrees
8 x 8 baking dish
Yield: 4 servings

4 artichokes
3 Tbs. lemon juice
1 tsp. salt

Wash artichokes, cut off stem and top, and remove center leaves and thistle so heart is exposed, clean and surrounded by 5 or 6 rows of outer leaves. Place close together in saucepan, add lemon juice, 1 tsp. salt and 1 inch boiling water. Cook uncovered for 5 minutes. Cover and cook 30-35 minutes until base of stem can be easily pierced with fork. Drain upside down.

Stuffing:
¼ cup margarine
½ cup water
1 Tbs. onion, finely chopped
¼ cup parsley, finely
   chopped
1 clove garlic
2 Tbs. Parmesan cheese
½ tsp. oregano
2 cups herb seasoned
   stuffing mix
lemon slices
melted butter

Heat ¼ cup margarine and water until margarine melts. Stir in remaining ingredients. Stuff artichokes and place close together in baking dish. Add ½ inch boiling water, bake at 350 degrees for 20 minutes. Garnish with lemon slices and serve with melted butter.

Mrs. Jerry Leadbetter (Tonii)

Asparagus Casserole I

350 degrees
Small casserole dish
Yield: 4 servings

1 (10¾-oz.) can mushroom
   soup
small amount canned milk
1 egg, hard-boiled, sliced
1 large can asparagus
potato chips, crushed

Mix soup and milk. Add sliced egg. Pour over asparagus. Sprinkle crushed chips on top. Bake for 30 minutes.

Mrs. Joe Stroud (Ruthie)

VEGETABLES

Asparagus Casserole II

400 degrees
1 quart casserole, greased
Yield: 4 servings
Freezes

5 slices hard toast made into
  crumbs
½ stick margarine, melted
1 cup Cheddar or Velveeta
  cheese, grated
1½ cups medium white sauce
1 large can green asparagus
  or fresh cooked

Add crumbs to melted margarine and
stir until well coated. Stir cheese into
white sauce before it cools. Place asparagus in bottom of greased casserole.
Cover with white sauce and sprinkle
crumbs on top. Bake until hot.

Mrs. Steven Zenthoefer (Ann)

Spanish Beans

325 degrees
Large pot
Yield: 12 servings

2 cups dry pinto beans
6 cups water
2 tsp. salt
½ lb. bacon
1 cup onion, coarsely
  chopped
2 cloves garlic, minced
1 small bay leaf
¼ tsp. oregano
2 (15½-16-oz.) cans tomatoes
½ cup bell pepper, chopped
2 Tbs. chili powder
2 Tbs. brown sugar
½ tsp. dry mustard

Soak beans overnight in water. Drain,
and add the 6 cups fresh water. Bring
beans to a boil; add salt. Reduce heat to
simmer. Cook 1-2 hours. Cut bacon
slices into fourths. Fry until partially
done. Add to beans with remaining ingredients. Cook uncovered at 325 degrees for 1½ hours.

Mrs. Charles Murray (Cynthia)

VEGETABLES

Baked Beans

350 degrees
2 quart baking dish
Yield: 6-8 servings

2 (16-oz.) cans of pork and
  beans
⅓ cup brown sugar
⅓ cup ketchup
1 Tbs. mustard
1 small onion, chopped
1 tsp. barbecue spice
4 slices bacon

Mix all ingredients together, except
bacon. Pour into baking dish and
arrange bacon on top of beans. Bake for
30 to 45 minutes.

Mrs. Bob Batte (Gerry)

Texas Caviar (Pickled Black Eyed Peas)   Yield: 8 servings

2 (1 lb.) cans black-eyed
  peas, drained
1 onion, sliced thin
½ cup salad oil or olive oil
¼ cup wine vinegar
2 cloves garlic, mashed
1 Tbs. Worcestershire sauce
1 tsp. salt
pepper

Put peas and onions in heatproof bowl.
Combine all other ingredients in a
saucepan. Bring to a boil and pour over
peas. Refrigerate for several hours.

Will keep several weeks in refrigerator.

Mrs. Jerry McGilvray (Jane)

Broccoli Casserole

350 degrees
Casserole dish, greased
Yield: 6-8 servings

2 (10-oz.) pkgs. broccoli,
  chopped
1 (10¾-oz.) can cream of
  mushroom soup
1 cup Pepperidge Farm
  dressing
½ cup Cheddar cheese,
  grated

Cook broccoli as directed on package—
put in large mixing bowl; add mushroom
soup and ¾ cup of dressing mix. Put in
greased casserole dish and on top
sprinkle ¼ cup dressing and Cheddar
cheese. Cook at 350 degrees for 30
minutes.

Mrs. Randy Davis (Lynn)

390

VEGETABLES

Almond Broccoli Casserole

350 degrees
2 quart casserole, buttered
Yield: 8 servings

½ cup celery, chopped
½ cup onions, chopped
½ stick margarine
½ roll garlic cheese
1 (10¾-oz.) can mushroom
   soup
1 Tbs. lemon juice
dash red pepper
1 Tbs. Worcestershire sauce
1 cup mushrooms, sliced
2 (10-oz.) pkgs. broccoli,
   cooked and drained
slivered almonds

Sauté celery and onions in margarine. Add next 6 ingredients and cook until cheese melts. Place broccoli in bottom of buttered casserole. Pour sauce over and sprinkle with slivered almonds. Bake until heated thoroughly.

Mrs. Charles Fox (Nancy)

Broccoli-Rice Casserole

350 degrees
3 quart casserole, greased
Yield: 12 servings

1¾ cups rice, raw
¾ cup onion, chopped
¾ cup green pepper,
   chopped
1 cup celery, chopped
4 Tbs. margarine
2 (10-oz.) pkgs. frozen
   broccoli, chopped
1 (8-oz.) Cheese Whiz
1 (10¾-oz.) can cream of
   chicken soup
1 (10¾-oz.) can cream of
   mushroom soup
1 (3-oz.) can mushrooms,
   chopped

Cook rice. Sauté onions, green pepper, and celery in margarine. Cook broccoli, drain and combine with Cheese Whiz, sautéed vegetables, undiluted soup and mushrooms. Fold in cooked rice and put into casserole. Bake 30 minutes.

Tip: Make a day ahead. Bake just before serving.

Mrs. F. H. Mangum (Maree)

VEGETABLES

Stuffed Broccoli

325 degrees
2 quart casserole, greased
Yield: 6 servings

½ pkg. Pepperidge Farm herb
  stuffing
2 tsp. butter
2 (10-oz.) pkgs. frozen
  broccoli
1 (10¾-oz.) can cream of
  mushroom soup
¼ cup milk

Brown stuffing in butter. Place some of the broccoli in bottom of casserole. Top with half of stuffing. Then top with rest of broccoli and remaining stuffing. Dilute soup with milk and pour over top. Bake 30 minutes at 325 degrees. Stir together before serving.

Variation: Celery may be added for a twist.

Mrs. Greg Morrow (Debbie)

Red Cabbage

Yield: 6 servings

1 medium head red cabbage
1 medium sweet onion
2 large apples
1 bay leaf
2 whole allspice
1 heaping Tbs. bacon fat
2 cloves (heads removed)
1 tsp. salt
6 peppercorns
½ cup sugar
1 cup vinegar
1½ cups water
2 Tbs. cornstarch

Remove outer leaves from cabbage and wash the head. Core cabbage and slice. Peel onion and apples and slice. Toss cabbage, onion and apple together. Add remaining ingredients to cabbage mixture and simmer 1½ hours in a covered pan. Thicken slightly with about 2 Tbs. cornstarch blended with cold water.

This dish is especially good with wild game of any kind and is excellent reheated.

Mrs. Scott Toothaker (Dorothy)

VEGETABLES

Candied Carrot Strips

Saucepan
Yield: 4 servings
Does not freeze

½ cup butter
6 Tbs. brown sugar
1 pkg. carrots, cut into
  quarters (split lengthwise,
  then cut in half)
¾ cup water

Blend butter and sugar; add carrots and water. Cook over medium heat until carrots are tender (about 15 minutes). Serve hot.

For variety, 2 Tbs. of fresh mint may be added.

Mrs. Glenn Jarvis (Pat)

Marinated Carrots

Yield: 10-12 servings

2 lbs. carrots
1 cup water
1 medium onion, diced or
  rings
1 bell pepper, chopped or
  rings

Slice carrots and boil in salted water for 10 minutes. Place carrots, onion and bell pepper in casserole.

Marinade:
¾ cup vinegar
½ cup oil
1 cup sugar
1 tsp. mustard
1 tsp. Worcestershire sauce
1 can tomato soup
salt and pepper to taste

In a saucepan combine the vinegar, oil, sugar, mustard, Worcestershire and tomato soup. Simmer for 15 minutes and pour over carrots. Store in refrigerator.

Mrs. Jim Henderson (Karen)

Variation: Canned carrots may be substituted for fresh.

Mrs. Madonna Johnson

393

VEGETABLES

Carrot Ring

350 degrees
Ring mold or
8-inch layer pan,
greased
Yield: 8 servings

1 cup shortening
½ cup brown sugar
1 Tbs. cold water
1 egg
1¼ cups flour
1 tsp. soda
½ tsp. salt
1 tsp. baking powder
1 cup carrots, grated
2 Tbs. lemon juice

Cream shortening and sugar. Mix in water and egg. Sift dry ingredients and add grated carrots. Add lemon juice and all other ingredients to shortening mixture. Pour in pan and bake 30 minutes.

Mrs. Leroy Lewin (Hilda)

Scalloped Carrots

325 degrees
Small casserole, greased
Yield: 4 servings

1 cup carrots, grated
1 small onion, grated
1 cup bread crumbs
salt and pepper to taste
1 cup milk
1 egg, beaten
5 Tbs. butter

Place half of the carrots, onions, crumbs and seasonings in greased casserole. Blend milk and egg together. Pour half of the milk mixture over carrot mixture in casserole. Add remaining carrots, crumbs, and seasonings. Pour remaining milk mixture over the top. Dot with butter. Cover. Bake at 325 degrees for 1 hour.

Mrs. Cayetano Barrera (Yolanda)

Corn Patch Pudding

325 degrees
1½ quart casserole, greased
Yield: 6 servings

1 (16-oz.) can cream style
  corn
1 cup sour cream
1 cup Parmesan cheese
½ cup corn meal
¼ cup butter, melted
salt and pepper
3 eggs, beaten

Mix all ingredients together, adding eggs last. Bake in greased (with Pam) casserole for 40 minutes or until done.

Variation:
1 cup cooked chicken, diced
¼ cup jalapeño pepper,
  chopped

Add 1 cup cooked chicken and ¼ cup chopped jalapeño peppers.

Mrs. Jerry McGilvray (Jane)

Corn Soufflé

325 degrees
2 quart casserole dish
Yield: 8-10 servings

1 (16-oz.) can cream style
  corn
⅔ stick margarine, melted
4 Tbs. flour
1 Tbs. sugar
½ tsp. salt
4 eggs
1 cup milk

Stir together the corn and the margarine. Blend the flour, sugar and salt together. Add to the corn mixture. Beat eggs well and add to milk. Combine this with the corn mixture. Pour into a 2 quart casserole (use Pam). Cook at 325 degrees for 45 minutes to 1 hour depending upon the depth of the casserole dish. Serve as soon as you take from oven.

VEGETABLES

Creole Corn

350 degrees
Casserole, greased
Yield: 10 servings

2 medium onions, chopped
2 green peppers, chopped
4-5 slices bacon, cut
  crosswise
1 large can pimiento,
  chopped
3 cans cream style corn
1½-2 cups rice, cooked
¾ cup Pet milk
salt, pepper, paprika
Cheddar cheese, grated
Parmesan cheese

Sauté onion, green pepper and bacon until soft. Add rest of ingredients except cheeses and heat. Salt and pepper to taste. Pour mixture into a greased casserole dish. Top with grated cheese, then Parmesan cheese. Sprinkle with paprika. Bake 20-30 minutes or until heated thoroughly.

Mrs. Charles Murray (Cynthia)

Frito-Corn Dressing

350 degrees
Casserole size is determined
by size of turkey
Yield: Serves 8

1 (9½-oz.) bag of Fritos
1 can cream-style corn
1 cup milk
2 slices bread
2 eggs
1 large onion, chopped
1 large green pepper,
  chopped
leaves of 6 stalks of celery
2 Tbs. oil

Crumble Fritos in bowl. Cover with corn, milk, bread, and eggs. Let stand while you brown onion, pepper, and celery in oil. Add this to Frito mixture and mash with potato masher just enough to coarsely blend all ingredients. Stuff in turkey and bake remaining dressing in casserole.

Delicious even without the turkey!

Mrs. Leroy Lewin (Hilda)

VEGETABLES

Savory Cucumbers

2 cucumbers, unpeeled
1 tsp. garlic salt

Slice cucumbers paper thin. Soak for at least one hour in ice water to which garlic salt has been added. Drain cucumbers until thoroughly dry (patting dry with paper towels if necessary).

1 cup sour cream
⅛ tsp. pepper
½ tsp. celery salt
½ tsp. onion salt

Combine and mix well the sour cream, pepper, celery salt, and onion salt. Add to cucumbers and toss lightly and serve.

Great with fish!

Mrs. Jerry Box (Deanna)

Eggplant and Sausage Casserole

350 degrees
Casserole, lightly greased
Yield: 4 servings

1 medium eggplant
½ lb. sausage
1 large onion, chopped
butter
2 eggs, hard-boiled
½ tsp. season salt
⅓ cup cracker crumbs

Peel eggplant and boil in salted water about 2 minutes or until soft. Brown sausage in skillet and pour off fat. Sauté onions in butter until translucent. Chop hard-boiled eggs. Mix ingredients and add salt. Mash and place in lightly greased casserole. Cover with crumbs. Bake 20 minutes at 350 degrees.

May be made day before and heated.

Mrs. Leroy Lewin (Hilda)

Do not salt water that is to be used for boiling corn. It toughens the corn.

VEGETABLES

Italian Eggplant Casserole

350 degrees
2 quart oblong baking dish
Yield: 6 servings

1 medium eggplant
1 egg, beaten
⅓ cup fine bread crumbs
cooking oil
salt and pepper to taste
1 Tbs. oregano, crushed
2 Tbs. parsley, chopped
¼ cup Parmesan cheese,
  grated
1 (6-oz.) pkg. Mozzarella
  cheese, sliced
1 (8-oz.) can tomato paste

Pare eggplant and slice into ½-inch slices. Dip in egg, then crumbs. Brown lightly in hot oil. Drain. Arrange slices in baking dish. Sprinkle with salt, pepper, oregano, parsley, and Parmesan cheese. Top with cheese slices. Pour tomato paste over all. Bake 30 minutes.

Mrs. F. H. Mangum (Maree)

Eggplant Patties

Yield: 4 servings

1 medium eggplant, pared
  and cubed
1 clove garlic, minced
1¼ cups Ritz cracker crumbs
  (20 crackers)
2 Tbs. green onion, sliced
5 oz. sharp cheese, shredded
½ tsp. salt
2 eggs, slightly beaten
⅛ tsp. pepper
2 Tbs. parsley, snipped
2 Tbs. cooking oil

In covered saucepan, cook eggplant in boiling water until tender (about 5 minutes). Drain well and mash. Stir in garlic, crumbs, onion, cheese, salt, eggs, pepper, and parsley. Shape into 8 patties about 3 inches in diameter. Cook in hot oil about 3 minutes on each side until brown.

Mrs. Cayetano Barrera (Yolanda)

Eggplant Casserole

350 degrees
1½ quart casserole, greased
Yield: 4 servings

2 large eggplant
¾ cup milk
salt and pepper
3 Tbs. Cheddar cheese,
  shredded
1 small onion, diced
1 cup crackers, crushed
2 Tbs. margarine
4 slices American cheese

Pare and slice eggplant and cook in salted water. Drain and mash. Add other ingredients except cheese slices. Place in casserole. Bake at 350 degrees for 40 minutes. Arrange cheese slices on top and bake 20 minutes longer.

Mrs. Julian Zipper (Sue)

Green Beans

Yield: 4 servings

1 can green beans
salt and pepper
1 small can mushrooms
1 (3-oz.) pkg. cream cheese

Drain bean juice into pan with salt and pepper to taste. Bring to a boil; add mushrooms and boil away ½ of the juice. Add cream cheese. When melted, add beans and heat.

Mrs. Shelley Collier, Jr. (Caryl)

Fancy Green Beans

300 degrees
1½ or 2 quart casserole
Yield: 8 servings

2 (16-oz.) cans French style
  green beans
1 (10¾-oz.) can cream of
  chicken soup, undiluted
1 can water chestnuts, thinly
  sliced
2 Tbs. butter (optional)
1 pkg. French fried onion
  rings
Parmesan cheese (optional)

Cook beans just to a boil, drain well. Mix soup, chestnuts, and butter with cooked beans and put into a 1½ or 2 quart casserole. Place the onion rings on top with the Parmesan cheese sprinkled over all. Bake at 300 degrees for 30-40 minutes.

Mrs. Bill Scurlock (Mary)

VEGETABLES

Green Beans with Sour Cream Dressing   Yield: 4 servings

1 can green beans
1 onion, sliced
salt, pepper to season
oil and vinegar dressing

Let the beans marinate with the onions overnight in the oil and vinegar dressing. Drain.

Dressing:
1 cup sour cream
½ cup mayonnaise
1 tsp. lemon juice
¼ tsp. dry mustard
1 Tbs. horseradish
¼ tsp. onion juice
2 tsp. chives, chopped

Mix dressing ingredients together and pour over marinated green beans.

Mrs. Robert Whitis (Linda)

Green Beans Amandine   Yield: 8 servings

2 (16-oz.) cans French style
   green beans
8-10 slices bacon
½ cup onions, chopped
5 Tbs. vinegar
salt and pepper
slivered almonds

Drain beans and set aside. Fry bacon, crumble and set aside. Brown onions in bacon fat; add beans, vinegar, salt, and pepper. Heat. Refrigerate. Just before serving, add bacon and almonds.

Mrs. Larry Fritz (Libby)

Marinated Green Beans   Yield: 8 servings

2 cans whole green beans
3 green onions, thin sliced
½ cup sugar
½ cup vinegar
¼ cup water
2 Tbs. salad oil
½ tsp. accent
salt and pepper

Drain the green beans. Slice the onions to make thin onion rings and combine with beans. Combine remaining ingredients in a saucepan, and bring to a boil. Pour over beans and onions. Chill for several hours.

Mrs. Margaret Colley

400

VEGETABLES

Bean Jumble Casserole

325 degrees
9 x 13 pyrex dish
Yield: 8 servings

1 (16-oz.) can lima beans
1 onion, chopped
1 (16-oz.) can butter beans
½ pint sour cream
1 (16-oz.) can French style
  green beans
salt and pepper to taste
1 (16-oz.) can English peas
1 small jar pimientos
1 (10¾-oz.) can tomato soup
1 (10¾-oz.) can mushroom
  soup
1 cup Cheddar cheese,
  grated

Mix all ingredients, except cheese. Sprinkle cheese on top. Bake for 20 minutes.

Mrs. Waite Law (Gladys)

Grits Casserole

350 degrees
2 quart casserole
Yield: 8 servings
Freezes

4 cups milk
1 cup grits
½ cup butter
1 roll garlic cheese
2 eggs, well beaten
salt

Bring milk to boil and add grits. Stir until thick, about 10 minutes. Remove from heat. Add butter and cheese. Stir until melted. Stir in eggs and salt and pour into 2 quart casserole. Bake uncovered 30 minutes.

Mrs. Leroy Lewin (Hilda)

VEGETABLES

Cheese and Grits

300 degrees
3 quart casserole dish
Yield: 10-12 servings
Freezes

6 cups water, boiling
1½ cups grits
2 tsp. salt
2 tsp. Lawry's salt
3 eggs, beaten
1½ sticks butter
1 lb. Cheddar cheese, grated

Boil grits in salted water for 25 minutes. Stir occasionally. Gradually add Lawry's salt to the beaten eggs. Add butter and cheese and mix well. Pour into a 3 quart casserole dish and bake at 300 degrees for 1 hour. Serve hot.

Mrs. E. F. Wallace (Janet)

Mushrooms Florentine

350 degrees
Shallow 10-inch baking dish
Yield: 6-8 servings

1 lb. fresh mushrooms
2 pkgs. frozen spinach
1 tsp. salt
¼ cup onions, chopped
¼ cup butter, melted
1 cup Cheddar cheese,
  freshly grated
garlic salt

Wash and dry mushrooms. Separate stems from caps and sauté all until brown. Mix cooked, drained spinach with salt, onion, and melted butter. Line baking dish with spinach. Sprinkle with ½ cup grated cheese. Arrange mushrooms over spinach. Sprinkle with garlic salt. Cover with remaining cheese. Bake 20 minutes or until cheese melts.

Tip: May be made ahead and refrigerated until baking time.

Mrs. Gary Gurwitz (Bailey)

Wash, dry and store mushrooms whole or sliced in freezer in plastic bags. No need to defrost when ready to use. If stems should become separated, save for use in stocks, soups, etc.

VEGETABLES

Creamy Grits Casserole

350 degrees
Casserole, greased
Yield: 10 servings
Freezes

1 cup grits, uncooked
¾ tsp. garlic salt (add to
  water for grits)
½ lb. Cheddar cheese, grated
1 (10-oz.) can condensed
  cream of chicken soup
⅛ tsp. cayenne, or less
paprika

Cook grits according to directions on package, adding garlic salt to boiling water. Add cheese, soup and cayenne. Mix well. Pour into greased casserole, sprinkle with paprika and bake for 40 to 50 minutes.

Bleu Cheese Noodles

350 degrees
2 quart casserole,
greased
Yield: 6 servings

8 oz. cooked noodles
1 cup cream-style cottage
  cheese
4 oz. Bleu cheese
¼ cup parsley, minced
¼ cup onion, grated
3 eggs, well beaten
¼ cup butter, melted
¾ tsp. garlic salt
paprika

Toss all together lightly. Add dash of paprika. Bake 30 minutes.

Mrs. Leroy Lewin (Hilda)

For a mouth watering rice, add a little white wine or sherry to melted butter before rice and liquid have been added. Cook as usual.

VEGETABLES

Cauliflower with Shrimp Sauce

Yield: 4 servings

1 head cauliflower
1 can frozen Campbell's
  shrimp soup
½ cup sour cream
salt and pepper to taste
¼ cup almonds, toasted

Boil cauliflower until tender but not over-cooked. Heat soup until steaming but do not boil. Add sour cream slowly. Add salt and pepper to taste. Stir in almonds. Pour over cauliflower.

Mrs. William Burke (Lynne)

Hot Hominy

350 degrees
9 x 13 glass dish
Yield: 8 servings

4 slices of bacon
1 large onion, chopped
1 (15-oz.) can hominy
1 (14½-oz.) can tomatoes
2 small cans jalapeños,
  seeded and slivered
½ lb. Cheddar cheese, grated

Fry bacon, drain and crumble. Cook on-ions to transparency in bacon fat. Add hominy and tomatoes, then add slivered jalapeños (more or less than 2 cans, according to taste). Put in casserole dish, sprinkle with grated cheese and bake at 350 degrees until bubbly.

Mrs. Robert H. Kern, Jr. (Carolyn)

French-Fried Onion Rings

Yield: 6-8 servings

3-4 large Spanish or Bermuda
  onions
2-3 cups buttermilk or ice
  water
1 egg, beaten
1 tsp. salt
1½ tsp. baking powder
⅔ cup water
1 cup all-purpose flour
1 Tbs. salad oil
1 tsp. lemon juice
¼ tsp. cayenne pepper
salad oil

Peel onions and slice about ⅜ inch thick; separate into rings. Pour butter-milk into a shallow pan; add onion rings to soak 30 minutes. Combine egg, salt, baking powder, water, flour, 1 Tbs. sal-ad oil, lemon juice, pepper; stir until smooth. Heat salad oil to 375 degrees. Remove onion rings from buttermilk and dip into batter; fry in hot oil until golden brown. Drain on absorbent paper.

Good batter for shrimp tempura.

Mrs. Billy Simpson (Ginger)

VEGETABLES

Onion Ring Batter

1 cup flour
1 cup cornstarch
¼ tsp. salt
3 Tbs. baking powder
1 egg
1 cup COLD water
3 Tbs. oil
onions, sliced and separated
   into rings

Sift dry ingredients and set aside. Beat egg, add water, oil, and mix. Add liquid to dry ingredients, mixing with fork (more water may be needed). Dip in onions and deep fry.

Tip: Good for shrimp, too. The batter really sticks!

Mrs. Hulon Webb (Carole)

Bar-B-Que Potatoes

400 degrees
1½ quart baking dish
Yield: 6 servings

3 cups potatoes (4 med.
   potatoes cooked with
   peeling)
3 Tbs. butter or margarine
3 Tbs. flour
1½ tsp. salt
2 cups milk
½ tsp. Tabasco sauce
2 Tbs. parsley, chopped
2 Tbs. pimientos, chopped
½ cup buttered soft bread
   crumbs
½ cup American cheese,
   grated
¼ tsp. paprika

Cook potatoes in skin until tender; peel and dice. Melt butter. Add flour and salt, stirring into a smooth paste. Add milk and cook, stirring constantly until mix thickens and comes to a boil. Stir in Tabasco, parsley and pimientos. Add potatoes and turn into a 1½ qt. (about 8 x 8 x 2) casserole. Combine bread crumbs, cheese, and paprika. Sprinkle around edge of casserole leaving center clear. Bake 30 minutes at 400 degrees. Hints: Dice potatoes evenly and rather fine. If doubled, fits nicely in 8 x 12 x 2 casserole dish. Heat the milk before mixing. Do not toast bread to make crumbs, but use soft crumbs. Casserole can be made day before. If refrigerated, bake 350 degrees for 50 minutes.

Mrs. Boone Slusher (Shirley)

VEGETABLES

Country Potatoes

325 degrees
1½ quart casserole, greased
Yield: 6 servings
Does not freeze

6 potatoes, mashed
½ cup butter
1 cup sour cream
salt and pepper
1½ cups cheese, grated

Place first four ingredients in casserole.
Top with cheese. Bake 30 minutes.

Mrs. Mike Frost (Sandra)

Variation:
¾ cup green onion tops,
   chopped
1 (2-oz.) jar pimiento

Add onions and pimiento to casserole.

Mrs. Glenn Jarvis (Pat)

Delmonico Potatoes

400 degrees
2 quart casserole,
greased
Yield: 6 servings

8 medium potatoes
8 Tbs. butter
6 Tbs. flour
2½ cups cream or
   half and half
½ tsp. salt
pepper
1 cup sharp Cheddar cheese,
   grated
½ cup fine dry bread crumbs

Wash, peel, and dice potatoes. Boil until just done, but not mushy. Drain and place in casserole. Melt 6 Tbs. butter, blend in flour; gradually add cream, stirring constantly. Heat to boiling while continuing to stir. Add salt and pepper and pour over potatoes. Top with grated cheese and bread crumbs buttered with remaining 2 Tbs. butter. Bake until cheese melts and casserole is bubbly, about 20-30 minutes.

Mrs. Walt Mielcarek (Betty)

VEGETABLES

Creamy Potato Bake

400 degrees
1 quart baking dish,
greased
Yield: 6 servings

instant mashed potatoes
4 oz. whipped cream cheese
1 egg, beaten
2 Tbs. green onion, finely
  chopped
1 Tbs. parsley, finely snipped
1 Tbs. butter or margarine
paprika

Prepare instant mashed potatoes—enough for 6 servings—according to package directions, omitting the butter or margarine. Add cream cheese. Beat well. Stir in egg, onion, parsley and blend thoroughly. Transfer to well-greased baking dish. Dot with butter or margarine. Sprinkle with paprika. Bake in 400 degree oven for 30 minutes.

Mrs. Scott Toothaker (Dorothy)

Fluffy Potato Casserole

300 degrees
9-inch square baking
dish, greased
Yield: 6-8 servings

2 cups cold or hot mashed
  potatoes (if using instant
  variety, follow package
  directions)
1 (8-oz.) pkg. cream cheese,
  at room temperature
1 very small onion, finely
  chopped
2 eggs
2 Tbs. all-purpose flour
salt and pepper to taste
1 (3½-oz.) can French fried
  onions

Put the potatoes into a large bowl of your electric mixer. Add the cream cheese, chopped onion, eggs, and flour. Beat at medium speed until the ingredients are blended, then beat at high speed until light and fluffy. Taste, and add salt and pepper, if needed. Spoon into a greased 9 inch square baking dish. Distribute the canned onions evenly over the top. Bake, uncovered, at 300 degrees for about 35 minutes. (If you prepare this dish ahead, add the onions just before putting it in the oven.) You can double this recipe. Use a 9 x 13-inch baking dish, and bake for about 1 hour and 10 minutes. Cover with foil if onions start to overbrown.

Mrs. Stanley Marcus (Marsha)

VEGETABLES

Hashed Brown Potato Casserole

350 degrees
Casserole, greased
Yield: 12 servings

2 (10-oz.) pkgs. frozen
   hashed brown potatoes
½ cup butter, melted
1 tsp. salt
¼ tsp. pepper
½ cup onion, chopped—less
   if you like
1 cup cream of chicken soup
1 pint sour cream
2 cups sharp Cheddar
   cheese, grated
2 cups corn flakes, crushed
¼ cup butter, melted

Defrost potatoes. Mix all ingredients thoroughly, then cover with corn flake crumbs that have been mixed in melted butter. Put in greased casserole dish. Bake at 350 degrees for 45 minutes.

Can be prepared the day before and put in the refrigerator. This recipe will half easily.

Mrs. P. D. Moore (Hortense)

Variation:
1 (10¾-oz.) can cream of
   celery soup
bell pepper, chopped

The cream of celery soup can be substituted for the cream of chicken soup. Chopped bell pepper can be added to taste.

Mrs. Larry Dooley (Jacqui)

Potato Casserole

350 degrees
9 x 13 casserole dish
Yield: 8-12 servings

½ cup butter, melted
2 cups sour cream
1 (10¾-oz.) can cream of
   chicken soup
⅓ cup onion, chopped
1½ cups Cheddar cheese,
   grated
6-8 medium potatoes, boiled,
   peeled and cut in chunks
2 Tbs. butter
½ cup cornflakes, crushed

Melt butter. Add sour cream, soup, onions and grated cheese. Add cream mixture to potatoes and mix well. Toss 2 Tbs. butter with cornflakes. Pour potato mixture into casserole dish and sprinkle cornflakes on top. Bake 45 minutes at 350 degrees.

Mrs. David Sulzbach (Judi)

VEGETABLES

Rice Casserole

350 degrees
1½ quart casserole
Yield: 6 servings

1 cup rice (not Minute Rice)
½ stick margarine
1 (10½-oz.) can beef broth
½ can water
1 tsp. salt
juice of ½ lemon
1 beef bouillon cube
1 tsp. oregano

Brown rice in margarine; add other ingredients and put in 1½ quart casserole and bake 1 hour covered.

Mrs. Vernon Neuhaus, Jr. (Gayle)

Rice and Cheese Fritters

Yield: 6 servings

2 Tbs. flour
1 Tbs. baking powder
¼ tsp. salt
1 egg, beaten lightly
1 cup rice, boiled
½ cup Cheddar cheese,
    grated
2 Tbs. milk
butter or oil for frying

Sift together three times the flour, baking powder, and salt. To the beaten egg, add rice, cheese, milk, and the flour mixture. Drop by spoonful into butter or oil. Cook until a delicate brown color, then turn. Serve hot.

Mrs. Mitchell Darby (Martha)

Baked Rice with Peas

350 degrees
Yield: 6 servings

¼ lb. butter
1 cup regular rice
1 (10½-oz.) can clear bouillon
1 (bouillon) can water
tiny green peas

Melt butter. Pour in rice, stirring until rice is coated. Add bouillon and water. Stir. Put in a baking dish and cover well with aluminum foil and bake about 1 hour at 350 degrees. Warm tiny green peas and scatter over the dish just before serving.

Mrs. P. D. Moore (Hortense)

VEGETABLES

California Casserole

375 degrees
12 x 8 x 2 dish, greased
Yield: 8 servings

¼ cup butter or margarine
1 cup onion, chopped
4 cups rice, cooked
2 cups sour cream
1 cup cottage cheese,
    cream-style
1 large bay leaf, crumbled
½ tsp. salt
⅛ tsp. pepper
3 (4-oz.) cans chiles, drained
    halves, with seeds
2 cups sharp natural cheese,
    grated
parsley, chopped

Sauté onion in butter until golden. Remove from heat. Stir in hot rice, sour cream, cottage cheese, bay leaf, salt, pepper; toss lightly to mix well. Layer half the rice mixture in bottom of baking dish, then half the chiles, sprinkle half the cheese, repeat. Bake uncovered 25 minutes or until bubbly. Sprinkle with parsley.

Mrs. J. W. Caldwell (Bernice)

Green Rice

350 degrees
Casserole dish, buttered
Yield: 5-6 servings

2 cups rice, cooked
1 cup milk
1 cup sharp Cheddar cheese,
    grated
¼ cup butter or margarine,
    melted or salad oil
1 egg, well beaten
2 Tbs. onion, chopped
salt and pepper
⅔ cup parsley, minced,
    spinach, chopped, or
    chives, chopped, or any
    combination of these

Combine all ingredients, with salt and pepper to taste, in a well-buttered medium casserole. Bake 15 minutes at 350 degrees.

Mrs. Neal King (Wileen)

VEGETABLES

Wild Rice and Mushroom Dressing

325 degrees
9 x 13 pan, greased
Freezes

2 cups wild rice, cooked
2 cups white rice, cooked
4 strips bacon, fried and
  crumbled
1 medium onion, chopped
½ tsp. thyme
1 bay leaf
2 Tbs. parsley, finely minced
1 large can mushrooms and
  liquid, sliced
¼-½ cup chicken broth
salt and pepper to taste

Cook rices according to package directions. Fry bacon until crisp; remove and crumble. Sauté onion in bacon drippings until soft and yellow. Place rices, bacon and onion in a greased casserole and add remaining ingredients, using enough chicken broth for a moist dressing. Season with salt and pepper; stir to mix. Bake 30 minutes at 325 degrees.

¾ cup uncooked rice is equal to 2 cups cooked rice. Good with turkey, duck, and other game birds.

Mrs. Jack Hart (Darlene)

Spinach Madeleine

325 degrees
Yield: 6 servings
Freezes

2 (10-oz.) pkgs. frozen
  spinach, chopped
4 Tbs. butter
2 Tbs. flour
2 Tbs. onion, chopped
½ cup evaporated milk
½ cup spinach liquid
½ tsp. pepper
¾ tsp. celery salt
¾ tsp. garlic salt
½ tsp. salt
1 (6-oz.) roll jalapeño cheese
1 tsp. Worcestershire sauce

Cook spinach as directed, drain well and reserve liquid. Melt butter, add flour and cook until smooth but not brown. Add onions and cook until soft. Slowly add spinach liquid and milk and cook until smooth. Add seasonings and cheese and stir until cheese melts. Stir in spinach. Can be served immediately or put into a casserole, topped with bread crumbs and served later. Heat in 325 degree oven until thoroughly heated.

Mrs. Charles Henson (Nancy)

VEGETABLES

Spinach Casserole I

350 degrees
2 quart casserole, greased
Yield: 6 servings

1 (No. 2) can spinach (with
juice)
1 (10¾-oz.) can cream of
mushroom soup
1 can water chestnuts,
drained and sliced
1 cup poultry dressing,
yellow sack
1 cup Cheddar cheese,
grated

Combine all in casserole. Top with some
of the stuffing. Bake until bubbly.

Mrs. Charles Murray (Cynthia)

Spinach Soufflé Crepes

Yield: 12-14 crepes

Crepes:
1½ cups milk
3 eggs
⅛ tsp. salt
1 cup all-purpose flour
vegetable oil

Put milk, eggs, salt and flour in a blender, cover, and blend at top speed for 30
seconds. Batter should be consistency
of heavy cream. Cover and refrigerate
for an hour or two to allow batter to thick-
en. Before preparing each crepe, brush
the crepe pan or small skillet with oil to
cover entire bottom. Heat pan until hot
but not smoking. Pour in about 2-3 Tbs.
batter, tilting pan to coat evenly. Cook
over medium heat about 1 minute until
the top of the crepe is dry and the bottom
is lightly browned. Turn crepe with spatula and cook on other side about 20
seconds.

Cheese sauce:
3 Tbs. butter or margarine
3 Tbs. flour
1 cup milk
¼ tsp. salt
dash pepper
1 cup Cheddar cheese,
grated

Heat butter in small saucepan until
melted. Stir in flour. Gradually add milk,
stirring. Heat to boiling, stirring until mixture thickens. Add remaining ingredients, stirring until cheese melts.

continued . . .

VEGETABLES

Spinach soufflé filling:

3 Tbs. butter or margarine
¼ cup onion, minced
¾ cup fresh spinach leaves,
  minced, (or defrosted
  chopped spinach)
3 Tbs. flour
1 cup milk, scalded
½ tsp. salt
⅛ tsp. nutmeg
4 eggs, separated
½ cup Swiss cheese, grated

Melt butter in medium saucepan. Add onion and cook, 5 minutes, stirring until tender. Add spinach and cook, stirring about 3 minutes to evaporate most of the moisture. Stir in flour smoothly. Add hot milk and cook, stirring, until mixture comes to boiling. Season with salt and nutmeg. Add egg yolks one at a time, stirring well until blended. Add grated cheese. Beat egg whites until stiff peaks form. Fold into egg-yolk mixture with a light hand. Pour into a well-buttered 1½-quart soufflé dish. Set pan in a pan containing 1 inch hot water. Bake at 375 degrees about 35 minutes, or until knife inserted in center comes out clean. To assemble: place about ⅓ cup of baked spinach soufflé in center of each crepe. Spread lightly. Roll up. Place in shallow baking dish. Top with cheese sauce. Place dish under broiler about 4 inches from heating element for 2-3 minutes, to brown sauce lightly.

Make crepes ahead, if you like, separating with waxed paper. Make sauce while soufflé is cooking.

Mrs. Morgan Talbot (Jane)

Spinach Casserole II

350 degrees
2 quart casserole
Yield: 6-8 servings

2 pkgs. frozen chopped
  spinach, cooked and
  drained
1 (3-oz.) pkg. cream cheese
1 (10¾-oz.) can cream of
  mushroom soup
1 can fried onion rings

Mix all ingredients, except ½ can of onion rings. Bake 15 minutes. Sprinkle remaining onion rings on top of casserole and bake 15 minutes longer.

Mrs. George Rabinowitz (Johanna)

413

VEGETABLES

Spinach Stuffed Tomatoes

325 degrees
Shallow pan
Yield: 12-15 servings

12-15 ripe tomatoes
salt and pepper

Drop tomatoes in kettle of boiling water. Leave for about 5 seconds. Remove and place in cold water (this loosens skins). Peel the tomatoes. Scoop out a little of the pulp and discard. Drain tomatoes if need be. Sprinkle each tomato with a little salt and pepper.

Filling:
2 (10-oz.) pkgs. frozen
  spinach, chopped
1 (⅜-oz.) pkg. onion soup
  mix
1 pint sour cream
salt and pepper

Place frozen spinach in a large saucepan over very low heat (add no water). Cover and watch carefully until spinach is thawed and cooked (about 10-15 minutes). Remove from heat, add the soup mix, sour cream and salt and pepper. Mound some of the filling in each tomato cavity. Bake at 325 degrees for 25 minutes.

Garnish:
12-15 strips raw bacon

Fry strips of bacon until brown, but not crisp. Remove skillet from heat. Removing one strip at a time, place the bacon strip on a paper towel. Run the tines of a fork under one end of the strip and quickly roll up (jelly-roll fashion). Secure the curl with a toothpick. It is best to cook 4-5 strips at the time as curls are difficult when bacon is cold. Place one curl atop each tomato.

May be made ahead about 6 hours and refrigerated until time to use.

Mrs. Shelly Collier, Jr. (Caryl)

414

VEGETABLES

Spinach Stuffed Zucchini

350 degrees
Shallow baking dish
Yield: 6 servings

3 zucchini
1 (10-oz.) pkg. frozen
   spinach, chopped, cooked
   and drained
2 Tbs. flour
½ cup milk
⅓ cup cheese, shredded
4 slices bacon, cooked
   crisply, drained, and
   crumbled (optional)

Trim off ends of zucchini and cook whole in boiling water 10 to 12 minutes. Drain. Halve lengthwise and scoop out centers. Chop centers and add to spinach. In saucepan, blend flour, milk and spinach mixture. Cook and stir until thickened. Place zucchini halves in baking dish. Sprinkle with salt. Spoon spinach mixture into zucchini shells. Top with cheese and/or bacon. Bake at 350 degrees for 15 to 20 minutes.

Mrs. Gary Gurwitz (Bailey)

Spinach-Cheese Casserole

350 degrees
2 quart shallow casserole
Yield: 8-10 servings
Freezes

1 pkg. frozen leaf spinach
1 (2-lb.) carton cottage
   cheese, large curd
¼ lb. butter or margarine
½ lb. Velveeta cheese
6 whole eggs

Snip coarse chunks of partially thawed spinach into bowl. Do not drain. Add cottage cheese, butter, Velveeta (cut into chunks) and eggs. Mix well; pour into casserole. Bake one hour.

Mrs. William Burke (Lynne)

Vegetables that grow underground should be cooked covered.
Vegetables that grow above ground should be cooked uncovered.

VEGETABLES

Squash Casserole

375 degrees
12 x 8 x 1 pan,
with non-stick spray
Yield: 8 servings

5 zucchini
5 yellow squash
1 medium onion
1 medium green pepper
leaves of 4 celery stalks
6 Tbs. margarine
1 egg, beaten
1¼ cups Cheddar cheese,
  grated
⅓ cup cracker crumbs
seasoned salt

Slice and boil squash until soft. Brown onion, green pepper, and celery in 2 Tbs. margarine. Drain squash and mash with browned mixture. Add 4 Tbs. margarine, ½ cup cheese, cracker crumbs, and seasoned salt to taste. Add beaten egg and cover with remaining cheese. Bake for 45 minutes.

Can be made a day ahead and refrigerated. If so, bake 30 minutes longer.

Mrs. Leroy Lewin (Hilda)

Baked Squash Casserole

350 degrees
9 x 12 pyrex dish,
greased
Yield: 6-8 servings

1½-2 lbs. yellow squash,
  cooked and strained
1 medium onion, chopped
  fine
1 jar pimientos, chopped
4 medium carrots, grated
1 cup sour cream
1 (10¾-oz.) can cream of
  chicken soup
1 stick butter
1 pkg. Pepperidge Farm herb
  stuffing mix

Cook squash, drain and mash well. Add rest of the ingredients except stuffing. Line a 9 x 12-inch greased casserole dish with ½ of the Pepperidge Farm herb stuffing. Pour in squash mixture and sprinkle the rest of the herb stuffing on top. Bake about 35 minutes in a shallow pan at 350 degrees. If a deeper pan is used, cook the dish a longer length of time.

Cheesy Squash Casserole

375 degrees
1 quart casserole
Yield: 6 servings

1 lb. crookneck squash,
   washed and sliced
¼ onion, chopped
salt
¼ lb. American cheese,
   grated
pepper, mill ground
2 pieces bacon, fried and
   crumbled
Parmesan cheese

Cook squash and onion in salted water until just tender; drain well. Stir in American cheese, pepper, and bacon. Pour into 1 quart casserole; top with Parmesan cheese to cover. Bake at 375 degrees for 20 minutes or until browned on top.

Italian Squash

Skillet
Yield: 6-8 servings

4 zucchini squash
1 medium onion, diced
1 medium tomato, diced
salt and pepper
garlic powder
¼ tsp. oregano

Wash zucchini and slice into thin slices. Sauté onion until golden, add tomato, then zucchini on top. Salt and pepper to taste. Dash garlic powder and sprinkle ¼ tsp. oregano over all. Add about 3 Tbs. water. Cover skillet and let simmer for about 25 minutes. More cooking time will make the squash less crisp.

Good accompaniment for pasta main dishes and beef main dishes.

Mrs. Philip Chaleff (Elsie)

Parsley will remain fresh and crisp longer by storing in a container with a tight lid.

VEGETABLES

Squash Boats

350 degrees
Large casserole dish
Yield: 12 servings

6 yellow squash
½ cup cottage cheese
1 Tbs. (heaping) mayonnaise
6 fresh green onions,
  chopped (using all parts)
1 Tbs. sour cream
½ cup Pepperidge Farm
  seasoned croutons,
  crushed
Cheddar cheese, grated

Parboil squash for 7-10 minutes. Slice lengthwise and scoop out center of squash. Chop up the center parts and set aside in a small mixing bowl. Mix together the cottage cheese, mayonnaise, onions, sour cream and croutons. Mix thoroughly with chopped squash. Spoon mixture into the squash boats and top each with grated Cheddar cheese. Heat 15-20 minutes at 350 degrees.

Swiss Vegetable Bake

375 degrees
1 quart baking dish,
ungreased
Yield: 4 servings

½ cup butter
1½ cups yellow squash (3
  small), sliced
1½ cups fresh broccoli, cut,
  or 1 (10-oz.) pkg. frozen
  broccoli, cut and thawed
1 egg, slightly beaten
½ cup Swiss cheese,
  shredded
¼ cup milk
1 tsp. salt
¼ tsp. dry mustard
dash of pepper
¼ cup Parmesan cheese,
  grated

In large skillet melt butter, sauté vegetables until tender. In a mixing bowl beat egg slightly; stir in cheese, milk, salt, mustard and pepper. Place vegetables in ungreased baking dish; pour egg mixture over and sprinkle with Parmesan cheese. Bake 15-20 minutes at 375 degrees.

Mrs. Ronald Imhoof (Sandra)

418

VEGETABLES

Parmesan Broiled Tomatoes

Baking dish, size
depending on tomatoes
Yield: 6 servings

3 large tomatoes
melted butter
salt and pepper
Parmesan cheese

Cut the tomatoes in half crosswise and brush with melted butter. Sprinkle with salt, pepper and Parmesan cheese. Broil 6 inches from heat 5-7 minutes or until golden brown.

Mrs. Shelley Collier, Jr. (Caryl)

Broiled Tomato Cups

Long, flat baking dish
Yield: 10-12 servings

5-6 tomatoes
½ cup sour cream
½ cup mayonnaise
¼ cup Parmesan cheese
1 tsp. garlic salt
juice of one lemon
3 green onions, chopped

Cut tomatoes in half. Combine remaining ingredients, and put on top of tomato half. Broil in long flat baking dish until bubbly. Watch closely.

Stuffed Zucchini Boats

350 degrees
Yield: 4 servings

4 medium zucchini
1 (12-oz.) can whole kernel
   corn, drained
2 tsp. seasoned salt
2 eggs, beaten
¼ cup chives, chopped
½ cup Cheddar cheese,
   grated

Scrub zucchini. Cut off ends, but do not pare. Cook whole in boiling water for about 10 minutes. Cut zucchini in half, lengthwise. With tip of spoon, carefully remove pulp of zucchini from shells. Chop into small pieces, combine with drained corn, seasoned salt, beaten eggs and chives. Pile lightly into shells and sprinkle with grated cheese. Bake uncovered for 30 minutes.

Mrs. T. B. Waite, Jr. (Thelma)

VEGETABLES

Zucchini Casserole

350 degrees
1 quart casserole, greased

3 cups zucchini, finely grated
1 cup cracker crumbs
1 cup Cheddar cheese,
   grated
2 eggs, beaten
2 Tbs. onion, chopped

Combine all ingredients and put in a well-buttered casserole dish. Bake 1 hour.

Mrs. Morgan Talbot (Jane)

Zucchini-Corn Casserole

350 degrees
2-3 quart casserole dish
Yield: 6 servings

5 large zucchini (4 cups)
½ onion, chopped
2½ cups cream style corn
1 small can green chiles,
   diced
1 (8-oz.) cream cheese
salt and pepper
buttered bread crumbs

Cook squash and onion until done. Drain well and chop. Add corn and cream cheese while hot. Add all other ingredients except bread crumbs. Do not drain chiles. You can add more onion if you desire. Pour into a casserole dish and top with buttered bread crumbs. Bake 45 minutes at 350 degrees.

Zucchini Supper

Skillet
Yield: 4-6 servings

2 Tbs. oil
2 stalks celery, chopped
1 small onion, chopped
1 lb. zucchini (about 3), cut
   up
2 tomatoes, cut up
2 Tbs. ketchup
1 cup American cheese,
   cubed
salt and pepper to taste

Sauté celery and onion in oil until golden. Add the zucchini, tomatoes, ketchup and salt and pepper. Simmer all together about 15 minutes. For a one dish meal, add the cubed cheese when you add the zucchini.

Mrs. Paul Moffitt (Marilyn)

VEGETABLES

Tomatoes and Onions Vinaigrette

9 x 9 dish
Yield: 4 servings

2 large tomatoes, sliced fairly
  thick
1 medium onion, sliced thin

Dressing:
1½ cups olive oil or
  vegetable oil
5 Tbs. wine vinegar
3 tsp. whole oregano
1½ tsp. salt
½ tsp. coarse black pepper
¾ tsp. dry mustard
3 small cloves garlic, minced
  or pressed
1 Tbs. minced parsley

Place the sliced tomatoes and onions in a flat-bottomed dish, alternating tomatoes and onions.

Combine all ingredients and pour over vegetables. Cover tightly and chill for 2-3 hours. Stir occasionally. Drain before serving on lettuce leaves. Dressing may be saved for other salads.

Mrs. Jerry Box (Deanna)

Three-Vegetable Casserole

350 degrees
2 quart casserole
Yield: 12 servings

2 (10-oz.) pkgs. French style
  frozen green beans or corn
2 (10-oz.) pkgs. frozen green
  peas
1 (10-oz.) pkg. frozen baby
  lima beans
salt and pepper
garlic powder
¼ cup Parmesan cheese,
  grated
1 cup whipping cream
1 pint Hellmann's
  mayonnaise

Cook each vegetable in a separate pan according to package directions. Drain and combine in large mixing bowl. Add salt, pepper, garlic powder, and cheese to vegetables and mix thoroughly. Whip cream until stiff. Add cream and mayonnaise to vegetables. Blend well and pour into casserole and top with cheese. Let stand at least 2-3 hours or overnight. Bake until heated thoroughly.

Mrs. Jerry Box (Deanna)

NOTES

WEIGHTS and MEASURES

EQUIVALENTS:

3 teaspoons = 1 tablespoon
2 tablespoons = ⅛ cup
4 tablespoons = ¼ cup
5 tablespoons plus
  1 teaspoon = ⅓ cup
8 tablespoons = ½ cup
12 tablespoons = ¾ cup
16 tablespoons = 1 cup
1 cup = ½ pint
2 cups = 1 pint
2 pints = 1 quart

4 cups = 1 quart
4 quarts = 1 gallon (liquid)
8 quarts = 1 peck (dry)
4 pecks = 1 bushel
pinch = as much as can be taken
  between tip of finger and thumb
1 ounce = 2 tablespoons
4 ounces = ½ cup
8 ounces = 1 cup
16 ounces = 1 pound
2 cups (liquid) = 1 pound

1 stick butter = ½ cup
4 sticks butter = 1 pound
1 square chocolate = 3 tablespoons chocolate, grated
8-10 egg whites = 1 cup
12-14 yolks = 1 cup
1 cup whipping cream = 2 cups whipped cream
1 medium lemon = 1 tablespoon grated rind = 3 tablespoons juice
1 medium orange = 2 tablespoons grated rind = ⅓ cup juice
1 dozen medium oranges = 4 cups juice

4 ounces uncooked macaroni = 2¼ cups cooked
7 ounces uncooked spaghetti = 4 cups cooked
4 ounces uncooked noodles = 2 cups cooked
1 cup uncooked rice = about 3 cups cooked

28 saltine crackers = 1 cup crumbs
4 slices bread = 1 cup crumbs
14 square graham crackers = 1 cup crumbs
22 vanilla wafers = 1 cup crumbs

No. 300 can = 14-16 oz. = 1¾ cups
No. 303 can = 16-17 oz. = 2 cups
No. 2 can = 1 lb. 4-oz. = 2½ cups
No. 3 can = 3 lbs. 3-oz. = 5¾ cups

THE FOLLOWING EQUAL 1 POUND:
2 cups butter or margarine
2 cups sugar
4 cups flour, sifted
3 cups corn meal
4 cups cheese, grated
4 cups pecans, shelled
2 cups crabmeat
4 small tomatoes
3 large onions

SUBSTITUTIONS:
1 teaspoon baking powder = ½ teaspoon cream of tartar plus
 ¼ teaspoon soda
1 tablespoon cornstarch = 3 tablespoons flour
1 cup milk = ½ cup evaporated milk plus ½ cup water
1 cup milk = 4 tablespoons dry whole milk plus 1 cup water
1 cup buttermilk = 1 cup fresh milk plus 1 tablespoon vinegar or lemon
 juice
1 cup fresh milk = 1 cup buttermilk plus ½ teaspoon soda
1 cup honey = ¾ cup sugar plus ¼ cup liquid
1 cup molasses = 1 cup honey
1 cup cake flour = 1 cup all-purpose flour less 2 tablespoons
1 square chocolate (1 ounce) = 3-4 tablespoons cocoa plus ½ tablespoon margarine
1 cup canned tomatoes = 1⅓ cups cut tomatoes, cut up and simmered
 10 minutes
¾ cup cracker crumbs = 1 cup bread crumbs
1 package active dry yeast = 1 cake compressed yeast
1 tablespoon instant minced onion = 1 small fresh onion = ¼ cup
 minced raw onions
1 teaspoon dehydrated parsley flakes = 2 sprigs fresh parsley
⅛ teaspoon garlic powder = 1 average size clove fresh garlic
1 tablespoon prepared mustard = 1 teaspoon dry mustard

Index

427

433

NOTES

ORDER FORM

Mail to:
Junior League of McAllen, Inc.
P.O. Box 2465
McAllen, TX 78502-2465

Please send _____copy(ies) Some Like It Hot @ $18.95* each $ _____
              _____copy(ies) *La Piñata* @ $18.95* each $ _____
  OR both books for $32.90
Postage & handling @ $ 4.00* each $ _____
           *Prices subject to change without notice
                         TOTAL $ _____

Name _____

Address _____

City _____ State _____ Zip _____

Make checks payable to *Junior League of McAllen, Inc.*

ORDER FORM

Mail to:
Junior League of McAllen, Inc.
P.O. Box 2465
McAllen, TX 78502-2465

Please send _____copy(ies) Some Like It Hot @ $18.95* each $ _____
              _____copy(ies) *La Piñata* @ $18.95* each $ _____
  OR both books for $32.90
Postage & handling @ $ 4.00* each $ _____
           *Prices subject to change without notice
                         TOTAL $ _____

Name _____

Address _____

City _____ State _____ Zip _____

Make checks payable to *Junior League of McAllen, Inc.*

Save $1.00 on your reorder. Just send us the name, address and phone number of the best stores in your town that sell cookbooks.

Name of store_____

Owner or managers name_____

Address_____

City_____ State_____ Zip_____
(Deduct $1.00 off your reorder when this is filled in)

Save $1.00 on your reorder. Just send us the name, address and phone number of the best stores in your town that sell cookbooks.

Name of store_____   _____

Owner or managers name_____

Address_____

City_____ State_____ Zip_____
(Deduct $1.00 off your reorder when this is filled in)

ORDER FORM

Mail to:
Junior League of McAllen, Inc.
P.O. Box 2465
McAllen, TX 78502-2465

Please send _____copy(ies) Some Like It Hot @ $18.95* each $ _____
_____copy(ies) *La Piñata* @ $18.95* each $ _____
OR both books for $32.90
Postage & handling @ $ 4.00* each $ _____
*Prices subject to change without notice
TOTAL $ _____

Name_____

Address _____

City _____ State _____ Zip _____

Make checks payable to *Junior League of McAllen, Inc.*

ORDER FORM

Mail to:
Junior League of McAllen, Inc.
P.O. Box 2465
McAllen, TX 78502-2465

Please send _____copy(ies) Some Like It Hot @ $18.95* each $ _____
_____copy(ies) *La Piñata* @ $18.95* each $ _____
OR both books for $32.90
Postage & handling @ $ 4.00* each $ _____
*Prices subject to change without notice
TOTAL $ _____

Name_____

Address _____

City _____ State _____ Zip _____

Make checks payable to *Junior League of McAllen, Inc.*

Save $1.00 on your reorder. Just send us the name, address and phone number of the best stores in your town that sell cookbooks.

Name of store_____

Owner or managers name_____

Address_____

City_____ State_____ Zip_____
(Deduct $1.00 off your reorder when this is filled in)

Save $1.00 on your reorder. Just send us the name, address and phone number of the best stores in your town that sell cookbooks.

Name of store_____

Owner or managers name_____

Address_____

City_____ State_____ Zip_____
(Deduct $1.00 off your reorder when this is filled in)